REVOLUTIONS OF 1848:
A SOCIAL HISTORY

REVOLUTIONS

OF 1848:

A SOCIAL HISTORY

———

PRISCILLA ROBERTSON

———

PRINCETON, NEW JERSEY
PRINCETON UNIVERSITY PRESS

To the memory of my father,

PRESERVED SMITH

Preface

No one has ever numbered the revolutions which broke out in Europe in 1848. Counting those in the small German states, the Italian states, and the provinces of the Austrian Empire, there must have been over fifty. Out of all these outbreaks I have picked the ones that were most important in themselves and that showed most clearly the intertwining strands that made up the opinions of the age and the ways men acted. To have included the story of the revolutions in Prussian Poland, in Bohemia, even the one in Naples, would have repeated the same patterns without bringing in much that was new.

This book is called a social history because its aim is to show how men lived and felt a hundred years ago rather than to describe at length other important factors like constitutions, battles, or Lord Palmerston's foreign policy, all of which have been adequately treated by other historians. My own purpose is to show what it was like to be a worker in Paris, or a student in Vienna, or an Italian patriot, or an aristocrat, or a king in those days. In a peculiar measure the men who were alive then had to face, in a simplified, almost a laboratory form, problems which have beset their descendants during the subsequent century—problems of socialism, nationality, power, and above all the meaning of democracy. I have tried to show how both sides looked—quite reasonably it seemed to each—at the same questions and came out with different answers.

I have not emphasized leaders. No leader was really very important in 1848 except as he typified for a while, and rode to power, the ideas current in some class or group. Because each one represented only one class or group and was unintelligible to the other side, none of them transcended the age and formed (as great leaders do) a new synthesis of ideas at a different level.

The people I have been most interested in, instead, are that large and paradoxical group who were for the revolution before it broke out and against it after it was over. Their dilemma derived, I think, from the conflict of their theories with the actual social conditions and unquestioned assumptions of their particular class or racial background. Nearly everyone was surprised at some phase or other of the revolutions, and that surprise is a measure of the miscalculation of their theories.

History is, after all, something that happened to people. No "force" whether economic or political can act except as it acts through the minds and bodies of human beings. It is of course true that much human activity is the result of conditions which are unknown to the participants. Many economic forces work seemingly outside the awareness of the individuals affected by them, and to uncover these forces is exciting and rewarding. The revelation of this mystery is one reason for the smashing success of the economic interpretations of history. It is not only economic motives that work mysteriously, however. Many of the social reasons for our behavior are imbedded in feelings too deep ever to be clearly voiced; and most prejudices, though partly conscious, create passions whose violence can only be understood by assuming that they go to the unconscious roots of a man's personality.

The 1848 period offers a peculiarly interesting opportunity to investigate what happens when people suddenly find their complacencies challenged or their ideals too suddenly fulfilled.

Looking at the year 1848 in this spirit some of the questions which have puzzled other historians disappear. Most students have found something "inexplicable" about the ferocity of the June revolts in Paris. Again it is impossible to begin to understand clashes within the Austrian Empire without untangling the different codes of loyalty, the different concepts of freedom, which pulled and pushed not only one race against another, but, more than in previous periods of history, each man against himself.

Since there was no revolution in England in 1848, I might have left the British Isles out of my story altogether. Instead I chose to put in some brief remarks which are intended to illuminate the continental revolutions by contrast and contradiction rather than to afford a complete history of Chartism, Young Ireland, or the British genius for muddling through.

I could never have written this book without the help, both physical and mental, of many other people. A large share of both kinds of help has been given by the staff of the Library of the University of Louisville, particularly Miss Evelyn Schneider, its head, and Miss Virginia Winstandley, who spent five untiring years in locating books at distant libraries and procuring them for my use through the inter-library loan service.

At the Harvard College Library, Mr. Robert H. Haynes has

PREFACE

smoothed my path as he has that of many guests at his incomparable institution.

I must also thank Harvard University for a generosity elsewhere unknown, in opening its facilities to the wives of that happy group of men, the Nieman fellows. The Curator of the Nieman Foundation, Mr. Louis F. Lyons, was possibly my severest critic, but I am grateful for his strictures as well as for his personal kindnesses.

If it had not been for the insistence of Professor Ernest C. Mossner, of the University of Texas, this book would never have been finished. He has also read the manuscript with considerable benefit to its readability.

Several historical scholars have been extremely generous with help; notably Professor Emeritus Sidney B. Fay, of Harvard, who advised me on the method of writing history as well as letting me draw on his wide knowledge of facts; Professor Alma Luckau, of Vassar College, who offered me dozens of carefully thought out suggestions; and Professor Donald C. McKay, of Harvard, who has given me unstintedly both information and encouragement. Professor Helen Lockwood of Vassar and Professor David Maurer of the University of Louisville have provided valuable criticism.

The maps are the result of the painstaking care of Mr. Edward Schmitz, of the Harvard Institute of Geographical Exploration.

Vivian Graves put many thoughtful hours into helping me organize the index.

Mrs. Herbie Koch did an unusually understanding and careful job of typing the bulk of the manuscript; and I was lucky also in the typists who did the other parts, particularly Mrs. Pal Littell.

As the mother of a young family I could not have pursued research without help in the management of my household and for this help at different times I am greatly indebted to Mrs. Annie Belle Taylor, Mrs. Emma Taylor, and their families. They have supported me with sympathy, understanding and cheerful assumption of responsibility. I am also deeply grateful to my niece, Nancy Easley Clifford, and my college classmate, Elizabeth Miller Davis. Each has run my home for a few weeks in order to allow me periods of study in a big library.

Cary Robertson has most generously given to this book his great skill as an editor, and I only wish it were more worthy of his talent.

i x

PREFACE

It is the case with all my friends and advisers that they have added learning and judgment to a book whose faults are entirely my own.

Thanks are due the following publishers for permission to quote from material copyrighted by them: Constable & Company, Ltd., Longmans Green & Co., Ltd., John Lane The Bodley Head, Ltd., Peter Davies, Ltd., Chatto and Windus, and Victor Gollancz, Ltd.

PRISCILLA ROBERTSON

Anchorage, Kentucky
May 16, 1951

Contents

INTRODUCTION

I

Start of a Hundred Year Cycle

WHEN the year 1848 broke upon Europe, everywhere men were waiting for the death of Louis Philippe, King of the French. Whenever or however it should occur, it was supposed to be the signal for the revolution which everyone was sure was coming, though some men looked for it with fear and some with hope.

The poet Heine, living in Paris, said that the fall of the King would be like the projected taking down of the conspicuous and disliked statue, the Elephant of the Bastille: thousands of rats would be let loose. Other men loved to talk of the great conspiracy to kill the King that was supposed to have been working for seven years. In Germany, too, the mounting fever of the 1840's was expected to mark its crisis with Louis Philippe's death. And in South America Garibaldi was waiting for this sign to bring him back to liberate Italy. Even in Austria, where another monarchy hung on the aged Metternich's survival, men counted the days of the King of the French.

As it turned out, Europe did not wait for the match to be applied. Louis Philippe was destined to die a natural, if unroyal, death in England late in 1850 after the outburst which his death was supposed to kindle had burned across Europe and had been extinguished. For Parisians were in a state of spontaneous combustion; in a swift struggle they ousted their King; and the university students of Germany, the plain patriots of Italy and Hungary tried to follow their example and make revolution.

In the end they all failed. What they fought for was brought about under different auspices, often ironically by specific enemies of the 1848 movement. Could the bloodshed have been avoided? The argument is the same after many wars. Battles have been won or lost for centuries without winning or losing what they were ostensibly fought for.

In the mélange of 1848 Europe, Louis Philippe was certainly neither the most wicked nor the most hated ruler. If law and order seemed symbolically attached to his life, it was partly because his heir was a child, so that there would be a fine chance for a coup amid the arguments about succession and regency; but mostly because ever since 1789 the rest of Europe looked to France as the natural source of revolutions.

Germany and Italy at this time were both divided into such tiny states that no one of them, not even Prussia, could hope to give the cue. As a matter of fact, revolution did break out in Naples before it did in France in this year of 1848, forcing the Bourbon who happened to be on that southern throne to grant a constitution. Yet no one paid much attention to the Neapolitan affair, while the news from Paris precipitated revolution in almost every other capital.

The lands that were ruled by the Hapsburgs—Austria, Hungary, Bohemia, northern Italy, and a large part of Poland—were far more oppressed and discontented than France. However, the Austrian monarchy was commonly considered to exist behind a Chinese wall where no modern ideas penetrated. Even the Napoleonic ferment had disquieted Vienna less than any other capital. So it seemed almost as hopeless to think of revolution coming out of Austria as out of Russia, the great dark reservoir of reaction.

The nations that were panting to be free from foreign rule— Poland, northern Italy, and Ireland—were too severely repressed to start a revolution by themselves, but they were the watchwords of liberals all over the continent. Many besides their own citizens were hoping for the chance these countries would get with the first crumbling of the regime that had endured, more or less unchanged, since 1815, when the Treaty of Vienna attempted to undo the work of Napoleon and to strait-jacket Europe against another attack of the madness of 1789.

Most men, however, suspected the truth, which was that conditions had changed since 1789. If Europeans were afraid of a revolution in 1848 it was because their uneasy consciences whispered that sixty years of the swiftest industrial progress the world had ever known had created a new working class whose miseries were likely to be explosive. Plenty of other people were restive in the strait-jacket, plenty of businessmen both large and small resented the eighteenth-century restrictions which limited their nineteenth-century opportunities. But the moral question centered around the proletariat and what freedom might or ought to mean to them.

Should they be given a vote, or would they use it immediately to destroy the whole precarious system by which even their own livelihoods were created? Or were they perhaps so much the creatures of their employers that only those who were what the Germans called *selbständig* could honestly be considered independent enough to vote? Or did freedom mean more than a vote? Was not productivity great enough for the first time so that society could now guarantee that no man should starve? Could not the state go further and guarantee each man a job in order to protect the pride of its citizens and to *make* them *selbständig*? If some of these things were not done, would not the proletariat itself rise up in hideous strength and demand them?

The social problem, then, was one to which most Europeans had given some worried thought, whether out of a desire for justice or out of fear. The other problem of 1848, the national one, which tangled with the social problem and almost smothered it outside of France, had not previously aroused nearly so much general apprehension. The Germans wanted to unite—but before 1848 they were not afraid of the idea, they did not yet know what there was to be afraid of. And similarly with the Italians. They did not foresee that they might have to choose between freedom as civil liberties and the greater opportunities that might come to them as citizens of powerful, unified, but autocratic states. Even in France the question arose, unexpectedly, whether they could have a revolution in one country or whether free France should not carry its arms to the oppressed of other nationalities. In Austria the ruling clique knew that it governed an uneasy hodgepodge of peoples but it is safe to say that it never dreamed how ferocious the clamor of these races to become nations would grow.

Of course, the socialism of an era is naive so long as the term means only a concern with the social problem. There were even some groups calling themselves "conservative socialists." In 1848, as at present, a great many people wanted to be democratic and simply did not know how. The psychological and economic barriers were far stronger than they could have imagined. Indeed the social lines that were drawn between classes did as much to make the revolutions take the shape they did as the more talked-of economic self-interest of those classes. An absurd example of how strictly these lines held occurred in the time of Louis Philippe, shortly before 1848. A group of political prisoners, charged with a common crime and serving sentence in a common jail, split into two groups which never spoke to each other. The only activity which the working class segment shared with their white collar prison mates, men who were being punished for defending workers' rights, was to sing the *Marseillaise* every day. After they had knelt together at the last verse the two groups always separated, and it was the occasion of remark when a good doctor strolled over from the side of the intellectuals to pass the time of day with the workers.

Because of this almost complete separation of life and thought it was easy for the intellectuals to imagine that the workers would be far-seeing and generous about social reorganization, and they imagined they would follow happily the lead of their sincere well-wishers from the upper classes. Incongruous as it may seem, these white collar "socialists," many of whom had never gone so far as to shake hands with a worker, believed in the fusion of classes.

Karl Marx saw that as society was set up they would not fuse, and in 1847 he had already laid down the doctrine of the class struggle in the *Communist Manifesto*. But the class struggle as a political actuality was rather the result of the 1848 revolutions than their cause. Hardly any of the leaders had had time or inclination to read the *Manifesto*, and they led their insurrections, some more and some less honestly, in the opinion that all classes could benefit together. Only after the liberals won power did they discover that they were afraid of the workers; when the workers found this out they turned to the Marxian gospel.

As for the nationalism of the period, it too was romantic. Nationality could give character and a mission to every people, so men said. They revived dying languages and cultures which would better have been left to die, and stressed military glory even in countries like France where the right to nationhood had long been won. Internationalism was made to seem materialistic and selfish, while the petty jealousies of Balkan nationalities, which have caused so much strife in a century, were made to seem like holy wars. Before 1848 Germans swam in a sea of vague patriotism; during that year they crystallized their decision that they cared more about power than civil liberty, and that their *Lebensraum* lay to the east. In this year Hungarians and Irishmen showed that they would prefer autonomy to power, if power was to be had by remaining within the empires that claimed them. In this year also hitherto less vocal groups, Croats and Czechs and Roumanians, began to turn their cultural revival into political excitement. And in this year Italy showed that she would not let the nineteenth century cheat her out of either unity or liberty.

It was therefore often difficult for a man to decide whether his greatest loyalty should be to his class or to his nation, but whichever he decided, after 1848, his loyalty was buttressed by hatred of opposing groups. What was lost, in 1848, was the idea that classes and nations had anything to give to each other.

It sometimes seems as if everyone who lived through the 1848 days wrote his recollections. A large part of the energy which might have been devoted to successful social action if the revolutions had turned out differently was cramped into the covers of books which purported to explain why so much hope, courage, and idealism had failed. Certainly part of the story as it has meaning for us today should tell what these men thought about themselves, what they wanted future generations to understand concerning these most beautiful days of their lives and their subsequent heartbreak.

It is lucky for an historian, however, that not all the observers were participants. Particularly the occasional Americans who were in Europe at the time make a refreshing class of their own. From Richard Rush, the minister at Paris who took it upon himself to recognize the Second French Republic, to William Stiles at Vienna who coolly told Prince Schwarzenberg that the Austrian Navy might sink an American frigate when they could catch her, American diplomatic agents did credit to their republic. Andrew Jackson Donelson at Berlin illuminated his legation in tribute to the victorious people; the American consul at Rome gave Mazzini a passport to escape. Untouched by the romantic dreams which kept Europeans of that period (as perhaps of most periods) from the direct perception of reality, they provide a touchstone which shows up the sickness of European society. These Americans were heartily in favor of peoples' movements, and they rejoiced at every victory over governments which they saw as stupid and vicious. Yet they could not but see that class distinctions in Europe, as well as a kind of wild impracticality in aims, prevented a happy outcome to the revolutions. With a healthy disgust they noted that the conditions of the lower classes in European capitals were so degraded that there were none to be found like them in the United States.

However, the greatest commentator upon the revolutions was a Russian, Alexander Herzen, a socialist who came to Western Europe for the first time in 1847. He hoped to discover there all the comforts and culture befitting the center of civilization, and instead he found bloodshed and reaction. Upon this scene he looked with a detachment like the Americans', yet, being European, he felt a tragedy which was quite beyond their experience. When, after the June days of Paris, he writes of the desolation of his soul in which he had not supposed there was so much left to be destroyed, when he tells how his wife no longer dared to wish her children to live for fear there was a fate as awful as the revolution in store for them, Herzen seems like no other writer of his time. His memoirs read as if a twentieth-century intelligence had somehow been sent back to record for us the meaning of those struggles that seem in so many ways the birth pangs of our modern era.

The insights which were choked off in 1848 were a real loss to the world. The psychologists, sociologists, and technologists of today continue to rediscover them. How many times have we heard, in the lingoes of these various disciplines, Victor Hugo's cry after the 1848 adventure was over: "We are a predestined generation. We have bigger and more frightening tasks than our ancestors. We have not time to hate each other"?

PART I · FRANCE

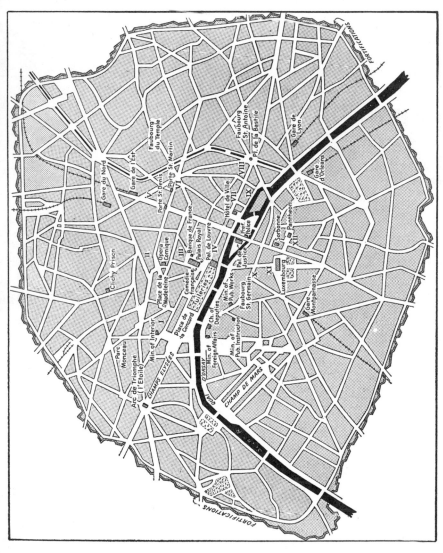

PARIS IN 1848

The Wind of Revolution

On Sunday, July 18, 1847, the citizens of Mâcon, forty miles north of Lyons in southern France, spread a banquet for their favorite son, Alphonse de Lamartine. Lamartine was France's most popular living poet as well as Mâcon's representative in the Chamber of Deputies, and the banquet was in honor of his recent completion of a history of the Girondins of 1790 which was the literary sensation of 1847.

The banquet place covered two acres, with 500 tables for 3,000 guests, and there were grandstand seats for 3,000 more who, as far as the record shows, did not share in the menu. The day was ferociously hot, until a thunderstorm ripped the tent wide open and drenched the listeners. By this time Lamartine was talking and he did not stop, so nobody thought of leaving. They were all electrified by his words: "It will fall, this royalty, be sure of that. It will fall, not in its blood like that of '89; but it will fall in its trap. And after having had the revolution of freedom and the counter-revolution of glory, you will have the revolution of public conscience and the revolution of contempt."[1] France was uneasy and this was what Frenchmen wanted, some action, some word on which their restlessness could crystallize.

The banquet was ostensibly in honor of a literary triumph, but the people who bought tickets did so as a political act. To put down money for a seat at the table and to put one's name on a list of subscribers to hear the government's most prominent critic, represented more political action than those who opposed the government had had a chance to show in a long time. And Lamartine himself gave them the word—"the revolution of contempt" flew over France, making everybody realize what it was he had been feeling for the government of Louis Philippe.

Louis Philippe was one of those kings who distinguished them-

[1] As reported by Daniel Stern, *Histoire de la révolution de 1848*, I, 21.

selves by being good men, and in the nineteenth century that meant being good to his wife and children. True, he had fought in battle on the side of the first French Revolution, taking his cue from his father, Philippe Egalité, the one member of the royal family who had voted to send Louis XVI to the scaffold; true, he showed a wide eagerness to see the world, including the sorts and conditions of men to be found clear down to the Mississippi Valley. An American story said he had even proposed marriage to a young Philadelphian, but her father cagily pointed out that while the heir to the House of Orleans was an exile he was not a good enough match for the girl, whereas if he should be restored to his fortune she would not be good enough for him. He finally married the daughter of the King of Naples, and with the restoration of the Bourbons to the French throne in 1815 he was able to come to Paris as the first peer of France, under the title of Duke of Orleans, and to devote himself to restoring his fortune and bringing up his eight children. He also set to work to build up his popularity. Aristocracy was scandalized that his sons went to public school, but the Duke, though he may have been an aristocrat at heart, was clever enough to realize that the future of the country lay with the bourgeoisie, who were, in turn, enraptured by the informal manners as well as by the expensive parties to be found at his establishment in the Palais-Royal.

Meanwhile the two dull old brothers of the beheaded Louis XVI who successively occupied the throne between 1815 and 1830 were becoming steadily more unpopular. At the end of this period Charles X flagrantly violated the charter of liberties which had been guaranteed to the French people after Waterloo in order to induce them to take back the Bourbons; and his subjects, who had acquired confidence and some ability in the technique of revolution, rose in three famous July days and overthrew him.

Apparently Louis Philippe was by no means surprised to find himself on the throne after those three days of 1830. He took scrupulous care not to engage in any of the fighting, but when it was over, when Charles X was being escorted out of the country, Louis Philippe allowed himself to be publicly embraced by Lafayette, the best guarantor to the people that the new king would enforce the Charter, that his would be a "monarchy surrounded by republican institutions," or even "the best of republics." To the bourgeoisie his fine, fat, pear-shaped figure seemed to promise that France would become rich, to the republicans his part in two revolutions held out the hope that she would become free. These promises he kept but indifferently well, while he ignored two other passions of his subjects completely, their love of glory and their need for social security. Although it was many years before France enjoyed either of these last satisfactions, events in 1848 showed how deeply she desired them.

People who visited France under the regime of Louis Philippe were usually favorably impressed. Railroads were being built, gas lights were beginning to illuminate the cities, the semaphore, that wig-wagging system proudly called the "telegraph," carried messages over the country with splendid speed. Looms were moving out of homes into factories, and other industries were developing. Guizot, the King's chief minister, told the bourgeoisie to get rich, and they were doing so busily. There were even noticeable improvements in the condition of the poor; one such sign was the quantities of wool and cotton which, thanks to machinery, they were now able to buy, so that poor girls could afford bright-colored cottons as well as the rich—the first sign of visible equality.

Furthermore, compared to other European countries, France was a home of liberty. The ministry governed through laws; the press was startlingly outspoken—a large part of its pages was given over to personal scurrility about the King and his family which would not have been allowed even in Britain with its theoretically wider tolerance; and trial by jury was so well established that for years a series of would-be assassins were acquitted. The American Minister to Paris, Richard Rush, wrote in December, 1847, "If I looked to the country, instead of the newspapers or speeches at political banquets, I should have thought I had come to a country abounding in prosperity of every kind and full of contentment. France appeared as well off as could be expected of any country where opulence, prosperity and power, existing on a large scale, must have drawbacks." Still, in spite of the pleasantness, drawbacks there were—enough, it proved, to make an eruption which blew Louis Philippe clear off his throne.

The man who applied the metaphor of the volcano to his country was Alexis de Tocqueville, he who had studied democracy in America and had impressed European political thinkers by his analysis of the tyranny of the majority. Early in 1848 he rose in the Chamber of Deputies to warn his colleagues. Looking back a few years later he admitted he was not actually so alarmed as he had allowed himself to sound, but it happened that events overtook his prophecy almost as soon as it was out of his mouth: "The working classes . . . are not bothered by political passions; but do you not see that, from political, the passions have become social? Ideas flow through their breasts that will shake the basis of society: they say that everything above them is incapable and unworthy of governing; that the distribution of goods to the profit of some is unjust. . . . When such ideas take root, they lead soon or late, I do not know when, to the most terrible revolutions. We are sleeping on a volcano. . . . Do you not see that the earth trembles anew? A wind of revolution blows, the storm is on the horizon."[2]

Tocqueville thus analyzed more acutely even than a sympathizer what was going on in the depths of society. He was observing, though more intuitively and less thoughtfully, the same phenomena which had caused Marx and Engels to get out the *Communist Manifesto* a few months before. Up to this time political revolutions had produced fairly satisfactory results in England, France, and America. In 1848 for the first time the working classes were going to assert, unsuccessfully, their demands for redistribution of goods.

The working classes were at the bottom of the volcano and Louis Philippe's government was on top. The first eruption, in February 1848, would blow off not only the King but also, indifferently, the top layer of men who had hoped to reform the monarchy and who had by their criticism helped prepare for the revolution. The volcano would cool off temporarily with political democrats, headed by Lamartine, on the surface, while underneath the social passions boiled with only a little less pressure than before. When socialists discovered the republic was quite as eager as the monarchy to suppress them, first a socialist newspaperman like Louis Blanc would try to crack the crust of the new government by stirring it from above and then a revolutionary, Auguste Blanqui, would try to make things boil up again from below. Finally, in June, there was to be a second eruption, one which just lacked the strength to carry the republicans down to destruction.

None of these types of leaders reckoned with the strength of the others. The men who wanted electoral reform would not believe that Lamartine could make a republic; Lamartine did not believe there was a great demand for Louis Blanc's socialism; and Louis Blanc

[2] Quoted from Barrot, *Mémoires Posthumes*, I, 478.

in turn could not see how workers might follow the cynical and sinister Blanqui rather than himself.

It was easy to miscalculate the variety of the opposition, because Louis Philippe's government made it expensive to publish newspapers and impossible to hold meetings of more than twenty people without police permission. Such repression of opinion naturally acted more heavily at the bottom of the social scale than at the top, where a political meeting could masquerade with wine and platters of cold veal. Those middle class citizens whose chief complaint was that they were not allowed to vote could voice their wishes more easily than the poor whose trouble was that they were starving.

Among the bourgeoisie the loudest clamor was for electoral reforms. The French election law of 1831 allowed only those persons to vote who paid a direct tax of 200 francs or more; there were never as many as 250,000 qualified voters out of an adult male population of 9,000,000. The situation may have been even worse than the figures show, but at any rate small and middling businessmen were excluded along with the learned and professional classes and, of course, the workers and peasants; and these disfranchised citizens began to look to England where the Reform Bill had passed in 1832, and to hope naïvely that France could have an equally easy transition. However, Prime Minister Guizot was not the Duke of Wellington, who shuddered for the future of England yet used his influence to keep the more intransigent peers from voting against the Reform Bill rather than see his country disrupted by open revolution. To every proposal for electoral reform Guizot replied, "Get rich; then you can vote," until even the advocates of reducing the electoral qualification to 50 francs (a mild measure which would very likely have saved the day) were forced to take extreme measures.

The answer of the government to its growing unpopularity was corruption. If it could not placate the majority of the people because it did not trust them, it could at least control its own minority by bribes. Its candidates were returned to the Chamber by promises of bridges, railroads, and hospitals to doubtful districts—a practice which led, incidentally, to an extraordinarily spotty development of railroad connections in those first years when they were being pushed through. Another common favor was the issuance of pardons or of exemptions from military service. Public morals sank below any recent remembrance. The director of the military bakery used state funds to speculate in wheat, leaving a tremendous deficit at his death. Two peers of France were actually tried and sentenced for dishonesty in a mining concession, and the case might never have come to trial if the principals had not quarreled and one published the other's incriminating letters. But the climax was the "affaire Petit," when Guizot himself, hitherto felt to be a rock of personal honesty, was shown to have paid 60,000 francs out of secret service money to recompense a man who had bought a place in the bureau of auditing and then not received the post.

Pervading dishonesty seemed to filter down through all classes, for people complained constantly of adulteration and false weights on the part of small shopkeepers. French wine was so constantly adulterated that it was difficult to export. Commercialism seemed everywhere; even pleasure became measured by price and art by income.

The young journalist, Louis Blanc, put his finger on one aspect of this discontent when he complained that France was a nation of warriors doomed to impotence because it was governed by shopkeepers; in those days the poor were all jingoistic. The King's devotion to peace won him the esteem of his brother monarchs in Europe, whom, as a parvenu, he was anxious to impress; and this quality may have endeared him to the Rothschilds. But in the breasts of the workers and peasants of France, of the liberal newspapermen, of the students in schools and universities, his policy aroused only shame and disgust. They recalled to each other the bright days of Empire when their fathers and grandfathers carried liberty across Europe on their bayonets. Yet, now, the Citizen King, himself raised to power by another revolution, calmly acquiesced in the treaties of 1815 which deprived France of Nice and Savoy on the south and— much the sorest point—of her frontier on the Rhine. He hesitated to spend money to put the army in first class shape. Nor did he show the least sympathy for oppressed nationalities like the Poles, whose revolt every liberal Frenchman burned to assist.

Jules Michelet, the historian of the great revolution, who was dismissed from his chair in the Sorbonne just before the 1848 outbreak, did his best for years to make his students feel that France was the hope of Europe. Each day, he told them, there is less sun, as Ireland, Italy, Poland perish. Germany is about to follow them into a state of reactionary oppression, and all the citizens of all these countries look to France, whose only true eternal name is Revolution. Michelet hoped that national feeling would grow stronger and deeper in every country, for did not the freedom of peoples seem part of the battle for freedom of the people?

Even the depression of 1847 was blamed on "external weakness" and "idle pacifism," as Ledru-Rollin charged in the Chamber. Perhaps Guizot was right when he said, "While other nations hated war, France actually liked it. It is an amusement she is sometimes forced to refuse herself, but it is always with regret. Peaceful policy is called—and in one sense *is*—anti-national." But republicans, though they still measured the nation's virtue by its military prowess, were beginning to feel that its arms must be used in a good cause. At any rate they had their past glory to capitalize on, and they played this tune as often as the Rights of Man. Their lunatic fringe shot at the King seventeen times in as many years, and the first reason, said the American Minister, for so many attempts at assassination was just that Louis Philippe wanted peace.

In spite of their belligerency, the intellectuals were the first to recognize that peace hath her victories. One of the ideas of their generation was that it was their particular mission to solve the social problem, and that meant giving decent security to every family. They knew the times were out of joint, and it seemed to them not a cursed spite, but a privilege, that they were born to set it right.

For France did not become the second industrial power in Europe without at the same time accumulating the second most miserable class of factory workers. England, of course, had the first. French orators were loud in the theme that France must not be allowed to sink to the level of Britain where squalor hit every passing eye, and where even eyes well chaperoned from misery were assaulted with books about the new problems of child labor, the inadequacy of working-class homes, the degradation of morals, of intelligence, of hope. In France, too, there were numbers of such studies,[3] but the only

---

[3] M. Georges Creveuil has made a careful study of the workers of Nantes under Louis Philippe. Those who earned over 600 francs a year, masons, carpenters and printers, were good workers, generally honest. They worked with spirit, often even joyously, because they were not completely deprived of every happy thought. By contrast, those who earned less than 300 francs showed physical suffering pushed to the limit. They raised only a fourth of their children, they lived mostly in under-

political action they produced during Louis Philippe's eighteen years was a single law against daytime labor by children under eight and night labor by those under twelve. Since this law was left to the enforcement of voluntary inspectors chosen from the manufacturing class, its effect was unnoticeable. The government probably agreed with Guizot that work was a desirable bridle to the ambitions of the lower classes, and the only effective one in the absence of those moral bridles whose lack he found deplorable.

Along with poverty came unemployment, endemic throughout the reign and a new problem for the nineteenth century. When an international financial crisis—the first of many—broke over Europe in 1846, it made matters much worse, and caused French production to fall by a billion francs out of a total of somewhat less than three billions. Skilled workers found themselves hurled back into the lower brackets, and unskilled ones into the casteless group of the unemployed. The harvest of 1846 was notoriously bad in places other than famine-stricken Ireland; but though the French government tried to help their hungry people by eliminating the tariff on wheat, their action came too late. The transportation system of the country was still too limited to prevent starvation in some places and hardship everywhere. There were peasant revolts which were sternly put down; and some estimates had a third of the population of Paris on relief in 1847. The city had been swollen to almost a million by earlier prosperity and by the need for labor on the extensive fortifications which Louis Philippe had pushed through in the early 1840's, and these workers hung on in town. They were to become the fighters at the barricades.

Socialism grew up to meet the problem of an industrial working class, and by 1848 there were a number of schools. In France these were mostly based upon the hard thinking which Saint-Simon and Fourier had done a quarter of a century before. In the 1830's and '40's their socialist doctrines, watered down, became almost fashionable, for their ideas were unusual enough to attract all literate classes, calling attention to evils which everyone saw in front of him. At the

ground houses with no furniture or heat, and as the price of bread rose in the 1847 crisis, a family of three or four children would eat over a franc's worth a day, while the father as a weaver could only earn 75 to 80 centimes. (See the periodical, *Révolutions de 1848*, for February and June, 1948.)

same time, their solutions, though often bizarre, seemed innocuous, since they mostly involved the construction of ideal communities. It was not until the streets of Paris ran with blood in June 1848 that the potential hatred of bourgeois and peasant toward the workers was uncovered; after that experience, socialism would create a hardier doctrine.

Of the socialist leaders just before 1848, Louis Blanc was the most popular because he seemed the most practical and was the author of the best-liked slogan of the period, "the right to work." In a way it was hardly fair to introduce him as a jingo—yet, that was part of his character, too. In 1848 the most earnest social reformers were usually the most nationalistic, and in this respect Blanc was only acting like Kossuth in Hungary or Mazzini in Italy.

He was born in Madrid in 1813, the son of a French official there, and when he arrived in Paris seventeen years later he was so utterly without resources that he nearly starved for a while. Eventually he got a position as tutor to the sons of a rising manufacturer and became interested in the employees as well as the children of his patron. Blanc was surprised to find what a passion for education these workers developed. As soon as he could, Blanc moved into the wider field of journalism,[4] and in 1840 he offered to the people his biggest work, *The History of Ten Years*, which was nothing but an exposé of Louis Philippe's government in the light of its campaign promises. Nothing else did as much to open the eyes of Frenchmen to the shams of their politics, and the King himself called the book "a battering ram against the bulwarks of loyalty."

Louis Blanc had taken "the oath of Hannibal," as he said, against the unjust social order—and for a contribution toward a just one he produced his most famous pamphlet on *The Organization of Work*, which he hoped would point the way to happiness for all classes. For he excoriated the idea of class struggle, and believed that the rich, who were "pale from fear," would welcome his way out as joyfully as the poor who were pale from undernourishment. To his mind competition, especially as it developed under the new English theories of free enterprise, was the source of incredible evil.

Labor was to be organized, according to Blanc, by setting up

[4] Blanc was a stickler for exactness. Once he insisted that a hurt dog does not "howl," it "yelps." Another time he refused to accept a patent medicine advertisement until the maker could produce one individual who had been cured by the product.

"social workshops," essentially producers' cooperatives, with state money. The state would not drive out capitalist enterprises directly, but would use competition to kill competition by offering employment to all who wished it. This was the nub of "the right to work," and Blanc not only assumed that most workers would prefer the social workshops but that they would be more efficient because of good morale and the "cheaper communal life" they would offer their workers in the way of housing, laundry service, and so on. For Blanc was not free of the idea so common in his day that ultimate social happiness would be found in planned community living.

It would be up to the government to keep prices from falling too low. Thus, though he talked about the possibility of the workshops' becoming independent of the state—buying themselves free—there was always in the back of Louis Blanc's mind something authoritarian and absolute. Heine, as subtle a psychologist as any modern Freudian, felt that Blanc's aversion to eminent individualism came from jealousy in his hidden mind against any superiority, a complex based on Blanc's stature. For Louis Blanc, with his dark eyes and shining white teeth, was only a bit taller than a dwarf.

Besides Heine one other person saw through Louis Blanc at the time of his popularity, Pierre Joseph Proudhon. Two *bons mots* were thrown out whenever his name came up, "Property is theft" and "God is evil." These were always quoted out of context, but they sounded sufficiently bitter, not to say sinister, to make him a bugaboo. People who only heard of him were terrified, but those who saw him were always struck with his broad smile. It was said that Venus herself might walk past him without being noticed, but whoever talked to him was sure to come back with a good story. "I dream of a society in which I should be beheaded as a conservative," he remarked to Louis Napoleon. Of all the societies existing, he liked ·the American system best because it governed least; in France he distrusted the republic at least as much as the monarchy, for he could not stand Louis Blanc's idea that all direction should come from the top. As he watched the progressive failure of Blanc's system through the revolutionary days of 1848, Proudhon's sharp criticisms stick out like the chorus of a Greek tragedy.

For the support of his principles Louis Blanc could rely on the most sophisticated working class leaders on the continent of Europe. For years French socialists and liberals had idealized the proletariat.

The historian Michelet, for example, wrote *The People* in 1846, a little essay in which he described the condition of each class of French society, all of them cramped by the conditions of the time, the poor by mortgages and factory conditions, the rich by fear of the lower classes and by the necessity to lie and flatter. But he found the hope of the future in the common people, who not only seemed to have a goodness of heart very rare among the rich, but who represented all the future of art and science, all the aspirations of the race. (When the revolution of 1848 was over, poor Michelet was disillusioned like thousands of other liberals. He remarked that he could never have written *The People* after that experience.) George Sand was another writer who not only glorified the working class hero in her novels, but who took the trouble to discover several working class poets. Other intellectuals planned courses in workers' education, and in response to all this flattery and interest, the skilled branches, at least, of the Paris proletariat were comparatively well-dressed, well-educated and well-read. A group of them even edited a newspaper, *L'Atelier*; white collar friends were expressly forbidden to sit on its board, though they occasionally contributed signed articles.

One result of the commiseration they received was that the workers grew used to having their sufferings described; they enjoyed feeling picturesque, and even snubbed Dumas because he refused to sound bitter enough about them.

Another result was that Paris was the only city where a true socialist revolt was possible in 1848. Other European capitals lacked the working-class leadership for such a fight; it is also true that their energies were more absorbed in the fight for nationality, which the French did not have to bother with.

Besides Louis Blanc's group of educated and presentable workmen, there was another active segment of the working classes far more revolutionary—the secret societies on which Metternich blamed all the trouble in Europe. In France under the Restoration they had been republican groups whose members were bound by a ritualistic oath to wash in the blood of kings. The candidate took this oath blindfolded, with a poignard in his hands, sure that death would be his own punishment for disloyalty.

After 1833 the laws against associations were made tighter—it became a crime to belong to one without official permission. But the general conditions of living were made easier, so when the secret societies, broken up that year, began covertly to reorganize, they had few middle class members save students, and became for the first time essentially proletarian. The workers had always known something of *Compagnonnage*, the freemasonry by which young skilled crafts-men were initiated into the social life of their trade and often made the tour of France before settling down. During the 1840's, descrip-tions of this happy way of life became part of the intellectual cult of the workers. But the Society of the Seasons had a different char-acter. Two young friends, Armand Barbès and Auguste Blanqui, undertook to set up in Paris a society with rational revolutionary aims. The plan of its organization was that six members were bossed by a man with the title of a Sunday: four complete weeks were grouped under a month, say a July; and three months would make a season. (Chesterton's novel *The Man Who Was Thursday* is taken from this scheme.)

The workers clung passionately to their old bloodthirsty rituals, somewhat to the dismay of their realistic leaders; but at the same time these leaders were able to extract regular contributions for the relief of political prisoners, for printing, and for laying up arms. Occasionally Blanqui or one of the others would hold a review. Sta-tioned in some obscure window he would memorize faces while his cohorts marched by with a secret sign to mark them, such as wearing their coats buttoned on the left or walking arm in arm by threes.

In 1839 the societies made an abortive insurrection for which both Barbès and Blanqui were sentenced to death. Public demonstra-tions against carrying out the executions were so powerful, added to appeals from the poet Lamartine and Barbès' stricken sister, and a protest from Victor Hugo, who heard the news at the theater and dashed off an appeal in verse to the King, that the soft-hearted monarch commuted the sentence. Thus it was that when the monarchy fell these two leaders were ready to step out of prison; but during their incarceration the Seasons fell into the hands of less energetic guides and became thronged with stool pigeons.

Perhaps the Seasons' most interesting connection, though it is a tenuous one, is in their German affiliate, the League of the Just, which Marx and Engels turned into the Communist League. These brother societies constituted "the specter which haunted Europe" in 1847. When people talked about communism in those days, they meant, so far as they knew what they were talking about, these materialistic non-religious socialists who were not afraid of the class struggle. All of these groups were in those days very small, however, numbering their members by hundreds rather than thousands, and if Marx had not used them as a springboard their influence on history would have been hard to detect.

To all the discontented groups in France, electoral reform seemed like a first step, one on which they could unite. It hardly seems inevitable a hundred years later, when everybody either has the vote or is accustomed to dictatorship, that social reform should be tied so closely to suffrage, but in those days all republicans were to a certain degree socialists (for instance, they favored the nationalization of railroads). And all but a few socialists professed to be republicans; they described their common aim as "the democratic and social republic." The conservative republic is supposed to have been invented by Thiers in 1871, but by that time Bismarck and Napoleon III had worn a good deal of the silver plate off the idea of votes for everybody.

III

The Revolution of Contempt

THE campaign of banquets did not start nor did it stop with the one at Mâcon. Political banquets were an old English custom, and, faced with the prohibition against big public assemblies, the opposition members of the Chamber of Deputies adopted it in order to force the issue of reform upon the government. Lamartine, undecided as yet what party to help, was too cautious to attend more than one of these affairs—his own. The others were in the hands of liberal deputies, those who wanted the English type of constitution, and the moderate republicans. The opposition that found its way into the Chamber under the existing election law was, as may be imagined, by no means the strongest anti-government force. But the Chamber was the place where infection could come to a head and burst, thus releasing other forces—the students, the secret societies, the disaffected national guard and the unpredictable people of Paris.

All this was far from the minds of the organizers of the first banquet, held near Paris on July 9, 1847, and attended by 1,200 Parisian voters. By "reform" they meant a loosening up of the election laws to include, not, indeed, the working and serving classes, but a far larger share of the substantial middle classes, together with a relaxing of the personal government of Guizot and Louis Philippe, so that there would be more commercial and intellectual freedom. The first banquet was such a success that the custom spread all over France and by the end of the year nearly every town had had one. Thousands of citizens pledged formal allegiance to the idea of reform by buying a ticket.

As might be expected, however, the more successful the banquets the more each faction wanted to claim credit and to urge its own propaganda. It was not long before the republicans and the liberal constitutional monarchists split—over the question of whether there should be a toast to the King. Odilon Barrot, head of the constitutionalists, discovered that Ledru-Rollin, the leader of the republicans, would attend the banquet at Lille, where there would be no toast to His Majesty, so Barrot canceled his acceptance. The resulting quarrel seemed likely to put an end to the whole campaign, except that a new wind came along to rekindle the flame.

For the authors of the plan for a culminating Paris banquet were far more radical than those that had planned the others: they were national guard officers and citizens of the 12th *arrondissement* of Paris. The 12th was on the Left Bank centering on the Pantheon, with the university near its fringes, and it had long been a center of working-class and student agitation—a fact which caused the police to raise objections to a banquet there. Liberals who had been banqueting all over France felt called upon to support this most dangerous fruit of their campaign, even though with misgivings. A few of the opposition deputies took over the plans for the affair and arranged that that bone of contention, the republican Ledru-Rollin, should be left out—for he himself agreed that his name was not worth the twenty-four respectable ones who would join the committee if he were not on it. Then as a further concession, plans for the banquet were postponed until the Chamber should have concluded a weeks-long debate on its reply to the speech from the throne.

On December 27 the King in person had opened parliament with an extremely self-satisfied speech, touching on the recovery from the commercial crisis of 1846, the growth of savings banks, peace in Europe, and his own devotion to France. "In the middle of the agitation which blind or hostile passions are fomenting, one conviction upholds me: it is that we possess in the constitutional monarchy the most certain means for satisfying for everyone the moral and material interests of our dear country. . . ."[1] The King's words were lost from then on. A glacial silence met his remark about blind and hostile passion, and every banqueteer, every member of the opposition felt an irrevocable, personal insult thrown in his face.

Guizot, the chief minister, who, of course, wrote the speech, had insisted on the poisoned words for the very reason, he said, that he wished to carry the war into the camp of the opposition.

So far it seemed as if the moderate forces in France were waging a clever campaign to win the moderate reforms that the middle classes needed. Whatever demands the working class may have had were being kept under, and the wishes, whatever they were, of the

[1] Quoted in Stern, *Histoire de la révolution de 1848*, I, 43.

12th *arrondissement* were apparently being stalemated by the safe and sane party.

Nevertheless, yeast was working. During the first weeks of 1848, Paris suffered from painful excitement. People in rags, with cadaverous faces, such as were never at other times seen by sunlight in the streets began to march in groups "like thunderclouds over the frivolous Paris sky." They showed first sticks, then guns. One of their leaders, tall and strong, carried a child's drum around his neck on which he kept beating. Others simply carried the fire of fanaticism in their eyes. One landlady was sure revolution was coming because the people sang so much, and to clinch her argument she pointed to her water carrier who had five loaves of bread under his arm. "For the three days. We always do such things in three days." At the same time the soldiers who were about looked distracted, as if they were afraid they would be ordered to shoot their fellow citizens.

Meanwhile, the banquet group was still concerned with its own small triumphs and did not delay to take up Guizot's challenge. On February 14 a new banquet committee was formed, including some leaders from each faction but few of the original 12th *arrondissement* group. The deputies, eager to avenge themselves on Guizot without taking up the cause of the workers and students, removed the scene of the banquet to the Right Bank and raised the price of admission. The first date set was Sunday, February 20. As the workers showed livelier and livelier interest, however—especially the infuriated citizens of the 12th—the time was moved to the following Tuesday when not so many working people could watch. A spot was engaged within four walls; a canvas cover was set up of a size to accommodate 6,000 guests; and it was carefully arranged with the police that the banquet should not be forbidden by force, but that at the entrance to the hall a police commissioner should read an act forbidding the guests to go in. The banqueteers were then to go in anyway, eat a token meal, and listen to a single toast, to be given by Odilon Barrot, "To reform and the right of assembly." Having thus broken the law, they were to go peacefully home and try the case in the courts.

Such a lily-livered scheme might have satisfied everybody. Gossip told the British Ambassador that the courts would have no choice but to declare the banquet legal.

But there were impatient as well as patient members of the opposition, and Odilon Barrot, one of the eminently patient ones, describes the horror with which on February 20 he read in the republican paper, the *National*, a long formal announcement of plans for the banquet. It was just what the committee had decided on, but Armand Marrast, the *National's* editor, had managed to give the description an official and battling air. At 11:30 on Tuesday, the 22nd, the deputies and peers who wished to attend would meet at the Place de la Madeleine and start off for the banqueting place in a body. At the Place de la Concorde other banquet subscribers would join them, including a few workers and students who had been given tickets, and the procession would pass through unarmed files of such members of the national guard as were supporting the demonstration. Everyone was urged to be peaceful, but everyone was obviously invited to watch, and the Ministry became scared by the evident size and discipline of the preparations. So the police announced hastily that it was illegal for any but constituted authorities to call out the national guard and that therefore they would prevent the meeting by force. Posters forbade the public to attend and threatened members of the national guard with severe punishment if they showed up in uniform.

Faced with this threat and the possibility of their peaceful banquet turning into a meeting of bloodshed, the deputies involved in the preparations met at Odilon Barrot's house on Monday and decided to give up the whole affair. Marrast, the editor of the *National*, indeed proposed the grand gesture that all the opposition deputies resign as a protest, but this was too much for most of the group, who weakly agreed only to sign a complaint which Barrot was to hand to the president of the Chamber. Barrot, the perfect parliamentarian, would have been happy with a purely parliamentary success like this; he was one of those who never appeared in the Chamber except in black, very well brushed, and while speaking in the tribune, he always kept his left hand behind him in the most correct form. A few deputies, led by Lamartine, who is supposed to have volunteered to go to the banquet alone, if necessary, "accompanied by his shadow," at first said they would go ahead with the plans anyway—but by Monday evening they, too, had been persuaded of the possibility of a massacre and abandoned the project.

The King was overjoyed at this news. "I told you it would all disappear in smoke," he told one of his advisers. The government saw only the superficiality of the banquets still, while even the most superficial of the banqueteers began to see the depths of trouble they were kindling. If the administration had left a single channel open for the political emotions of its citizens, it might not have been completely destroyed.

Fury boiled in the 12th *arrondissement* and in the national guard, but the people no longer had any leaders. Of the republican newspapers, the *National* naturally reflected the decision Marrast had helped to make, while even the more radical *Réforme* counseled no action. Meetings were held at its offices, but even on the 22nd, when all Paris seethed with angry indecision, citizens could get no clue from the leading radical paper. Three days later the Second Republic was practically to be born in their offices—but before they could act the newspaper men had to draw courage from the people.

Except in the Tuileries, where Louis Philippe laughed at the "storm in the teapot" that was brewing, Monday night was spent uneasily in Paris. Odilon Barrot was busy planning the storm in *his* teapot, the signed protest of the opposition to the forbidding of their banquet which he was to hand over to the Chamber.

The workers, excited by hunger as many of their depositions show, as well as by inflammatory placards on the city walls, planned in large numbers to take the next day off and see what happened. They did not prepare for a battle.

The secret societies, crowded with stool pigeons, assumed an air of watchful waiting. The British Ambassador was told they would wait for their old signal, the death of Louis Philippe. Lucien Delahodde, who was one of the top officers of the Society of the Seasons, secretly reported to the police that his society had positive orders not to move—probably he himself had a voice in giving those orders.

But there was an offshoot of the Seasons, formed by militants who distrusted Delahodde's soothing leadership of the old society without knowing his true connections as a stool pigeon. They separated into a club known as the Dissenting Society, a group which had at this time, according to Delahodde, about 400 members, among them the inevitable twelve police spies. We hear that these 400 men organized the February revolution, spreading out during the night to all the suburbs, urging workmen to take the day off; organizing columns of people to march down the boulevards the next morning; and erecting the first barricades.

The police, though warned by their twelve men of the Dissenting Society's intention (100 sous went to each informer), were on the whole so confident of their own strength that, with the approval of the military and the King, they countermanded orders for the troops to occupy strategic zones and told them to stay in their barracks. Also, in order not to antagonize the people, the police were told not to appear in uniform on Tuesday. A list of 150 key men to arrest was made up, but was carelessly forgotten.

It is doubtful how much the Dissenting Society accomplished. Most witnesses, especially those having no contact with the working classes, loved to speak with horror of the vast underground network; Lamartine, who enjoyed making the best possible story, described hordes marching with a discipline that could only have come from practice; yet most of the depositions taken later from active fighters show that the people who took over the February revolution were swept away by enthusiasm and were totally unprepared to seize the power that fell into their hands.

If anybody crystallized their feeling, it was more likely the students. When the student leaders, editors of the Latin Quarter papers, *L'Avant-Garde* and *La Lanterne du Quartier Latin*, heard that the deputies and the grown-up newspapers had given up the banquet, they decided it must then be held by the schools. (The medical and law students were the revolutionary ones—no one could enlist the engineers until the third day, when they helped restore order.) All Monday night the students prepared for battle, collecting arms and casting musket balls, and in the morning, 700 strong, they marched to the Palais-Bourbon where the Chamber was sitting, and then across the river to the Champs Elysées—all the time singing the *Marseillaise* or the still more popular Girondin chorus, which came from a Dumas drama that had opened the previous summer.

All that really happened on that Tuesday was the milling of steadily increasing crowds. They gathered at the Palais-Bourbon until some dragoons came out of their barracks on the Quai d'Orsay, at a trot and with drawn swords. When they reached the crowd, the soldiers reined in their horses and sheathed their weapons. The crowd cheered them wildly, and the dragoons saluted—an ominous sign for the King. Later in the day the government decided to call out more troops and to summon the national guard, a step they had hesitated to take thus far because of plausible doubts of their loyalty. In any case, on this occasion the orders got mixed and the guard showed up in small numbers.

The gamins of Paris, forever eager for excitement, found this a good day to practice their favorite sport of stone-throwing, and towards evening their older brothers got the fever and began to put up a few barricades. As the sun sank behind two broad red clouds, it glinted on a musket at every street corner. By this time everybody on both sides who had a uniform put it on. An Englishman says he was the only person in the street in mufti; in his restaurant the proprietor was in uniform, and "our fillet of beef was brought to us by a corporal and our coffee poured out by a sergeant."

Nothing had happened the whole day, there was only one man dead. Yet the theaters were closed, and "when the *Comédie-française* shuts its doors in perilous times it is like the battening down of the hatches in dirty weather."

At seven o'clock the next morning (February 23) troops marched in and took their places at various points in the city—the Place de la Concorde, the Hôtel de Ville, the Porte Saint-Denis, and the Porte Saint-Martin. Then the drums went through all *arrondissements* to beat the *rappel* and summon the national guard.

The national guard ought to have been Louis Philippe's most loyal defender, for its establishment was one of the triumphs of the July days of 1830. The right of citizens to bear arms was one of the most insistent liberal demands throughout this period, and when Louis Philippe was willing to grant it, this seemed proof that his new monarchy would have a force to guard its constitution. Since 1830 the guard had always responded to the call of monarchy in trouble, and it enjoyed the exclusive privilege of service at the Tuileries and attendance on the King's carriage. Eligibility was on a somewhat broader basis than suffrage, for any man between 20 and 60 who paid a property tax could join. Each citizen supplied his own uniform, though this was theoretically optional, and the cavalry their horses as well, so there was a good measure of snob appeal in belonging. In spite of these attractions, by 1848 plenty of members were thoroughly bored with guard service. There is a tale that Balzac, a few years previously, neglected his duties so determinedly that officers hunted all over Paris to find him, and finally snagged him by pretending to deliver a handsome Italian vase to his suspected hiding place. When he signed for the parcel they ran in and dragged him off to prison for a week. Something similar befell Dumas.

Added to the general boredom was the fact that the men enrolled in the guard were mostly of the self-sufficient middle class that was particularly conscious of the need for just such reforms as the banquet campaign had been pushing. On the very eve of the uprising a friend of Lamartine tried to puncture the complacency of a general officer by declaring that he belonged to the best company of the best battalion of the best legion of the guard and the spirit of all the men was detestable.

Doubts were felt therefore even in the highest quarters, but the troops were supposed to fight better if they had the citizen guard beside them. Dumas says the first drum beat came to his ears about eleven, and "when we heard that cry of royalty we understood that affairs were serious." But the guard had its own mind. In the famous 12th *arrondissement* it decided to gather in force in order to be able to act for reform; the 8th pursued the opposite tactic of not obeying the call. By noon several legions had made their way to the Tuileries to petition the King for concessions. There is a legend that many guards gave up their arms and uniforms to the people, either from force or from sympathy. And as for the regulars, if any soldier were separated an instant from his line the mob immediately seized him; he was embraced in the friendliest way, deftly disarmed and sent back.

Barricades were building all this time and cries of *"Vive la Réforme"* and *"A bas Guizot"* became louder. By two-thirty the King was talking to Guizot and saying he would rather abdicate than lose his favorite minister. Later the King said that Guizot abandoned him in this critical moment. Guizot, on the other hand, states that the King pushed him into it. Guizot was probably right about this, for he explained that *he* could not grant reform, with his record—and though the King embraced him with tears, he listened to the cries outside the window and finally announced he would send for the reactionary Count Molé to return to office and form a new cabinet.

When Guizot went to the Assembly in the Palais-Bourbon to tell them of his dismissal, Odilon Barrot had turned in his petition regarding the forbidding of the banquet, and the president had received it in stony silence and refused to allow discussion. Then Guizot walked in, his face pale and contracted, his head thrown back for fear of seeming to lower it, and his tone of voice charging Louis Philippe with black ingratitude. The news hit the members of the majority just where it would hurt most. It seemed to them, accustomed to living on their votes, like treason—and Tocqueville noted on their faces "surprise, anger, fear, avarice."

At the fall of Guizot everything lapsed into worse disorder than ever. Delessert, the usually mild and able chief of police, urged the arrest of political enemies of the monarchy, the opposition deputies and such, but no one was in a position to give such a drastic order. Guizot was determined to let his successor stew in the juice that he had left simmering, and in view of the hotness of the pot it was many hours before anyone could be found. Count Molé sensibly refused; the voices of the people when they heard of Guizot's dismissal were enough to indicate that only a liberal ministry could possibly control them. The news was all over the city by three o'clock, and the large bourgeois elements broke into immediate rejoicing. Women and children began to come out into the streets and bands of people went around forcing everyone to illuminate his house. Rothschild's mansion was lit up, and even Guizot's residence at the Foreign Affairs building, though Guizot himself had departed.

The workers, however, were still distrustful. They had been badly disillusioned in 1830, having made a revolution then and let the bourgeoisie run off with the profits, and until Guizot's successor had been found they would maintain their barricades. An excitable young man named Marie-Joseph Sobrier, who was both radical and rich, "one of those light-headed young men whom the imprudence of parents allows to remain their own masters in Paris," ran from barricade to barricade until he fell exhausted, telling the workers that the fall of Guizot was not enough, that they should go to the Chamber of Deputies and demand their rights.

In the middle of this double-edged excitement came a massacre. Along in the evening a column of singing people, with a red flag at the head, marched from the office of the republican *National* to the Ministry of Justice, where they forced the minister to light up his windows, then to the Ministry of Foreign Affairs. By this time the crowd around them was enormous, but the officer guarding the Ministry ordered his troops not to let them pass. The crowd was continually pushed forward from the rear; to back up would have been impossible. The officer took his horse, which was scared by the red torches, behind the line of troops and ordered his men to fix bayonets. They had to step back a few paces to do this, and as they handled their loaded guns a shot went off. It was almost certainly an accident, although scores of fantastic stories were worked up later to explain the event to the satisfaction of either side.

At any rate the soldiers reacted with a volley of musket fire straight into the crowd.

People scattered in terror, leaving the street bloody and groaning with wounded. Fifty-two people were killed by this fusillade, and no one counted the number of wounded who were carried into apothecary shops and nearby houses.

Afterwards the soldiers who had been in that company had the numbers taken off their hats; they had to be mixed up with other regiments to save them from the anger of the people.

That night the genius of revolution was working, as Odilon Barrot put it. Someone found a huge wagon with a white horse and piled the corpses on it. A man on the shaft of the wagon held a torch so that everyone might see the dead. Some witnesses described a young woman's body on top of the heap with her bloody breast exposed, while a workingman kept lifting the corpse and embracing it, crying "Vengeance."

This funeral wagon went all over Paris until dawn. Its followers knocked on the doors of poor homes and made people wake up and look at the bodies. Church bells rang out the tocsin; and people— 100,000, they say—began to seize arms and build more barricades. New processions of fantastic nature filled the streets—Dumas describes a group whose leader was dressed only in blue trousers and a shirt. His bare arm held up a red flag, while two men beside him carried torches. Then a fourth man came along holding a straw image dipped in pitch, alight on a high stick.

The students of *L'Avant-Garde* spent the night preparing to lead the struggle and making more powder and balls. Their editorial explained, "We understand that it is up to democracy to conquer or die." The people were in fact so well prepared that when Marshal

Bugeaud attacked at five on Thursday morning (the 24th) his plans failed. He thought that Paris would not be awake so early.

For Marshal Bugeaud, Duke of Isly, was the one leader who had been found to help the King. He received the appointment about midnight to command all forces in the fight against the insurrection, both the army and the national guard, and immediately took energetic action. His very name heartened the men under him, who had been allowed to remain wet, cold, ill-fed, and ill-armed. Munitions were ordered from Vincennes, one of the nearest fortresses, to be pushed right through the rioting districts, and plans were made to occupy important spots. At last the military had the leadership it needed to quell the rebellion, or so it seemed.

On the parliamentary front, the King finally summoned Louis Adolphe Thiers, the titular leader of the opposition, who had been prime minister in 1840 and was to become president of the Third Republic after 1871. Thiers told His Majesty that in order to form a ministry he would require the assistance of Odilon Barrot. It was a bitter pill for Louis Philippe to have to take into his cabinet one of the men most conspicuously labeled the month before as having a blind and hostile passion. (Thiers throughout the banquet campaign had carefully kept his coattails out, while instigating Barrot to involve himself as deeply as possible. It was Barrot's fate never to realize how he was exploited.)

The new ministry, for Thiers was his last hope and the King had to give in, demanded two things, Bugeaud's dismissal and the dissolution of the Chamber with a new election. The marshal had been one of the most hated men in Paris ever since he brutally repressed some riots in 1834, in what the working classes knew evermore as a "massacre." On the very day of his new appointment he declared in the Chamber of the Peers that he would still fire if he had 50,000 women and children in front of him. No liberal ministry could have taken office with the odium of his name attached. The King demurred, but realized he was in a corner and finally compromised by giving the order that Bugeaud should withdraw all regular troops outside the city while the national guard, which would now have to bear the defense of the monarchy, should be commanded by a more popular general. Thiers and Barrot, who only became ministers about eight in the morning of the 24th, signed an order to all troops not to fire. This order was printed and posted all over Paris as quickly as possible, but whereas it thoroughly demoralized the troops, the common people were afraid it was a trick, especially as no copy of the order had been sent to the official newspaper, the *Moniteur*, nor were the new cabinet's names listed. (Guizot, though it was after his dismissal, had thoughtfully inserted the notice of Bugeaud's appointment in the *Moniteur's* pages.)

By this time Paris streets were everywhere dammed with barricades, 1,512 in all at the final count. In small streets they seemed to rise almost every ten feet, while at important squares huge ones rose that were to become legends. Enthusiastic Paris citizens had used barricades ever since 1588 (against the Duke of Guise) and now they went methodically to work with crowbars to dig up the foot-square paving stones. They politely stopped omnibuses, unhitched the horses, assisted the passengers to alight, and turned the vehicles over to be weighted down with stones. They tore iron railings from houses, cut down four thousand trees along the boulevards and destroyed nearly as many lampposts, so that afterwards the streets looked as if they had been swept by a tornado. Between the barricades men crouched around huge fires casting lead balls. All over town, houses had been ransacked for arms, and chalked on doors one could read, "Arms Given Up,"—some added, "With Pleasure." Through the incessant tocsin, the *Marseillaise* sounded everywhere, or *Mourir pour la Patrie*, the Girondin chorus. Poor Heine, who lived through these days, tried to hum old German folksongs to himself to break the monotony in his ears, but utterly without success.

Outside Paris the railways, stations, and bridges were destroyed for distances as great as thirty miles—partly because people were angry at the speculative exploitation which had gone on in building them, but also because there were enough coachmen and other drivers who felt the railroads were taking their jobs to direct this particular destruction. Inside the city, too, many workers tried to destroy their machines, although a poster from some of their leaders was spread around saying that to do so was to "stifle the voice of the Revolution."

The worst fight came at the Château d'Eau, a military post on the south side of the square of the Palais-Royal. It owed its name to the large fountain where water from the Seine was piped to this section of Paris. Water carriers with their carts came every day to

fill their oaken buckets there. On this 24th of February the crowd
heard that troops were holding prisoners there and also that it was
defended by a detachment of municipal guards. (The municipal
guards were a kind of militarized police, in great popular odium
not to be confused with the national guard.) The Château had a
thick oak door which no effort of the crowd succeeded in breaking
down, so they dragged eighteen carriages to the door and set them
on fire. When the Château itself caught fire, the defenders had to
surrender. And what happened then makes a study in the psychology
of historical witnesses. Delahodde, the conservative police spy, would
have it that as the municipal guards threw down their arms and
marched out, the crowd shot every one. On the other hand the liberal
Daniel Stern says that once they surrendered the crowd received
even the hated municipal guards with open arms and, with chivalry
typical of the working class, nursed the wounded as tenderly as their
own brothers. What probably happened is that the first few out of
the building, trying to shout that they were surrendering, were shot,
but that the rest were spared, whether or not to be nursed no impartial witness remembers.

As the fight moved from the Château d'Eau over to the Palais-
Royal a woman led a band of fifty people to the attack. She was
dressed in a chemise and a skirt, with stockings which fell spirally
about her legs. Her brown hair fell to her waist, and her shoulders,
arms and most of her breast were bare. As men rushed up to embrace
her she brushed them off, for all her ardor was devoted to the revolution.

As might be guessed, the unhappy King was becoming every
minute more discouraged Marshal Bugeaud refused to obey the
orders given by a civilian minister such as Odilon Barrot, and had
to be told expressly by one of the King's sons to give the order not
to fire, and to withdraw his troops. Thereupon Bugeaud placarded
the walls with the order, signed with his name, not realizing that the
public would not trust any conciliation coming from him. Still, by
eleven o'clock the order was out everywhere and the trumpets
sounded retreat.

Barrot himself became a pompous walking placard, as he conceived
it his duty to go from barricade to barricade explaining the new
deal to the fighters. At first he felt his efforts were successful, but
as the day wore on he became dusty and hollow-cheeked, and his hat

became crushed down over his eyes. When the workers at the Porte Saint-Denis, behind their formidable two-story barricade, met him with derision, even he began to understand how the temper of the people was changing. For the first time men started to cry for a republic.

The policing of the city was now up to the national guard which took to marching around with drums, but they had voted heavily not to support the King with arms until he had granted reform. Most of its members probably did not want a republic, but by failing to hold firmly to the monarchy, they decisively laid the path open for one. In the hope of building up their morale, the King, in the uniform of a general of the guard, reviewed them; but when some of the members began calling for reform from the parade ground, the King turned gray and went suddenly back into his palace.

The people meanwhile were seizing the Hôtel de Ville with its cannon and beginning to converge on the royal palace of the Tuileries.

There, the King was no more happy inside with his new cabinet than he had been outside with his national guard. Thiers kept insisting on the dissolution of the Chamber with new elections forthwith. When His Majesty demurred, he heartlessly proposed that perhaps he had better summon M. Guizot again.

Abdication was the natural course of action for such an unhappy monarch, and towards the end of the morning it was put to Louis Philippe dramatically by Emile de Girardin, director of *La Presse*,[2] who rushed in apparently unannounced and dared to tell the King to get off his throne.

Now the heir was Louis Philippe's nine-year-old grandson, the Count of Paris, son of the Duke of Orleans, who had been killed in a carriage accident in 1842. His mother, the Duchess of Orleans,

---

[2] *La Presse* was the first cheap paper in Paris. In 1836 Girardin reduced its subscription price from 80 francs to 40 for the year, with the novel idea that ads would pay the expenses. Girardin was not disappointed. His paper had 60,000 subscribers, winning popularity not only by its price (which the other papers had to imitate) but by its general news coverage. Lamartine, Dumas, and Chateaubriand were among its contributors.

Before he bought *La Presse*, in his early days of poverty Girardin made his start with a fabulously successful little sheet called *Le Voleur* (literally, *The Thief*). Since he could not at that time afford to pay for contributions, *Le Voleur* announced that it would reprint in each issue the most interesting articles from all other publications.

was a German princess who had been a friend of Goethe in his lifetime, and was still one of Humboldt and Victor Hugo. She was young, beautiful, and serious, but not too popular with other members of the French royal family because of her Protestantism and her intellect.

French law stated clearly that in case of the accession of the Count of Paris while still a minor, his oldest uncle, the Duke of Nemours, would be regent. Before his death the Duke of Orleans had specifically stated that he would not want a woman regent, on the theory that the head of the government of France ought always to be able to mount his horse within a quarter of an hour. Or, as Louis Philippe is said to have put it more vulgarly, "Ce qui accouche ne doit pas régner."

In spite of these hindrances many liberals were hoping that some way could be found to make the Duchess regent.

The Duchess herself begged her father-in-law on her knees not to abdicate; the Queen told her husband to die at his place; but his sons urged him to get off the throne. Slowly Louis Philippe sat down and wrote that he abandoned the throne in favor of the Count of Paris. Not a word about the regency. The paper was snatched from his hesitating old fingers and Louis Philippe offered his arm to his Queen and led her into exile. Looking back afterwards he thought he had done right, since his motive was to spare bloodshed, but he took the step, he said, only after "a general abdication of the public conscience."

The royal family had no difficulty in getting to England, even though Louis Philippe forgot to take the half-million francs he had gotten ready for just such an emergency. Lord Palmerston told British consuls to offer any aid they could, and the new provisional government that was soon set up in Paris also budgeted money to have the ex-king secretly kept safe, though this sum was never needed.

Louis Philippe was a humane and conscientious ruler, by no means proud of his office like Frederick William of Prussia or the Hapsburgs who felt God owed them a throne; but he became vain in his old age, and conceit put a veil between him and his people. He could not see what they wanted because he was so sure they ought to want just what he was giving them.

At the end, therefore, support slipped away from him like the final caving-in of land that has been slowly washing away for years. His first active mistake in the catastrophe was to alienate what should have been his loyal opposition by branding their wishes blind and hostile, driving them into actions more daring and far-reaching than they would have wished. Then, by forbidding their banquet, he disorganized these moderate, not to say timid leaders.

Royalty's next line of defense should have been the national guard, but to these men, too, the forbidding of the banquet and the appointment of Marshal Bugeaud over them seemed to cap a long age of restriction and autocracy. They were unwilling to assume responsibility for this kind of law and order—therefore, Paris fell to the mob.

The mob, in turn, was infuriated beyond any hope of pacification by the unfortunate shooting at the Ministry of Foreign Affairs. Now came the real moment of blind and hostile passions, sweeping the old government out of office, heedless of where a new group of leaders were to be found. Paris was luckier than Berlin or Vienna later that summer, for there had been enough political activity in France to create leaders eager and able to take command of the situation. To a large extent they came out of the republican newspaper offices, and when they consolidated their power, several members of the left wing of the reforming banquet group assumed office —Lamartine, Ledru-Rollin, and Louis Blanc.

Hardly had the King and Queen left the Tuileries when the people burst in. Finding the table set for lunch, a group of workers sat down and ate it with much hilarity and ironically elegant manners. Everybody sat on the throne in turn and began carrying off souvenirs and breaking china, while someone put up a sign, "House for Rent." However, they did not touch the pictures, because (Dumas tells us) they obscurely felt they could never replace works of art, though it took ten wagons later to carry off chipped porcelain and burnt tapestries. They managed to break 23,000 pieces of glassware, and the gold leaf on the broken table china was still worth 20,000 francs.[3] So the mob lived on for days in squalid splendor, using the palace servants, until finally the new government had to drive them out by force.

Since it was up to the Chamber of Deputies to pass on the question

[3] A franc was worth about 18.6 cents in those days.

of regency, friends of the Duchess of Orleans urged her to go thither in person and plead her case. Victor Hugo even tried to make her ride through the streets and appeal to the people, but she was too shy to do this. She did appear in the Chamber, dressed in heavy mourning, leading her two sons in short black jackets and pleated white collars, and made a sight so touching that Lamartine, who had just decided to support a republic, was afraid she would melt all hearts. He induced her to take a back seat and proceeded with his oration in favor of the republic, though he tells us his heart bled as he did so. When the Duchess asked permission to speak it was denied her, and when someone moved that a provisional government be established, everyone applauded, including the small pretender.

The Chamber was filling up with citizens who poured in and overflowed the galleries, the halls, the aisles. Before things became too dangerous the Duchess and her children were helped to escape, but the meeting soon became too rowdy for the president to manage, so he put on his hat, a sign of adjournment. The crowd refused to let themselves be cheated by this maneuver and immediately raised an old and valiant republican leader, Dupont de l'Eure, to the chair. The duty before the house was to select names for the provisional government.

Nearly every group of politically minded citizens in Paris had spent the afternoon preparing lists for such a government, but the two most important meetings for this purpose were held in the newspaper offices of the *National* and the *Réforme*.

The *National* was the paper of the moderate republicans. It was the only paper in Paris that had refused to accept bribes of railroad shares in the 1830's. (At that time nearly all republicans were in favor of state-owned railroads.) Its editor was Armand Marrast. The *Réforme*, founded in 1843, was much more radical, but was considered less dangerous because it had barely 2,000 subscribers and was going on the rocks financially. Its editor was Ferdinand Flocon; its angel, Ledru-Rollin of banqueting fame; and it supported the policies of Louis Blanc.

On this February 24, the partisans of both papers gathered at the journals' offices and started writing out their tickets. Some names, like Lamartine and François Arago, the famous republican astronomer, headed both lists, but further down each group tried to inscribe as many of its own editors and contributors as possible. A hurried consultation was carried out between the two factions and the joint list and various reasonable facsimiles were hurried over to the Palais-Bourbon.

Significantly the radical meeting at the *Réforme* took one extra precautionary step. They ordered two of their own men to take immediate charge of the police and post offices. Etienne Arago, brother of the astronomer, rushed to the post office and ordered that the mails should start moving immediately, barricades or no barricades. Subsequently, he helped popularize the republic by introducing cheap postal service.[4] But far more important, since every revolutionary group at that time, as at this, recognized the importance of controlling the police, they sent one of their most efficient organizers to the Prefecture, Marc Caussidière.

Caussidière had a tremendous heavy body with a sugar-loaf head sunk between his shoulders, and small pig eyes that shone with wariness and finesse. Otherwise his person betokened good nature, and many are the tales of how much he could eat and drink. He had earlier thought up several good ideas for starting in business, like lighting house numbers at night and developing a waterproof fabric, but he never worked hard enough to be financially successful. He lived off his friends, particularly Ledru-Rollin, who seems to have used his wife's fortune to keep half the republican party going, including the *Réforme*. But in jobs requiring less constant application than making a living, Caussidière's success was sensational. In 1845, for instance, he joined and reactivated the secret society of Seasons. In 1847 he was sent all over France to raise money for the *Réforme*, and succeeded in keeping the paper alive.

When he was given the congenial task of installing himself in the police headquarters, he met no resistance from the demoralized officials. What he slyly calls "his only revolutionary threat" was to gather all the police captains and officers together and tell them he would shoot anyone who was treasonable to the new regime.

His next move was to draw up a proclamation to the people of Paris, urging the citizens to keep their arms at hand and their revolutionary spirits up, reminding them that they had often been betrayed before. Since the police always regulated retail stores, he also decreed that food shops should stay open for the remainder of

[4] Postal reform began in England, with a penny rate for letters set in 1840. The U.S.A. followed in 1847. In France, in August 1848, the rate was set at 20 centimes.

the emergency, for he was anxious to make the new regime popular and that things should be easy and pleasant for the people.

These duties attended to, he inspected his new office. First he found where the money was kept, then he discovered the records of police spies, which he was to find most interesting reading in the course of ensuing weeks. All his republican friends enjoyed coming in to look up their own names in the police record.

(In spite of the irregularity of their appointments by a mere citizens' meeting, Caussidière and Arago were to entrench themselves too well for the new legal government to do anything but accept them and keep them on. The chief of police was always willing to give jobs to deserving republicans and to help people out with friendship, advice, and money. His devotion to the party did not, however, go to the length of hiring republican cooks—the excellent servants of the old regime were kept on, and they served up fine food for the revels which Caussidière delighted in giving for his friends.)

Back at the Palais-Bourbon the serious business of choosing the provisional government was in hand. The scene was tumultuous and doubtless would have lost all order if everyone there had not had in his mind a perfect picture of how a revolution should be conducted. Luckily the pattern was clear to all. They did not remember the history of 1830 in vain. After Dupont de l'Eure took the chair Lamartine sorted out the lists of names for a provisional government that were handed to him on behalf of various groups. After several false starts he got Ledru-Rollin, who was in the tribune, to read the names aloud. As each one was called, the crowd roared its applause—Dupont de l'Eure, Lamartine, Arago, Marie, Garnier-Pagès, Crémieux. But this procedure was only a start. Ritual required the new provisional government to march to the Hôtel de Ville, there to be consecrated by the people's applause. The new ministers set off together for this ceremony. On the way they passed a military post where some dragoons were sitting, apparently none too happy over the situation. Lamartine stopped, begged them for a drink of their red wine, and as he touched it to his lips recalled the almost forgotten beginning of the story: "Here is your banquet."

The revolution of contempt was neither as bloody nor as passionate as the revolution of freedom had been, but as far as its participants could manage it had been played along the same lines; and like a good play, it produced its feeling of catharsis.

The Republic of Intellectuals

AT THE Hôtel de Ville every room was full of people, wounded still lying on straw, orators making speeches from window sills, and the mass just watching to see what was going to happen. When the members of the provisional government arrived by ones and twos, for they could not keep together, they could hardly force their way in, and there seemed no place where they could sit down, let alone deliberate. At last someone found them a small private office where they barred the door with heavy furniture and posted a few well-disposed youths outside to guard them. Here they sat down to a session that lasted fifteen stormy hours. Crowds kept beating on the door with their demands, and seven times Lamartine had to go out and pacify the people with his "purple and golden" words; some of the others took turns at this job, too. And more than once an inordinately obstinate republican forced his way into the very presence of the cabinet.

The first of such interruptions was perhaps the most unwelcome to the seven men in conference. It consisted of Louis Blanc, borne on the shoulders of some workers or he could never have forced his small frame through the crowd, together with Ferdinand Flocon, editor of the *Réforme*, announcing that they were also members of the provisional government, chosen by the meeting at the *Réforme* and consecrated by the people just like the seven gentlemen already sitting.

"Consecration" of the new rulers was accomplished by the roar of the people's applause as each of them presented himself to the crowd at the Hôtel de Ville and explained his principles. Each of the first group had done this, and now the newcomers also; and it was true that in this probation the new ones were as popular as the others, probably more so. It would be dangerous if not impossible to exclude these radicals after they had been endorsed by the crowd, yet the original conservative seven felt reluctant to admit them. Then the practical Garnier-Pagès thought of a formula: let them be "secretaries" to the new government, secretaries with consultative voices. This seemed to make Lamartine and his colleagues happier; the new arrivals agreed, but said they must include also the name of Albert, a workingman. For it had been decided at the *Réforme* meeting that a worker should by all means have his name in the new government, and Albert was proposed though he was not present. Now Louis Blanc had explained about him to the crowd and they had consecrated him *in absentia*. Although the new cabinet accepted a working-class member, no one ever bothered to call him anything but Albert, which was his given name (his surname was Martin)—a beautiful example of nineteenth century class feeling, and possibly one reason why Albert said he felt patronized and soon wanted to retire.

Somehow or other Flocon's rival editor of the *National*, Armand Marrast, was also included in the new government, and so the original seven became eleven. Within two days the pretense of secretaryships was dropped and the new members were accepted, and acted, on perfect equality with the old.

This was emphatically not because they liked each other. Tocqueville, indeed, commented that it would be hard to find a body of men who mutually hated each other more sincerely, but the balance of power was so delicate that they simply could not allow resignations. Except for Albert and possibly Arago they were all conceited men; by reading their memoirs it is easy to confirm the sarcasm of Odilon Barrot that it was as if Providence had deliberately thrown together all varieties of human pride, in order to show how little this sentiment could accomplish. They were also suspicious. Ledru, Lamartine, and Marrast are known to have kept secret operatives to spy on the others; and when the government fell, each delighted to hint in delicate Gallic manner which of his colleagues, in his opinion, should receive the blame.

Decidedly this is to put the lowest estimate of them first. In the test they all proved honest. No later investigation could ever show either mismanagement of funds or even undue extravagance. And they all stuck by the republic and their own convictions, even if each one believed his own conception of a republic was the only possible one. What they lacked, what all the continental republicans of 1848 lacked, was experience in the practice of democracy which lets men allow time for changes, and tolerance by which opposing sides may rub each others' corners off instead of splitting them into pieces.

Here they sat, then, this uneasy fellowship, with the people still ready to burst in and demand immediate confirmation of all their wishes. The first demand was the republic. In its creation the people could understand no delay, and in fact set delegates of their own to remain in the council room and make sure the government did not equivocate. In vain the hesitant legalists around the table said they should leave the proclamation of a republic up to popular vote. Louis Blanc, with the masses at the door to back him up, forced the other members to decree that they "wished" a republic now, and decreed one, subject to immediate ratification at the polls. And to quiet the crowd someone broke out a huge banner on which was written with a piece of charcoal, "The Republic one and indivisible is declared."

When morning came the new ministers, who had spent the night drafting decrees and distributing portfolios, breakfasted on black bread and cheese left by the soldiers and drank red wine and water out of a cracked sugar bowl which they passed from mouth to mouth. "A good beginning for economy in government," remarked Lamartine.

All that first day of peace, February 25, things would not quiet down. Workers still circulated through the streets of Paris, not knowing exactly what to ask for next. About noon an armed man came into the deliberating chamber and pounded with his musket on the floor. "*Droit au travail*," he said, "the right to work." Blanc says he was handsome, pale, and savage, with the people's electricity in his eye; and Lamartine for once felt himself at somewhat of a loss when he drew him aside, trying to remonstrate, and was told, "No more poetry." Meanwhile, Blanc was hastily drawing up a decree which he read to the man. It pledged the republic to give work to all citizens who needed it, but Blanc pointed out the impossibility of doing this overnight. "Very well, Monsieur," said the worker. "The people are waiting. They will put three months of misery at the service of the Republic."

Next came the delegation that wanted the red flag adopted as the standard of the new republic instead of the tricolor which had been "dishonored" under Louis Philippe. The red flag had been used on some of the barricades and was accepted as the color of socialism; now a passion hit the crowd to make it their own forever. It was a dark wet day, but when boys began distributing bits of red cloth, the street was soon brilliant with flashes of color. Once again the mob gathered around the Hôtel de Ville and demanded a concession. But this time the provisional government did not give in because their financial advisor said the red flag would absolutely ruin their credit. So Lamartine, himself just barely convinced, went out to face the mob again and even with their loaded muskets leveled at him he produced an oration powerful enough to turn the emotion of his hearers. "The tricolor has gone around the world in triumph," he said, "the red flag has only been dragged through mud and blood around the Champ de Mars." He was referring to a famous "massacre" of the people that occurred in the Champ de Mars in 1791. Reminded of their national glory, the people accepted the tricolor. As a concession, under the Second Republic, it was always to have a red rosette at its staff; and members of the provisional government, who were already arrayed with large blue-white-and-red sashes over their shoulders, agreed to wear red rosettes in their buttonholes to remind themselves of the barricades.

Having met this first slowing of their momentum, the multitude was willing to give up for a while and go home, leaving the new government more or less at peace. For a brief moment, hardly long enough to be called a honeymoon, everyone was enthusiastic, from the wealthy inhabitants and diplomats living in the Faubourg Saint-Germain to the poorest ragpicker. Egoism seemed to have disappeared; property was safe; someone was always at hand to help ladies politely over barricades, while every man that passed was asked to pull down one stone. Even Prince Louis Napoleon, rushing from England to put himself at the disposition of his country, performed this service. People were all called "laborer," and Trees of Liberty began to be planted over the city, affectionately decorated with flowers, flags, and ribbons.

In the Champs Elysées, boys in jockey jackets shot at a clay image of the King—if they hit him in the eye, their prize was a statue of liberty. On Punch's stand "Egalité" was printed, and Judy wore a Phrygian cap. And the crowds that rode out to see the shows jammed the busses, for hackney cabs suddenly became unfashionable.

It was mid-March before the first conservative notice dared to appear among the rows of friendly libertarian placards pasted on the walls of every street. It took the conservatives almost a month to rally their forces and begin to oppose the new government. By April the moderates began to doubt; and by May, "society was cut in two; those who possessed nothing united in a common greed, those who possessed something united in a common terror."[1] In June the split ended with a bloodier battle than that of February.

The members of the new government were all republicans—why then did they not agree? It was extraordinary how what had seemed like a small left wing under the monarchy should suddenly expand to include nearly all France, with as many views and interests as France itself.

The biggest split was between the advocates of the social welfare republic and the democratic republic. By censoring the lists handed to him at the last meeting of the Chamber of Deputies, Lamartine had practically selected the names of the government members there chosen; these seven he fairly dominated during their term of office, even Ledru Rollin, by far the most radical of the group. But Ledru stood for property and order in the end, for his radicalism consisted mostly in more willingness than the others that the people should vote for what they really wanted instead of what Lamartine wanted them to want.

The new members of the government, the four that burst in, headed by Louis Blanc and backed by Caussidière in the police office, were the left wing of the government; yet they were only at the center of opinion as expressed by a very vocal Paris. The real left wing was to be found in the radical clubs, headed by Blanqui, just out of prison; and because these clubs were always threatening even more radical action, Louis Blanc's group were practically driven away from their social republic into the arms of the law and order democrats.

The great questions before the government were the elections and the right to work. The elections were ardently awaited by the first group which hoped they would clearly establish the will of France as conservative, but the two more radical parties hoped that they could be postponed until "all the good that was to be done was accomplished," in the words of Louis Blanc.

By saying that they wanted to guarantee the right to work, Lamartine's group cleverly took the initiative for social reform

[1] Alexis de Tocqueville, *Recollections*, London, 1896, p. 132.

away from Louis Blanc, who was, after all, the author of the idea.

By quietly building up armed forces this first group likewise fortified itself against the real left, Blanqui and the proletariat of Paris.

They hoped to make a unified country, but being without candor or tolerance they failed. When the right to work proved a sham, as organized by those not really sympathetic, when in June the armed force was brought out into the open against half of Paris, the country was as disgusted with Lamartine as it had been afraid of Blanqui. All the February leaders equally lost authority, and by summer France had to look for a new name to cling to.

But to get back to the new government, which startled Europe by including a lyric poet, an astronomer, a radical lawyer, and a workman. Dupont de l'Eure had been given top position because nearly all his eighty years had been spent as a republican, but he was too old to take much responsibility. The real leadership fell on Lamartine in the ministry of foreign affairs. And Lamartine had only decided to press for the republic on the very morning of the day it was declared.

During the 1840's everyone saw revolution coming as their grand-children foresaw war ninety years later, with intellectual pleasure at their own cynical intelligence together with a kind of hope that after all it would not break out tomorrow. But there were at that time on the French scene two individuals who were carefully preparing themselves to take power, Alphonse de Lamartine and Louis Napoleon. Both won it, and both lost it, the one soon, and the other late.

Lamartine was born an aristocrat, with more ties to the Bourbon than to the Orleans dynasty. In 1830 he seemed too conservative for the new government of Louis Philippe, and people expected that he would retire and write more of the lyrics that made him one of France's leading poets. But Lamartine wanted to be a statesmen, and in 1833 won election to the Chamber. When people asked him whether he would sit on the right or the left, he laughingly answered, "on the ceiling," for his design was to keep away from party intrigues for a period, well out of trouble, while he polished up his public speaking. In order to learn how to make his words purple and golden (as Louis Blanc assures us they were in 1848) he practised on social and humanitarian subjects rather than on political ones.

It is no wonder that his colleagues did not know what to make of him, or that when he formally entered the left in 1843 its members were alarmed.

All this time he was busy writing, his climactic work being the history of the Girondins, the moderate republicans of 1791. It came from the press during 1847 in installments for which all literate France waited in fascination; for this he was tendered his banquet at Mâcon. It was a work which "gilded the guillotine," retelling the story of France's most stirring period in such terms that it seemed the earlier revolution had failed not because it wished for too much but because it did not dare enough. Lamartine concluded by urging his readers to carry on that interrupted work.

He once said of himself that he always appreciated events in the fashion in which they could be recounted; and indeed his imagination, particularly regarding himself, showed very fancy touches. Tocqueville's judgment of the man was stern:

"I do not know that I have ever . . . met a mind so void of any thought of the public welfare as his. . . . Neither have I ever known a mind less sincere. . . . When speaking or writing he spoke the truth or lied, without caring which he did, occupied only with the effect he wished to produce at the moment. . . . [He was] always ready to turn the world upside down in order to divert himself. [He was] capable of everything except cowardly behavior or vulgar oratory."[2] And George Sand said that he handled all kinds of ideas and all kinds of men without believing a single idea or loving a single man.[3]

He was singularly handsome, tall, slender, with finely chiseled features, and an expression of subdued melancholy; there was no passion in his lips or in his eyes. In style he was the perfect gentleman, and the master of those exquisite nothings which make for spontaneous elegance.

Now this man, who had turned down embassies under Louis Philippe, assumed the congenial responsibility of Minister of Foreign Affairs. Since he was too polite to move immediately into the apartment vacated in such haste by M. Guizot, he slept the first night on the floor of his new office. There were plenty of problems to face in the morning.

In the first place many people both in France and other countries

[2] Tocqueville, p. 147.
[3] George Monin, in *Révolution française*, 1899, xxxvii, 58.

assumed that a republican France would automatically start a war of conquest. The King of Prussia tried to use this fear to strengthen his control over the small states of Germany, mostly those near the Rhine. Metternich at Vienna felt Austria was not up to a war with France at the moment and sounded out the Czar as to possible aid. The Czar felt considerable scorn for Austria, but agreed to support her if she were attacked.

French sentiment ran to the notion that the republic could only fulfill her destiny by helping enslaved nationalities like the Italians and the Poles. "The Republic seemed to open of itself the gates of war; the army aspired to it; the people sang it; the superabundance of the idle and the active population furnished the motive for it,"[4] said Lamartine analyzing his own difficulties.

For Lamartine himself had no more wish to enter a war than had the despised Louis Philippe, yet he had to step carefully to keep peace and still to disappoint as few hopes as possible.[5] He therefore drew up a *Manifesto to Europe* which shocked established diplomatic channels by its appeal to the peoples as well as to the sovereigns, but it relieved them by expressing the intention of France to remain at peace. They learned that France no longer accepted the hated treaties and boundaries of 1815 in law—but would accept them in fact. And that France would "protect" legitimate movements of growth and nationality (referring to the Poles and Italians), although she acted as if she believed her example was almost help enough.

The *Manifesto* seemed tepid when published, but in the light of what was actually accomplished it was sufficiently energetic. Thus the people of Italy were led to hope they would receive support from France in throwing off tyranny, especially that of Austria in the north; but the agents of Rothschild, through their connections in all capitals, were able to assure the Imperial Government of Vienna

---

[4] Lamartine, *History of the French Revolution of 1848*, II, 12.

[5] The direct relationship between war and social progress (which seems curious to us) was deeply felt by most men of 1848, and shows its force as an historical tradition when A. J. P. Taylor calls Lamartine's failure to intervene in Poland "the first step toward Munich." The French historian, E. Tersen, says Lamartine adopted this policy with full consciousness that he was thereby undermining real revolution within France. For him, as for Guizot before him, the price of peace abroad seemed to be using force to govern at home—or was it that if they needed the force at home to preserve "order" they could not waste it abroad?

that French non-intervention was a sure thing long before the Italian patriots had given up hope of active assistance.

The United States of America was the first country to recognize the young republic. Within a few days the American Minister, Richard Rush, broke with the diplomatic corps and on his own initiative announced that his country would gladly accept the new government. As soon as the news of his action reached Washington, he was enthusiastically backed by President Polk and the Senate. Great Britain did not immediately offer recognition ("the Queen could not write to the Constituent Assembly"), but Lord Palmerston, who hated Louis Philippe, privately assured Lamartine of British help in case France were attacked.

In spite of his peaceful declarations Lamartine was determined to increase the army, and this apparently not only because of the danger of attack but because he very early foresaw the possibility that troops might be needed internally. He tells us how much happier he was after he was able to get some troops back into Paris in April. He also arranged to call some of the forces from Algeria to strengthen the frontiers, and he laid the basis for the program which increased the army from 370,000 to 500,000 by the end of the year. In the time of Louis Philippe, any young man was liable to be chosen by lot for military duty for a seven-year term at pay of roughly a cent a day. Under the provisional government, the term was reduced to two years, and conditions in the service, including pay, food, and promotion by merit, were vastly improved.

There was slight sentiment for disarmament in such a bellicose society, though someone noticed that when two Frenchmen got together, they talked of the necessity for reducing the military budget —but *three* Frenchmen would always talk of extending French influence over Europe. In 1848 one socialist (Cabet, who had sent off a group of colonists to found an ideal community in Texas) tried to have protection for conscientious objectors put into the law, but without success. Strangely enough Emile de Girardin, the hardheaded publisher of *La Presse*, advocated immediate and unconditional reduction of the armed forces by 200,000, with the hope that France would also press for universal disarmament. No one else thought of such a thing, and they all considered Girardin a materialist.

The armed forces, first the navy and soon the army also, were put into the hands of François Arago, the distinguished director of the observatory. Though he was consistently known as a republican, his life and adventures up to this time had been in the service of science. Even in science, however, he had shown his democratic principles and had welcomed visits of workingmen to the observatory.

In 1806, as a young man, Arago was chosen to run the meridian through Spain, and had to spend six months on a mountaintop with two Carthusians who broke their vow of silence to talk to him. At one time the natives thought his fires must be signals to the enemy, for it was during the Napoleonic wars, and he had to take refuge in a fortress for fear of being lynched. On the way home from Spain, he was captured by Corsairs, but he refused to try to escape for fear of losing his instruments and notes, which he was finally able to bring safely to Paris after more than a year on the journey. Later on he became interested in the polarization of light, and devised the demonstration which convinced the nineteenth century that light was waves, not particles. On the day when he showed this experiment to the Academy of Science, he rushed home, tramped on his wife's hat, tore his daughter's shawl in two, and said, "I have just solved the problem of light and I can very well buy you a shawl and a hat."

Arago did not believe in God (incredible in an astronomer, commented Victor Hugo) but he was a strong believer in the republic, and now in its service he renewed his youth. He improved the navy's rations, and abolished flogging; and for a crowning achievement he was able to get the provisional government to abolish slavery in the French colonies, with an indemnity to the owners.

Meanwhile, Ledru-Rollin, who had led the republican faction during the banquet campaign (he had been the first outspoken republican elected to the Chamber under Louis Philippe) was working twenty hours a day at the Ministry of the Interior to establish the republic solidly inside France. Ledru's first concern was to send commissioners to each department to see that the regime was run right, and he had a hard time finding sufficient men who were both capable and loyal. Most of the commissioners were native to the districts to which they were sent and were not very radical, but an outstanding exception was Emmanuel Arago. This fanatical son of the astronomer was sent to Lyons, where he dissolved the religious orders, levied a huge property tax, and established the right to work with such radical vehemence that his name became a byword. In general, however, it was not the activity of Ledru's commissioners so much as his instructions that stood conservative hair on end. "Your powers are unlimited. Agents of a revolutionary power, you are revolutionary, too." To be sure, he added, "To us belongs the duty of reassuring the public," but alas, the public was far from being reassured.

Ledru himself was a steady and consistent republican, more interested in the political than the social trappings of the government and, therefore, not very close to the most radical party headed by Louis Blanc. But it seemed to be Ledru's misfortune to stir up more hornets' nests than his colleagues. A second furor came up over the *Bulletins of the Republic*.

One of his workers was George Sand, then no longer young, but an extremely emotional republican who rushed to Paris from her country home at the first news of the revolution and settled in the Ministry of the Interior, devoting herself to the writing of propaganda. The stories passed around Paris about her included every scandalous possibility and went to such fantastic lengths as that she sent roses dipped in blood to Ledru. Her actual sentiments were expressed in her own words: "I have seen the people, grand, sublime, generous, the most admirable people in the universe."[6] (A few months later she was to reverse herself: "The majority of the French people are blind, credulous, ignorant, ungrateful, bad, and stupid; bourgeois, in fine!"[7]) Largely from her pen came the *Bulletins* which were posted every other day all over France. An effort on the part of the government to explain its doings to the citizens, these bulletins at various times urged faith in the possibility of a republic; they explained in fatherly terms why an extraordinary tax was necessary; in tones considered unduly moving by some, one number analyzed the plight of girls driven to prostitution; but it was Number 16, on the subject of the elections, which blew off the lid:

"The elections, if they do not lead to the triumph of social truth, if they express the interests of a caste . . . the elections which ought to be the salvation of the republic will be its damnation. . . . There will then be but one way of salvation for the people who made the barricades; that will be to show their will for a second time and to eliminate the decisions of a false national representation."[8]

[6] Quoted from John Charpentier, *George Sand*, p. 218.
[7] Charpentier, p. 222.
[8] Quoted from Wallon, *La Presse de 1848* . . . , p. 39.

5 3

This threat of new barricades played up the very aspect of the revolution which the respectable members of the government were desperately trying to hide. All that Lamartine and his partisans wanted was to pilot the country safely through to the elections, and the possibility that the workers of Paris would not accept the results from the rest of France was their nightmare. *Bulletin 16* got printed by accident, for the proper censors, including Ledru, were not on their job that day—but afterwards it was agreed that every minister would have to see each bulletin before it could be printed.

Another function of Ledru's department was to foster art. For the first time in Paris free theater tickets were distributed. The government granted money so that twenty theaters could send tickets to the Hôtel de Ville and to police headquarters, where they were given out to factories, clubs, and schools, and the poorest citizens had a chance to draw them by lot. On the first night for these performances, Ledru-Rollin sat in the orchestra, not in a box (although the provisional government maintained a box on the *left* at the *Théâtre Français*, the opposite side from the old royal box).

Most of the rich people had left Paris, so the theaters might have had to close if it were not for such efforts. Dumas went to great expense to keep the *Théâtre Historique* going out of his own pocket. The hit of the season was *Le Chiffonier* by Felix Pyat, the story of a ragpicker, which had opened first in the spring of 1847 and had been so popular that it had played every day, contrary to Paris custom. Queen Victoria is said to have wept when she saw this drama of the lower classes and to have asked Frédéric Lemaître, the leading actor, whether there were really such poor people in Paris. "There are many, Your Majesty; they are the Irish of Paris." Now, under the republic, Lemaître put back passages that had been censored under Louis Philippe, and even added touches so that when the ragpicker sorted out his pile of junk on the stage, he now dragged out a royal crown to the great hilarity of the masses. Satires about the new regime were also welcomed. In the Guignol, Punch beat up the provisional government's policeman as thoroughly as he ever had a royal officer; and Proudhon himself is said to have laughed heartily at a show entitled *Property is Theft*, showing Paris turned to a desert by socialism.

The ministry also tried to encourage republican art and poetry, offering prizes for suitable examples, but the blight that always attends such efforts hit this one. Even their most ardent partisans admitted that the results of the competitions were disappointing.

Victor Hugo was asked by Lamartine to accept the portfolio of education, but Hugo was not certain that he wished to become a republican and declined. So the job was given to Hippolyte Carnot, son of one of the figures of the first revolution. Carnot was a Spartan republican. He entered his ministry with a single trunk on the back of a porter, out of which he lived for many weeks. When he departed he had but to carry the trunk out again. His accomplishments in the field of public instruction included instituting a course for women at the *Collège de France*, starting schools for agriculture and for civil service, opening public libraries and public lecture courses. But he did not, or could not, push fast enough his program for free compulsory schools for children up to fourteen; and in the end he became so entangled with the Catholic church, which was fighting against him to make education "free" in the sense that would allow it to extend its large teaching establishment, that his ministry was commonly accounted a failure. Like George Sand he had a penchant for tactless remarks. At the time of the elections he hoped the schools would be centers of republicanism. "Let us make new men as well as new institutions," he cried. But he let fall the suggestion that an honest, sensible, uneducated peasant would make a better deputy than an educated rich man who was unaware of what was going on. This remark was taken up by his enemies as an attack on education itself and proved a potent weapon. When the Assembly was finally elected the education committee was one of two which the Catholic party was careful to control; it soon reintroduced the use of the catechism and did away with the policy of education for everybody at state expense.

Using their new-found freedom of the press, the people of Paris started 479 newspapers between February and December of 1848, and plastered the whole city with wall placards. It soon became a hobby to collect a copy of each paper; and by the end of the year not only were there several catalogues with lists and descriptions for collectors, but there developed a tidy little business in issuing reprints so cheap as to be profitable if bought only by ten or twenty collectors apiece.

The government forbade private persons to use white paper for posters, in order to distinguish its own bulletins and proclamations, but other colors were open to all. So the advocates of rights for women spread their views on yellow, old age pensions were proposed on blue, some favored eating more meat in lilac. An especially ubiquitous poster in bright pink demanded divorce; deaf mutes reminded the world of their problems in green. By February 26, three members of the Bonaparte family already had letters on the walls. Various workers' groups publicly offered one day's pay to the republic. And a group called *Vésuviennes* recruited unmarried girls from 15 to 30 for a year's semi-military training.

When the elections approached, all the earlier posters were smothered under election appeals—every one, they would have it believed, coming from convinced republicans, all glorifying the heroic people. Yet, there was one telltale word by which conservative candidates could be distinguished, "order." At first this word appeared hesitantly, hedged with apology, but it became more frequent and bolder until it fairly dominated the streets.

The actual comfort of living in Paris depended more on Caussidière than any other one man, and he set about genially to make the police an agency for conciliation rather than terrorism. All Paris was pleased by the general good humor of the gendarmes during this period. Caussidière sent agents to the country to get in more wheat, so he was able to lower the price officially on March 2. By the middle of April he abolished duties on meat entering the city, and he fixed wine duties so as to encourage more sound wine. He wanted to start regular inspection of meat and wine, and to spread sand on the streets to keep them from being slippery, and to disinfect the sewers which let horrible smells rise through the city every night —but these reforms required more money than his department had to spend.

In checking crime Caussidière was highly successful. During his three months in office there was only one murder in the city, and theft was greatly reduced. He closed many gambling places, and tried to get amateur and uninspected prostitutes off the streets, for he favored big legalized houses under the responsibility of a matron, where the girls would not be exploited by pimps and could be inspected for disease. (Anti-republicans complained that one reason why prostitution was increasing was the high wages paid to the various new republican police forces, Caussidière's and others. A whole new class of smart young men had money to spend.) Venereal disease increased markedly during the gaiety of the first weeks of the republic, but in April and May it went down again under the police campaign. Even for criminals Caussidière did his part; he improved the prisons, which he took pains to inspect personally, by improving the diet, and created more work especially for the younger prisoners who, he felt, would deteriorate fast from enforced idleness.

Labor arbitration, too, devolved on the broad shoulders of the chief of police. His office opened free employment agencies, getting rid of an old-time racket among bakers' and butchers' helpers; and he corrected other abuses. This done, he would not allow strikes. To the cab drivers and bus drivers he issued peremptory orders not to strike, pointing out that the government had given them a wage increase and that they must show their gratitude by setting a good example to other workers. Likewise when the bakers complained too violently against long hours, Caussidière told them that although their complaints were justified, violence was not the part of good citizens, so he would postpone the edicts they desired for a month.

All the time he was building up a force of young men, 2,700 in all, called Montagnards—a most picturesque police, uniformed in blue blouses with red belts, paid the high sum of 2 francs 25 a day, and provided with arms and barracks. The entrance requirements for this force were that a man must have fought on the barricades, or have been a member of one of the secret societies, or have been a political prisoner.

Caussidière thus offered one of the few openings where a political prisoner could get a good job, for most members of the government distrusted them and preferred to give them jobs such as the care of parks where their radicalism would not become contagious. These prisoners had been let out of jail the minute news of the republic reached the prison doors, and a fierce rivalry grew up between them and the men who had been lucky enough to do the actual fighting on the barricades of February. The prisoners made the same sort of problem for the provisional government that the returning émigrés had for the Restoration in 1815.

While nearly everyone was grateful for Caussidière's reforms, he sat in his office and amused the world by his antics. Lamartine's wing of the government was afraid of his militarized police, to be sure, while the radical clubs considered him materialistic; but his Montagnards called him affectionately "the big sun of the republic," and used to beg him to sing the one song he knew at all their banquets. He showed his good humor on countless occasions, as once when some national guards arrested him unknowingly for walking on the streets at two in the morning. When they all reached the police station, Caussidière invited them to stay and drink with him. It seemed hard to believe that this friendly benefactor had been schooled in the secret societies and still believed in their discipline.

Caussidière, however, spent many hours over the records of the secret police of Louis Philippe, and finally became convinced that his friend, Lucien Delahodde, had been passing information about the secret societies for years. Delahodde was not a man to cashier lightly, for at the very time he was discovered he was holding down an important job at police headquarters—giving out passports—and he was also known to have a number of friends both armed and devoted.

It was in the tradition of the secret societies, accordingly, that the chief of police gave a rendezvous to Delahodde and other people who might be interested at the Luxembourg palace at midnight. All the important officers of the secret societies were there. Delahodde suspected that someone was going to be tried but did not believe that it could be himself, since he trusted to the elaborate system of numbers and false names he had used in his dealings with Caussidière's predecessors. Nevertheless he carried a pistol to the meeting and stationed friends who were to come to his aid at the sound of a shot.

Caussidière opened the meeting by reading the indictment, then presented his proofs that Delahodde had been a traitor. The accused had become a high officer in the Seasons, and not only kept the government informed about its doings, but had endeavored to turn its activity into safe non-revolutionary channels. Now his judges gave him a chance to defend himself, but Delahodde knew with sick certainty that there was nothing to say; and he knew that every one of his listeners had been sworn under such circumstances to bring about his death. First they urged him to shoot himself but his hand faltered. Then Caussidière drew poison from his own pocket, but Delahodde refused to drink it. Nobody seemed quite willing to murder him on the spot, and finally Albert, the worker member of the government, spoke up and reminded the group that after all

Delahodde had fought at the barricades in February. Let him live, but in chains. So during the rest of Caussidière's term of office there was a secret prisoner in the cellar of the Prefecture.

Partly because the Montagnards seemed dangerous and partly because he was worried about the general attitude of the people of Paris, Lamartine persuaded Marrast, now the mayor of Paris, to set up the Garde Mobile. This force, which reached 15,000, was composed like the Montagnards of young men from the working classes, but they were to be kept loyal and uninterested in social problems. Marrast worked hard to prepare them to defend the government by military drill and to cultivate their loyalty by providing flashy uniforms and pay at the rate of six times what the regular army received; thus he effectively siphoned them away from the interests of their fathers and brothers.

The government was clothing everybody, remarked Delphine de Girardin, poetess wife of the editor, Girardin. Students, policemen, guards, representatives, and cabinet ministers all had their uniforms —everyone, in fact, but the poor.

All the time that the bright young unemployed were being recruited as Montagnards or Gardes Mobiles, the national guard was also being rapidly expanded. Every adult Frenchman was now supposed to be a member, and 90,000 new ones were actually clothed and armed in Paris. But soon a great division began to appear between those who had been in the force for a long time and the newcomers. The old members already had uniforms, paid for by themselves, and they knew their way around; so the new members, mostly proletarians who were waiting for government issue uniforms, felt excluded in spite of the fact that in some companies they outnumbered the oldtimers ten to one.

Some of the old bourgeois companies arranged to parade to the Hôtel de Ville on March 16, to beg the government not to dissolve or dilute them. They were proud of their appearance, especially of their huge bearskin caps, and they tried to explain to the members of the government and to the new members of the guard that they had no wish to be snooty, but they had drilled together for many years and wanted to keep up their old friendship and *esprit de corps*. On the day this demonstration was to take place, Caussidière massed long lines of workers so the bearskins had to march between them, and when they arrived at the Hôtel de Ville they were informed coldly that the original plans for breaking up their companies would be pushed through.

The workers now felt that it was necessary for them, too, to stage a demonstration. It may have been Louis Blanc's idea originally so that he could show off his popular backing and get the power he needed to do good (at least that was Proudhon's analysis). His nerve failed, though, when 100,000 workers, marching with incredible discipline on March 17, the very day after the bearskins, arrived at the Hôtel de Ville and stared Blanc in the face. The marchers were organized by Blanqui, the greatest secret society leader, as his first bid for attention after his release from prison, and Blanc tells how their faces appeared sinister and menacing as he gazed into them. On this day, significantly, Caussidière, no friend of extremists like Blanqui, had ordered his Montagnards to stay around and protect the lives of Louis Blanc and his colleagues.

The demands of Blanqui's cohorts were that the election for officers of the national guard be postponed until April 5, in order to give the new members a chance to get acquainted; more importantly, they wanted the elections for the Constitutional Assembly to be put off till May 31, so as to make time for democratic propaganda in the province. As a matter of fact, a great many socialists, including Louis Blanc himself, would have preferred to postpone the elections indefinitely until they had had a chance to set up their reforms. The marchers' last demand was the removal of the remaining troops from Paris.

Lamartine, who had secretly arranged for extra troops to be sent from Lille in case the radicals succeeded in seizing the city, blandly reassured the crowd on this occasion that the republic would never use arms against the people. Nevertheless, it was not he but Louis Blanc who was finally able to talk the marchers into going home, aided by the mobilization of the national guard, after the government had decided to refuse all their demands. As the delegates left the council chamber, one worker called out bitterly to Blanc, "Then you are a traitor, even you." From this moment the working people no longer felt they had a friend in power, since Blanc proved to be so easily intimidated—and Proudhon called this day "the reaction of Louis Blanc."

The great crowds that could now be mobilized for any occasion were partly the work of the radical clubs. Determined to enjoy liberty of association as well as liberty of the press, Parisians formed hundreds of clubs representing every conceivable interest, and all meeting places were crammed with people every evening. The mayor was instructed to find and rent rooms to them for a nominal sum, and any group was free to apply. Karl Marx, for one, set up a new headquarters for his Communist League that spring in Paris. But people talked more about a woman's club at which, so the story went, in a clumsy attempt to favor woman suffrage, it was moved to "abolish all age and all sex."

The two best-known clubs belonged to Blanqui and Barbès.

Blanqui, released from his imprisonment on February 25, had come immediately to Paris, where he was enthusiastically welcomed by his old admirers and at once set up the Central Republican Society. Blanqui at first rather expected to summon his followers to make another insurrection on the heels of the first, enforcing a more radical program, but within a few hours he decided to give the provisional government a chance, tore up his proclamation and restrained his partisans from an immediate *coup d'état*.

Blanqui was the most mysterious and sinister figure in Paris, a disagreeable ghost to those in power and a fascinating spectacle to gaping crowds. Every evening from eight until eleven except on Sundays, and then at two, the Central Republican Society met for discussion. Only affiliated members could vote and discuss from the floor, and to become a member one had to have two backers and sign a profession of faith—but the public was admitted to the gallery, which was always full of both sexes.

In appearance Blanqui was small, with white hair and white lips and deeply lined cheeks. "He seemed to have passed his life in a sewer and to have just left it," wrote Tocqueville, who saw him in those days—perhaps because he always wore the same clothes he had had in prison. They were black, in mourning for his young wife who died while he was incarcerated, with no shirt, no speck of white linen showing. Even his hands were always encased in black gloves.

In doctrine he was the most complete revolutionary of his time, even more than Marx who felt the temporary domination of bourgeoisie over the proletariat was inevitable and so did not oppose it. Thirty-seven years of Blanqui's fairly long life were spent in prison, but on each release he was more determined to destroy society than before. "Society is nothing more than organized cannibalism," he said, and, "Hunger is slavery." And, more bitterly still, "Every protection to weakness against the holy rights of force is an attack on *social principles*, on liberty, on the natural order, on the essential nature of man."[9] Nothing in the existing system seemed worth retaining or repairing, the social order must be started over again from the bottom with a proletarian dictatorship. No one has recorded a more genial emotion from Blanqui than irony; he repaid love with disdain, admiration with sarcasm (said the sentimental Victor Hugo), but nonetheless he inspired an extraordinary devotion.

Such a character could not long remain content with the temporizing provisional government, and soon he began to attack it in his club and organize his workers against it. In this labor he was incredibly active, and a result was the demonstration of March 17 which struck such terror into all members of the government. It was obvious after March 17 that even Blanc would not support Blanqui and that he could no longer hope for anything from anyone in power.

Although Barbès was customarily mentioned in the same breath with Blanqui, and was his prisonmate for years before and after 1848, he was actually Blanqui's complete opposite and his enemy personally and politically. Barbès was handsome, and according to Delahodde, he consciously modeled himself on a James Fenimore Cooper hero. In gratitude to Lamartine for having saved his life nine years earlier, he threw himself into support of the provisional government. He was also a great friend of Ledru-Rollin and used to hang around the Ministry of the Interior along with George Sand at Ledru's midnight periods of relaxation. At the request of these friends, he opened the Club of the Revolution in rivalry to Blanqui's. He also accepted the colonelcy of the 12th legion of the national guard—or, as Blanqui put it, put his blind passion at the service of the bourgeois circle which exploited his vanity and animosity for its own benefit.

In the scare after March 17, the administration began to prepare its revenge on Blanqui, which they accomplished by printing an unsigned document from their old police files containing details of the plot of May 1839, when Blanqui and Barbès had both been im-

[9] Quoted from Dommanget, *Blanqui*, p. 49.

prisoned. Ledru-Rollin had thrown open the Orleanist archives to a newspaperman named Taschereau who kept himself alive by digging up and publishing juicy bits of scandal. Sainte-Beuve among others was tarred with this brush, as having received money improperly. But Taschereau's greatest sensation was this anonymous paper from the secret societies, for as soon as they showed it to Barbès he swore publicly that only Blanqui could have composed it. Blanqui was therefore branded a traitor and a police stooge.

The day after this publication, Blanqui resigned from his club, but he was immediately reëlected and carried home in triumph by 600 members. Nevertheless, his prestige was hurt with many people who were not his immediate followers, and the scandal hung like a shadow over the rest of his life. The authenticity of the document was never proved, since it was not in Blanqui's handwriting, and in any case all it amounted to, if true (and it probably was), was that Blanqui, when sick and broken in prison after the plot had failed, gave the police a too detailed account of how it had been planned.

Blanqui did not help his own case by refusing Barbès' "jury of honor" to try him, but he wrote a defense which sold 100,000 copies, in which the most telling proof of his innocence was evidence that he had gotten nothing out of the deal.

"Who among my companions has drunk as deeply as I of the cup of anguish? After a year my wife died of despair. For four years, in the solitude of my cell, I lived alone in this Dante's Inferno. When I left it my hair was white, my heart and my body were broken. Now I hear in my ears, 'Death to the traitor, let us crucify him! . . . You have sold your brothers for gold,' they cry. Gold? To go to a slow death in a tomb on black bread and water? . . . I live in a garret on 50 centimes a day."[10]

The workers trusted him and did not forget him. In 1871 the Paris Commune made an offer to Thiers, then head of the Third French Republic, to exchange all their hostages for Blanqui alone, and were refused.

Ledru may have let fear get the better of him in allowing the Taschereau piece to be published, but Lamartine never lost faith in his own power to win anybody over. He prevented Blanqui's arrest, and arranged that he should call on him at six one morning. "Well, M. Blanqui, you have come to assassinate me. . . . You see I

[10] Quoted from Stewart, *Blanqui*, p. 121.

wear no cuirass," said the head of the government to open the conversation. They talked for a long time, and though he extracted the story of Blanqui's life, Lamartine was utterly unable to change his mind. Later, accused of conspiracy with such a dangerous character, Lamartine defended himself by saying, "Yes, I conspired with him— but only as the lightning conductor conspires with the thunderbolt."

The Right to Work

THE records of the struggle against the Paris depression of 1848 read something like dispatches from Washington in 1932, even to the arguments of their enemies.

The number of businesses in Paris declined during 1848 by 54 per cent, partly because, when the rich fled the revolution, luxury trades were killed, partly because many small shops could no longer obtain credit. When Richard Rush, the American Minister, went to buy a pair of gloves in a fashionable shop shortly after the republic was established, he was the only customer in the entire day. Victor Hugo described in detail how a small businessman, a maker of figurines, met the crisis—when no one wished to buy these wares any longer, the man had to sell his knickknacks, to pawn his watch.

Every day some of the unemployed, offering various things for sale, showed up on the Champs Elysées, where under the monarchy they had been allowed only on holidays. Dentists' chairs, side shows, and stalls where cutlets were fried filled the walks, also weighing machines—although people did not like to get weighed because they were all thinner. Life was so gay that many of the thoughtless rich assumed that the workers were having too much fun, with their clubs, demonstrations, and military duties, to be in any hurry to return to their workshops. Stories passed around that under a republic one could live for nothing, that even rent need not be paid—and house owners who refused to remit their rents found the buildings decorated with black flags and piles of straw suggesting arson.

Among serious students of the workers' needs there were, as usual, two lines of thought. One group believed in helping the workers directly, another argued that the best way was to put the employers back on their feet. Many small businessmen were begging the government to take over their enterprises just so they could discount their paper—for in the absence of the yet unknown bank checks, commercial bills of exchange customarily passed from hand to hand as commonly as money, but now no one would take them.

The portfolio of finance was first entrusted to a worthy Parisian banker. He told the provisional government that their position was hopeless and that he would commit suicide rather than carry the responsibility. Almost in despair the cabinet turned to one of their original members, Louis Antoine Garnier-Pagès, who was big and honest and imperturbable, looking something like a cherub, with his long gray hair curling behind his ears. This gentleman succeeded in restoring credit by two great measures—declaring the notes of the Bank of France to be legal tender, not redeemable in specie, and raising the land tax.

The provisional government would have preferred an income tax, which suited their philosophy, but in their immediate need for money they had not time to set up the machinery for a new tax. The tax on real estate was already in working order, so in desperation they decreed that for every franc in taxes that had been paid the year before an additional 45 centimes should be paid in 1848. Such a tax fell hardest on the peasants, and it made almost the only change they could see in their lives from this revolution. In the great revolution they had received land, and thus became a strong support for the republican regime. Now, however, they were violently prejudiced against this new republic. Since the money was to be used partly to establish the famous right to work for city dwellers, the peasants felt they were paying to keep the Paris workers idle, even though the *Bulletin of the Republic* explained that while private charity degrades, state responsibility rehabilitates the unemployed and makes of them a national asset. So many people complained of the tax that the provisional government made the extraordinarily silly rule that the mayors in each town could make out a list of those persons for whom payment of the tax would constitute a hardship, and they were to be exempted. Naturally this made the tax very hard to collect, and its total revenue to the treasury was only about half what Garnier-Pagès had estimated.

The 45-centime tax may have saved the republic from bankruptcy, but it also killed it by arousing the hatred of the countryside. From that day all the propagandists, including Louis Napoleon, who tried to win the peasants, promised its repeal, though when Louis Napoleon came to power he found it too useful to give up.

The House of Rothschild, which was quite friendly to the new government, helped to avoid a large-scale panic by getting in shipments of specie from its London office. To raise funds for meeting a run of depositors, the Rothschilds took huge losses, selling at 33 French government 3 per cent securities which had sold at 73 the day before the revolution. They also donated a sum to be used for the families of the men who had fallen in the February battle.

To help the credit of small firms, Garnier-Pagès ordered public warehouses to be set up all over France where goods could be stored and graded, so that their receipts could be used as security. Unfortunately these became unpopular, since it was assumed that anyone whose credit was otherwise good would not resort to the warehouses.

This was what was done for capital, and it was enough to convince Karl Marx that the intentions of the government were thoroughly bourgeois. Still, the republic could not get out of its promises to labor. If the regime of Louis Philippe was "a monarchy surrounded by republican institutions," the new republic intended to be a republic surrounded by social institutions. Thus the affairs of labor were now turned over to Louis Blanc, though in a rather left-handed manner.

He was given the Luxembourg palace (which had housed the defunct house of peers) to live in, and was directed to set up a conference to study working conditions. Garnier-Pagès, who had earlier thought of making Blanc a "secretary" instead of a regular member of the government, now thought of this solution to avoid giving him a regular portfolio as "Minister of Progress," which the workers had requested. Another member of the cabinet later explained that Blanc had been given the Luxembourg so that he could "disorganize" labor only in theory, not in practice.

And in fact Garnier-Pagès' strategy worked. When Louis Blanc accepted the job at the Luxembourg he took an opportunity to talk instead of to act, cutting himself off from power. Incidentally, the Luxembourg meetings turned out to be quite large, and took so much of his time that he carried less of the responsibility of the provisional government than he had up to this time. People said he began to look like a beaten man, one who knew he had not lived up to his expectations.

Nevertheless the Luxembourg Commission, as it was called, the first workers' congress in the world, had a certain aura of excitement. The very first day they met they ordered the working day to be reduced to ten hours in Paris and to eleven in the provinces, where it had been as high as fourteen or fifteen. At the same time they voted to abolish the practice of subcontracting in house building, a system that had long operated to reduce wages, since the less each subcontractor paid his laborers the greater his own profits.

Employers were invited to separate sessions at the Luxembourg, and the second day they met and accepted both these reforms. Soon a joint committee was set up, consisting of ten workers, chosen by lot—a favorite method with the equalitarians—and ten employers chosen the same way. This group settled a great many disputes on wages and hours, a task which had been handled up to this time by the police and upon which Caussidière had prided himself.

There was never another large-scale victory so easy for the Luxembourg workers, though they tried to abolish work in prisons and convents as competitive with free labor, and to establish public responsibility in industrial accidents.

Each industry in Paris was invited to send three workers as delegates. The methods of their choice were apt to be informal. Some women sat as representatives of women's trades like copper burnishing. Altogether there were three or four hundred members who met to debate and to hear speakers of all shades of opinion.

Blanc called his commission "a school where I was called to give a course in hunger in front of famished people." He was not unaware that many of the delegates, who were unpaid, lost their jobs because of the time they gave to the work of the commission and were subsequently blacklisted from further employment. Other members of the government objected that when Blanc reduced the food allowance for his office help, from 6 francs apiece at each meal to 2 francs 50 for lunch, and 3 francs 50 for supper, this seemed like a reproach to his colleagues. Blanc answered that they had to eat with bankers and diplomats but he, face to face with workers lacking many of the necessities of life, could not insult their misery by the display of a feast. (He was still spending on food three times a workman's daily wages.)

When the Luxembourg Commission finally drew up its report, it offered a plan for moving toward state socialism that not unnaturally took in many of Louis Blanc's ideas. It proposed setting up in each department of France an agricultural colony for a hundred families, having a common laundry and a big kitchen where wholesome food would be prepared for everybody. Other colonies could be formed by industrial workers, who would borrow enough money from the state to enable them to become self-supporting. All these projects were to have a full system of social security for illness and old age.

During this spring of 1848 Blanc actually succeeded in founding one such cooperative, the Clichy tailors. The government was unwilling to grant him money but it let him have the use of the Clichy prison which had been used for debtors and now was vacated, since the republic had abolished imprisonment for debt. He then obtained for his 2,000 journeymen tailors a contract for the uniforms of the national guard, and with this help the group were able to make a modest profit, enough to raise their wages to 2 francs 15, as compared with the flat 2 francs which the national workshops paid for a day's work. One of Blanc's favorite plans, which he vainly hoped the Luxembourg Commission could implement, was to build four model housing projects where four hundred working class families could save in rent, fuel, food, and also enjoy the privileges of a common library, nursery, school, garden, and baths. Lamartine's republic was indifferent; it remained for Napoleon III and the Second Empire to start workers' housing.

But what, meanwhile, of the famous organization of labor? What of the right to work? Blanc was only allowed to theorize, while unemployment and the state's solemn promise toward it stared the government in the face. The man with the musket who broke into the first meeting of the government had voiced the most insistent need of the Paris workers.

On February 26 the government decreed that national workshops be set up immediately to give employment to out-of-work persons, and on February 28 the workers who wished to apply were directed to register at the mayors' offices.

Unfortunately, advertising the guarantee of the right to work irresistibly lured Frenchmen from the provinces to Paris. Probably 100,000 arrived during the three spring months to dump themselves upon authorities who were already at their wits' end to find work for as many as 10,000. On June 20, the day before the national workshops were ordered dissolved, there were 120,000 men enrolled in them and 50,000 more unemployed hanging around Paris who had been refused admission.

During the first few days there were enough problems facing

those in charge without their worrying about extra numbers. Obviously the provisional government promised employment to its citizens without having given any thought to the practical set-up, though determined to keep the management out of the dangerous hands of the member who had thought about it most, the author of the *Organization of Work.*

In this circumstance it devolved upon the suspicious and gloomy Minister of Public Works, Alexandre Thomas Marie, whose opposition to Louis Blanc was well enough known to make it certain that he would never let socialism in at the back door of his project.

Though possessing the requisite negative qualifications, Marie had few positive ones and got nowhere in the first few days while angry mobs gathered around the mayors' offices to register. So he fairly embraced a young engineer named Emile Thomas who presented himself at the ministry and announced that he had worked out a plan to keep order by organizing the national workshops along military lines, using the polytechnic students of the Central School of Arts and Manufactures as officers. Thomas himself was a graduate of this school, only 26 years old at the time, and his student friends and he were chagrined over the noise and disorder at the central bureau for the workshops, which was right across the street from his home.

Marie was hardly willing to give Thomas the four days he said he would need to get his organization started. The government donated one of Louis Philippe's small chateaux, the Pavillon Monceaux, for an office, whither Thomas moved with his staff and his mother to keep house for them.

Thomas' plan, briefly, was to organize the men in the national workshops into squads of ten who would elect a squad leader. Five squads chose a brigadier, four brigades a lieutenant; over four lieutenants and 800 men was a commander who was to be one of the engineering students. The men were to receive 2 francs for every day that work was found for them and 1 franc 50 in case there was no work, later reduced to 1 franc. Brigadiers received 3 francs and all student officers 5 francs. Since this was the first money many of the students had ever earned they entered the project with enthusiasm. The system of paying the rank and file was worked out in such a way as never to provide an occasion for more than ten of them to get together when they were not working—one small example of the innumerable precautions taken to keep the workshops politically safe.

In addition to their officers the squads elected "delegates" who combined the functions of spies and grievance committees. They were expected to report complaints, but also to check up on addresses, number of children, and other facts on the registration cards of the members.

Like everyone else in Paris the national workshop members had a uniform, or at least insignia—a golden bee to adorn their caps. Their officers also wore woolen armbands, while the students wore silk armbands with silver or gold fringes.

The chief trouble with the workshops was that they never had work for more than 10,000 men. As the numbers increased, it came to be the custom to pay each member as if he had worked for two days in the week regardless of whether even that much work had been available.

Their projects mostly required unskilled labor, such as leveling the Champ de Mars and planting trees on the boulevards to replace those cut down in February. Thomas put his skilled workers to mending equipment or to making shoes and clothes for the members of the workshops in spite of the objections of his shoemakers and tailors against working for only 2 francs.[1] When he received a contingent of 600 out-of-work artists, actors, and bank tellers (who wore coats instead of the habitual blue working-class blouse, but who were just as needy as the others, Thomas found to his surprise) he made them paymasters. His plan to set up a studio where the artists might paint republican propaganda pictures was not adopted.

To Emile Thomas' fertile mind, it was easy to think up projects that would have kept his men busy if only he could have obtained the government's approval; but this kept being mysteriously denied. He would have liked to have them work on building railroads, on an underground canal to join the Seine above and below Paris (in Marseilles the workshops labored on a canal that everyone felt was needed, and they became much more popular than in Paris) and on

[1] The cost of living in Paris was not high. A member of the Hungarian Choral Society wrote in May, 1848, that it would be easy to live on a franc a day. He never saw such fruit or such harvests in Hungary, a good lunch could be had for 10 sous, a luxurious one for 14. The best meat was 8 cents a pound. In three months in Paris he spent 194 francs of which 70 went for clothes, the rest for food, lodging and laundry. But of course he was not trying to support a family. (Bouteiller, 131.)

housing projects with community centers. He hoped builders would be allowed to contract for the labor of some of his men for socially useful structures, paying half their wages, and earning the right to tax-exemption on the buildings. He would have approved government loans to employers so they could take workers back, and he wanted to make a study of seasonality of employment.

In short, Thomas disapproved of payment for idleness and of the centralization that kept so many unemployed in Paris, but the government obliged him to continue these two characteristics of his organization. Marie suggested why on March 23 by asking Thomas if he could count on his workers. Thomas replied that he thought he could, though the numbers grew so fast it was hard to exercise the personal influence he would have liked. Marie then told him as far as money was concerned not to worry, for he would provide any sum Thomas required out of secret state funds. Apparently it was the policy of the government to keep yet another semi-militarized, loyal force in Paris. Three quarters of the members joined the national guard and were given the same pay for days with the militia as for work days, and they were able to drill even in the rain in the Monceaux riding school. It was frankly Lamartine's hope that the workshops would justify their existence by becoming a counterweight to the "sectarian workmen of the Luxembourg, the seditious workmen of the clubs"—and in the back of Lamartine's mind a counterweight was always military.

Another time Marie told Thomas he hoped the workshops would disgust the workers with socialism. Although Louis Blanc felt that the workshops perverted everything he believed in, he was ingeniously made to seem responsible for them—as if the government of which he was a member were trying out his ideas. Marx thought the confusion of the workshops with socialism was half naïve, only half intentional. In any case, they were pilloried together.

For there was no doubt that they failed. They scandalized the good citizens by their boondoggling. The workers themselves either raged at a government whose promise of work turned out to be a lie or laughed contemptuously at it for paying good money for idleness. After the elections their morale became so bad that the director had to spend every day figuring out how to calm them on the morrow. On May 16 a Representative Dupin in the Assembly stood up and declared that "good Paris" wanted the end of the worshops; the next day he received a moving plea signed by members of the work-shops saying that they did not like living on charity—the government should blush at giving them only alms. They said they wanted to work at their own trades, and that those who did not work, including bureaucrats, should not eat.

In one aspect alone were the workshops successful, in the social services they offered. They not only distributed extra food, bread, meat, and soup to members, depending on the size of their families, but put some of their members to work making shoes and clothes which were sold to other members for the cost of the material. Many of the men enrolled could hardly come to work, especially in the rain, for lack of clothing. But since it was hard for an individual to save up as much as four francs for a pair of shoes, for example, every member was asked to put in two or three sous a day out of his pay, and this jackpot went to buy shoes for the neediest members first.

More than this, members of the workshops and their families were entitled to free medical service. Twelve doctors served the project and in the forty-one days the plan was in operation they treated 14,000 patients at an average cost per case of 51 centimes. The doctors involved were very much pleased with this arrangement and pointed out that this sort of medical care, including office calls, house visits, free medicine, and even cash donations if needed, was much cheaper than the maintenance of hospital care. They urged that the project be continued.

Thomas also planned for a club for the recreation of his workers, though whether this should be classed as a social service in view of his purposes is doubtful. For he used the club as a sounding board to detect and eliminate the most dangerous thinkers and orators. Since there was not room for everyone, delegates were elected to this club by the members and given cards of admission, to the number of about 400. All the engineering students also attended. Thomas asked the group to think how to help their brothers, but to exclude political or social subjects from their discussion. They were to be given no chance for political action, although they were as politically-minded as any workers in the world at that time; no chance, in spite of the democratic procedure of electing their officers, to have a voice in their own affairs. The workers of Paris were coming to know what they wanted, but it was almost too much to expect that one set over them like Thomas should go much beyond the nineteenth-century idea of how to dispense charity. It was nearly a hundred years before social workers and personnel officials discovered the importance of letting people help themselves, of giving them status by real responsibility, and it was a hard lesson even in an age which set workers apart less class-consciously.

On April 16 the Luxembourg Workers' Commission planned another huge demonstration. They were to march to the Hôtel de Ville, bearing a gift of money to show their gratitude for the republic, but at the same time to press a petition for the *true* organization of labor.

The great question about this day is whether there was behind it a radical plot to destroy the government. Lamartine, who got the news from his spies, was sure that there was, and he prepared for it by making his will and burning his compromising papers, for he barely expected to survive. George Sand told later how she, with Barbès, Flocon, Louis Blanc, and Caussidière planned to use this occasion to get rid of the conservative members of the government and to put Ledru-Rollin at the head of a more radical one, and she asserted that they showed Ledru ahead of time some of the measures they imagined such an administration should adopt. However, when this group heard that Blanqui was going to exploit the demonstration, they decided they preferred to keep the government that existed and to continue as the left wing themselves, rather than run the risk of having Blanqui as the new left wing in power. According to this side of the story, Ledru spent the night in a sweat wondering on which side to play ball; when morning broke he rushed to Lamartine to tell him all he knew.

On the other hand, Marx says that this was all a sham, that the government arranged a frightening show in order to "defeat the shadow" of working class revolt.

The right to call out the national guard was the exclusive prerogative of Ledru as the Minister of the Interior. To Lamartine's immense relief, at noon Ledru ordered the *rappel* beaten through the streets. This was his decisive action.

It was still uncertain in how large numbers the guard would show up, but to the admiration of the friends of order they turned out 100,000 strong, surrounded the parading workers with bayonets, and were congratulated on "saving France." Most of the national workshop members of the guard went out with them for the gov-

ernment, but a few marched with the Luxembourg. Barbès, induced
by his hatred of Blanqui, also appeared at the head of his 12th
legion; but he later became ashamed of this action and his club felt
they had been duped into supporting the wrong side.

When the demonstration collapsed, Lamartine felt it was the happiest day of his political life. Crane Brinton, who examined the great
revolutions of history in *The Anatomy of Revolution*, awards Lamartine, for his energy, a distinction which no moderate in any of the
big outbreaks achieved—that of using force to stop the left. Proudhon, however, dubs April 16 "the reaction of Ledru-Rollin."

The elections so long and hotly fought over were finally set for
Easter Sunday, which came late that year. The date was two weeks
after the one Lamartine had hoped for, a postponement that might
seem like a concession to the radicals, but was also needed to complete
the arrangements. Frenchmen were to be allowed to vote under the
broadest election law the world had ever seen, even including classes
like domestic servants that had been excluded in 1789.

Voting was by slates. Every department was given a certain number of representatives according to population, so that in the Department of the Seine, the Paris district, everyone voted for 34
candidates, in the Upper Alps for only three. Various parties drew
up lists which they busily passed out for days ahead of time on
busses, at street corners and polling places; for this service Emile
Thomas engaged 500 members of the national workshops, at 5 francs
a day, to distribute the lists which were approved by the Department of Public Works.

The most active electioneering agency was the Luxembourg,
which sent out worker propagandists all over France at government
expense. For their Paris list they interviewed seventy candidates on
their attitudes about everything from the right to work to divorce,
and finally made a list of thirty-four which coldly excluded Lamartine. They offered, however, to put Emile Thomas' name on their list
if Thomas would let the workshops support it—a deal which Thomas
declined.

To judge by their posters, *all* candidates who solicited votes were
sons either of delegates to the Convention of 1792, or of workers or
peasants. One Negro son of slaves advertised that he had been condemned to the galleys for life but was pardoned, and had fought on

the February barricades. One man was elected after describing himself as a worker, but when it was discovered he was really a functionary of Louis Philippe his election was annulled. More flagrant deceits were more successful. Monarchists like the Vicomte de Falloux ran as republicans; Louis Napoleon, later to be crowned emperor, described himself (for the June election) as a socialist. (He did not run in April, but was a candidate in the by-elections six weeks later.) The worst reactionaries got in on the most advanced platforms; all candidates either explained their past or explained it away. Some stressed order, as we have seen, but all shouted for liberty, equality, and fraternity. The placards make very monotonous reading.

George Sand was proposed as a candidate by a ladies' club, but she publicly disclaimed any relationship with them and expressed the hope that no one would be so foolish as to waste a vote on her, and no one did.

Emile de Girardin, publisher of the *Presse*, was the only one who dared come out with a one-line campaign. "I am not an old-line republican" was his response to Ledru's request for that sort. Most conservatives were more mealy-mouthed, but by asking the double-edged question, "If the Assembly votes to restore a monarchy, what will you do?" they tossed the old-liners on the horns of dilemma fundamental in republican philosophy.

On Easter Sunday priests all over France sang mass at dawn and urged their flocks to vote. Eighty-two per cent of the eligible voters did so, and the result was a complete vindication of Lamartine's opinion that the elections would save property. As Caussidière put it, the peasants voted for their landlords, the workers for their employers, small merchants for bankers, and small owners for usurers. The radical oratory and patriotic protestations had pleased everybody as show-window dressing, but France was not really ready to give in to the Paris workers. Only one in twenty of the Luxembourg worker candidates was chosen.

Still, Caussidière himself was elected, and handsomely, both in the Easter voting and again in the run-off elections which were held on June 4 to compensate for duplications and annulments. The second time he got more votes than any other candidate, twice as many as that cloud now first appearing on the horizon, Louis Napoleon.

In these June by-elections it was shown that the Parisian workers could profit by their mistakes. The Luxembourg and the national workshops stood much closer together by that time and elected four out of eleven successful candidates, instead of one out of twenty. But for that rapprochement there were reasons. For if France was not ready to give in to Paris, neither were the Paris proletariat willing to be balked in their expectations by the slow-moving, property-loving provinces which did not even try to understand their problems.

As soon as the Constitutional Assembly and the Paris workers saw each other they hated each other. On the opening day, May 4, the workers immediately made a threat by placarding the walls of the city with the Declaration of the Rights of Man and soon began to think of arming themselves once more. Though the Assembly was not so quickly bellicose it proved in the mass to be ignorant, intransigent, and tactless, very far from that force which should unite France in brotherly love. Thus society, the organism whose two nuclei had been pulling against each other since early March, was splitting at last; and the process led, in June, to the first real class war of modern times. It was, of course, unfortunate that the Assembly had to meet in Paris, the only place where the two groups would have been sufficiently equal to fight each other. No one proposed another city, however, perhaps remembering how during the great revolution the magnetism of the capital had forced the Assembly of 1789 to move in from Versailles.

The great mass of the French people hated the national workshops, feared Louis Blanc, and were beginning to distrust Lamartine because he had not been strong enough to oppose these socialistic forces. They had very little notion of the temper of the Paris working class, or perhaps they would have appreciated Lamartine's finesse in keeping them divided and at bay. Naturally, the other half of Paris, the well-to-do half, was pleased at the Assembly's arrival. At last, they hoped, here was an authority capable of enforcing order, for they were sick and tired of watching members of the workshops idling on the streets or performing useless labor at the expense of the taxpayers. The national guards, which had betrayed Louis Philippe and wavered under the provisional government, were to prove, except for a few of the new labor contingents, consistently loyal defenders of the Assembly.

Although a representative body elected by universal suffrage ought in theory to represent all classes, there were more landlords and noblemen than in any of Louis Philippe's chambers, and many more ecclesiastical members. Two-thirds of the members were considered moderate republicans—for the republic "pure and simple" rather than for one "social and democratic." Among the delegates were only eighteen workers, and the whole revolutionary left barely totaled sixty, although a noisy and voluble sixty.

Actually few new leaders had been shaken out by universal suffrage. The old parliamentary left of the monarchy, Odilon Barrot and Tocqueville, moved over to the right, while on the new left sat such figures as Barbès and Proudhon (who remarked that the other members were surprised he had neither horns nor claws), Albert, and Louis Blanc. On the extreme right a Catholic who would eventually suffer excommunication, Viscount Frédéric Pierre Falloux (du Coudray), trod quietly the path of the Jesuits, boring secretly but irresistibly against secular education and the national workshops, the two accomplishments of the republic which were felt as a threat by the Church.

These were the leaders, but the bright minds were almost lost amid the "stupid faces, the greedy eyes, the big noses, the rapacious provincialism"[2] of the rest of the Assembly. Most of them did not know how to talk or how to listen; they often voted and unvoted the same proposition several times, for they were unused to parliamentary procedure. And the huge oblong building hastily erected for them in the courtyard of the Palais-Bourbon did not make it easy for them to hear or see one another. Someone asked Tocqueville how the Assembly of 1789 succeeded with equal numbers and equal difficulties. "Ah, they had the cream of France, we have only the skim milk."[3]

Lamartine remembers the whole nine hundred springing to their feet with cheers when the provisional government was presented to them for the first time, but Lamartine was always over-responsive to praise; the British Ambassador's contrary observation that the government was received coldly is buttressed by the fact that the vote of thanks to the government was passed by only twelve votes.

For president, the Assembly nominated Philippe Joseph Buchez, a moderate Christian socialist; and they gave him an editor of the greatly admired workers' paper, *L'Atelier*, for a vice-president—

[2] Herzen, *Letters*, 236.   [3] Nassau Senior, I, 106.

this was one way for the Assembly to show it was not hostile to labor without truckling to the Luxembourg Congress or to Louis Blanc. To make the other side happy they also made a vice-president out of Antoine Marie Jules Senard, a national guard officer who was responsible for the Rouen "massacres"—an election affair in which some workers, rioting because they had been deprived of their votes, were shot down. Senard was widely touted as a champion of order for this service, though, of course, he was execrated by the class-conscious proletariat.

The deputies listened perforce to the whipped cream of Lamartine's oratory, glorifying his term of office in words in which he was careful to explain, for the left, that the troops in Paris were only a "guard of honor," for the right, that the Luxembourg was only "a laboratory of ideas." But they voted down a proposal to retain the provisional government intact because that would have meant keeping on with Louis Blanc and Albert. It might have been better if they had listened to Louis Blanc's speech in which he predicted "a revolution of hunger," but he was utterly unable to move them. They also wanted to drop Ledru-Rollin, but here Lamartine drew the line and astonished everybody by saying that he, Lamartine, would not serve without Ledru.

Ledru's manner was so easy, his bearing so confident that it was hard for his friends to imagine that in the salons he was called an ogre, in the provinces a Bluebeard, that the Assembly itself, "this compact mass of bald prudence," regarded him as the criminal author of those incendiary proclamations which had resulted in its own election. The members obviously felt no gratitude, for they finally chose an executive commission of five members, of whom Arago got the most votes because of his popularity with both sides; then Garnier-Pagès; then Marie, for his services against the workshops, then Lamartine who was pulled down by his loyalty to Ledru-Rollin, and finally Ledru himself.

No one could quite figure out why Lamartine stuck to Ledru. He himself said he felt it was important to have Ledru's sort of republicanism represented in the new executive. He may have felt the currents running too fast towards the conservatives, and he may have been grateful to Ledru for his support in calling out the national guard on April 16. It was certainly not personal friendship, for their natures were too far apart and after a month their collaboration ceased. It is interesting, however, that Ledru was still a political force to be reckoned with a year later when he was thundering against an invasion of the Roman Republic by the French army, while Lamartine never recovered any influence after the idolatry with which he was held in the spring of 1848 had melted away.

The Assembly then turned to the problem of costuming itself. They decided at once that a mere ribbon in the buttonhole was not showy enough, and spent some time debating whether a tri-colored sash was more effective over the shoulder or around the waist. After both had been modeled in the tribune, the shoulder style won. At one point it was proposed that they should adopt the costume of the Convention—the white waistcoat in which Robespierre was familiar on the stage—but Caussidière was the only member who was uninhibited enough to appear in this outfit.

This was exactly the kind of Assembly against which the Paris workers had predicted new barricades. If their friends like Louis Blanc were to be pushed out of power, the workers would make another revolution; and on May 15 they did so—though if the February assault seemed like play-acting in the light of the past, this one was farcical. Again the Assembly Hall was invaded by the mob, again a provisional government was formed, this time with Barbès at its head, and again there was a march to the Hôtel de Ville where proclamations of revolt were issued.

The occasion for this outbreak was a parliamentary debate on Poland, that favorite subject of the left. The radical clubs arranged to meet at the Place de la Bastille at the time the debate was scheduled and to prepare a petition demanding war with Prussia and Russia if these countries refused to restore Poland within twenty-four hours. As usual they were swayed more by slogans than by possibilities. From this meeting, 20,000 men marched silently to the Assembly Hall; then with one terrible shout they demanded admittance. General Courtais, who was in charge of the national guards defending the Assembly, refused to fire on the mob and agreed to admit twenty-five to the Chamber to present the petition. Once the door was open he could never get it shut again and thousands poured in. The galleries filled up and began to break under the weight of humanity, and as men began to drop to safety over the sides of the galleries to the floor of the house the noise was like cannon fire.

The leaders of this invasion were Aloysius Huber, a former police spy, now even on this day accused of working for the government to make the demonstration fail, and the young Sobrier who pranced so gaily along the February barricades and who had spent the intervening time gathering a supply of weapons at his Rue de Rivoli house, perhaps with Lamartine's connivance. (Lamartine's confidence in his own power over human nature was unbounded, if misplaced.)

Barbès had been opposed to the whole idea of the demonstration, possibly because he was a member of the Assembly. His club had voted against it the evening before and refused to take part. Now, with the mob actually in the Assembly Hall, Barbès leapt into the tribune and tried to get the petitioners to go away, while he also moved to the Assembly the war for Poland. But as soon as Barbès saw Blanqui in the crowd he lost his head, determined not to let his archenemy get ahead of him; and when the sound of the *rappel* being beaten for the national guards penetrated the Assembly room, Barbès cried "We are betrayed!" and led the march to the Hôtel de Ville. Ledru had promised Barbès not to beat the *rappel*, but President Buchez had slipped out an order to General Courtais.

Blanqui also, it appears, was opposed to the demonstration, careful revolutionary that he was, on the grounds that the times were not yet ripe. His club, however, was for action, and because of the Taschereau scandal he was afraid that if he didn't participate he would lose influence, so he led them in the parade and into the Assembly. Once there he was forced into the tribune and began to orate about Poland. Gradually he tried to switch, to get to things nearer home, the election massacres ordered by Senard at Rouen, the sufferings of the unemployed, but the people's minds were on a single track. "Talk about Poland," they yelled.

The tumult became more and more frightening, though Taschereau, who had exposed Blanqui and, therefore, had a personal fear, was the only representative who fled from the building. Every possible spot was filled with sweaty, bare-armed workers wearing red sashes. President Buchez was pulled out of his chair, and finally Huber called out in his terrific voice that the Assembly was dissolved. The people cheered and cried, "To the Hôtel de Ville."

Barbès and Marrast, whose job was that of Mayor of Paris, ran a race to get there first, and installed themselves in different wings when they arrived. Barbès had time to make two proclamations. One was the conventional declaration of a provisional government and the other sent an ultimatum to Russia and Germany on the Polish question. Barbès also announced that if Blanqui came in he would break his head. He did not use, perhaps did not even know, the seven decrees that had been printed ahead of time at Sobrier's house, one stating that the workers had been fired on—a revolutionary expectation which General Courtais had steadfastly failed to gratify. Marrast, meanwhile, in the other end of the Hôtel de Ville was printing a counter-proclamation on a small press and dropping it from the windows to the crowd below. Before very long he was rescued by the national guards who came to arrest Barbès.

At the Assembly Hall guards and deputies were embracing each other, happy to have escaped without bloodshed or injury. Louis Blanc was the only member who ran any real danger. During the invasion of the Assembly Blanc looked like a snake having its tail pinched. His thoughts were various: he was angry at the way the Assembly had tossed him out of the government, yet scared by the mob. Later he started to go to the Hôtel de Ville with the rebels, then thought better of it and returned, only to be seized by national guards who almost tore him to pieces, since they, like most conservatives, blamed him for the whole affair. With his coat in rags, his hair a tangle, he finally managed to reach the tribune, where he defended himself so bravely that even his enemies were impressed.

That other famous radical, Caussidière, had maintained a more than prudent inactivity during the day, saying he had a sore leg. His Montagnards were not allowed to help guard the Assembly, and revenged themselves on the national guard by fêting and releasing the prisoners the latter brought into the police station. After this day the Montagnards were immediately disbanded—adding to the forces of disaffected radicals in Paris. But Caussidière, like Louis Blanc, pleaded his case so well that he won over his enemies. The executive commission was at first unanimously determined on his dismissal; he convinced a majority of his good faith, and then resigned anyway, both as police chief and as deputy. Only two weeks later he won a brilliant reelection in the by-elections.

The unhappy results of May 15 were that the workers were left almost leaderless for the graver crisis ahead, for Barbès was thrown into prison immediately, Blanqui was caught after two weeks—and the other leaders were silenced. The Assembly, meanwhile, looked at the bootmarks on its velvet seats and became convinced that measures to curb the spirit of Paris could not come too soon nor be too drastic.

It was arranged that on May 21 the Assembly should review the armed forces in a ceremony incongruously called the Feast of Concord. For the occasion Paris was brilliantly illuminated, with rows of lights picking out the lines of all buildings along the Place de la Concorde and for a mile and a half up to the Arc de l'Etoile. A huge statue of the republic guarded by four lions was set up in the Champ de Mars, while floats representing agriculture, commerce, arts, music, and even international friendship went by. The last was represented by France, Germany, and Italy hand-in-hand. The richer and uniformed national guards went by crying, "Long live the National Assembly!" some of the poorer ones still in blouses cried, "Long live the democratic and social republic!" while troops of the line marched past in silence.

Concord may have been present—if so, it was most certainly for the last time in Paris that spring; yet the Assembly lacked faith. Most of the members secretly strapped a pistol or dagger under their coats before entrusting themselves to this contact with the people.

On June 4 occurred the by-elections already mentioned, at which the sensation was the election of Louis Napoleon Bonaparte, nephew and heir of the late Emperor. This prince had dashed to Paris in the first days of the republic, but Lamartine, who hated Bonapartism in every form, was so inhospitable that the young man returned at once to London and settled down to watch events with his usual cynical, cautious, and patient eye. He positively refused to run in the April elections because, he told his friends, he was waiting for the illusions of springtime to fade before he placed himself before the people as a man of order. For the June elections these devoted partisans covered Paris with tiny posters—they could not afford big ones—and stimulated working class support by songs, medals, and little flags for buttonholes.

At least five Napoleonic papers were circulating in Paris in June —one conservative, one demagogic, one historical, one literarily pink, and one stressing military glory. As usual, Louis Napoleon played all sides. Just as kings had at one time sought the support of the middle classes against the feudal nobility, so in the nineteenth century they often came to courting the workers against the middle class. Napoleon III as Emperor, and Bismarck, both did this later; in 1848 Radowitz advised the King of Prussia that it was the policy he ought to follow.

The Prince was the author of a work entitled *The Extinction of Pauperism* and he loved to quote from his uncle at St. Helena, "I wish for the worker to be happy and to earn his six francs a day" (three times the pay of the national workshops). On this basis Louis Napoleon was made to seem almost a socialist and he won the support of large numbers of the workers. The ex-Luxembourg Committee endorsed him, and Louis Blanc and Emile Thomas both became Bonapartists, although it is only fair to mention that some members of both the Luxembourg and national workshops signed posters against him.

But Louis Napoleon was one socialist the Assembly was not afraid of, even with Louis Blanc's endorsement. Perhaps the party of order can recognize its champions under any disguise. Lamartine and Ledru fumed against the Prince, urging not only that he should not be allowed to take his seat but that he should be banished—and on the very day after Lamartine's oration against him the delegates voted to seat him. Louis Napoleon, however, declined the honor sensationally, and in so doing seemed to reproach the Chamber. He had said that if people imposed duties on him he would know how to fulfill them, but now, since his name, which ought to unite France, caused dissension, he would remain away. Perhaps he was discouraged at the opposition, perhaps he felt his tide was not yet at the flood, but for a while longer he remained inscrutable in London while the crisis of the national workshops grew more acute. When France was really ready he would emerge again.

V I

The Revolution of Despair

THROUGHOUT the country nearly a million francs a day were now being spent for the wages of the unemployed, and this fact alone was sufficient to burden the hearts of an Assembly devoted to order. Order in the streets is not enough, an orator told them, what we need is *order in ideas*. This is impossible so long as the poor are being demoralized and the rich bankrupted.

As early as May 13 the executive commission decided to abolish the workshops. As a first step they instructed Emile Thomas, on May 24, to enlist the young unmarried members in the army, to pay the traveling expenses home of those workers who had not lived in Paris for at least six months, to fire the members who refused jobs in private industry, to send some units remaining on the payroll to the country for public works projects outside Paris, and to pay those still working in Paris at piece rates. Some of these measures seemed designed simply to infuriate the workers, especially the one forcing men into private industry, which gave employers a fine chance for wage-cutting, and the one decreeing rural public works, for the first group of workers to go out of Paris was known to have been sent to the unhealthful swamps of Sologne.

Thomas, now in charge of 120,000 workers, was appalled at this series of orders and begged for delay. He was angry that none of his constructive measures had been discussed, and he knew that violence would result from the governmental program. But he soon learned how much in earnest were the cabinet. On May 26 he was summoned to the Ministry of the Interior and ordered to resign on the spot. He was also informed that he must leave Paris at once, under police escort, for Bordeaux, where he was to "study canals." The post chaise was waiting outside the door and he was not allowed to see his mother or even to write to her before taking off. He was kept at Bordeaux, under surveillance, until after the June elections—a procedure so high-handed that Louis Philippe's police would never have dared to try it.

No one at Thomas' office at Monceaux believed that their beloved director had been sent on "an important mission," and when the Minister of the Interior showed up at the Pavillon, they tried to kidnap him in protest. Failing in this, the workshop members became steadily more aggrieved, willing now for the first time to listen to the words of their more sophisticated rivals, the Luxembourg workers, from whose contaminating propaganda Thomas had so carefully preserved them.

So long as Louis Blanc had been a member of the government, and Thomas kept the workshops working, labor, however uneasy, was divided by its various and almost justified hopes; Marie's and Lamartine's efforts to keep it compartmented into Luxembourg and workshops succeeded in fooling part of the people part of the time. Now at last the two groups united, first for electioneering, and soon, finding ballots did not give them what they wanted, for fighting behind new barricades.

As a protective measure early in June, all the clubs were ordered closed, and the penalty for attending an armed meeting was set at twelve years' imprisonment. So ferocious was the law that to stand unknowingly next to a person bearing a concealed weapon became a crime. The monarchy's decrees seemed mild in comparison. Nevertheless, outdoor meetings, the "clubs of despair," were common in spite of the law, and the workers began making cartridges again in their suburbs. National guards were kept in uniform during the month and made all their business and pleasure engagements with the proviso, "if they don't beat the *rappel*." The rich guards, too, in a burst of fraternity, began giving parties for the poor guards, to keep them loyal.

During these days Tocqueville met George Sand for the first time, at a dinner party. He did not expect to like her, having a prejudice against women writers, but discovered in her the natural simplicity of great minds, and he was impressed in spite of himself by her stories of her working-class friends. They were desperate, she said, ready to fight to the death, and she begged him to try to keep his side from forcing the issue. Unfortunately, for minds on opposite sides to meet like this was the rarest thing in the Paris of that day.

Adolphe Blanqui's young servants showed a simplicity of mind that must have been fairly common. (This Blanqui was a perfectly respectable economist in spite of being the club leader's brother; he is said to have been the one who invented the term "industrial revolution.") Just before the outbreak, these servants were heard remarking, "Next Sunday *we* shall be eating chicken wings and wearing silk clothes," an incident much quoted in histories of the period. What is not so often told, though it is almost more significant, is that their master did not dare to fire them for saying this until after the victory.

The Catholic party in the Assembly was determined to abolish the workshops even before the government's preliminary measures to diminish them had time to take effect. In the public mind they were socialistic, and that meant that they were an attack on the Church and the family. No other issue, except education, seemed nearly so important.

Falloux, the workshops' archenemy, exploited every parliamentary trick to rush first the Committee on Labor, then the Assembly itself, into a precipitate vote against the workshops.

Falloux had chosen to work in the Committee on Labor, he tells us, because the Committee on Public Instruction was already under the influence of as good a Catholic as himself, Vicomte de Montalembert. Falloux also pointed out that whereas most people were not interested in labor, he felt he understood the problems involved because of the large amount of charity work he had done among the poor. Being a legitimist, he had not been distracted from good works by parties and social life under the Orleans regime.

Although the platform on which Falloux ran for the Assembly was one of undiluted democratic sentiments, his earlier writings had glorified the Inquisition. "Liberty," he said, although not to the electorate, "is the instrument of modern centuries to reestablish the institutions of the age of faith. Tolerance is not a virtue except in ages of doubt."

He was clever enough in his attack to convince, temporarily, both Proudhon and Victor Hugo, and Hugo made his maiden speech in support of Falloux's bill. Proudhon later said he felt as if he had been an imbecile, and as for Hugo, he was so ashamed of his speech that he altered the text when he printed his papers.

The executive commission realized that they were all playing with explosives and tried once more to slow down the process of dissolution. They suggested taking a census, as one expedient, and they hoped to work out a way to use the men on state-owned railroads. Caussidière rose to echo this plea—let us do important things, let us clear land, let us use this labor to make France happy. But no palliative would subdue Falloux's tireless hatred. On June 23 he insisted on presenting a decree to dissolve the workshops within three days, reading without emotion in spite of the fact that barricades were rising even as he spoke. However, the Assembly voted him down.

Later Falloux was cool enough to say that his report could not have been responsible for the street battle because it was read after the fighting began—ignoring the fact that for days ahead all Paris knew his bill was coming. But even though the Assembly had wished to temporize, by this time the people were unwilling to wait for whatever mollifying laws their representatives might be planning.

On June 18 the Luxembourg commission, which had kept its organization intact after being officially dissolved, and the leaders of the national workshop members issued a joint proclamation in favor of the democratic and social republic. On the 21st the two worker groups had a meeting to plan a demonstration against closing the workshops, and the following day a lieutenant in the workshops, Louis Pujol, led a group of men to interview Marie on the subject.

"If the workers don't want to go to the provinces," declared Marie, "we shall make them go by force. Do you understand?"

"By force," said Pujol. "Good. Now we know what we wanted to know."

"And what was that?"

"That the Executive Commission never sincerely wanted the organization of labor."

Pujol emerged from Marie's office to report to the crowd in his apocalyptic manner that they would be forced to join the army or to leave for the provinces, and cried to them, "Swear vengeance." "We swear it," they replied in chorus. And Pujol gave them an assignation, "Tomorrow at six o'clock"—the day army enlistments were scheduled to start among workshop members. That evening Maxime Du Camp, Flaubert's friend, walking in from dinner in the country, met 2,000 unarmed men marching by threes, crying monotonously, "Bread or lead." He noticed that shop windows and doors slammed shut as the marchers passed.

Pujol came to the fore at the start of this insurrection because all the men who had planned the earlier demonstrations were in jail like Barbès or powerless like Louis Blanc. He was a mystic of sorts and had written a *Prophecy of Bloody Days* in Biblical style which had the power of strangely moving the people. Perhaps now he felt a responsibility for making his prophecy come true. In his subsequent career, he was pardoned by Napoleon after his part in this June uprising, but found that he was persecuted in France for his ideas. He fled to Spain, kidnaped a woman, took her to London, became a teacher, abandoned the woman, married an Englishwoman, and carried her to the United States, where he opened a girls' school and eventually fought for the North in the Civil War.

At six o'clock on the morning of Friday, June 23, the workers who wished to fight for their rights met at the Pantheon as pledged, and marched solemnly to the Place de la Bastille. Pujol ordered them to uncover and to kneel in honor of those who had died here for liberty. When they arose they set to building barricades. Though it was a stormy day with thunder in the air and rain falling, it was not the weather that made these barricades more forbidding than those of February. Wet, gloomy, determined figures, with women and children among them, dragged the stones, making structures that were thicker, sturdier, and neater than those of February, built with more determination and less verve. Those June barricades were systematically built with small openings for passage near the houses. Even mail wagons were upset this time, even water wagons. And when a flag was raised over a completed barricade, the very *Marseillaise* sounded mournful, though the singing was almost drowned out by the alarm bell ringing from the tower of Saint-Sulpice to call the builders' brothers to guard duty.

For a few hours the barricade builders worked almost unopposed, since the government had decided to let the insurrection get its head so that it could be more effectively attacked with troops. This policy must have been a favorite one among friends of order, for it had been advocated by the military party in the outbreak of 1830, and by Thiers to Louis Philippe in February 1848; in the Paris Commune of 1871, Thiers was to put it into action again. Now, in June 1848, it was insisted on by General Eugene Cavaignac, though bitterly opposed by the Executive Commission. Lamartine and his colleagues argued all night that it would be more humane and civilian in spirit to attack each barricade as it was built. The Commission, which was still the governing organ, had asked for 60,000 troops for Cavaignac, which he had failed to provide. It was a bitter disillusionment to them to find that he still continued reluctant to send for reinforcements and that there were not enough troops in Paris to attack all the vital places. Finally Ledru-Rollin telegraphed to other cities for troops and ammunition.

The *rappel* for the national guards was, of course, beaten early, but by mid-morning this was changed to the *générale*, a mixture of drums and trumpets in double quick time which was used only in the greatest emergencies. Tocqueville never heard it before or afterwards. Now the guards poured out of their houses and ran to duty while the workers watched them cynically and listened to the cannon which were beginning to boom.

Shortly after noon the first blood was shed near the Porte Saint-Denis, where the national guards summoned a barricade to surrender and were met with fire. Thirty guardsmen were killed in a bloodthirsty volley from the defenders; and for their part the attackers shot down in succession two beautiful, disheveled young prostitutes who stood atop the barricade, lifting their skirts up to their waists and screaming in unprintable language, "Cowards, do you dare to fire on the belly of a woman?"

Ledru's summons brought immediate help, professional and amateur, from all over France. The first day the government sent a man who passed himself off as an Englishman in order to get to the railroad station, which was in the hands of the insurgents. He carried his orders in the sole of his boot. Once there he managed to mount a locomotive and drive it to Amiens, whence he returned in five hours with 3,000 national guards. Other towns sent reinforcements. Peasants and shopkeepers and nobles could now get their revenge on the workshops, and they poured into Paris until by the last day of fighting they were coming from 500 miles away. From Brittany came 1,500 who had had to make their way over 200 miles where there were as yet no railroads. There was no doubt what the rest of France wanted, no doubt that the Paris workers suffered a complete ideological separation from the country.

The new Minister of War, General Cavaignac, came from a family long prominent for its republicanism and all his life had had to suffer from social pressure on that account. It was hard for him as a boy to get into Polytechnic School, and later in the army he found promotion slower than it might have been for an officer of his ability with somewhat more flexible principles. His military fame was gained in Algeria, then undergoing pacification by France; his formula for governing was never to seem to admire the boldness and courage of the natives, but to make them feel inferior by impressing them with French force and stability. Another of his rules was to give the French colonists private property to defend. His long devotion to republicanism, if not to democracy, found its natural reward when the provisional government summoned him to Paris in April to take over the War Office.

In character someone described him as a surly drill sergeant. A fanatic on obedience, he disliked final responsibility and wanted to get orders from the Assembly—an attitude which charmed those worthies after their dealings with the self-sufficient Executive Commission. Cavaignac's face was rigid even in repose, his eyes were mean; he was the sort of general who could give orders to storm the particular barricade behind which one of his officers was held as hostage. Yet, when the insurrection was over he was found sobbing at the knees of his mother, to whom he was deeply bound.

Concerning the honor as well as the comfort of his troops, he was a perfect fussbudget. Before he would allow them to attack, he laid in ample supplies, so that every soldier had four days' provisions; and he preferred to let national guards police the city and attack what barricades were necessary because he heard that in February some troops had been disarmed by the people. Cavaignac said that he would blow his own brains out if that happened to a single soldier under his command. His contempt for the insurgents surpassed his hatred for a foreign enemy, for he insisted he could never make terms with rebels; he must receive an unconditional and formal surrender.

The workers, under Cavaignac's policy of temporary laissez-faire, had managed to win control over the eastern half of Paris, and inside their territory they performed prodigies. They opened indoor communications from house to house over long distances to make getting around less dangerous. In one of the city's foundries they cast a cannon, and to cool it quickly they hung it in the air and rocked it while children threw sand against it. To get munitions to the barricades women sometimes carried sacks of powder in such a way as to make themselves look pregnant, and men carried rifles in coffins. Meanwhile, civil order was perfectly maintained. No rape or theft was committed in the insurgent area; even jewelry shops were safe, though gunshops were ransacked. When the crowd swept through Victor Hugo's house, probably looking for arms, they left everything untouched down to the unfinished manuscript of *Les Misérables* which was lying on a table. (Eventually, the work was revised and became a masterpiece in the light of those June days.) Taxes were collected at the city gates as usual, and even the stations of the semaphore telegraph within the area wigwagged all dispatches forward except about the battle. The insurgents were so eager to show they were good citizens that they often set prisoners free, even lent them blouses to cover their uniforms until they reached safety.

The Assembly was in permanent and agitated session all this time, comparing themselves to soldiers who kept their posts on the barricades all night. Senard, who was now president, possibly for the very reason that having quelled the election riot at Rouen he was supposed to know how to handle such affairs, voiced the general opinion. The insurgents are not asking for the republic, he said—they have one; they do not ask for suffrage—they have it; they are only looking for anarchy and pillage. Thus, when Caussidière proposed treating with the insurgents he was howled down.

Arago felt it his duty to walk to the barricades and to talk to some of the people on the other side. All they told him was, "Ah, M. Arago, you have never suffered from hunger." He came back from this encounter convinced of the need to use force. With tears in his eyes he ordered the troops to attack. Lamartine likewise went out to parley and was told, "We are not bad citizens. We wish to live and die for the republic." But he was not moved to take their side either. It seemed almost impossible for anyone who had ever owned property to extend his sympathy across those June barricades.

The best the government could think of to do was to continue to pay the members of the national workshops, a policy which undoubtedly kept many workers neutral. Later—on Sunday—the Assembly voted three million francs to be used for relieving the unemployed, a sum which seemed to naïve members of the party of order (and they were as naïve as the workers) to prove complete and indeed overwhelming generosity on the part of the Assembly. Then, just as if to prove that there was no use offering the insurgents anything, a brave officer, General Bréa, was killed when he tried to carry this news to the insurgents. The workers took him inside a barricade to parley, and there, because some of them had heard that he ordered prisoners killed, they shot him.

Atrocity stories, however, were not all on one side. The young firebrands of the militarized police, Lamartine's garde mobile and even Louis Philippe's hated municipal guards (which Cavaignac ordered back from the country, where Emile Thomas had sent them to the ironworks to save them from Parisian wrath after February) now found the chance to cut loose, and horrified the insurgents with their barbarity. No matter how the tales about them are toned down, it seems that they shot a good many prisoners (one story was they threw them into the Seine and shot them while swimming) and left a thousand more in the Tuileries without food and water. When asked to have these latter removed to a more decent place, President Senard said he simply could not guarantee their safety—if they were marched out, the national guards were so inflamed as to shoot them en route. Even Cavaignac, the disciplinarian, said his orders would be ineffective in stopping atrocities.

On Saturday (June 24) the Assembly decided to take power away from the Executive Commission and to make Cavaignac dictator. Up to this point the Commission had shown considerable sense and energy—they had at least tried talking to the workers, and they had sent for reinforcements—yet apparently the deputies rejoiced at the chance to get rid of the five men who had so many ideas of their own that they paid too little attention to the Assembly's.

By Sunday morning the government forces had succeeded in freeing the left bank of the Seine, but the working-class districts on the right bank seemed more tightly organized and more hostile than ever. It was impossible to exchange parleys any longer, until in the afternoon the Archbishop of Paris, Monsignor Denis Auguste Affre, offered to carry a message from Cavaignac to urge the workers to come back like repentant brothers. The good Archbishop had long been concerned with the social problem, particularly with the dechristianization of workers, and to counteract this tendency he had opened history classes in church, and started a medical insurance society which had 15,000 members in 1845. After the revolution, he supported the provisional government at every step and ordered his curates to sing "God save the people" instead of "the King."

Now he was a member of the Assembly. Cavaignac warned him that he could not offer to send a military escort to protect him at the barricades, but Monsignor Affre went ahead anyway. Unfortunately the parley to get him behind the barricades turned into a fight, and he was hit by a bullet from a window in one of the insurgents' houses. Other workers gathered around. They begged him to come into their houses and let them nurse him, they brought clean linen to him and kissed his hand. But Affre knew he was dying and raised his voice in one final prayer, "May my blood be the last that is shed," a wish that almost came true.

For by the following morning the workers held only the Faubourg Saint-Antoine; but no news had reached inside their sixty-four barricades for three days and they did not know that theirs **was** the last stronghold of revolt. Cavaignac gave them a truce until ten o'clock, time for the Faubourg to send a delegation out to the Assembly and to spread news inside their own lines of the governmental victory. But there were still so many workers unwilling to give up that they kept on arguing past the deadline when the truce was to end. At ten minutes past the appointed moment firing began. This time the battle was short and quick. Within an hour it was all over.

That night Alexander Herzen and his family were sitting in their house when they heard shots being fired at short regular intervals. "We glanced at one another, all our faces were livid. . . . 'They are shooting prisoners,' we said with one voice, and turned away from one another. I pressed my forehead against the window pane. Such moments provoke ten years of hatred, a lifetime of revenge: *Woe to him who forgives at such moments*."[1]

After complaints were received about the shooting (so the story went) General Lamoricière gave orders in the future to use bayonets. (Like the inmates of modern concentration camps, officially these prisoners were shot "while attempting to escape.")

In all, these four days of fighting cost 1,460 lives, counting 150 as the number of prisoners who were shot or bayoneted. Four generals were lost as well as four Assembly members. Somebody figured that in no victory of the First Empire were so many French officers killed as during these June days.

Not more than 50,000 took active part in the insurrection, by no

[1] Herzen, *My Past and Thoughts*, IV, 3.

means a large proportion of the working population of Paris if one remembers that 120,000 were registered in the national workshops alone. The morale of those who fought came not from enthusiasm this time, but from despair, yet it was so fierce that they did not give up the Faubourg du Temple until they had fired their last cartridge. No other possibility seemed open to them than to fight over again for what they thought they would win in February, protection against poverty, which they believed was contrary to morality. Women fought as fiercely as men, for the comfort of their husbands, the education of their children. What the insurgents asked for when they attempted to treat with the government was continuance of the workshops, withdrawal of the army from Paris, release of their beloved leaders who had been imprisoned since May 15, and assurance that the "people" should make the constitution. Naïve these suggestions may have been, but they were certainly not bloodthirsty nor vengeful, and they form a painful contrast with the double dealing and determined misunderstanding with which their troubles were always handled by the other side.

Paris was left with houses smoking; many rooms broken open by cannon fire were visible from the street, with smashed furniture and scattered glass; inhabitants, of course were gone. Soldiers were bivouacked on the streets, lying on straw, making soup in the gardens of the Tuileries, their horses tethered to iron palisades or left where they could nibble trees on the Champs Élysées. As for the Luxembourg Gardens, they were closed until after the first big storm, which washed away (people said) the blood of the executions that took place there. Boys of sixteen swaggered through the streets boasting of the men they had killed while shop girls of the same age ran out and pelted them with flowers. The city was quiet, however, though ears still rang with the echoes of shots, the tramp of cavalry, the heavy rumbling of cannon wheels. Herzen, again, told how he felt, and in so doing summed up perhaps for the first time the sort of shock intellectuals were to suffer in many future decades:

"Byron has a description of a battlefield at night; its bloodstained details are hidden in the darkness; at dawn, when the battle has long been over, its traces—a sword and bloodstained clothes—are seen. It was just such a dawn that rose now in the soul, it lighted up a scene of fearful desolation. Half of our hopes, half of our beliefs were slain, ideas of skepticism and despair haunted the brain and took root in it. One could never have supposed that, after passing through so many trials, after being schooled by contemporary skepticism, we had so much left in our souls to be destroyed.

"Natalie wrote about this time to Moscow: 'I look at the children and weep, I am terrified. I no longer dare to wish them to live, perhaps there is a fate as awful in store for them, too.' "[2]

On June 28 Cavaignac, the perfect republican, resigned his powers to the Assembly, which voted them right back to him with the decree that he deserved well of the country.

For vengeance on the workers, the Assembly declared subject to transportation without trial all who were caught with arms in their hands or who worked on the barricades. Louis Menard insists that they picked up women in childbed, paralytics, and some who were not even in Paris at the time of the fight. Of 15,000 prisoners, 6,000 were released after a few days, and batches of others were freed at intervals stretching over a year and a half. By January 1850, 468 were still held and nearly all these were actually sent to Algeria at this time. Some of them turned into colonists, some returned home when they were pardoned in 1859. Only 12 had escaped.

Blanqui, the economist, spoke of the heart breaking distress, and Lamennais, the unfrocked mystic, reproached middle-class women especially for their indifference. Louis Blanc quotes from the police report concerning the president of the Luxembourg delegates, who was sentenced without trial, that he was "of incontestible integrity, of peaceful disposition . . . well-informed . . . well-liked, and for this reason very dangerous in the propagation of socialist ideas."

The only place in the whole city where families of insurgents could go for relief that summer was the office of Proudhon's newspaper (supported by Herzen, incidentally), for Proudhon was deeply ashamed of the way he had been taken in by the Assembly's propaganda during the fighting.

To Cavaignac goes the distinction of setting the first example of permanent martial law, so effectively copied at Berlin and Vienna later in the year. Paris was officially considered "in a state of siege" until October 19, with 50,000 troops encamped there, and a law against the press more restrictive than under the monarchy. Eleven presses were closed, and what publications kept running had to put

[2] Herzen, *op. cit.*

up such a huge guaranty sum in advance that this rule decreed "silence to the poor." The working day was set back at twelve hours, imprisonment for debt was reestablished, and those deluded souls who thought they would not have to pay rent under a republic and for whom Caussidière had kept trying to negotiate some gentler settlement, were now thrown out into the streets with their possessions.

The first draft of the new constitution had been written with the right to work guaranteed. After June this right was torn out, and the "right to support" substituted.

In education the Catholic party worked more slowly but no less thoroughly; in 1850 they laid down a law which made it possible for the Church to control most of the schools of France.

The flight to reaction made Proudhon laugh, and deceived Marx and Engels into thinking, temporarily, that capitalism had not much longer to live. The great gain, as they saw it, was that the June defeat freed the revolutionaries from "pre-revolutionary traditional appendages" of personages, illusions, and ideas. But the bourgeoisie too had lost illusions, all those friendly thoughts about the noble worker and the solidarity of classes which led them to the same side of the barricades in February. Now, these workers, these propertyless individuals whom they had helped to free, had ungratefully turned on their betters in irrational and dangerous fury; the fear that gripped the upper classes was like that in Rome at the invasion of the barbarians.

Society hurled itself backwards (said Daniel Stern) as if it wanted to return to the forms which it had just destroyed, when all at once a name appeared that gave form and energy and a new existence to revolution.

This name, of course, was Louis Napoleon's. As his uncle had taken over the First Republic, using power for both liberal and illiberal ends, so the nephew, now ready to emerge from obscurity, bestrode the Second Republic. He took what strength it had for his own and abandoned the shell when it was empty.

After Napoleon had turned down his seat in the Assembly, he doubtless congratulated himself (or would he think it only natural?) that he escaped contact with the June battle. His attitude toward the revolution is as mysterious as everything else about him, only one may be sure that he would have capitalized on it equally if the workers had won. However, he was not bloodthirsty, and it seems almost certain that he did not try to start this particular trouble, loud though he was in sympathy for the members of the workshops and bitter in denunciations of the law forbidding public meetings. But as the trouble grew nearer he ordered his partisans to play dead. If one-third of the insurgents were Bonapartists, as was estimated, they were without active leadership in the battle, and the new Napoleon who emerged in the fall was far less demagogic and far more the man of order than the one who had campaigned for election in June. In the middle of Cavaignac's summer-long dictatorship, the prince remarked that the general was merely clearing the way for him; a Bonaparte could hardly have been sorry to watch odium piling up on another's reputation while the Napoleonic ideal was kept shining and untarnished. His was the only one whose promise had not yet betrayed the people. Louis Napoleon came as the bearer of a new fantastic hope of peace and liberalism.

In September he at last allowed himself to be elected to the Assembly, though he told his friend and campaign manager, Fialin de Persigny, that he did not feel his place was in that body and he would try not to take his seat. Nevertheless, once elected, he arrived in Paris on the 24th and two days later made his appearance at the Assembly hall, where he responded to the moderate acclaim which greeted him with a short speech (in a pronounced German accent). After that he seldom appeared on the floor but let his two cousins who were also members speak for him. In his first days at Paris he arranged talks with several socialists, including Proudhon. And he instructed Persigny never to let any private or public conversation intimate that he had any other ambition than to serve France in legitimately established channels.

In October the Assembly created the berth for which he aspired, one both legitimate and eminent. If the new constitution, in creating a four-year presidency and forbidding the incumbent to succeed himself, hoped to erect a barrier against monarchy, four years would at least give the country a chance to see how it liked a republic and Napoleon a chance to work peacefully from the top.

The great question in drafting the constitution was whether to elect the president in the Assembly or by popular vote. The Assembly at that date would unquestionably have chosen Cavaignac, and, knowing that, Lamartine threw himself into a passionate appeal for universal suffrage. The purple and golden words worked—once more. It was Lamartine's last parliamentary victory, and one cannot be sure whether he made the effort out of vain conceit that he himself would be the people's candidate—for he spent the rest of his life in self-admiration, and kept nine portraits of himself in his living room—or whether he recognized that Napoleon would win and cynically felt that that was what the country deserved. "The more I see of representatives of the people, the more I like my dogs," he is supposed to have said, and he may have felt that way about the presidency.

The constitution was quickly ratified; it turned out to be excessively cumbrous, drawn so that if the president and Assembly got into a deadlock there was almost no way they could get out again. Also, it was almost impossible to amend it. It was these provisions which, Napoleon's apologists say, made the *coup d'état* of 1851 in which he took power into his own hands, coupled with his later crowning as Napoleon III, the only possible way to break the log jam. This would be easier to believe if the Napoleonic dream had not been an imperial dream from the beginning; and this Napoleon was certainly clever enough to outsmart any constitution whatever.

A proposal was introduced to the Assembly to bar pretenders from the presidency, but even Cavaignac felt this idea showed lack of trust in the electorate and opposed it. The Prince himself was asked to explain his position, and said in a few sentences that he just wanted to be a French citizen and wished people would stop calling him a pretender. He spoke so haltingly that the member who introduced the amendment withdrew it in scorn, saying he perceived it was not needed. He grossly underestimated the Prince, but then so did nearly everybody else who knew him. That was part of his strength.

Shortly after the presidential elections were arranged, the Central Bonapartist Committee set itself up in Paris to push the Prince's candidacy. The elections were to take place on December 10. Persigny, warned by having been imprisoned in June, slept every night in a different bed but between naps was indefatigable in electioneering. Emile de Girardin, also furious at having been thrown into prison in June, supported Napoleon in the *Presse*; and Thiers, whose eye was on the presidency for himself in four years, supported him on the theory that this was a weak scion of the Bonapartes whose course he, Thiers, could direct. For weeks it was a private joke between Napoleon and Persigny that Thiers, who was short, came to the Prince begging him not to wear a uniform in office lest his successor happen to be a very small man whom the military garb did not become. The truth was, Napoleon was nearly everybody's candidate. Conservatives did not dare name one of their own men, radicals were furious at Cavaignac and would support anybody to beat him, socialists were misled by Napoleon's apparent sympathy, peasants adored his uncle, and workers wanted to live and eat without another battle. Also, he was the candidate of other millions who felt that Napoleon was a synonym for national glory. Persigny explained that his candidacy did not exclude any party but called eminent men from all parties; and for many people, including Persigny himself, the cause was like a religious faith. It was Heine who noticed that the pictures of the first Napoleon which decorated every peasant's cottage usually showed him either visiting the sick and wounded, or lying on his deathbed of expiation, and he was struck by the religious connotations of these two poses.

Yet the campaign was not all sweetness. Persigny knew how to appeal to hatred and envy and ambition. (He even tried, unsuccessfully, anti-Semitism.) Napoleon explained to the friends of order that he wished to discipline the workers, for his projected workers' colonies were more like the labor camps of Hitler than the cooperatives of Louis Blanc. To the workers he explained that though he was going to run the country cheaply, the few little moneys that he did require would be extracted from the rich. "The Napoleonic cause goes to the soul," said the Prince at one time, and no one knew better than he that souls have evil passions as well as good. He believed in exploiting all depths.

In Louis Napoleon's mind, ends were more important than means, and the end was that France should be Napoleonic once again. It seems fair to divorce his ambition this far from personal advancement. If one were to ask what he really believed beneath his almost impenetrable reserve, his statement that he would put efficiency ahead of liberty, and that the chief thing France needed was prosperity, seems more to agree with his actions than some other remarks. His uncle, he said, would have planted liberty in France if he had been given more time, because he had already planted "all that ought to go ahead of liberty." Tocqueville found in the young man no real taste for freedom, only "a sort of abstract adoration of the people," whom he genuinely wanted to be happy on their six francs a day. Because he wanted to be a great ruler he had to make France a great nation and one unified in spirit; unlike the hereditary rulers of Germany and Austria, he had brains enough to see at least some of the things that were required.

With such an ambition and such an ideal he felt no loyalty to friends nor to his own statements. Many persons complained of his disloyalty, but never while they were still useful to him. When he dropped them he became, not unfriendly, but indifferent. The strength of his character lay in his immense self-possession. No one ever saw him angry, or excited, or depressed, or impatient; yet though he rarely gave his confidence to anyone, people who talked to him came away heartened and excited.

The extraordinary effect of his personality is best described by an Englishman who met him about this time:

"Though I had not the slightest ground for expecting to see a fine man, I did not expect to see so utterly insignificant a one, and badly dressed into the bargain. . . . When Prince Louis Napoleon held out his hand and I looked into his face, I felt almost tempted to put him down as an opium eater. Ten minutes afterwards I felt convinced . . . that he himself was the drug, and that everyone with whom he came in contact was bound to yield to its influence."[3]

It was this man who drafted as a campaign pledge, "I will make it a point of honor to leave to my successor at the end of four years power consolidated, liberty untouched, and real progress accomplished." Some of his friends asked him why he insisted on promising to get out of office. Napoleon turned to Emile de Girardin and asked his opinion whether to take this out or not. The editor told him to leave it in if he meant to act on it, otherwise to take it out. The promise stayed in, but it was not kept.

Napoleon's only serious opponent in the election was Cavaignac, who was busily flooding the country with campaign biographies and portraits of himself on horseback. When asked whether he believed the country was sincerely republican, the general replied he knew it was not, but he was seeking office solely with the object of making it so. One of his gestures was to send 3,500 troops to Rome to sup-

[3] Vandam, *An Englishman in Paris*, II, 7ff.

port the Pope and to escort him to France if revolutionary troubles in Italy made him flee. However, this gesture (though it was followed up energetically by Napoleon) got Cavaignac nowhere with the voters. The Pope, perhaps partly because he disliked Cavaignac's publicity, took refuge in Naples instead of France.

Hardly anyone was surprised when Napoleon drew 5,434,266 votes to Cavaignac's 1,448,107. Lamartine's complete discrediting showed in his 17,910. To avoid a demonstration the Prince took his oath as president a day ahead of schedule, on December 20, and at once installed a ministry including Odilon Barrot, Falloux, and Tocqueville—the old left, the Catholic right, and the cynical student of democracy.

To his opponents Napoleon tried to be generous, though Cavaignac almost refused to shake his hand and turned down the grand cordon of the Legion of Honor, and Lamartine refused a portfolio under the new regime. Though he was deeply in debt, the poet also refused to let the Prince pay his debts. Later on Napoleon was secretly able to save Lamartine's face by giving him a house, the origin of which Lamartine never knew. And three times during his first six months as president, Napoleon tried to pardon the June insurgents condemned to transportation; but each time his ministers threatened to resign or the Assembly blocked him. It was like him to feel strong enough to make this gesture, and it formed a heart-warming contrast to the executive powers throughout the rest of Europe when they faced their defeated 1848 revolutionaries.

Inevitably, however, the Napoleonic promises came to prove as false as Louis Philippe's or Lamartine's. A professed democrat and nationalist, the future emperor was to kill democracy and nationalism in the Roman republic; a boastful friend of peace, he led France into several wars; though he publicly courted socialists, he used reactionary ministers and soon cut off his left-wing friends.

Universal suffrage, then, did not give a very good account of itself in its first try in nineteenth-century Europe. Marx, to be sure, thought votes for all were a good thing because they would unite all the bourgeoisie into one camp against the lower classes and thereby unchain the class struggle; but Marx was an optimist. Proudhon, who was a pessimist, expressed the opinion that universal suffrage means counter-revolution. "Put an end to our quarrels by taking away our liberties," he apostrophized Napoleon, "come and complete the shame of the French people." Herzen was the only observer on the French scene who believed that something specific rather than something general was wrong with the elections in France. He felt that local self-government was an essential foundation for national self-government, and that the French had had no practice in either. For centuries they had expected all initiative to come from the top (except for a few months after 1789), had supposed the state would solve all their big problems. Those who had power, like both Napoleons, and those who wanted power, like Louis Blanc, envisaged its use in this way. They used the electorate as a tool for mass emotion, and although Napoleon never equaled Hitler's percentages, he made a good first try in this direction. There were not many places in Europe to test Herzen's theory of local self-government as a foundation, but in Hungary, where local politics were the liveliest and most responsible, the 1848 revolution was carried through with the least bloodshed and the most sensible program of reform.

PART II · GERMANY

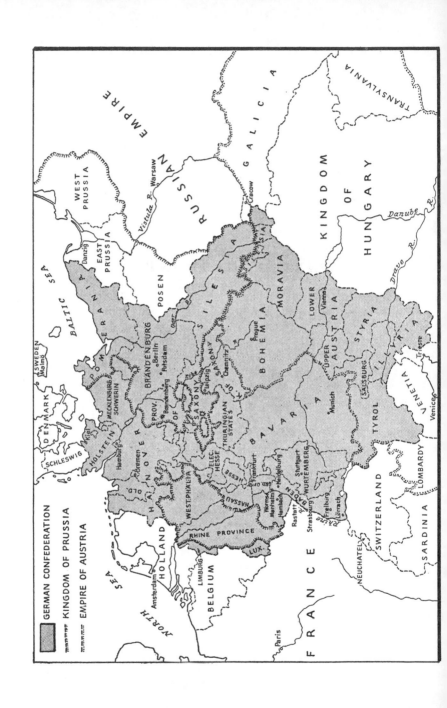

King of Prussia by the Grace of God

FREDERICK WILLIAM IV of Prussia was one individual who could scarcely conceal his satisfaction at the fall of Louis Philippe. Though he deplored revolutionary activity anywhere, that it should strike in France against a monarch who had not scrupled to take advantage of it in 1830, seemed to Frederick William only the revenge of a just God. That the same providence barely gave him three weeks to indulge his complacency before letting revolution strike in Berlin might suggest to a more candid eye that even strict Prussian legitimacy had its faults and miscalculations—but since Frederick William was still on his throne at the end of the disturbance, his faith in himself may have been justified to a certain extent.

He occupied accordingly the positions of both Louis Philippe and Louis Napoleon, in respect to the revolution, and he shared something of the weakness of one and the strength of the other. Like Louis Philippe he shrank from bloodshed even at the moment of his greatest danger; like Louis Napoleon he was confident in his destiny. Both French rulers had knocked around the world enough to respect the power of its new ideas, so that one succumbed to the new age, the other manipulated it to his own fashion. But Frederick William consistently ignored it, and by ignoring it succeeded in driving it back for twenty—or a hundred—years.

In this effort he was helped by the nature and backwardness of the Prussian state, but a large share of the credit must go to his own character. By temperament he would have made a better subject than ruler, so deep was his reverence for himself and his office, so mystical his approval of his own royal course of action. His reign began in 1840 with a deceptively idealistic policy which seemed liberal for a while because it was friendly, but whose object was to cultivate old-time religion, morals, and customs. He was consciously working against not only the then widely held ideas of the French Revolution, but against the ideas of the English Revolution which he deemed responsible for the French Revolution. This was his attitude especially because many German reformers were advocating the British kind of constitutional monarchy for Germany.

Like Louis Napoleon, Frederick William lived in a dream about himself. But Napoleon believed he needed and should win the people, whom he "adored abstractly"; Frederick William could do without them, since he had the grace of God behind him. Both men felt that they themselves were the incarnation of their own ideal.

All this was not immediately easy for Frederick William's subjects to notice. In the first place, observers agreed that his personality was rich and charming, so that many great men like Humboldt and Radowitz, his chief adviser, were fascinated by him. When he broke all precedent and spoke to his people in person at his coronation he was rewarded by a thunderous popular "*Ja*." And then, wishing to rule by confidence, he pardoned many distinguished political prisoners and exiles, among them the poet Moritz Arndt and famous old *Turnvater* Jahn, who had stirred up the youth of the 1810's to fervent patriotism by gymnastic exercises. He was kind to many poets, among them the revolutionary Georg Herwegh, to whom he remarked in an interview in 1842, "I love a convinced opposition." Nevertheless when Herwegh protested because a newspaper he was editing was suppressed, he was exiled.

As only one sign of how the honey dripped away—the treasury's handsome surplus, left by Frederick William III, was spent within two years on court festivals and grants to the nobility, while the unhappy middle class soon saw that modern trade had neither the understanding nor the sympathy of their medieval-minded monarch.

On the other hand, he was more careful of his poor people than one might have expected, for he felt it was his kingly duty to protect them. For instance he honored the Association for the Welfare of the Working Classes with a gift of money, thereby endorsing its program of education and savings banks. Nevertheless, when he said he was a father to his people he had in mind a distinctly Prussian type of fatherhood. He would be just to his children and protect them from unrighteous laws and officials, but it was not his duty to listen to their ideas. The King's friend, Baron Bunsen, remarked that he was like a child who was glad when the bird he held by a string acted like one that was free; nevertheless, at no price would he cut the string to make it really free. And another friend, the brilliantly conservative Radowitz, explained that the Prussian state existed not to further people's material or intellectual welfare but to help them lead earthly lives that would prepare them for heavenly ones.

Greece had lost its leadership, according to the historian Lorenz von Stein, by the victory of the lower classes over the upper; Rome, by the triumph of the patricians over the plebeians. The German way was to prevent either catastrophe, with the King as an umpire. Naturally this idea was far from pleasing either to the middle class, just beginning to feel its power in Prussia, or to the infant proletariat, stimulated by ideas of the rights of man and the first rumors of socialism.

Most of the King's notions and his duty-ridden conscience stemmed from a profound though not precise religious conviction. He seemed to one French observer to float between Protestantism and Catholicism, as between feudalism and parliamentarianism. But the fuzziness was superficial. His beliefs came out clearly to Bettina von Arnim, who was pestering him with letters about liberalism. He said that although the Bible was for her a partly interesting, partly objectionable human product, for him it was the real work of God, commanding obedience.

And kings had special insight into the mind of God. Frederick William verily believed he knew things no statesman could know, things which had been dark even to himself as crown prince—hence he did not care to govern through ministers. He presided at his cabinet meetings and tartly set down any contradiction as presumptuous.

Thus he spent his first eight years on the throne in a gradually increasing fog of misunderstanding. Austria and Russia were both terrified at his appearance of reform—liberalizing press laws and so on—which they could only interpret as desire for aggrandizement by winning the favor of the small states. His own subjects soon found these reforms were in appearance only, and they came to despair of explaining anything to a ruler so despotic and so dreamy.

It takes two sides to make a revolution, and if the Hohenzollern temperament was better fitted to withstand attack than the house of Orleans, at the same time Prussian subjects were by no means so wide awake or articulate as the French. The peasants were mostly silent, not from having their wishes satisfied as the French had been in 1789, but from not yet realizing their grievances; the city workers made a picturesque fringe to the outbreak, but never managed to voice effectively any separate demands. The class that was able to ask something from the government in 1848 was the middle class which needed civil rights, a constitution which would give them a share in running the country and greater opportunities for carrying on business, some of the same things the French had revolted for in 1830.

Unlike the bourgeoisie of France and England, however, the Prussian middle class had been so surrounded by dictatorial members of the nobility, the army, and the bureaucracy that they had never quite made of themselves a ruling class. In Prussia they always needed the support of either those below them or those above them, and the history of 1848 is partly a story of their being pushed from one camp into the other. When they felt their property was being threatened by worker support they turned back to their King. It was all too easy to induce them to prefer "order" to the "freedom" they thought they wanted at the beginning of the period. And since the workers by themselves were even weaker than their employers, things in Berlin never reached anywhere near the point of the June insurrection in Paris. They would have had to defeat the absolute monarchy before they could quarrel about their share of the spoils.

Three-quarters of Prussia was rural, and though serfdom was legally dead there were parts of the country where the Junkers still dispensed justice and claimed all their old feudal dues, even the *jus primae noctis*. The nobility were everywhere provincial, and though they sat in their provincial diets, the provinces were kept apart; there was no central organ of government in Berlin to draw them together, and little else there to attract them in the manner of Vienna or Paris.[1]

Indeed, Berlin was described at that time as a magnet which attracted only poverty. What high society existed was luxurious but inelegant, the streets were broad but dead, the opera house pretty but uncomfortable. The brilliant Rahel von Ense complained how everything there sank into the commonplace; even the Pope himself, she thought, would sink there to the standard of a groom. The

[1] Herzen found the possibility of living comfortably in Europe in those days started at the Rhine. He was enchanted at the conveniences of Paris, especially the numbers of quick efficient services, from catering to house-cleaning, which made it unnecessary to employ private servants.

well-to-do citizens were stuffy, frightened by intellect. They coveted friendship with the police so that if their sidewalks were not cleaned promptly it would be overlooked, and so that they might obtain passports for their relatives from out of town to visit.

Of the 400,000 inhabitants, only 712 were large merchants, while something over a tenth of the population worked in factories and could barely live on their earnings. Six thousand received alms, including soup, bread, and land to raise potatoes; six thousand got sick relief; and there were three or four thousand beggars. Housing too was wretched. In seven big new tenements 400 rooms held 2,500 people. The labor of children was forbidden under nine years of age, and until sixteen it was limited to ten hours, supposedly to give the children a chance to go to school and learn what was needful in their station of life. But only 55 per cent of school-age children actually attended these classes (a much lower percentage than in any of the Prussian provinces) and there were many heartbreaking stories of working children's suicides.[2]

Guilds still controlled the labor in many handcrafts, and in these fields a man could theoretically rise to become an artisan or shop-keeper. But the number of apprentices was increasing faster than the general population which meant statistically that their chances of rising were growing less, and this, as well as the competition of textile and printing machinery made the young men of the guilds restless and angry.

The common people nevertheless had the reputation of being very gay in every way in which they were allowed to be by the police. They adored picnics, bonfires, parades, festivals. Berlin popular wit, with its love of puns, was famous.

The leaders of the workers, furthermore, were beginning to be trained to think about their problems. A fair number of them traveled to France and Switzerland in their *Wanderjahre*, bringing back ideas which were overrunning western Europe. At home a series of organizations, each one short-lived, seems to have kept their minds busy. The Worker's Club, for example, used to exhibit samples of its members' craftsmanship; and in different years were instituted

---

[2] The strikes of the Silesian weavers, about whom Hauptmann wrote his famous play, had taken place in 1844. These workers were Prussian subjects. Sunday work was so common in Silesia in this period that many workers promised their pastors to work from Friday noon until Saturday night at nine in one unbroken stretch in order to avoid laboring on the Sabbath.

a workers' chorus; club meetings where workers could meet poets and intellectuals; workers' classes in geography, history, physics, architecture, and literature; and in 1846 a newspaper reading room and lending library.

About 1840 the houses of prostitution, formerly under police and medical supervision, had been closed, and some people attributed the city's new nervousness partly to this fact. Certain it is that the year after the revolution they were reopened.

In April 1847, the worst disturbance which any Berliner could imagine up to that time occurred. Crowds of women, enraged because everything became more expensive that spring, began raiding the markets and food shops. They swept through the streets cleaning out the food but not hurting the other property of merchants who showed themselves good-natured. In bakeries they weighed the loaves, and if they found a certain product up to standard they congratulated the maker and wrote on his door that he was honest—signs that were respected by the crowds that came along later. A number of substantial citizens offered to serve as extra police to keep order in the city, but the government was afraid to trust any of its civilians with arms, and on the fourth day ordered soldiers to clear the streets. In the wake of this disturbance, a hundred people were imprisoned, to be released only in 1848 in the revolution's amnesty.

This affair, like the Silesian weavers' strike of 1844, was a blow to the Prussian conscience, and people began everywhere to do what they could to better the condition of the poor. But not much could be done while Prussia was ruled by its army and its bureaucrats.

All the hatred which in Vienna was concentrated on Metternich, in Berlin found its object in the Prussian army, the proudest in Europe, and deliberately organized to keep the people down. Each big city had its garrison—Berlin, for instance, quartered 15,000 soldiers but maintained only 209 policemen—and the policy was to move each regiment every four years to prevent any great friendliness or attachment to special localities even in the ranks. As for the officer corps, it was open only to aristocrats and was as famous for its contempt of the lower classes as of civil affairs generally. The arrogance of both officers and troops made them detested so bitterly that no concession during the revolution could make the citizens happy until the soldiers had been completely withdrawn.

Prussian bureaucracy had aroused Cobden's praise ten years earlier by its progressiveness and incorruptibility. Nevertheless, most Germans, both above and below on the social scale, hated it. Frederick William particularly felt the dangers of letting "salaried, lettered, uninterested, unpropertied officials" (the phrase was Stein's, the great reforming Prussian statesman of the Napoleonic period) run his country for him—and this was one reason for the King's appearance of liberalism.

In the various parts of his country the popularity of the new King waned at different speeds. The Rhinelanders never had liked being under Prussia, to which they had been attached only since 1815, often openly preferring the French Napoleonic rule. Carl Schurz tells how in his boyhood "the word Prussian served for an opprobrious invective, and when one schoolboy flung it out at another it was difficult to find a more stinging invective to fling back."[3] It was the adults of the Rhineland, middle-class burghers who needed progress faster than it was coming their way, who supported young Karl Marx in his early efforts at editing the *Rheinische Zeitung* in 1842.

By 1847 only the feudal nobility and their loyal ignorant peasants stuck wholeheartedly to the King.

Even Frederick William knew something had to be done. Proposals for reform ranged from the ideas of the French Revolution to those of German Catholicism—but Frederick William as usual had his own peculiar revelation. Partly because under a law of 1820 he could not get any taxes to build railroads without the consent of a representative body which Prussia had never had, and partly because he imagined it was going back to the old German way, he summoned the eight provincial diets of the kingdom to meet in Berlin as the "United Diet." It was a solution which proved to be neither old German nor new German, and besides it did not give him his money.

The provincial diets consisted only of landowners, in two chambers according to their rank, and although they were more ornamental than useful to the body politic, most of them had pulled themselves together sufficiently during Frederick William's reign to petition the crown for a new constitution, or a constitutional assembly. Such an innovation had been promised by Frederick William's

[3] Schurz, *Reminiscences*, I, 72.

father in the wake of the Napoleonic struggle, but had never come to birth. As early as 1841 Frederick William refused to accept a fete as he was passing through the city of Breslau because the local diet had been so presumptuous.

United, the diets proved more rather than less refractory. The King opened the meetings with a speech complimenting the members on their organic unity with the crown. Prussia, he was confident, like England, would never need a scrap of paper to come between the ruler and his subjects. And as if he suspected that these remarks would rub his subjects the wrong way, he added that he was going to act in such a way as to deserve the thanks of the people whether he got them or not. The effect was so uncompromising that the Crown Princess of Prussia retired to her chambers and wept. The Diet exhibited a more masculine rage. It announced to the King that unless he granted them the right to regular periodical meetings it would not feel competent to guarantee the money for his railroads. Naïvely, however, they begged the King not on that account to stop work on the construction; but naturally the furious monarch ordered all work stopped immediately. In fact, he almost had to. Even the House of Rothschild had refused to lend money to the railroad project without the Diet's confirmation.

The question of periodicity was crucial, because the members of the Diet felt if they were assured of being summoned regularly they would be able to keep watch over the interests of the country and force some modern rights out of the King. This was what Metternich had cynically prophesied—that even though Frederick William thought what he was summoning was only the old diets, they would leave Berlin as a regular representative legislative body.

With this problem still unresolved, in late 1847, the King's mind went on to something else. He liberalized the press laws of his kingdom to allow for discussion of another of his pet projects—turning the German Confederation into a federal union. "The word Germany," said the King, "has sent thrills of ecstasy for fifty years quivering through my soul." Imagine his disappointment to find that his subjects at the moment quivered more easily to the notion of a constitution for Prussia.

Nor were the two ideas quite so unrelated as they seem. In the minds of most Germans at that time was the fixed idea that a liberal Prussia was the only state that could lead the rest of Germany into union. Later in the century Bismarck and Marx both showed in their separate ways that there was no necessary connection between freedom and nationalism, but this was not apparent to the patriots of pre-1848. The American Chargé d'Affaires in Vienna remarked acutely that in 1848 both Germany and Italy could have won either unification or liberalism, but because they tried for both, they did not win either.

The picture in the mind of the King of Prussia as March 1848 approached was not the same as his compatriots'. He was considering plans for both a congress of German sovereigns and a congress of representatives from all the German diets, neither of which ever came off. But his picture, fixed in such detail that his mind could hardly accommodate to any other, was medieval. He wanted to restore to the House of Austria the crown of the Holy Roman Empire, defunct since Napoleonic times, but he also imagined there might be room for a "King of the Germans," or just for an hereditary Imperial Military Commander to run the Empire's armies. Either of these posts he would have been glad to fill, even while carrying a silver basin in the coronation procession of the Emperor. The King's mind had evidences of practicality after all—let the old German forms be mystically preserved, yet let Prussia be the real executive, "compelling Austria," with its millions of other races, "to be German."

The fall of Louis Philippe was the catalytic agent that precipitated revolution in Prussia. Paul Boerner, a university student at Berlin, tells us how the news hit him. When he first heard of the events in Paris he had to go out in the cold and walk until he was exhausted in order to quiet his blood. He says he could have embraced anybody. After that for many evenings he would go and listen to the papers being read aloud in Stehely's café. One group would listen and go away and another would come in, but Boerner would sit through all of the readings, waiting until late so that perhaps he could then snatch a look at the papers himself.[4]

[4] Carl Schurz, who was a student at the University of Bonn, describes in a classic way what happened to him and his friends at the news of the French outbreak: "The first practical service we had to perform turned out to be a very merry one. Shortly after the arrival of the tidings from France the burgomeister of Bonn, a somewhat timid man, believed the public safety in his town to be in imminent danger. In point of fact, in spite of the general excitement there were really no serious disturbances of the public order. But the burgomeister insisted that a civic guard must at once be

The revolutionary students in Berlin never numbered much more than a hundred out of 1,500 enrolled. But these few immediately sent a delegation to General von Pfuehl, governor of the city, to ask that they should be armed, as a student wing of the citizens' militia that all were hoping for. The general sent away the bodyguard that had come along to protect the leaders, and turned the leaders over to the police for grilling.

Other and more important groups were forming. Spring was early that year, with March evenings as warm as May, and the citizens of Berlin began to congregate in increasing numbers in their favorite outdoor spot, the *Zelte*. The *Zelte* had at one time been real tents, as the name indicates, but long before 1848 permanent buildings were erected in the park along the Spree—cafés, concert halls, amusement stands among the trees, overlooking the water. While old women sold cucumbers in vinegar, sausages, white beer, and cherry brandy, revolutionary news and views spread and people began to organize informal public forums. For the first time in Prussian history huge groups of citizens began to talk over measures of their government, now that it seemed at last as if the King were trying to catch up with the times.

On March 6, 1848, for instance, he dissolved the committees that were still sitting as a hang-over from the United Diet, and gave the long-awaited promise that he would summon the full Diet regularly. Meanwhile, with smaller German regimes on every side collapsing or capitulating to reform, he exhorted his own subjects to gather around him like a wall of brass. On March 7 a great assembly in the *Zelte* mulled over this concession and drafted a petition to the King asking for immediate calling of the Diet, and freedom of the press.

---

organized, to patrol the city and the surrounding country during the night. The students too were called upon to join it, and as this forming of such a guard was part of our political program, we at once willingly obeyed the summons, and we did this in such numbers that soon the civic guard consisted in great part of university men. . . . Armed with our rapiers, the iron sheaths of which were made to rattle on the pavement to the best of our ability, we marched through the streets. Every solitary citizen whom we met late at night was summoned with pompous phrases to 'disperse' and to betake himself to his 'respective habitation,' or, if it pleased him better, to follow us to the guardhouse and have a glass of wine with us. Whenever we happened to run across a patrol not composed of students, but of citizens, we at once denounced them as a dangerous mob, arrested them and took them to the guardhouse, where with cheers for the new empire we drank as many glasses together as there were points of reform in the political program. The good burghers of Bonn fully appreciated the humorous situation and entered heartily into the fun."

They wanted to send a deputation to the King with these requests, but were told the King would never receive such representatives. So the petition, read out loud and signed by thousands, was sent through the mail.

On March 8 the government came out with a pious hope for freedom of the press some day, meanwhile pointing out that the rules of the German Confederation forbade Prussia to grant it at present. (The Confederation was a league of German states, dominated by Austria, which felt that censorship was as important to national defense as an army.)

This was countered, as might have been expected, by a still bigger crowd at the *Zelte*. Berlin was beginning to be hard to police. The soldiers, on whom officialdom counted for keeping order, began to feel unsure of themselves as the officers censured them for irritating the people when they were only obeying previous commands. By the 13th, it was noted, the public began to whistle and hoot at the military for the first time, and to talk openly of getting them out of the city. The city gates were closed against mobs pushing in from the suburbs, yet nevertheless the tumult was great enough to drive the audience away from the new ballet at the Opera House. At this point someone asked a high officer if the soldiers would really shoot at civilians and got the answer, "If the King commands, we shall shoot, and gladly." Indeed, on this very day some of them proved their willingness by attacking women with broadswords to dispel the crowds. Fury rose on both sides. The soldiers in Berlin were mostly new recruits with many grievances, and they probably understood very little of what was going on. But the entire hatred of the populace in Berlin was concentrated on the military machine that had shoved them off the streets and given them insolent orders for so many years.

On March 16 two people were killed by a volley from a group of dragoons trying to clear a square. That was the end of the chance for peace in Berlin, though the real battle started two days later. The King was fussing around with two proclamations, one of them to call a constitutional assembly, and the other broader and vaguer. In it His Majesty talked of revision of the Confederation, the idea of a German flag, a German fleet, common German law, and freedom of the press. Many people thought that he was trying to snatch the leadership of Germany away from Austria at this critical juncture, although his later acts made this hypothesis hard to prove. But this was just exactly what the burghers, at least the prosperous ones, in Berlin wanted to hear. Bodelschwingh, retiring Minister of the Interior (a change of ministry being one of the conventions of such an occasion, in spite of the fact that Bodelschwingh had been trying to work in a constitutional direction for years while the King would neither let him go ahead nor let him resign)—Bodelschwingh remarked on the eve of March 18, "Prussia has already had her revolution."

By eleven o'clock the next morning the streets were crowded with people waiting to hear the reading of the happy news that had been promised. Well-dressed women sat in shop windows to observe the goings-on, and nearly everybody was cheerful and eager. In the restaurants collections were taken for the poor. Some workers, it is true, began to mutter, "This sort of thing won't help us poor people at all," but their betters warned them to be quiet. Shortly after one o'clock the proclamations were read to a mass of openly enthusiastic people. In the city council room citizens came up to embrace the councillors. Near the palace greater crowds collected to cheer the King.

In the middle of this rejoicing came the two mysterious shots that seem like the hallmark of the 1848 revolutions. To please the army the King had that day appointed General von Prittwitz, an old-fashioned martinet, to be Governor of Berlin, and ordered him to clear the square. A squadron of dragoons trotted out and rode right into the crowd with drawn swords. Then some foot soldiers began marching toward the square—and the two shots rang out into the air. No explanation has ever sounded plausible.

No one was hurt, but the people were terrified and began to spread rumors. Within an hour barricades began to rise. The first one was made of two hackney coaches, a carriage, a sentry box, some curbing and a few barrels. The main ingredient of another was a fruit stall, of another, fire pumps. People brought bedding and sacks of flour out of their homes to help. It seemed to the newly arrived envoy from the French republic that these Berlin barricades were far more tragic, built with far more passion, than the ones he had seen the month before in Paris.

The turning of joy into rage was so swift that later people asked themselves how it could have happened. One young man whose first thought was to get to his mother, who had gone to watch the procession when everything seemed quiet at noon, could not get across the city. Already pavements were torn up, the boards and planks that reached across the gutters lifted from their places, and vehicles overturned. A number of university students galloped on horseback through the city gate to summon the locomotive builders in the suburbs, and 900 workers marched back, carrying heavy iron bars. Bullets were molded in the streets, and women came out with coffee and sandwiches for the barricade fighters. That night, in bright moonlight, with most of the city's windows illuminated, the sentry boxes near the city gates were set on fire, and these shone red all over the city.

Troops were called out, of course, and, led by General von Prittwitz, they made a good beginning of conquering the barricades. They would have done better in this job if the King had let them. But the unhappy Frederick William met the first news of the uprising with, "It can't be. My people love me." All through the night, whenever his permission was asked to take a certain barricaded position, he would answer, "Yes, but do not fire."

Nevertheless, the fighting on all sides was fierce. The soldiers were particularly embittered by some of the improvised weapons used by their opponents—one soldier received a shot of steel pens in his face, and others complained of having boiling oil poured on them from above. Meanwhile, the people were taking out old grudges. "People's justice" was supposed to consist in not stealing anything, but breaking and burning the property of "enemies of the people." A glove maker named Wernicke gave coffee to the troops—an extremely rare offense, apparently—and for this his shop was burned. Years later it became fashionable in conservative circles to buy his gloves, although they were both bad and expensive.

By morning the principal streets were red, not only with blood but with piles of roof tiles. All the windows on the Königstrasse, for instance, were broken, and most of its roofs left open.

Army men liked to think their contempt for the rebels was justified. A dashing young officer, Prinz zu Hohenlohe Ingelfingen, complained that the rebels were such cowards they stopped fighting in the Königstrasse as soon as one of them was wounded, and that they only defended their houses at the entrance, and possibly, out of desperation, on the top floor. But in contradiction to this, he complained of the insurgents' ferocity, which he attributed to a decoction of tobacco mixed with brandy that was supposed to be passed around their lines.

On the other hand a liberal like Varnhagen von Ense would write of the same rebels as follows: "Never have I seen greater courage, a more resolute contempt of death, than in those young men who were beaten down and lost beyond all hope of rescue. Well-bred students in fine clothing, men-servants, apprentices, youths, old laborers, all went to make up a single company and vied with one another in courage and endurance." In the histories of the liberals, feats abound like the one of the poor student who picked up a metal boundary marker for a barricade and took it across the avenue. An hour later three soldiers could hardly get it back into place.

The King was the one whose courage and endurance gave out first. His night was poisoned with doubts and horrors, and he spent a large part of it composing an appeal "to his dear Berliners":

"It is up to you, inhabitants of my beloved native city, to prevent greater evil. . . . Turn back to peaceful ways, clear the barricades that are still standing and send to me men full of real old Berlin spirit with words such as are seemly to address your King, and I give you my kingly word that all streets and squares shall be cleared of troops at once and the military occupation shall extend only to necessary buildings, palaces, arsenals and a few others and even there only for a short while. Hear the fatherly words of your King, inhabitants of my loyal and beautiful Berlin and forget what has happened as I will forget it. . . ."[5] This poster, printed in haste, was spread around the city during the first hours of the morning in a truce which had been arranged to allow people to go to church, it being a Sunday. It met an ill reception. The people would believe no word of kindness while troops were still in the city, and were afraid to parley with the King for fear of the army. They tore copies of the proclamation to bits, and where it was being read aloud they interrupted with bitter comments.

When his officers, possibly trying to scare the King into more decisive action, exaggerated to him the possibility of a people's victory, the King reacted in the opposite way and told the appalled generals to retire the troops. This was the suggestion of the liberal

[5] Klein, *Der Vorkampf*, 178.

party. Its spokesman for the moment was Georg von Vincke, a modern-minded Westphalian aristocrat who had posted many hard hours to reach the King and was received in audience on this morning of March 19 in his travelling clothes, an unheard-of concession in etiquette. Vincke's idea was that the troops were the main sticking point in the people's confidence in their sovereign; hence for the King to show that he trusted his people by sending away his troops would increase their loyalty. The King's usual advisers began to laugh when Vincke expounded this plan, but he turned on them. "Today you may laugh, gentlemen. Tomorrow perhaps you will not laugh."

The actual chance of success of the rebels in a military way at this point in the struggle was probably not great. But certainly they had not been defeated. Many years later Engels warned workers not to assume from the apparent victory of these Berlin fighters that mere citizens, no matter how brave and well organized and armed, could ever win against trained military forces. The Prussian troops at this time, he said, were exhausted, bedraggled, and hungry, and the rulers learned enough in this battle not to allow such conditions to occur again.

The King, in any case, made up his mind, and at noon Bodelschwingh, although he had resigned his portfolio, had to give the order to the army to withdraw in the face of the still standing barricades. The Prince of Prussia tried to stop him, throwing his sword on the table in anger. Bodelschwingh, his face on fire, said, "We cannot change the words of the King." High officers of the army refused to take such orders from a civilian, however, and finally Prittwitz himself had to give the order.[6] Prittwitz, who had given several signs of bad temper already, became even more careless and spiteful. When his maneuver of withdrawal was completed, there were not left on the streets of Berlin enough troops to guard the palace. The King did not know that no soldiers at all stood between him and the mob.

People pressed in, closer and closer to the palace, and suddenly, perhaps remembering stories of Paris, Berliners decided to have a

---

[6] The whole army was in low morale. Hohenlohe, for instance, tells us that he refused an offer of civil dress after the order for withdrawal had been completed, because he hoped to be killed walking around. A few stones were thrown at him, but he also received kisses from other citizens, leading him to the disgusted opinion that Berlin was an insane asylum.

parade of their fallen heroes. Only, remarked the French envoy, the Germans had the poor taste to attempt it in the middle of the day. The bodies of those killed in the fight were called for, and as they were put on biers, someone called out their names and where they were killed. In a few cases only the latter fact was known, and some of the corpses were first recognized and claimed at this time. Half-naked, many of them, bloody and covered with flowers, they were held up to stare at the mob. Soon someone called out loudly, "The King ought to come, he must see the bodies," a cry which became a clamor. Prince Lichnowsky appeared at the palace window and told the people the King was in bed. "Bring him out," the people shouted, "or we will throw these dead right down in front of his door." So the King appeared, and the Queen too, clinging to his arm. As the corpses were brought closer the King was forced to take off his hat, while the Queen fainted. The crowd burst into a dignified chorale, and when they were through singing, seemed satisfied and willing to move away. One story says that Prince Lichnowsky appeared again and hurried them off by telling them all their demands were granted. "Smoking, too?" he was asked. "Yes, smoking, too." "Even in the Tiergarten?" "You may smoke in the Tiergarten, gentlemen." And with this small easing of a pinching restriction, the revolution in Berlin was really over.

That night the American legation was most brilliantly illuminated, not only in tribute to the noble and gallant people, but also, it was explained, in justice to the King, now that he was on a firmer footing.

Afterwards the King remembered the parade of the dead with particular disgust. "We all crawled on our stomachs," he said. Still, at the time he made his concessions they came from apparent goodwill. Chagrin, suspicion, anger were to come to him all too soon, but for a few days yet, the days when he still believed in his pan-Germanic destiny, he played his revolutionary role with spirit.

On March 21 he rode through the streets of his capital wearing the German tricolor, protected by the newly armed citizens' militia, the troops having left the city. The veterinarian, Urban, a famous figure with his long white beard and unkempt hair, walked near him carrying a painted imperial crown. When the King met the officers of the new militia he told them he could not clothe in words his gratitude to them, for it had been this force, armed in a hurry, which had finally cleared the streets and restored order on March 19. They answered him, shouting "Long live the German Emperor!" Frederick William bowed his head. "Not that," he said. "That I will not, may not, have."

This remark only proved that the King was stimulating hopes which he was actually unwilling to gratify. For the black-red-gold colors were the colors of united Germany, the ancient colors of the Empire to which all German hearts were looking back. They were being displayed all over Germany that year as the colors also of liberty, in the common ecstasy which imagined nothing less than a united, free, and constitutional Germany.

To confuse his compatriots still more, the King of Prussia that day chose to make an appeal to the German nation, that he was willing to take the leadership of all Germany for the period of danger. Alas, the period of danger (from French aggression) was over as he spoke, and the other princes and their subjects became more afraid of being devoured by Prussia than attacked from across the Rhine.

Frederick William's delicate way of phrasing his plan was that Prussia would "merge into" Germany, which might have been possible if Prussia had been willing to separate into her eight provinces, which would then be units comparable in size to the other states that were expected to join with them. Such, however, was not the intention of the King by the Grace of God. The grand gesture began to seem ridiculous, and the King snapped miserably out of his delusions of moral grandeur into fury at the citizens who had watched and abetted him.

On March 22 the barricade fighters were buried, 230 civilians (as compared to twenty soldiers, who enjoyed a separate and inconspicuous funeral). Their battle must have seemed justified, for on that day the King expressed a royal wish to consider a new constitution with popular representation, possibly even including ministerial responsibility. It was to be his last concession, but it seemed like a conclusive one.

Shortly after this the royal family left Berlin for Potsdam. Such a move had been ardently pushed by the officers, some of whom had even planned to kidnap the King and carry him out of the reach of the revolutionaries. But until the great funeral he was kept in

Berlin by the new liberal civilian ministers whose appointment had followed the battle and the resignation of Bodelschwingh.

Prussian prestige sank to a low level after the March days. The rest of Germany felt the King had given a poor example of leadership, and also it seemed that a stronger, constitutional Prussia would be harder to "merge" into Germany than ever. For many months after this those who wanted to revive the Empire looked everywhere else than toward Prussia for possible leadership, and when a year later they came back to Prussia as their only practical hope, it was too late.

In the new, soldierless Berlin, the job of guarding the palace was given to students, who relaxed cheerily in the King's guardroom, discussing democracy over the coffee, bread, butter, and sausages which he ordered sent to them from his own kitchen. Their self-importance and conspicuousness were enhanced by their uniforms of white hose, Calabrian hat with a high feather, cloak and sword.

Other divisions of the militia had compensations also, though they did not look so snappy. The fat, middle-aged, middle-class citizens looked, in fact, rather silly in their uniforms, often improvised, so that some people felt the simple green blouse of the handworkers, and the blue blouse of the factory workers, the best-looking turnouts in the streets. Sights like a stout butcher, whose equally stout wife brought him lunch while he was on guard at the Brandenburger Tor and then carried his gun back and forth while he ate, struck Berlin wits as frightfully incongruous. But the wives were so delighted with the new titles—lieutenant and such—of their husbands, that they were reconciled to their absence at the somewhat merry guardhouses. It was remarked, however, that under the new policing, drunken fathers of families and prostitutes were hauled in much more ruthlessly.

Prussian workers, too, found a certain new dignity in those weeks. The Brandenburger Tor no longer saw princely carriages roll through, but the plain people walked by with as proud a step as any sovereign, since that was what they felt themselves to be. Some of them even expected to be called "sie" instead of "du," which completely changed the character of Berlin street life.

Some of the wounded barricade fighters were housed in the palace, the Queen providing bedding. Others were in hospitals, where they were visited by the wife of the French Ambassador, who was surprised to find this custom unknown among upper class Berlin women, for she considered it "a measure of prudence as well as charity." She found the wounded smugly sure they had won a great victory, and naïvely happy.

Printing presses began to test their new freedom, and were so successful that boys who had formerly sold cakes, flowers, or matches now found they could make more money peddling papers and pamphlets.

Public works in the pattern of Paris were quickly set up for the unemployed. The first assignment was to cultivate and plant "a small America on the Spree." Unemployed artists formed an orchestra to play to the men at work on the project, and when the magistrates complained that not enough work was done, the workers staged a funeral, complete with orchestra, for the Berlin Municipal Board. When the board sent militia to stop such nonsense, the workers invited them to a joint ball which lasted late into the night. The matter was settled, rather bitterly for a joke, by shipping the headstrong workers off into the country to build the new railroads.

However, in spite of such merry stories (Engels pointed this out), the tragedy of the Berlin revolution was that everybody, even the liberals, was scared by the power of the workers. The reaction exploited this terror to the full, so that if a group of workers so much as carried a flag, they were described as wishing to found a republic, and the militia were called out against them. Having society partially armed, by class, was a sad substitute for the armed citizenry that all liberals demanded, but admittance to the militia in Prussia required a special citizen's certificate which workers could not get. The members of the Prussian militia were horrified to learn that workers were now admitted regularly to the national guard in France.

The Democratic Club, a small middle-class group, worked tirelessly to stop this mood of mutual distrust, with word and with deed. It fed a hundred unemployed workers for three weeks, giving each man a loaf of bread and a quarter of a pound of fat every day, but the authorities disapproved, because they could not control the giving, and denied the club supplies, saying that all relief must be handled by the local poor authorities. The locomotive workers also announced that they stood for peace. Once, after things had come to bloodshed between the militia and the mob, they declared that they would go unarmed between them to stop the fighting, and one of their members was killed as a result of carrying out this policy.

Still, fear made many liberals turn suddenly toward the King. After all, the bourgeoisie were trying to set up in Germany the kind of regime which the French had just destroyed. There are ridiculous stories about the funk of the ruling classes. Police chief Duncker was so afraid of the plain citizens that he closed all the apertures to his apartment, including the flue of his stove, and then began burning papers. He made so much smoke that the plain citizens thought it was a fire and broke in to save him. The serious side appears in the fact that 70,000 people left Berlin because they were afraid to be left there without any soldiers to protect them. There was fear of a general communist movement. By March 30, when the first troops returned, solid citizens wept for joy and crowned with garlands one regiment, which had not been involved in the recent unpleasantness, and in which many Berliners served.

Here we see how dependent the Prussians were on their army, since the troops at the barricades had actually behaved abominably. Because they were angry at the uprising, and at the citizens' refusal of food and drink during the battle, they whipped, starved, and even shot at prisoners taken on the barricades. They treated the King's orders, and all civilian influence, with contempt. One old officer is said to have killed himself rather than put the German black-red-gold colors above the black-and-white Prussian cockade which he had always worn. When the King, safe in Potsdam, addressed his officers only to tell them that he had felt as safe under the protection of his good Berlin citizens as he did in the midst of themselves, there was such a murmuring and rattling of sabers as no King of Prussia had ever heard from his officers. Hohenlohe tells us that most of them immediately began to consider taking up other occupations, Hohenlohe himself a career in scientific agriculture.

They need not have been so concerned, for Frederick William, isolated in Potsdam, began to take a new view of the revolution he had just been through. One so consciously pious, and so convinced of his own rightness, can hardly be accused of open hypocrisy, but it is certain that his attitudes were for a while ambivalent and ended up by being hostile. "The people of Berlin have behaved to me so nobly and magnanimously that it could hardly have happened in another big city in the whole world," he declared to a deputation of citizens on March 31. Yet the previous day he had written in a letter to his new liberal minister, Ludolf Camphausen, "So long as Berlin is not cleared of the clubs and murder-rings, I cannot and will not return there." He began talking of the barricade fighters as riffraff and the opposition to the return of the troops as childish; and gradually he became convinced that his dear and lovely capital had risen against him as the result of a plot by foreign agitators. Were there not barricades where no German words were heard? Were there not many unidentifiable corpses among the dead? His friend and envoy to London, Baron Bunsen, lightly rallied his master on seeing ghosts—and received in return a hot letter on liberalism, which Frederick William diagnosed as a disease, as much so as disease of the spine. Disbelief in conspiracies, he said, is the first infallible symptom, and the only medicine is the sign of the holy cross on breast and forehead.

Against protests from the more obstreperous radicals, who were afraid that it would prove too conservative, the United Diet was summoned, as had been promised, and quickly finished its work of granting the long awaited loan and of drawing up plans for the elections of the new Prussian Assembly. For convenience this Assembly may be called a constitutional assembly, but its legal powers were carefully limited by the King who described it as a parliament to "agree" with the King upon making a new constitution for Prussia.

The law for voting was fairly radical, although young Otto von Bismarck managed to get expunged from the draft actual congratulations to the barricade fighters. Every man twenty-four years of age and six months in residence could vote in the first election, to be held May 1. In order to avoid the supposedly great dangers of universal suffrage, the first voters would only choose electors, to meet on May 8 and select representatives to the Assembly.

Hans Viktor von Unruh, subsequently president of the Assembly, described just how his own election went. Because of his belonging to the small nobility, he took it for granted that he would not be wanted by the voters in his area, but he went along to the meeting in his precinct and was shocked at the confusion among the voters and candidates. Unruh lost his patience—though he was careful to explain that he was unaccustomed to public speaking, being a railroad man—and told them sharply to explain what they meant by terms like unlimited monarchy, the republic, and a constitution, the kind of veto power they wished the King to have, and so on. He modestly defined his own position as favorable to a constitutional monarchy, and everyone was so pleased that Unruh found himself chosen elector, one of six. In the electors' meeting things went the same way. By asking definite questions of the candidates Unruh showed them up; and though he did not announce himself as one, he was asked to run. He received some liberal votes, and all the conservative ones, since these were unable to elect their own man. So he was elected, along with another liberal and a radical from that district.

The representatives, finally assembled, proved to be quite an assortment. There were many peasants from Silesia who could not read nor write, but who kissed the hand of the man who paid their expense allowances. These members often voted blindly in absolute contradiction to the way they had voted before, because they were confused by the issues. Then there were Polish noblemen, who always voted from patriotic motives with the democratic faction, though their sympathies lay far away. Unruh was shocked to see one of them let his highly educated secretary kiss the hem of his robe. The cities sent no member of the working class, though there were a number of artisans, and some of the democratic demagogues, the *Wilde Rotte*, who wore fur caps and long beards. A few sported sixteenth-century student costumes, in black velvet, with feathers in their hats, and tried hard to look fierce, says one reporter, like cows at a bull-fight.

The Prince of Prussia was the most distinguished single member. He had used his election as an excuse to return from London, where he had fled early in the revolution, and where he had ostentatiously studied constitutions. He appeared once on the floor of the Assembly. The members of the right rose, while the left cried, "Keep your seats." After a more or less gracious speech, His Royal Highness retired, never to return to the floor.

It was a gathering all too easy to make fun of, and all too hard to weld into a parliament. With the possible exception of the Prince, there was no single member of the Assembly who had ever in his wildest imagination dreamed that he might some day be called to help draft a constitution for his country. Yet the difficult thing was done. With all the dead wood, there were enough bright and hard-working representatives to create a constitution; and it was such a good one that the King himself took over most of its points.

They met for the first time May 22, with an address from the throne in the White Room of the palace. There had been some talk among the democrats that the King should present himself at their place of meeting, like the King of England, but this disagreement was composed and the mountain went to Mohammed. If they had not done so, the choleric monarch threatened to dissolve them. He privately determined to do the same thing if the Assembly tampered with the King's relation to the army (even the American constitution did not require democracy in control of the army); if they meddled in the question of succession; if they declared the sovereignty of the people; or, of course, if they declared a republic. In case things went too far and the revolution seemed to be taking its head again, Frederick William was already turning over the idea of getting troops from the Czar.

None of these emergencies arose. From now on Frederick William was destined to endure nothing worse from the revolution than the "pain, mortification and indignation" that it cost him to attend meetings of his new cabinet. "I thought I would die," he said when the ministers were discussing the draft of a constitution of their own. For, he wrote to his prime minister, it makes the King look undignified and unworthy for the ministers to come out with a concerted plan before the King has spoken.

The new prime minister was Ludolf Camphausen, a well-to-do Rhineland business man, strong for railroads, customs union, and parliamentary reform, but devoted to moderation and the monarchy. The romantic King, for his part, often addressed him in letters as "Best and dearest Camphausen," but privately thought him too practical, without ideals.

Camphausen was appointed out of the March crisis; hence he had already been in office two months when the Assembly met, and owed nothing to it. Nor had anything yet been put on paper about making ministers responsible to the parliament—or the parliament actually responsible for anything at all. It turned out that Camphausen could not manage the Assembly, and after a decisively hostile vote he tried to resign. The King urged him to pin his faith on the conservative strength of the country and to ignore the mobs of Berlin, who, said the King, were intimidating the conservative members of the Assembly into staying away from meetings. Camphausen hung on for a few days, then, realizing that his position was hopeless, he resigned anyway, on June 20.

To the people of the time, Camphausen's failure was an added proof that the Berlin Assembly was running wildly to the left. All the oratory and all the imagination seemed to be on that side, while the monarchists were scorned even by the King for maintaining what he considered an obvious position and for being so easily scared. The actual concrete proposals put out by the Assembly were greater than it was commonly given credit for. It considered a tremendous number of laws, many of which, concerning taxation, workers, servants, were put into force by the Weimar Republic seventy years later—but it passed only a few of these laws, and the King signed only eight.

In September another ministry fell, on a resolution passed by the Assembly declaring that any army officer who could not wholeheartedly support the constitution they were going to draft had a duty of honor to resign his commission. The incoming minister was a conservative, General von Pfuehl, and the court party were horrified that he made an honest effort to carry out the wishes of the Assembly in regard to the army's loyalty. But by this time the King was almost through governing with the aid of an Assembly. King, in Potsdam, and parliament, in Berlin, carried on without seeing each other and almost without communication. Conditions seemed so disorderly and hopeless that the Princess of Prussia, who had been the court liberal, said she would rather see the land attacked by cholera. As for the King's conservative intimates who had watched affairs nervously for so long, they were more than ever eager to convince the King that what he needed were armies, not diets.

There was actually no hope of democratizing the army, but the democrats realized the problem was crucial. They never let up in their letters "To our brothers, the soldiers," and in their insistence on getting the officers sworn faithfully to the hypothetical constitution.

We have mentioned the King's complaints that the Assembly kept giving in to threats by the mob. The mob was feeling its oats, and according to the point of view of the observer, was either trying to disrupt all orderly government with impossible demands, or was trying to see that the fruits of the barricade fight should go to those who were in the battle.

For purposes of broad generalization, perhaps the mob after March 18 can be divided into the followers of Stephan Born and the followers of Friedrich Wilhelm Alexander Held.

Born was a printer who in 1848 was still too young to be eligible for either of the parliaments of that year, in Berlin or at Frankfurt. He was only twenty-three but he had already quite a history behind him. While his brother was studying to be a doctor at the University of Berlin, Stephan was a printer's apprentice, and every day during his two-hour lunch period he would steal over and attend lectures at the university. By 1845 he was working hard to carry education to workers' circles in Berlin and had published a pamphlet on justice to the working class. In 1847 he took the year of travel that was still customary for up-and-coming young craftsmen. He worked his way to Brussels, Paris, and Switzerland, meeting the far more class-conscious workers of western Europe. In Paris he was taken up by Engels and introduced to Marx; and this pair, who were busy organizing the Communist League, supported him all through 1848, although they later turned against him with the peculiar bitterness they saved for ex-friends.

Born got back to Berlin just in time to throw himself into organizing the workers' party. Incidentally, the Prussian police could not conceive of a genuine working-class leader, and always referred to Born in their reports as a "helper" of the more advanced workers. They did not know that Born himself was particularly opposed to using such helpers, or *Menschenfreunde*. "We take our affairs into our own hands," was his motto, and he was determined for the workers to build up their own treasury, no matter how little each one earned. Out of small but regular contributions he foresaw eventually housing developments and libraries built by the working class alone. "Germany is not so poor that part of her children must be in need," he cried.

All crafts were organizing in Berlin at this time, grocers, hair-dressers, factory workers, the German cooks who issued a manifesto against the custom of hiring French cooks, the cab drivers who complained of the use of busses. They asked for higher wages and they asked that the shops be shut at eight instead of ten at night, so as to make their day only twelve hours long. On March 29 a workers' deputation even waited on the King, petitioning for a ministry of labor, popular education at the expense of the state, and economical government. "They go well together," muttered the King under his breath, and stalked out of the audience chamber.

But the workers would not be stopped. A chain of workers' clubs began to form all over Germany. They began to meet in congresses and to consider politics and the long view. Considering the short view also, they managed several strikes.

Of all their efforts, the most appealing was the tiny Workers' Congress in Berlin in August. The clubs spent months discussing who should be eligible to vote, and who to come; the call, when it was finally issued in June was signed by members from Berlin, Hamburg, and Königsberg. Forty delegates finally assembled, representing thirty-one clubs from many parts of Germany. It was their intention to compose a people's charter, copying the English Chartists, and their plans were so inclusive that they worked out nearly all the reforms which were granted in the next fifty years—unemployment insurance, consumer cooperatives, free secular schools, with free books, and teachers who, though licensed by the state, were to be elected by the community in which they served. They demanded workers' housing, equality for women, income taxes, a ten-hour day, and foremen with some technical knowledge.

Such were the reforms which labor felt would benefit them, not the free press, the armed militia, and commercial reforms which were the revolutionary demands of the middle classes. The workers' groups were splitting off from their co-revolutionists in perfect Marxian form. Yet Born wrote to Marx that he would be laughed at if he called himself a Communist, and the Communist League could not get a foothold in Berlin.

Held's followers cut a much wider swath than Born's thoughtful, skilled craftsmen. Held fitted the popular notion of what a demagogue should be—he was a blond giant with a voice that could be heard from the Brandenburger Tor to the Belle-Alliance-Platze. He won his influence over crowds, not with hackneyed flattery but with wit and sarcasm, tricks he had learned in his varied past as lieutenant, actor, and newspaperman. He left the army to run away with an actress, left the stage when he did not get enough recognition to suit him, and finally started the first cheap newspaper in Germany, the *Lokomotive*, which became immensely profitable until it was suppressed. The government could not bear to have a paper which would bring for a year, to all who could afford one thaler, news, wit, and countless digs too subtle for the censors. When the revolution broke in Prussia, Held was in prison, but he was freed in the general amnesty of political prisoners and immediately took up the *Lokomotive* again.

There was no doubt that he became the idol of Berlin. His portrait seemed to be in every house, his bust in every restaurant, women flocked to his club to hear him and showered him with love letters. He was the only man allowed inside the Democratic Woman's Club, which spent its time on such projects as how to take care of unemployed servant girls by womanly work. When a scandal developed between Held and one of the ladies, he was ejected. He had a bodyguard of 4,000 well-armed locomotive shop workers who were presumed ready to obey his slightest command. The King and the friends of order were frantic to get Held out of the way. And yet he was one of the safer demagogues, since he had no definite plans to offer, except that he was intensely nationalistic. On at least two occasions he used his immense prestige with the masses to prevent violence.

Held's influence was finally killed by what seems like an absurdly small incident. A meeting, which Held expected to be a private tea party, was arranged between him and one of the conservative ministers. The news, by fair means or foul, was publicized everywhere, so that people lost their trust in him. In October his fame was at its peak; by December his lion's voice was subdued to a puppet's, for he was last heard of running a Christmas marionette show in the Tiergarten.

As in Paris, the progress of the revolution was marked by workers' demonstrations, the first of which in Berlin was caused by a cabinet order in May to recall the Prince of Prussia from England. Now the Prince, though later to become William I, the first German Emperor and a figure of pride for his country, was at this time so cordially hated that his name was omitted from public prayers. He was the King's brother, and heir to the throne because Frederick William and his queen were childless; but he was far more military and far less dreamy than the King—"leathery" he called himself, and "practical." His wife was named Augusta, a princess whose life was consistently unhappy from an unloved childhood through an unloved marriage—but she had been brought up by Goethe in a liberal court and was considered in Berlin the advocate of liberal measures. Her husband twitted her on the common saying, "If Prince William ever comes to the throne, the Princess will see to it that Prussia gets a constitution," and he was indifferent to her pleas against bitterness in his handling of the people. A king, he replied, must show that he is master.

In the wild days of March Augusta asked Bismarck, then the most promising conservative member of the United Diet, to wait upon her, and begged for his support for her young son in case Frederick William could not hold the throne. But Bismarck, who had started to arm the peasants on his estate and bring them to Berlin to save the King, repudiated her notion so flatly that she never liked him again.

While in England, the Prince of Prussia had been bracketed by cartoonists with such deposed exiles as Louis Philippe, Metternich, and Lola Montez. This was too much for his royal brother to stand. Hence the command for his return early in May. Fifteen thousand workers met in the Tiergarten to protest, and it was Held who managed to get them to disperse peaceably.

A month later a more serious outbreak occurred. The democrats, led by Held, had been demanding arms for all the people, not just those with the correct police endorsement of property or income, and they soon found out that the government's countermove was to withdraw arms from the Berlin arsenal. On the moonlit night of June 14 they marched up, beat a roll of drums in front of the gate of the arsenal, and told the commandant and his two hundred soldiers that the revolution had broken out in Potsdam so he could expect no relief. Then they ran a ladder to the second floor and created such a panic that soldiers began running out of the second story windows. As they ran along the cornices to the fire escapes each one considerately brought a gun, of which he was relieved at the bottom. The only casualty was a soldier who jumped right out of a window.

This affair created a perfect storm among the reactionaries; it was a lucky turn of affairs for them, since they could now clearly claim that Berlin needed soldiers and more rigid control. Indeed, Stephan Born, who rather looked down on the locomotive shop workers and the others that attacked the arsenal as plunderers, also brought evidence to show that the reactionary party had stirred them up.

No doubt the reaction was gaining in unity, coherence, and emphasis. Its course might be graphed by the flags on the Hohenzollern palace. In March a big black-red-gold tricolor flew alone—this was the symbol both of German unity and liberty which Frederick William adopted in the first flush of yielding. In April a small black-and-white Prussian flag appeared beneath the new standard and seemed to grow gradually bigger. On August 6, a big black-and-white standard flew above a small tricolor.

Some intellectuals began to remember the quiet of the police state. David Friedrich Strauss, for one, voiced his feelings about the whole revolutionary process. He was the author of a radical and rationalistic life of Jesus, one of those who had done the most to stir up new thought in Germany.

"To a nature like mine it was much better under the old police state, when we had quiet on the streets and were not always meeting with excited people, new-fashioned slouch hats, and beards. In society a man could talk a bit of literature and art, of odd characters and such things, he could let himself go, which is no longer possible . . . I simply don't go out any more. . . . I have learned to know myself better in these days than ever before, that I am one of those decadent hang-overs from the period of individual education, of the type Goethe describes, and beyond these limits I neither can nor wish to go. To all this effusion on the part of boys and girls, to this pouring out of wisdom on the streets, I can only respond with cutting irony or disdainful contempt."[7]

Just before the outbreak Strauss had declared himself in favor of liberal ideas, but he was not the only German who proved too thin-skinned to stand them when they came.

Landowners were forming an association to protect their rights, while peasants wrote (or were quoted as writing) threatening letters urging Berliners to restore decency in their "damned hole," not to butcher the peasants' sons in the army and not to abuse the King. The army officers, of course, still smarting under their March humiliation, were the most dangerous single reactionary force.

Frederick William was the leader of all the reactionary groups,

7 Klein, 118.

gradually pulling their strength together around himself. By leaving the city in May he cut himself off completely from both his ministers and the Assembly—from any possible liberal influence. He éven refused to let his ministers consult him as often as they needed to, "in order not to take up their time." His chosen friends, the men he was really sympathetic to, closed around him in a camarilla and would only let trusted persons be received in audience. Prince Consort Albert of England, who took a lively interest in German affairs, tried to explain to him that democracy was not un-German, but instead of listening even to this high source, Frederick William began to say, "Only soldiers can help against democrats."

He himself might not have felt strong enough to bring in a full complement of soldiers against the democrats immediately, but his new commander, Count von Wrangel, ordered a military review to be held in September. Von Pfuehl, the more moderate prime minister, although he was a general and was picked as a conservative, was doing his best to carry out the wishes of the Assembly in forcing loyalty to the constitution on the army, and he felt that a review would be the worst thing to stir people up. Hotly, Wrangel offered to resign rather than give up the review—so it was held, embellished with a speech to the citizens of Berlin in which Wrangel commiserated them for the grass growing in their streets, for the empty shops, the unemployed workers, and promised, by bringing back a full garrison soon, to restore true liberty, order, and with order, all that was good. "The swords are sharpened to a point, the balls are in the guns," he said.

Immediately Berlin wits announced a "grass auction," to sell off the grass in the streets. Every customer was to receive a picture of a small man riding through tall grass as a gift, and the proceeds were to go into buying powder and lead for the "sovereign Linden Club" (which was their name for the public meetings held *unter den Linden*.)

In October more people than ever before went to the Linden clubs. Held reached his zenith, the Democratic Club called meetings so packed that no leaf could have fallen to earth between the people, meetings with the serious intent of forcing democracy to mean something to the masses of the people. Huge placards covered the city providing news and opinions from every side; and night after night was made hideous with Berlin's special contribution of

Katzenmusik in front of the houses of reactionaries, a shrieking, whistling, squeaking, bellowing, grunting, howling, miauling, hitting of kettles and shouting up the downspouts. *Agents provocateurs* were known to be active among the mob, which became wild. On the 20th they threatened to hang members of the Assembly who did not vote for sending troops to help the democratic party in Vienna, then under siege. Next day the King, disappointed in plain conservatives and acting on Bismarck's advice, asked his uncle, Count von Brandenburg, to form a truly reactionary ministry. Brandenburg was an illegitimate son of Frederick William II, and was a cavalry officer with no experience of affairs beyond the army. The outraged Assembly worked more feverishly than before on the constitution with which they hoped to bind the King, but instead of baiting the trap, they went out of their way to eliminate "by Grace of God" from his title. So infuriated was His Majesty, when the Assembly sent a deputation, headed by Unruh, to ask for a ministry with whom they could work, that he stamped impatiently out of the room without so much as a refusal. An excitable deputy called after him, "That's the trouble with kings, they won't listen to the truth." Unruh was almost as deeply offended by this outbreak as the King, because by protocol none but himself was supposed to address the throne in such an audience. Unruh wanted a constitution and he wanted reform, but he was as easily shocked by a violation of etiquette as a society climber. As long as big businessmen could show such sensitivity towards the feelings of royalty it was no wonder they shrank from the rougher manners of the lower classes who might have supported them in their demands.

The final excuse, so ardently desired, for bringing back the troops came after a wild and disorganized effort of the democrats called the Second Democratic Congress. (The first had been held in Frankfurt.) The meetings of this body were so noisy that the president asked for a brace of pistols to keep order instead of his bell, and so unrealistic as to pass a resolution "that the German people by a great majority desire a republic." For a first step it organized a huge mass meeting and besieged the Constitutional Assembly. No one knows whether anyone received for this the 25,000 thalers[8] that Held declared had been offered him if he provoked a disturbance great enough to call the troops back. In any case

---

[8] Equivalent to $32,000 U.S.

the army marched in to music—dismayed, according to Hohenlohe, that it was not a battery of guns that led them into the city.

The Assembly meanwhile realized that it was going to be dissolved, and as a protest conceived the idea of drafting a resolution urging Prussian subjects not to pay taxes to their high-handed ruler. Unruh did not want any "revolutionary" or "disrespectful" (the two words were synonymous in his mind) acts on the part of his Assembly, and refused to call a meeting to discuss this subject until a majority signed a petition for it, signatures which despite his attitude were quickly obtained.

While this meeting was in session, the militia rallied around the hall to protect the Assembly. It was reasonable to expect a big battle. All the militia had served in the regular army, and all were sworn to defend the Assembly with their lives. Someone who watched them said they made sour faces, some with fear and some with joy. Wrangel rode along the Charlottenstrasse and greeted them politely, but they did not respond, except that their commander said they would yield only to force. Wrangel answered pleasantly that he had plenty of that, and that in fifteen minutes the Assembly would be dissolved.

Inside the hall a staff officer was telling Unruh that he had authority to close the session, but that it would save trouble if Unruh would do it for him. This Unruh refused, though he was privately gratified that the matter of nonpayment of taxes would not come to a vote. The members, however, clamored for a division and before the soldiers could get back they passed the resolution by acclamation. Then they filed two by two down the steps of their hall and disappeared. The militia likewise disappeared. It was less than fifteen minutes after Wrangel's ultimatum.

The appeal to Prussians not to pay taxes aroused tremendous interest all over Germany. Radicals felt that the Prussian Assembly had at last justified itself and looked for a chance to start a new fight for democracy. Carl Schurz tells how he and his fellow students at Bonn tried to help by driving the revenue officers from their posts at the city gates so that the peasants could bring goods in duty-free. When soldiers came up to take charge, the peasants rallied to defend their student friends, and were kept from bloodshed only by student remonstrances.

A good deal of the bite of this action of the Prussian Assembly was taken away when the Frankfurt Parliament, representing the people of all Germany, denounced the tax-withholding idea, even though with the same breath they deplored the forcible dissolution of the Prussian body.

The Frankfurt Parliament, which was engaged in trying to unite all the states of Germany under a single constitution, rather looked down on the Berlin Assembly. Its members also felt that a strong separate Prussian constitution would only enhance Prussiandom, splitting Germany so that it could never be united. They wanted no constitution in separate states until their federal one was completed. In the back of their minds was still another idea, that they could win Frederick William's support for a German Empire by supporting him against his own Assembly, and that in this way the King's victory would not be entirely one of bayonets.

Unfortunately they underestimated the depth of the royal contempt for parliaments. The King of Prussia was as indifferent to the help of Frankfurt as to the hostile resolutions of the Assembly he himself had summoned. With his army behind him and his conscience made up, he was able to cope with any situation out of his own resources.

A day or two after the Assembly was closed, Berlin found itself under martial law. All clubs were closed, all strangers that looked queer were made to leave town, no papers or posters could appear without official sanction.

Also the citizens' militia was disbanded. Thirty thousand rifles had been issued to them in March; in November all but 150 were returned, in spite of the fact that the officers burned the membership lists to make disarming more difficult. This figure reveals the depth of Prussian passivity. How could a revolution ever have been successful? In the same spirit the citizenry went right on paying their taxes. There is no record that the Assembly's hot insistence on the illegality of these taxes made any difficulty for the collectors.

The working classes naturally were left totally without allies or power. When the printers of the shut-down opposition papers complained that their livelihood was taken away, General Wrangel contemptuously sent them forty thalers' relief. Democracy was stopped in its tracks.

The final blow, on an almost insensible body politic, was the constitution which the King promulgated in December. When people read it they were at first astonished at its similarity to that which the Assembly had worked on. Whenever possible the King's advisers had taken over the words and even the liberal ideas of the Assembly. Later they noticed that the King received an absolute veto, that elections were subtly made indirect, and that the power to levy taxes was ambiguously placed. On the other hand, religions were free, the church was to be disestablished, letters were to be uncensored, the press was to be free under restrictions, and feudal privileges were curtailed.

The Assembly, formally reopened at Brandenburg and slightly purged, agreed with the King on this document. After all, this had been their original duty—to agree. Then the Assembly expired. The elections, which followed in January 1849, took a reactionary turn, but the resulting legislative Assembly was dissolved in April for daring to protest against the martial law which had never been relaxed in Berlin.

After that show of independent spirit the electoral law was changed so that those who paid one-third of the taxes elected one-third of the representatives. According to this scheme, electors of the first class, with a third of the power in the Assembly, numbered three per cent of the population; electors of the second class ten per cent; of the third eighty-seven, which included those who paid no taxes at all. The government showed that it had learned to rely on property rather than on censorship. With this change, the constitution, promulgated in January 1850, remained in force until 1918—during which interval Prussia suffered no more revolutionary attacks.

The truth of the matter was that the middle classes who made the revolution in Prussia were satisfied by what they got out of it. Unruh himself, in summing up the events of the year 1848, admitted that he and the other liberals had been naïve to think that what they needed was a better constitution. They found out in practice that what they really needed was a better administration. And Prussia shortly developed the best administrative system in the world.[9]

[9] The Germans in 1848 seemed peculiarly loathe to develop what sociologists call a "role conflict." They hated to get into a position where their duties to their class, as businessmen, or to their professional honor, or to their personal wishes as private citizens, were at variance with their obligations as subjects. The French historian, Vermeil (see the book edited by Fejtö), pointed out that Adam Smith's demarcation between state and private interests went against the German grain. Goethe and Stein both realized the importance of responsible individuals as the basis for a state built on cooperation of its citizens but they were almost unique in Germany. It is, after

Frederick William, after 1848, lived in an increasing cloud of bitterness which ended some years later in madness. The Prince of Prussia who succeeded him and became the first German emperor forgot his 1848 lessons no more than Frederick William. He placed no reliance on the constitutions he had studied in England. Instead he had learned to rely on his army.

The immediate drama in early 1849 turned to Frankfurt. In spite of Prussia, there still seemed some hope in that city that a liberal German Empire might be created.

---

all, out of role conflicts that creative solutions to social problems come. (See W. Mommsen on German citizenship.)

VIII

A Crown from the Gutter

Professor Dahlmann, the constitutional historian, remarked in 1849 that Germans had found out that their thirst for freedom could only be satisfied by power. Though this was almost like saying their thirst for water could only be satisfied by *schnapps*, Dahlmann here puts his finger on the nationalism that characterizes, one might almost say corrupts, every one of the 1848 revolutions outside of France.

To be sure, the Prussian revolution seemed like a copy of the Parisian though twenty years behind the times. The same sort of orderly legalists demanded the same sort of orderly change; these groups split similarly from the working classes, though with less noise in Prussia; and in the end all hands gave in to military dictatorship and skillful repression.

But only half of German energy went into efforts of reform, even though nearly every one of the thirty-odd German states yielded to demands for constitution, militia, free presses, and liberal ministers. The other half of German idealism showed up in the fierce insistence from every section that now, 1848, was the time for Germany to unite, for a German Empire to be created. In the light of the hundred years since, when national feeling has caused so much trouble, it may be hard to realize how noble national freedom seemed before it had been well tested. Dahlmann was probably unconscious of any cynicism in his remark about German thirst for power. It only seems cynical to us. Dahlmann watched 1848 liberalism fail through its own weakness and leaped to the simple conclusion that any strong Germany would satisfy its citizens' desires. Perhaps, also, the freedom that had been fought for and lost in 1848 began to seem, a year later, less desirable than the power which seemed momentarily within the Germans' grasp.

Early in 1848 a group of Germans from many states was working on the problem of uniting all Germany into one grand new constitutional empire. These patriots succeeded in calling a parliament of the entire German speaking population of Europe which drafted a constitution for their huge, hoped-for fatherland. If Austria had not chosen to withhold its German subjects from such a combination, preferring to add them to its other subjects, Slav and Magyar; if Prussia had not refused to consider the work of mere upstart common citizens, the parliament would not have failed. As it was the parliament has remained a dream to liberal Germans ever since, a stepping stone on which they hoped to build; its debates throw light on all Germany's subsequent history.

Napoleon had, of course, abolished the Holy Roman Empire of the German people, and there was in 1848 no such thing as Germany except in the hearts of its patriots. The German-speaking people were divided among some thirty-nine sovereignties, topped by the giant states of Prussia and Austria; and tapering down through the kingdoms of Bavaria and Saxony, into princedoms, grand duchies and free cities such as Hamburg and Frankfurt. The list took in moreover two or three territories like Alsace and Schleswig-Holstein that every German soul claimed for the fatherland although they were under the rule of foreign countries.

The same German souls as a rule did not throb at all for the national aspirations of non-German subjects of Prussia and Austria. Yet Prussia's huge minority of Poles and the Hapsburgs' huge majority of Slav and Hungarian subjects were to prove the most upsetting of the obstacles to German unification. French liberals we have seen agitating for Poland; German liberals began by singing the same tune, along with the other French catchwords, but soon the Germans caught themselves and realized that to give up their Poles meant to weaken the fatherland.

Much as they wanted to unite, most Germans hated the single political bond that tied German states together in the period after 1815. They had been organized by the Congress of Vienna into a Confederation whose members promised not to make war on one another. It was also part of the original plan that each state should be guaranteed a representative constitution, but these promises which had been made originally by rulers in order to induce their subjects to fight Napoleon had become halfhearted even by 1815. In 1848 not half the members of the Confederation had paper constitutions, and neither Prussia nor Austria was among those that did.

The Confederation was intended for pure Germans alone, so only one-third of the Austrian monarchy and only the German parts of

Prussia were included. And still more curiously, even some Germans under foreign rule were represented. One bit of Switzerland, one piece of Holland, and the Danish duchy of Holstein were all inside the line.

But the Confederation represented only the princes of Germany, not the people—and it was admittedly dominated by Austria which used it as an instrument to impose her own dark standards on other German peoples. The organization was designed to be weak—too many foreign statesmen were afraid of a strong Germany—but by using the press laws Austria was able to keep the other members gagged, and she did her best to discourage constitutionalism throughout the other states and even to control such small matters as freedom of movement among the working classes. For workmen who were allowed to see the world brought back all kinds of ideas, like Stephan Born of the Berlin Workers' Congress.

The organ of the Confederation was a diet which met at Frankfurt. Its meetings were secret, and so often ended up in bad news for the German people that a man in the 1848 parliament compared it to the Inquisition:

"There are institutions which are so hated, and rightly so hated that no modification can appease public opinion. They can only be rooted out, trunk and branches. The Inquisition was such an institution; the censorship was such an institution; such an institution is, I would gladly say was, the Federal Diet. . . . Have not most of us seen with our own eyes the living ruins of men whose strength of body and character the abominable government of the Federal Diet completely destroyed through years of imprisonment?"[1]

Up until March 1848 the Diet seemed so well entrenched and so lethargic that nothing could move it. Frederick William IV, indeed, had asked his friend and councillor, General Joseph Maria von Radowitz, to work out a plan of reform, but the German people did not realize this when they heard one March day, like a spring hurricane, that those separate governments that wished to abolish censorship were now free to do so (with restrictions); that a black-red-gold flag (the colors of German union) was now flying over the Diet itself; and that a constitutional assembly for the whole German people was to convene at Frankfurt.

Actually it was the people, not the Diet, least of all the Prussian

[1] Quoted from Petzet and Sutter, *Der Geist der Paulskirche*, p. 47.

King, that was creating the hurricane. The Diet made these concessions in the spring of revolutions before being swept out of existence—but the people were taking things into their own hands anyway.

The division of Germany seemed to most Germans their chief grievance. It was a condition which hampered their progress whichever way they turned, intellectually, commercially, and patriotically. Their pride and their pocketbooks were equally offended.

The censorship, which Metternich persuaded the Confederation to impose on all the petty states, was so severe that all the brightest men in Germany were persecuted. Some lost their jobs; some, like Heine and Herwegh, were exiled; a shocking number were actually imprisoned.

Those intellectuals that stayed at their jobs were deliberately separated from public life even before 1848, though later Bismarck was to make this separation a fine art. No one could get a state appointment unless he professed to believe in absolutism, and it was hard for a university graduate to live any other way since all the universities as well as administrative positions were controlled by the governments. Censorship also tended to make the intellectuals lose their sense of proportion by exaggerating unimportant items. The effects of these tendencies showed up all too plainly in the deliberations of all the popular assemblies called during 1848, especially in the great parliament at Frankfurt.

Students, on the other hand, were the freest part of the community. Though the government was always trying to put them down they were irrepressible, and the festivals which they arranged at intervals may be compared to the French banquets as the nearest preparation of the public to act upon public affairs. The first and most famous of these celebrations was at the Wartburg in 1817, when a great mass of young men climbed the mountain, lit a huge bonfire on top, and swore to each other to believe in kings but not in officials, not to fight other Germans, not to become censors nor members of the secret police. The most recent such affair had been held in Hambach in 1842.

The businessmen, the class which in Prussia agitated for reform, in the smaller states needed a bigger country even more than they needed reform. The tariff union, headed by Prussia, was the first considerable help they received, for it included three-quarters of the German population, although Austria and a few other states did not belong. Trade had been much easier ever since January 1, 1834, on which date long wagon trains, backed up at many frontiers, were allowed to carry their goods across free for the first time. In 1835 the first big railroad was built in Germany, and by 1848 there were 3,000 miles of track.

Naturally a country so burgeoning with fast transport and free trade was not going to be hampered forever by an oldfangled confederation, nor with the innumerable systems of weight, money, and commercial law to be found in the various states. Either Prussia or Austria could easily have taken over all the rest of Germany by granting a few reforms, as Bismarck demonstrated later.

But as it happened, in 1848 the rulers of Germany lagged behind their subjects. They almost had to be anti-patriotic, that is, anti-German in order to maintain their separate thrones, and they clung to their expensive little courts, their small evidences of sovereignty with an eighteenth-century tenacity. And indeed the loyalty of their subjects proved, in the test of revolution, to be strong enough to keep most of them on their pedestals; no German dynasty was unseated. Nevertheless the princes were jealous and afraid of each other and their subjects. Even the King of Prussia, who held the center of the stage with his attempts to save Germany, failed more bitterly even than the professors and radical revolutionaries who had the same aim at heart.

But their class structure was also a handicap for it was rigid in a way that is hard for an American to understand. Carl Schurz tells how his grandfather, a well-to-do manager of a large estate, yet classed as a peasant, could go to town or ride out to pay visits in a two-wheeled chaise but not in a four-wheeled carriage; while the women in his family could have caps or hoods as pretty as they pleased, trimmed with expensive lace or even jewels, but never a bonnet such as city women wore. After the daughter of a tenant with certain rights to the use of the land married a cottager who had only the use of a house, no tenant families would speak to her.

The middle classes were beginning to be able to rise through money or education, and were sometimes ennobled. Still, the old aristocracy stuck to its pedigrees, and it seemed as undesirable to them that a ruling house should lose its prerogatives of sovereignty as that anyone else should change his station in life. Europe was in fact full of ex-princes who had lost their tiny territories when

the Holy Roman Empire was abolished, and yet who were treated
with all the etiquette, the forms of address, the backing out of com-
moners from their presence, that they had been entitled to when
they were actually sovereigns.

Of the thousands of men who had been thinking hard about a free
united Germany, two groups were especially vocal. First there was
a group of liberals from the smaller states, led by Heinrich von
Gagern, Prime Minister of Hesse-Darmstadt, which included a
large number of prominent liberals from Baden, the most advanced
of all the German states. The second group consisted of republicans, led by Friedrich Hecker and Gustav von Struve. These
gentlemen turned out to be such ardent revolutionaries that they
preferred to lead an army for a republic rather than to compromise
with the commonplace ideas of the first group.

Heinrich von Gagern was the son of a German diplomat who
happened to be in the service of the Netherlands, a man whose deep
broodings on German unity were passed on to his sons. The eldest
of these was General Friedrich von Gagern, also employed by the
Netherlands, though the main interest of his life was Germany.
After profound thought he came to the conclusion that Prussia
was the only natural center for a free Germany, though he seemed
to hope that Prussia would be willing to separate into its eight
provinces and lose its national identity in a greater Germany.
Widely discussed throughout the country, these views had their
deepest influence on Friedrich's brother, Heinrich, who was a member of the left in the Hessian chamber until, in March 1848, the
revolutionary turn of things made him minister of that small state.
On March 24 he made a speech to the Chamber which was almost
a call to arms for all Germany, urging freedom and unity, and
expressing the view that Germany must turn in the immediate
future to Prussia (at that very moment rapidly giving in to liberal
demands) without, however, permanently cutting off Austria.

In the early spring of 1848 the two groups, constitutionalist and
republican, met together fifty-one strong at Heidelberg and agreed
to ignore their differences for the moment in the effort to organize
a parliament to represent the entire German nation. Their first
step was to invite to Frankfurt on March 31 all the past and present members of legislative bodies of German states together with
prominent intellectuals and friends of the committee.

This preliminary parliament was a haphazard gathering since attendance depended on how the individuals who were invited happened to feel. Only two Austrians showed up, 114 Prussians, and from tiny little Baden 72. The debates likewise were of a miscellaneous character; one observer said they were like a musical composition combining *Rule Britannia* with the *Marseillaise*. Gradually, however, Heinrich von Gagern clinched the victory of reform over revolution by his simple statement that most Germans were not ready for the republic, a remark in which all non-fanatics agreed. Struve, the republican, gagged by a rule limiting speeches to ten minutes, barely had a chance to read out the radical demands; cursing the moderates, he stamped out of the meeting to raise an army. From this moment the parliamentarians were purged of their left wing and became mere liberals.

The preliminary parliament's only accomplishment was to call for elections. The German people had never had an election before and the preliminary parliament could not lay very good claim to the authority to set one up, but bravely took the chance, and declared that every 50,000 Germans were to choose one representative by direct universal suffrage. (The preliminary parliament voted unanimously for universal suffrage. The word limiting the vote to individuals who were *selbständig* was lost in a stenographic error, but most people felt that such a qualification was nevertheless "implied.") In May, they boldly stated, this Assembly was to meet, with the right and duty to draw up a constitution for all Germany. The beaten-down Federal Diet (whose members were appointed by the separate governments) concurred in the call for the Assembly, giving it its only show of legality, but only because the Diet realized that control had slipped out of its hands.

On the sly, nonetheless, the Diet sent out suggestions to the various governments to influence the elections as they could. In some states residence requirements and the necessity of being an "independent" citizen kept large numbers of servants, workers, and apprentices from voting. Some states even went ahead and arranged for indirect voting, and in Bavaria a tax-paying requirement was used. But these attempts at evasion had little effect in most places. More decisive in the composition of the body was the varied interest shown by different sections. Many Austrian Germans failed to vote, so their country was badly underrepresented. Some people who were elected refused point blank to take part in such revolutionary swindles, among them Baron Alexander von Humboldt and Prince Hohenlohe's father. Incidentally, both these gentlemen fell into disgrace with the King of Prussia for their refusal to serve. Frederick William came to hate the Assembly, but at first, apparently, he thought some good might come of it, especially if enough of his own supporters took seats. On the other hand Friedrich Hecker, the idol of the democrats, was elected but not allowed to sit, on the ground that he had recently led an armed rebellion in Baden for a republic. Perhaps the fact that General Friedrich von Gagern was killed in the battle against him stimulated distaste, in a parliament led by Gagern's brother, for seating such a rabid republican. When his application for the seat was refused, Hecker sailed for the United States.

This was the German people's first and, as a matter of fact, only parliament. Five hundred and eighty-six members were finally seated, including at least isolated specimens from nearly every rank: one small sovereign prince on one hand, and on the other, a single Silesian peasant who was (perhaps poetically) credited with having built his homestead with his own hands, and who seemed not unable to hold his own in debate on the miseries of his countryside. However, the overwhelming majority were educated men, 95 lawyers, 104 professors, 124 bureaucrats, and 100 judicial officials, together with 34 landowners and 13 businessmen. Nearly all the famous names in the field of thought were there—old *Turnvater* Friedrich Ludwig Jahn showed up, the man who had rallied a generation of German youth toward patriotism and health by his gymnastic meetings in the 1810's, work for which he suffered in prison. He was almost too old to function when he got to Frankfurt, but he looked handsome, with a white beard to his waist and a black velvet cap on his snow white hair; and he reminded the others of the ideals of the first movement of German youth for freedom. Jacob Grimm, the story teller and philologist, was another distinguished and distinguished-looking member. Moritz Arndt was another ancient, an ornament to the body because everybody there knew by heart his patriotic poetry and was grateful for it.

The man universally wanted for president of the Assembly was Heinrich von Gagern because he had done such a fine job of conciliation in the preliminary parliament. His talent was to rule the meetings not like an assembly of enemies but like a group of friends with differing opinions. "It is always easier for me to love than to hate," he said of himself, and in fact he was so trusting, modest, and unselfish that he began to seem like a medieval knight fighting for German freedom. Women tore his gloves into ribbons for souvenirs, and rumor said that an admirer set one of his buttons in diamonds.

The members of the left soon began to realize that in spite of his charms he lacked any decisive originality. His oratory grew monotonous once one got over its almost irresistible pathos; and though he was brave and talented, he could not see over the rather low fences which bounded the range of vision of the average imagination of 1848. "I can be a republican, for I have learned to live simply, but I will have no mob rule,"[2] he said, betraying the common confusion of the period. In Frankfurt all the aristocratic forces in his nature pulled him away from his first sympathy with the left, where he had sat so long in the Hessian chamber. The death of his adored brother Friedrich in combat against the republicans in Baden had a painful effect on his mind, too.

Possibly the most popular member of the Assembly, certainly the unchallenged leader of the left, was Robert Blum of Leipzig. The son of a servant girl and of a cooper who had died when he was eight, Blum lived through desperate poverty in his childhood. He remembered standing in a long line at a bakery at five in the morning because cheap bread was so scarce in those days; once when he was robbed of it on the way home his mother and sisters had nothing to eat all day long. Apprenticed to several masters in turn and not liking any trade particularly, he did manage nevertheless, like Stephan Born, to attend a few university lectures in off hours and to get around Germany. In 1840 he became cashier for the Leipzig theater, and since Leipzig was the center of the book industry he fell in with a group of intellectuals and became extremely popular both with them and with the working classes. But when he was elected a city councilor in 1847 the Saxon government would not let so dangerous a liberal serve, even though he had on several occasions used his strength to maintain order and the authorities should have been grateful.

At Frankfurt Blum was acknowledged to be the leader of the whole working class. He dressed in a blouse, which some wit called

---

[2] Quoted from Legge, *Rhyme and Revolution in Germany*, 247.

the cowl of the period, and he seemed to have the exact knack of charming his hearers by talking of his own early struggles without dragging them into the deeper and deeper waters of revolution. The women of Frankfurt must have been peculiarly impressionable, for, as Blum afterwards described their actions to his wife, they pelted him with flowers, kissed their hands to him, and sometimes almost swam in tears. It was only by looking in his mirror, to see that he was an unhandsome forty, and by remembering that it was his party they were applauding, not himself, that he kept his head, he said. His own sex were less easily overwhelmed, and eventually people noticed that his speeches all sounded like Antony's in *Julius Caesar*, only he never quite brought the excitement of his hearers to a head—he was always willing to leave the door open for a compromise. Engels called him shallow, ill-educated, and impractical, but also added that at the end, when he went to fight and die in Vienna, his sound instincts and energy raised him far above the usual standard of his own capacities.

The intellectual power of the right had much less public appeal. Joseph Maria von Radowitz, probably the most sophisticated intelligence at Frankfurt, made people think of a magician like Cagliostro, with his small round head, dark brown eyes, and such an uncanny knowledge of history that it was easy to imagine he must have been alive in many previous epochs. He was born in Hungary, educated in France, had fought with the French army in 1814, and subsequently became instructor of military science in a small German city. Technical education, he found, left him spiritually empty, but after he came to Prussia, in 1823, he suddenly found the two loyalties that absorbed his genius for the rest of his life, the Prussian throne and the Catholic church. He became one of the closest advisors to Frederick William IV, who used him in various delicate missions to Austria and Frankfurt. But when Radowitz reported to his royal master his election to the Frankfurt Assembly, Frederick William's congratulations were cool. His reply voiced the fear that Radowitz would be wasted at the Assembly, for "Satan and Adramelech have their headquarters there."

The liberal party felt that those two personages were adequately represented in Radowitz himself, listen as they might to his enchanted oratory. He was considered the evil genius of Prussian politics, and Radowitz wrote to his wife how much he was hated and feared. Many people came to consult him, he said, but they always begged for secrecy. And no one understood what he was really driving at. As a matter of fact his ideas were far from blackly reactionary; they were in many respects the same ones by which Bismarck and Napoleon III later won success. His advice to the King of Prussia was to make an ally of labor, as a bulwark against the middle class; having labor laws, social security, and progressive income taxes would be as far as the workers cared to go, he thought, whereas the bourgeois liberals were after the essence of kingly power. For Germany, he tried to achieve a united nation under Prussian leadership, with a close relationship to a separate Austria (like Bismarck again); he drafted a free press law for Prussia, and though he wanted a conservative power on top, he felt that the Frankfurt Assembly would be justified in compelling all the states to accept the constitution.

For a constitutionalist, the Assembly turned to Friedrich Christoph Dahlmann, from whom everybody expected more than he could perform. He had been one of the seven professors at Göttingen with the courage to protest when the Hanover constitution was abrogated by the new ruler. This was in 1837; the Kingdom of Hanover was separated from Great Britain because Victoria could not succeed in the German state. Dahlmann, living under liberal British rule at Göttingen, had acquired an immense admiration for British institutions, and his careful study of the English Revolution had had an immense sale throughout Germany. He also studied the French Revolution, with far less sympathy. It was the British system, with local autonomy, hereditary monarchy, and a strong representative legislative body that he wished to adapt for his fatherland. He and his six colleagues had been expelled from their chairs in Hanover for their courage and convictions, and were, therefore, considered martyrs to liberty. Dahlmann, however, and some of the others, were taken in and treated rather generously by the King of Prussia; by 1848 Dahlmann was teaching at the Prussian University of Bonn. In the Assembly he acted like a doctrinaire, and once remarked acidly that while he demanded of no one that he should have read his books, still, he would like those that quoted from them to have perused them. At the same time he was brave and incorruptible, and the only fault of the constitution he produced (for the job of drawing up the document was more or less given into his hands) was that it did not suit the passionate kings of Germany nor their passionately revolutionary subjects.

Frankfurt, the meeting place of the Assembly, as it had been of the Diet, was one of the famous free cities of Germany. The Rothschilds had a branch there, for it was a natural financial capital, and other banks too throve on changing the seven monetary systems then circulating in Germany. Of the 58,000 people who lived inside the city, barely half had citizenship rights, and of course none of the several thousand suburbanites held them. Only sons of citizens could become masters in trade and could get permission to marry. The other people who lived in the town did so only by permission and under severe restrictions. The Jewish community, for example, had been granted equal rights in court with Christians, but could only celebrate fifteen marriages a year. But against this antique respectability new forces were pushing. Just at the time of the opening of the Assembly in May, the city council banished two "foreign" labor agitators from another German state who were accompanied to the city gates by a huge procession of workers. At first the workers were as enthusiastic about the Assembly as everybody else, but when they found it was neither radical enough nor patriotic enough to suit them, they were ready to riot against it, and it took only four months to change their minds.

In Frankfurt, then, on May 18, the Assembly opened, adored by the German people, and set off with great panoply. The meeting place was St. Paul's Church, the altar covered with a huge picture of Germania and the galleries crowded with journalists from scores of papers, even French and British ones. Ladies were also in constant attendance. If reports can be credited the ladies leaned far to the left; even many wives and daughters of conservative members preferred to stand for several hours on the left rather than sit in the box which Prince Lichnowsky had arranged for them on the right. After the split with Austria the following year the Prussian ladies, ostentatiously attired in black and white, moved over to the left in a body.

An unaccustomed democracy was practiced in these sessions. Only generals and ministers were honored with their titles; everyone else, even professors, was addressed simply *Herr*. Radowitz wrote his wife how hard all the members worked, saying that he often sat from nine to six in unbroken session, and then from eight to midnight the various blocs would meet in their clubs for more talk. Blum, too, wrote of getting only three or four hours' sleep a night. Each shade of opinion had its own inn, and parties were identified by the names of the hostelries where they foregathered. In St. Paul's Church itself there were no committee rooms, so the members had to use all kinds of makeshifts when they wanted to get together in small groups. Sometimes important consultations had to be held outside even in pouring rain.

The second day Heinrich von Gagern was chosen president; he made a moving address on national sovereignty and the great position waiting for the German people. A committee of thirty was chosen to work on the constitution and a committee of fifteen to think about a provisional government, which seemed essential if the parliament was to achieve authority. So far, freedom and power seemed to be moving along hand in hand.

The constitution was not to be ready for months, but by June the question of the executive came to a head. Some people declared the Assembly itself was the German republic, even if it did not want to be; others denied its competence to set up a ruler for Germany. It was Gagern who proposed the formula of salvation. He told the members they must make a bold stroke and themselves establish a provisional government, and he proposed the name of the Archduke John of Austria to be the Imperial Administrator. This prince was to have executive power over the whole territory[3] represented in the Assembly for security, welfare, defense, and the right of exchanging diplomatic representatives. And he was to work through a ministry responsible to the Assembly.

The nomination of this particular Archduke was a minor stroke of genius because, since he was a Hapsburg, the princes would feel a certain hesitancy about repudiating him, while he had married a postmaster's daughter and was supposed to be democratic. In Vienna he had made a good first but bad final impression on the discerning Radowitz, who found out his character was weak though his ambitions were high.

When he arrived at Frankfurt to take office he was escorted to St. Paul's Church on foot to show how democratic he was. He wore black

---

[3] The territory represented was almost the same as that in the confederation; but representatives from Schleswig and Prussian Poland were also welcomed.

civil dress with no gloves and no orders, though he wore the German black, red, and gold cockade prominently. In the Assembly, though he was gracious, he carefully did not sit down on the throne which was placed a bit below the president's chair; and during the winter, though he gave weekly receptions to the Assembly members, he would not partake of food at their parties. Robert Blum noted that his face was expressionless and effete and felt that it was horrible to entrust Germany to such a man.

Almost everybody else went momentarily wild over what seemed like an enormous step forward. It was as if united Germany were being born painlessly; no one knew yet that the child was too weak to live. Even the Federal Diet dissolved itself, the last link of the old Germany, feeling that it would be entirely proper to give over its power into the hands of an imperial and royal highness, even though it could not succumb before the plain people. And with the Diet gone, the conquest of freedom seemed deceptively easy. Now for power.

First the Prussian and Austrian governments, however, and later all the others that considered themselves graced by God, treated the new Imperial decrees with contempt. One of the supposed homages to be received by the new authority was the swearing of allegiance by all troops in the service of any German state. Hohenlohe's story of the way this maneuver was carried out in Prussia is that the troops were assembled, the bulletin was read to them telling them to obey the Archduke; and then instead of swearing to it they gave three cheers for their own king. It was the same everywhere; even in Austria, weakened that summer by the worst civil war of any German state, the government at Vienna in which Archduke John served as regent refused to comply with the decrees of Archduke John the Imperial Administrator.

Undeterred by such signs of weakness, the Assembly went ahead with its plans for aggrandizement. There was no doubt about what the French Ambassador noted, that a spirit of vertigo filled the Assembly at the idea of conquest. Even the most cosmopolitan German—and all liberals were cosmopolitan—insisted that Trieste and Danzig must belong to the fatherland. Persons as various as Radowitz and Karl Marx felt that a big war would be the only way to clear the air. So the Assembly devoted a fair amount of its time to the nurture of the new German army and fleet. They ordered the armies to be increased by conscription to two per cent of the inhabitants of each state.[4] A navy was also commissioned although the Assembly's only funds for this purpose came from voluntary subscriptions.[5] Lord Palmerston said he would order British ships to treat the black-red-gold flag as a pirate's; and the United States would not allow a ship being built for the new Empire in the Brooklyn navy yard to leave New York until Germany promised not to use it in the war against Denmark which was going on at the time, the first of the efforts to expand German territory.

But within Germany the protests against war were few. Even Blum, who realized that the money spent on an army would be better used in making Germany industrially self-supporting, at one time looked forward to a war with Russia as a means of driving Frederick William IV from his throne. Only two members of the Assembly spoke for peace. Arnold Ruge, who had been a collaborator of Marx, tried to explain to the Assembly that armed peace is barbarous and that it would block the new democratic freedom they hoped to establish; but in vain. Karl Vogt, the free-thinking zoologist who later propagandized Darwin's theories on the continent, felt that the most important goal of Frankfurt policy would be the setting up of a disarmed peace in Europe. Everyone admired Vogt's intellect, which distinguished itself again in the debate on the church in relation to schools; nevertheless, people did not listen to what he had to say because he was considered "unhallowed by moral worth." In the 1830's and 1840's the exact sciences were at war with what was called philosophy, one of the symptoms of German idealism, and though science was supposed to be on the democratic or radical side (Vogt and his friends made a point of writing in a clear direct style for the benefit of the common people), most democrats and radicals

[4] The middle class liberals who advocated war as an instrument of progress in those days felt that it was a means of arousing people to take their share of responsibility in the state. Arndt wrote a "Soldier-Catechism" designed to show conscripts their duties as citizens. (For this reason Metternich and the Czar felt that universal military training would be revolutionary.) How far the patriots realized that war and military preparations could also be used to control and limit the freedom of the lower classes is not clear; that effect certainly followed—it was noticed by Proudhon—and, consciously or unconsciously, was not unwelcome to the middle class liberals who at the same time excoriated the idea of social welfare legislation.

Later on, social welfare laws were indeed turned against the middle class, by Bismarck and others, who saw how thus to limit the freedom of that class which to them was more dangerous to the state than the lower class.

[5] The salaries of the Archduke and his ministers were paid out of funds collected by the confederation in 1840 for common defense.

were still too idealistic to welcome support which they deemed materialistic.

The Assembly enjoyed not only excitement and popularity in its first few months but also a small war for freedom, to help it forget that it was only playing at power. For a short while it moved ahead unchecked. To the people of Germany who expected salvation from it the Assembly was sovereign. So great was their faith in it that when the *Neue Rheinische Zeitung*, then being edited in Cologne by Karl Marx, expressed contempt for the meetings at Frankfurt, the paper lost half its subscribers.

In July the King of Prussia invited the whole Assembly to Cologne, where the cathedral was being dedicated. This was the high point of the golden illusion, when the representatives sailed down the Rhine by boat in summer heat and were greeted and dined by the King and Archduke. The latter created a bad first impression by appearing in a Prussian general's uniform, but he quickly changed. Frederick William on the other hand added an ominous and unchangeable note to the party when he inserted in his supposedly gracious speech the remark, "Do not forget that there are still princes in Germany and that I am one of them."

By the end of the summer the Assembly was beginning to find this out, although in their first quarrel Frederick William was the one who seemed unkingly.

The source of this particular trouble was in the two duchies of Schleswig and Holstein, which were under the rule of the King of Denmark. Schleswig, it is true, was partly Danish and had not been admitted to the German Confederation, but Holstein was pure German and did belong. Furthermore, the duchies, right at the neck of the Danish peninsula and possessing the fine harbor of Kiel, were strategic territory for any future German empire if it was to develop a fleet and become a North Sea power. The hearts of all true Germans yearned after their kinsmen in this country, and since the King of Denmark had no direct male heirs, it seemed like a good time to pry them loose from Danish suzerainty by applying a kind of Salic law. King Christian VIII of Denmark had tried to prevent this with a decree, but when on March 23, 1848, the duchies revolted and set up a provisional government, and when shortly thereafter Prussian troops came in to support the insurgents, all Germany went wild with excitement. Representatives from both duchies were enthusiastically welcomed and seated at Frankfurt, volunteers from every quarter of the fatherland thronged toward the battle, and it seemed as if Denmark had no chance to hold the territory. A goodly number of radical proletarians and students were drained out of Berlin (one of whom invented submarine mines to defend the harbor at Kiel); and cynics said that to get rid of these inconvenient citizens was one of Prussia's purposes in fostering the war. But Marx, the unconscious nationalist, considered this the first war of revolutionary Germany; it took the French ambassador at Berlin to note that the Schleswig revolution contradicted all the others of its time in being led by the aristocracy and including almost no liberal demands. But the enthusiasm of the other revolutionaries showed how beautifully easy it was to mix up "Germany" and "liberty" in their minds.

The shock of the news that Prussia had granted an armistice at Malmö in this holy war without consulting the gentlemen at Frankfurt was a stunning blow both to the Assembly's feeling for German manifest destiny and to its self-esteem. Great Britain and Russia had both come to the side of Denmark, for obvious reasons of policy. Not only that, but the conscience of the King of Prussia had been disturbed at the thought he was supporting a revolt against a legitimate ruler, and that it was among his own liberal subjects that the war was most popular. Besides, the war had not been going very well for Prussia in a military way.

While the common people of Frankfurt prepared to riot at this example of royal perfidy, the Assembly tensely listened to Dahlmann on the subject of German honor, which he told them would never recover if they ratified the armistice. Robert Blum, hoping at any time for a break with the Prussian ministry ("never with the Prussian people"), was one of Dahlmann's loudest supporters. Furthermore, the people, Blum's people, were pressing. "If you want to create an uprising, ratify the armistice," he told his colleagues. For the working class was especially chauvinistic here as it was in France. So though calmer heads feared to crack the still unfired bowl of German unity, the Assembly voted to denounce Malmö. Blum's face at this moment radiated sinister joy (so we are told by a conservative witness), old Jahn acted like a caged wolf, while Radowitz's features registered masculine sadness. Radowitz, Frederick William's confidant, was the only one who knew the reasons of policy behind the act.

This vote took place on September 5. The Imperial Ministry handed in their resignations to the Archduke John, just as if they were well-trained British parliamentarians, and he then dumped in Dahlmann's lap the duty to set up a new ministry. In a few days poor Dahlmann had to give up the responsibility again, so impossible was it actually to go against Prussian power, and on September 16 the Assembly reversed itself and endorsed the armistice.

The governments changed their minds, but nothing had happened in the interim to make the patriotic people change theirs. As soon as the news of the Assembly's reversal reached them a furious mob gathered near Frankfurt which lost no time in declaring the majority of the Assembly to be traitors. With red feathers in their hats and pistols in their belts, 10,000 listened to an orator who urged them to make barricades of their bodies. Next morning they attacked St. Paul's Church.

Up until this time the Assembly had distrusted military protection and there were only a few troops in the city. When trouble seemed at hand the Imperial Ministry sent to Mainz, where Austrian and Prussian troops were garrisoned, and these arrived (the Austrians looking handsome with their white coats and gleaming muskets) just in time to prevent the mob from beating in the front door of the church. A few did break in the back door, partly because the Czech soldiers on guard there did not understand German, but Gagern adjourned the meeting with his customary dignity, leaving the troops free to quell the people.

As usual the soldiers were particularly brutal with their civilian enemies. Their prisoners were stowed away in what threatened to be another black hole of Calcutta without air, water, or medical attention until one of the members of the Assembly telegraphed the Governor of Mainz and had them removed from the city by railroad.

The riot at Frankfurt was remembered longest for the murder of Prince Felix Lichnowsky and his companion, General Hans von Auerswald, both members of the Assembly on the right. Lichnowsky was a brilliant, spoiled, and perverse Prussian officer who had fought for the legitimists in Spain, sided with the Silesian weavers in Berlin, and seemed too giddy to be trusted by his own party in the Assembly. They enjoyed his tormenting of the left, however. He used to adore to call out in his shrill voice "Name, please," whenever Robert Blum, the best-known man in St. Paul's Church, rose to speak. On the fatal day of the riot he borrowed a horse to go and look at the shooting, along with Auerswald, and the insurgents began to pursue them. One excuse was that they mistook Lichnowsky for Radowitz. The two friends fled to a house where Auerswald was given a nightshirt to make him look like the man of the house, while the Prince was hidden in a fruit cellar. Unfortunately, the people searched even there, and found him by a corner of his coat hanging out. He was dragged forth and through the streets, wounded by bullets, and by the time he was rescued he was dying. As he expired he uttered a deathbed will leaving his fortune to a duchess.

Later in the fall, a far more tragic death occurred. After the riot was suppressed, Robert Blum began to have premonitions of the failure of the democratic party. He gave his last penny to help the victims of the riot and their families, so that he did not even have money to send to his wife and four children in Leipzig. His letters show how deeply he suffered from persecution in the Assembly and from watching the waste of forces which he believed could transform Germany. Sometimes, hiking in the country on Sunday, he would see his own picture in a remote peasant's hut; the sense that he got in this way of the confidence of the common people, and of their loyalty to his party, was all that kept him on a job he found more and more disagreeable and hopeless. When the chance came to go to Vienna, then in the final stages of its revolutionary battle against Austrian Imperial troops, he welcomed it. He was supposed to carry greetings from the left-wing clubs of the Assembly to the embattled students of Vienna, but after he reached Vienna and made his speeches to the students (who elected him an honorary member of their famous Academic Legion) and to the committee of the new Austrian Diet, he wrote that he had never seen such a fine city, and stayed on to fight. In fact, he lost his former caution so completely that his old friends could hardly recognize him. The former peacemaker realized that democracy for all of Germany would be won or lost on the Vienna barricades, not in any parliament. Nothing in Frankfurt could reverse the verdict of these arms.

When Vienna fell he was arrested by the victorious Austrian

troops, and though he pleaded parliamentary inviolability, the new prime minister, Prince Felix zu Schwarzenberg, gave special orders to have him shot. The news of the sentence came as a complete surprise to Blum one morning at six, so that he had barely time to write a few heartbroken words to his wife before he was executed.

The Assembly at Frankfurt declared a holiday in respect to his memory and directed their shadow ministry to punish those responsible, but nothing was done—nothing could be. The success of the Austrian army against the democrats put an end to more important liberal hopes than that one and gave courage to counter-revolution in more places than Vienna alone.

Meanwhile work on the federal constitution was pushed slowly forward, undeterred by the Assembly's lack of success in fields of power politics. The almost interminable debate on the bill of rights was deliberately prolonged by parties who felt they could not get— in 1848—the kind of constitution they wanted. No constitution putting Prussia at the head of Germany could have passed in those early days, nor was there any chance of a republic to suit the left. So while waiting to see if their chances improved, both sides talked of common citizenship, freedom of speech, writing, printing, and making pictures, all of which were written into the document; they abolished the nobility and all titles except professional ones, and the special rights of police and justice which landowners still possessed. (A favorite cartoon of the period shows Jacob Grimm as a monkey, saying, "Man is abolished. We are all of one race.") They tried to loosen up other parts of German life too; many more minutiae were included than are covered in the American constitution, like hunting rights and the question of free emigration. Also, education. It is stated in the Frankfurt bill of rights that learning and teaching were to be free, though supervised by the state; that no tuition was to be charged in elementary schools; and that parents might not leave their children uninstructed. German schools were clamoring loudly for reform; teachers wanted more science and modern languages and German history, and there was a long debate on this at Frankfurt, as well as on the relation of the school to the church. (The school, said one ingenious separationist, is the daughter of the church but marries the state, which knows that a mother-in-law should not live with a couple.) But, significantly, the motion to guarantee to non-German-speaking subjects their own schools and cultural rights was defeated.

The right to work was voted down in spite of numberless petitions from proletarian groups, all of whose petitions were ignored so regularly by the political economy committee that the working population lost its confidence in the Assembly.

The vote for direct, secret, and universal suffrage was, on the other hand, a triumph for the left. To win votes for this measure they had to swap support for an hereditary monarch. Many true democrats, quoting Thomas Jefferson, who had said that votes for everyone would not work in Europe, felt that servants and factory workers would vote only as their masters told them and destroy democracy. A look across the Rhine, where Louis Napoleon was maneuvering, tended to confirm this suspicion. It is a tribute to the drafters of the constitution that they were willing to take the risk.

These lectures on political science, as one bored member called them, could not forestall forever consideration of the more fundamental German problem—how to handle a monster with two heads. To lop off the Austrian one and accept Prussian hegemony over the rest of Germany was an operation no one was willing to face at first —particularly the small states, which were sufficiently terrified by Prussia's power though they needed her army, but also those who felt that Austria was a "lantern for the East," Germany's path to the Black Sea as well as to Venice and the Adriatic, the necessary and only direction for expansion (later called *Lebensraum*) for the greater Germany that was to be. Idealism made its customary neat tie-up with imperialism, though the problem of forwarding both future interests and present political possibilities wrenched even the most lucid and practical intelligences at Frankfurt.

The Confederation had ruled with such a loose rein that Austrian Germans were scarcely conscious of suffering double authority, especially as Metternich had made things go Austria's way ever since the union was started. But how to fit this fraction of Hapsburg subjects into a new, tight federal union with a representative assembly, the very idea of which was an abomination to their government, and with power over their army and to some extent their laws —that would be a different question. The alternative, however, was bitter: leave Austria out and accept Prussia as top dog. It was bitter but it began to seem inexorable. Radowitz, the conservative, who wanted lines of power kept open to the south (he always took the long view), and the liberal Gagern, who had hoped that the people along the Danube who "have neither vocation nor claim to independence" could be set up as satellites around the German planetary system (he was always a sentimental *kultur* man)—both these leaders came around to the idea of Prussian hegemony. Gagern would couple this with a complicated alliance between Hapsburg and Hohenzollern lands, to keep Austria on the German side instead of letting it fall to the Slavs; while Radowitz toyed with a system of rings within rings, a small, Prussian-led Germany within a larger union of German-speaking peoples within a larger union including all the Slavic and other satellites. Only the left still stuck out directly for a big Germany against a little Germany. But in taking the first step toward separation the right and center broke the mechanical deadlock. A clause in the new constitution was drafted to prohibit the union within one state of German and non-German peoples. The Hapsburg emperor could, by this proviso, still be king of Hungary and other dominions, but he must rule these lands separately from his German territory with a personal union in the crown only.

Once this question was settled the problem fell apart of itself. When a vote on unity (in connection with a motion which would give the Frankfurt ministry power to treat with Austria as a separate power) came up in January, emotion during the roll call was tense but the conclusion was inevitable. Every man in turn was called to announce his vote, and when the old poet Arndt's choked "yes" came, the left broke out into an ironical chant—*Das Ganze Deutschland soll es sein* ("It must be *all* Germany")—one of his most famous lines. But the motion carried.

On March 4, 1849, Austria herself settled the whole subject even more definitely by promulgating a constitution declaring the entire Hapsburg Empire to be an indivisible monarchy with a common army, revenue system, and administration. No personal union in the crown alone for her. At last there seemed to be no room for doubt in anybody's mind at Frankfurt that Prussia would have to take over.

This was the point at which Dahlmann made his discovery about power and freedom; the whole debate turned unconsciously more toward strength and less toward liberty. In 1848 it was quite commonly felt that Prussia was too big to be a single state and ought to divide into its eight provinces which would be comparable in size to the other states which would join the new union. This was one of the notions of Friedrich von Gagern, Heinrich's dead brother, who felt that even the Prussian name must be given up for the German one. There was also talk of keeping Prussia from being too powerful by rotating the job of emperor among different ruling houses, or by putting a committee of five at the head of Germany. By 1849 people seemed glad of Prussian protection and glory; perhaps they were tired of revolutions, though the left was still against Prussia and the vote was close.

Things began to move faster now. By March the constitution was all ready to be voted on, complete with a clause giving the hereditary kaisership to some ruling German prince. Dahlmann felt this would give the state the warmth of family life as well as guarantee the power he craved. Someone moved to accept the document as a whole and offer the crown to the King of Prussia, and when this enthusiastic motion failed many of the strongest men broke down and wept. It must have been a tearful month in St. Paul's Church, after such long exertion—for later, when they started to vote on the constitution section by section and one of the important paragraphs was lost, the leaders sat there stunned with their heads on their desks. "Oh, let us die," said one—to which Gagern replied, "I am already dead." But still, miraculously, things came to life again, the constitution was passed in sections, and 290 votes were cast for Frederick William IV as emperor, against 248 who abstained from voting. Bells and cannons greeted the news all over Germany, and the first long electric telegraph wire in the world carried the news from Frankfurt to Berlin within an hour.

Gagern had already talked to the King in November on the subject of his election, which he had hoped could be put through even so early if Frederick William were willing. Gagern's interest at this time had been to prevent a separate Prussian constitution, one such as the Prussian national assembly was busily drafting at just that moment, which Gagern felt would increase the difficulty of German amalgamation. At that time the King told him plainly that the only election he would consider valid would be to be chosen by the other princes. Gagern assured him this formality could be arranged—a promise which to the King was more like a threat. He called Gagern his friend publicly, remarking privately that he hoped he would never need such friendship. Gagern's attitude was, "the King must whether he wants to or not," and so he kept working at the idea. Nothing in the King's remarks warned him that His Majesty would become hysterical when the crown was formally proffered.

Frederick William, indeed, gave signs of ambivalence in wanting the crown. He would have liked an election in the medieval manner, like Emperor Conrad's, made while the German nations were encamped at Worms, under their dukes, ready to acclaim the choice. Was the Assembly a substitute for this encampment, ironically asked the King's friends? The King actually went so far as to write to Schwarzenberg, Austrian Prime Minister, in April, asking if he could be made Imperial Administrator instead of Archduke John— a suggestion which offered a neat way out of many difficulties. Frederick the Great, remarked his descendant wistfully, would have taken the gift as offered by the parliament and made what he wanted of it, "but I am not a great ruler."

Even when the formal delegation from Frankfurt waited on him (after having been extensively feted on its way from Frankfurt to Berlin), Frederick William's refusal was so ambiguous that the members could not be quite sure that he meant to turn them down. They stewed for a while, trying to get ratification from the various states while the King's anger boiled up. All his loyalty to Austria, his horror of the humiliations which the revolution in Berlin had piled on him, his moral and religious convictions poured over him until he reached the point of calling the Assembly's crown a dog's collar, a pig's crown, a fictitious coronet baked of mire and clay. "I want neither the *consent* of the princes to the *election* nor the *crown* itself. Do you understand the words underlined?"[6]

His friend Baron Bunsen, his most liberal advisor, could not but feel that the King's character had been changed by the events of the Berlin revolution. Bunsen, lately from England, was horrified at

[6] Letter to Bunsen, December 13, 1848. In a letter to Arndt, Frederick William made things still clearer. "What is offered me? Is this birth of the hideous labor of the year 1848 a crown? The thing which we are talking about does not carry the sign of the holy cross, does not bear the stamp 'by the Grace of God' on its head, is no crown. It is the iron collar of servitude, by which the heir of more than twenty-four rulers, electors and kings, the head of 16,000,000, the master of the most loyal and bravest army in the world, would be made the bondservant of the revolution. . . . The revolution is the abolition of the godly order, the despite, the setting aside of legitimate order, it lives and breathes its deadly breath so long as bottom is top and top is bottom." Quoted in Legge.

the atmosphere of the Prussian court, where everybody seemed to be choking from suppressed rage. Even the palace servants refused to give a glass of water to the president of the Frankfurt Assembly when he arrived for his audience. Bunsen felt the King's mind had been systematically poisoned until he had lost his old conviction of right, and all his energy seemed to expend itself in talk. (During the next decade Frederick William actually lost his mind, so that the Prince of Prussia had to assume the regency; but it seems doubtful whether the symptoms of that later illness showed up as early as 1849.)

The King's close advisors, of course, were dead against compromise with either the King's medievalism or the Assembly's democracy. Most officers, including the Prince of Prussia, felt that for Prussia to merge into a reconstituted Roman Empire would be a step down, and they were sure that in the natural course of things the country would achieve dominance by its own force. "It cannot be done à la Gagern," said the future first Kaiser in a way that showed he knew he was right. The politicians at Berlin were willing to use their monarch's fancies to play against the Gagern policies, just as they wanted to play Austria and St. Paul's Church off against each other, without, however, encouraging the latter's lust for sovereignty.

Meanwhile, all the separate parliaments of Germany, including that of Prussia, voted for the Frankfurt constitution and for a Prussian emperor. So did most of the rulers, especially in the small states. Frederick William wrote grateful letters to the King of Bavaria and some of the others who had prevented unanimity among the princes by *not* endorsing him, but at the same time he made them angry and jealous merely by his having been offered the job of emperor. As for the German people, their rage was mingled with despair. After sporadic fierce rebellion, especially in Baden and Saxony, they settled back into a period of greater and more skillful repression than they had yet known. In the end Bismarck took over some of the 1848 Assembly's ideas without its idealism, either for liberalism or for pan-Germanism—and without its weakness.

The Assembly, naturally, appealed to the people to support their constitution—the center hoped by legal means, the left by revolution. But members kept drifting away or being recalled, so that it was a much diminished body that moved from Frankfurt to Stuttgart, deposed the imperial administrator, and elected five of their own number to be a regency. On June 18 Württemberg troops drove these die-hards out of their chamber. The Assembly was dead, killed by its own inexperience, by the jealousy of states and rulers, and, paradoxically enough, by the very constitutions of Prussia and Austria, which established those states so firmly as conservative entities that they could never be amalgamated into any liberal empire.

IX

Light Cases of Fever

OF ALL the states of Germany the tiny Grand Duchy of Baden was the most liberal politically. Apparently it was also the most revolutionary corner of Europe in temperament, for while other countries were having one or possibly two outbreaks during 1848 and 1849, Baden had three. The first was a gay little affair inspired by the news of the republic in Paris. The second came at the time when the Frankfurt Assembly seemed to be turning away from the people's demands, at the time of the September riots. The third and most important was a fierce battle in the spring of 1849, which revolutionists hoped would spearhead a gigantic protest all over Germany to force the acceptance of the Frankfurt constitution. There were plenty of men in Germany sore with disappointment when the Assembly collapsed, and it seemed as if there ought to be plenty of support for an armed movement. Only it turned out that most Germans would rather suffer in silence.

In the southwest corner of Germany, Baden, like other Rhine territory, was greatly struck with so-called "French ideas." After 1815 its citizens had maintained a constitution, and in 1831 even dared to establish freedom of the press, a step which other members of the German Confederation forced them to take back almost immediately, since one free state was almost as dangerous to Metternich's system as many. From that time on, however, Baden statesmen were leaders in all liberal plans for German unity. In numbers out of all proportion to the size of their state they helped set up the Frankfurt Assembly, and the die-hard republicans who were frozen out of this organization were also mostly Baden subjects.

When the news of the Paris revolution was announced, Carl Mathy, the leader of the liberal opposition in the Baden Chamber, foiled the revolutionary party for the moment by getting the government to grant their demands before they had a chance for a demonstration. But the idea of revolution was in the air, and to the dismay of both Mathy, the liberal, and Friedrich Hecker, the republican leader, the peasants in the whole Rhineland began to seize land, to burn castles[1] and tithe-books, and to persecute Jews wherever they could find them. This was far from the ideal of human brotherhood that the would-be remakers of Germany had set themselves.

Hecker was called the most popular man in Germany at this time —certainly he was the idol of the republicans. He was a generous, hot-headed fellow of good family, tall and handsome, and he always wore a blue blouse with high boots and a couple of pistols in his belt. He had been head of the most liberal party in Baden for years, and during the revolutionary period the common greeting throughout the whole Rhineland was "Hecker hoch!" When he retired to Switzerland after his defeat in the spring of 1848, crowds used to come across the border every Sunday just to look at him—occasions which he laughingly called "menagerie day." But in spite of his good humor and enthusiasm he was no more easy to work with than most of the republican leaders, for he was untrained and obstinate.

His best friend and partner at this time was Gustav Struve, whose principles dictated that he should leave out of his name the *von* to which he was entitled. Struve was a newspaper man; he was small and bloodless, the sort that ate no meat, drank no wine, and took cold baths. His face showed the moral rigidity of the fanatic (said Alexander Herzen) with uncombed beard and untroubled eyes. At one time he devised a special calendar for German meditation, with every day devoted to two human leaders, such as Washington and Lafayette. Every tenth day, however, was given over to two human enemies, like Nicholas of Russia and Metternich. He was also a phrenologist, and (so swears Herzen) deliberately chose a wife who lacked the bump of passions. But she had beautiful eyes, whose luster induced more than one volunteer into Struve's army, and she was tactful and shrewd and loyal. During the three Baden revolutions she bought supplies for the army and organized a nursing corps. Alas, her husband was hardly her equal as a leader, for he was so careless about details like burning incriminating papers that he

[1] The poor peasants were beginning to feel more insecurity by the middle of the nineteenth century than at any time since the time of the Peasants' War—in a way reminiscent of the American sharecroppers in the twentieth. After 1807 they were no longer tied to their land and one natural result was that many of them sold it or lost it and had to turn to the still lower status of day laborer. This process was far more evident around the Frenchified Rhineland than in East Prussia. This is why we hear of castle-burning in Baden while Bismarck's peasants were so loyal to the King that they would have liked to march on Berlin to crush the revolution there themselves.

landed his friend Gottfried Kinkel in prison, so naïve that he fell for stories cooked up for him by spies, and so impractical that he was capable of ordering men with scythes to attack regular troops. When his rebellion was finally beaten, he kept thinking that it could have succeeded if this or that detail had been different.

The first idea of Hecker and Struve was to declare the German Republic, to match that of France; this they accomplished in the Baden town of Constance. Then they traveled around Baden trying to arouse the people. "Who is *unripe* for the Republic?" asked Struve, cleverly taking the question out of the mouths of the conservatives; and of course his answer was that the kings and princes were unripe, the timid constitutionalists, and those professors and pastors who lived on scientific and religious superstition. For allies they counted on winning the army, the large numbers of unemployed workingmen who were being sent back from France half-starved, and the peasants who wanted to keep the land they had seized.

To meet the army which the republicans were raising, the Baden government summoned Friedrich von Gagern, brother of the man about to be chosen president of the Frankfurt Assembly, from his job as general in the Dutch service. This Gagern was as patriotic as his brother Heinrich and had given even deeper thought to the problems facing Germany; when he received a letter from the Netherlands which he suspected might recall him, he left it unopened and went to command the Baden campaign in civilian dress.

The republicans were counting hard on winning over the soldiers. "Don't shoot your brothers," they called across the lines, and with enough success to make the troops waver. Gagern and Hecker had a personal meeting just before the battle (which took place April 20) and in a high-minded conversation each accused the other of fanaticism. Finally, Gagern, realizing the danger from his uncertain soldiers, ordered the attack. He was killed on the field the same day, but his troops easily overpowered the poorly armed republicans. Struve was captured and jailed, along with 3,500 others, until the prisons overflowed. Hecker fled to Switzerland, and from there, after finding out that his armed revolt had cost him his seat in the Frankfurt Assembly, he went to Illinois and bought a farm. In America he became a strong Republican, fought in the Civil War, and made orations against slavery which were famous among all German-speaking people in the United States.

The little history of the romantic and disorganized German Legion of Paris, which tried to march to the help of Hecker and Struve in those days, is an epitome of the whole German revolution.

Among the Paris clubs during the spring of 1848 was, naturally, one for Germans, the German Democratic Society. Its members were mostly workingmen who had been employed in France and whose jobs failed with depression and revolution. The French Republic was anxious to relieve its own unemployment situation by getting rid of the foreigners, so it agreed to pay transportation expenses plus a daily allowance for each man to go to his own home. Several thousands of these men who had fought on the Paris barricades were enthusiastic about carrying the revolution back to their own country.

For president the society elected a poet named Georg Herwegh, a despotic and dreamy young man who hated to be forced to explain his large and vaguely idealistic ideas. As a youth he had fled from Germany to Switzerland to avoid military service, and through publication of some best-selling poems gained an enormous reputation. He was called the iron lark, the songbird of war, for his *Poems of the Living* were all political, urging his Germany to stretch her limbs. His wife Emma, the daughter of a rich Jewish banker of Berlin, was a young woman of outstanding common sense and devotion who was able to pour her father's fortune into the German Legion. She deserved better than she got out of life, for Herwegh disintegrated completely a few years later in a love affair with Alexander Herzen's wife.

While Herwegh was still in Paris his chief faults were merely bossiness in the management of his supposedly democratic committee, and ineptitude in running either financial or military affairs. He paraded through the streets with his Germans, carrying a huge banner labeled "German Republic" which amused everybody greatly, while he appealed to French citizens to turn over to him the arms they were laying down. Yet he was unwilling to allow his legion to be subjected to military discipline.

In appealing for help from the French government to arm his little band and dispatch it to the Rhineland, Herwegh had to deal with Flocon, the official in charge of relations with foreign republicans, who was one of the most amicably disposed radicals in the government. One day Flocon summoned the poet to ask him how much money he would require for his legion, and as a hint to the recipients he held fifty 1,000 franc notes in his hand and lightly ruffled through them. Herwegh gulped and replied he could use 2,000 francs. Flocon counted these out, with a look of disgust on his face at such lack of realism, and when Herwegh's equally disgusted comrades went back the next day to ask for the rest of the money, Flocon told them it was gone.

At the end of March the legion began to march to Strasbourg in small groups. There was no railway yet. The French people with whom the legion was quartered were so enthusiastic that they mostly refused money and offered their best food for nothing; but when the travelers arrived at the Rhine they seemed to be stuck. Emma Herwegh went twice to hunt for Hecker in Baden and offer him the help of the 800 fighters who were ready, but Hecker was not very eager to use what he considered French support—especially unarmed French support. The legion had never succeeded in finding guns for its men. Likewise the Frankfurt Assembly turned down Herwegh's offer to provide a military force for its defense; and no German government was willing even to let the legion go through its territory and fight in the war with Schleswig-Holstein. The Baden government, to be sure, offered to pay the way of any unarmed individual to his own home, but only 16 members accepted this offer. The rest were determined not to go home without tasting battle. Finally Hecker was talked into naming a date and place on the Rhine for the legion to cross over to Baden, and he promised to have an escort ready to meet them at the Baden shore. Unfortunately, by the time the date had come, Hecker's army was defeated and he himself was in Switzerland. The legion crossed the river in ignorance of this and tried to figure out what had happened.

The Herweghs marched at the head, Georg with his "sinister-looking Italian brigand's face" topped by a black peaked cap, and wearing a wide black cloak; Emma in black trousers, a black velvet blouse and broad-brimmed hat. She carried two small pistols and a dagger in her belt. The uniform of the legion consisted of white or light gray blouses, gray hats with feathers,—and as they marched through the valleys with their black-red-gold banners beating against the scythes which were almost their only weapons, they looked as if they had come out of the Thirty Years' War.

By this time troops from Württemberg were policing the whole area, since the Baden army was demoralized by the fight with Hecker. Much to the pleasure of the legion, they had one skirmish with the regulars, in which the legion came out very creditably. Herwegh and his wife sat on a cart and passed out gunpowder to those who had guns, but it turned out that what really scared the Württembergians were the scythes, of which they had heard tall tales. After this incident the legion made its way to the Swiss border as best it could. The Herweghs were sheltered en route by a kind peasant couple, who lent them native clothes and let them work in the fields for a day while the soldiers were searching for them.

The second Baden revolution began September 21, after the Frankfurt riots. Struve, who had gotten out of prison, walked with a dozen unarmed friends across the bridge from Switzerland to the small town of Lörrach, took possession of the Rathhaus, and once more proclaimed the German Republic. They seized the printing press and immediately began to print republican proclamations, all headed:

GERMAN REPUBLIC
WELFARE, EDUCATION AND FREEDOM FOR ALL!

They issued appeals for troops, gave instructions to burgomasters to gather provisions for the new army, and ordered officials to leave lights burning to guide the troops. They declared that feudal dues and most other taxes were abolished and that a progressive income tax would be levied. The program and its leaders seemed radical enough to scare all the liberals, yet the true socialists of the time laughed at Struve and pointed out that his program was basically not much more than what the professors at Frankfurt were after. The truth of the matter was that the unlucky Germans in 1848 had to struggle at the same time for things which Anglo-Saxon countries got in the seventeenth and in the twentieth centuries. Lumping everything from habeas corpus to social security in one set of demands makes those demands occasionally very old-fashioned, occasionally startlingly modern; invariably, however, the rebels were biting off more than they could chew.

Volunteers kept streaming in, and thirty-six hours after the republic was declared its army of 10,000 was able to march toward Freiburg. Unhappily the fighting men consisted largely of riffraff; the light-hearted adventurers of the first uprising had almost dis-

appeared. So when they were beaten by troops in a few days hardly
anyone was sorry.

Struve was imprisoned in the fortress at Rastatt after this affair,
and his wife at Freiburg. She was released April 16, 1849, and went
immediately to Rastatt, where she stayed to arouse the townspeople
and garrison on Struve's behalf. But by this time the third Baden
revolution was gathering.

The failure of the Frankfurt efforts for an empire and a constitution brought renewed outbreaks of revolution all over Germany, but
only in Saxony and along the Rhine did they become spectacular.
Democratic clubs had been forming everywhere since the danger to
liberalism had begun to seem imminent, specifically after the debacle
of the Prussian Assembly in November. In Baden these groups were
especially successful, where they were led by Lorenz Brentano, a
lawyer who had the courage to defend Struve and the other revolutionists of the first uprising. Over half the male citizens of the
Grand Duchy were enlisted openly in the democratic cause, including many soldiers.

What they hoped for, of course, was that all over Germany people
would fight for the Frankfurt constitution which the King of Prussia had rejected. Most people except Struve realized that the spirit
for creating a republic in 1848 was missing in this spring of 1849;
but a fight for the constitution occurred all over the Rhineland—not
with the same hope, not with ecstasy, but with a sense that the duty
was inescapable. No one who took part, of course, knew for sure that
the rest of Germany would not rise too. When the Cologne outbreak
was put down, Marx and Engels printed the last edition of their
Neue Rheinische Zeitung in red; and Engels went off to fight in the
Palatinate, where he was soon disgusted by the amateurishness of
the effort. Carl Schurz was also in this fight, and tells us that since
the rebels had no uniforms they dressed so as to look as wild as
possible, an effect which they could have achieved, he says, if their
faces had not been so strikingly good-natured.

Meanwhile in Baden, on May 1, the committee in charge of the
people's clubs issued a call to be ready with arms. Shortly another
notice went out to the soldiers, exhorting them to stand by their
brothers. On May 13 a people's congress met, in which many soldiers
were delegates. It voted not only to support the Frankfurt constitu-

tion, but also favored a pension fund for workers who were incapacitated, and included several other touching humanitarian reforms on its list. Then the army suddenly mutinied; the Grand Duke, finding himself without a carriage, fled on the ammunition chest of a cannon; a crowd freed Struve from Rastatt; and a permanent State Committee of the People's Clubs took power and moved into Carlsruhe. In one breath it organized general elections for Baden and set up the pension fund.

On May 15, Prussia declared war on the Baden revolutionaries.

Most officers in the Baden army remained loyal to the Grand Duke, while the soldiers went over to the revolution in a body. These soldiers were supposed, in revolutionary theory, to elect their own officers, which they proceeded to do, usually choosing their own noncommissioned officers. At the same time the new government advertised in newspapers for trained military men to fill the higher ranks. For a commander-in-chief they sent to Paris for the Polish officer, Mieroslawski, who was recovering there from a wound. After his release from prison in Berlin in the general enthusiasm for Poland which the March days brought even to the Prussian capital, Mieroslawski had gone straight back to Posen where within a week he began to lead a revolt against Prussia; when that was quelled he moved on to Sicily, where he received his wound. Now he seemed happy to be invited to Baden. He arrived in red trousers, a blue overcoat heavily trimmed with brass, a golden sword belt, his blond hair carefully parted and combed. He seemed almost too picturesque to be useful, but when his first review was held his troops surprised everybody with the evidence of spirit and discipline which he had instilled into them.

The financial machinery of the Grand Duchy also fell untouched into the hands of the revolutionaries, and only ineptitude kept them from using it fully. The new finance minister, however, did not know where to look for several millions in paper money that was lying around, and he would not coin silver because the only stamp available had the Grand Duke's image on it. But the new government pledged the pig iron owned by the state against new paper money, and it decreed a forced loan at five per cent interest.

The elections on June 3 chose a constitutional assembly for Baden which set up a dictatorship with Brentano at the head, much against his wishes. Though at first he won confidence by his moderation, he lacked both resolution and training. On June 26 he resigned and fled, and wrote a letter full of recrimination back to Baden from Switzerland. From there he emigrated to America and was eventually elected to Congress.

Brentano's mistake (though his cause was doomed anyway) was to neglect the rest of Germany. He believed in revolution in one country, while Struve was the Trotsky of this little world and kept pushing for a general uprising. It is probable that an attack into Württemberg would have brought that small state into the fight as an ally; and a plan was even drafted to unite Baden with another of its neighbors, the Bavarian Palatinate, into one single country—a first step toward world government. The plan fell through because Baden, which was richer, haggled about divisions of financial responsibility until the unhappy Palatinate fell to the Prussians, leaving Baden's own flank completely uncovered.

The Prussian army naturally kept on. Into Mannheim they shot red-hot cannonballs, seeking to fire the houses or the cotton bales which were used for gun emplacements. The water supply was so well organized, however, that not a house burned; and a certain shoemaker's apprentice spent all day putting out sparks in the cotton bales.

On July 1 Mieroslawski resigned, feeling that nothing more was to be gained from carrying on the fight. Among the conditions that he blamed for his failure at arms was that neither the citizens nor the soldiers knew what they were fighting for. They stood for no exact revolutionary aims, and were inclined to interpret "freedom" in a way that meant fulfilling their own whims. Mieroslawski himself escaped safely, and was still leading revolutionary battles in Poland in 1863.

As the Prussians swept through the rebels were driven back until most of them were inside the fortress of Rastatt. This was one of the so-called imperial fortresses, whose up-to-date defense works had been commissioned by the German Confederation and constructed by Austria after the threat of war with France in 1840. In fact, the work was not quite finished, but even so it was strong enough to withstand an almost indefinite siege. On June 25 men and horses crowded inside its walls together, pellmell, sleeping on the streets, in the schools, wherever there happened to be a spot to lie down. When organized and counted, the garrison proved to contain about 6,000 men. Another equally strong revolutionary army, under General Sigel, was still outside, and had promised to relieve them before their provisions gave out. By July 2 the Prussians had completely surrounded the fortress and began urging the garrison to surrender, but they took pains not to tell them, nor let them find out, that the Grand Duke of Baden promised amnesty to any of his rebel subjects who gave themselves up by July 15. Inside the fortress discipline was good, food seemed adequate, though the military leaders could not extract a definite statement about provisions from the civil authorities; and when the supply of leeches for their wounded gave out, the Prussian surgeon general handsomely sent in a boxful. A newspaper was published, and even a branch of Struve's radical club established. So the besieged force could not bear to surrender or to believe that hope was lost to them. It came as a sharp surprise to the military commanders to learn on July 21 that only three days' food supply was on hand. Still hoping for relief, they arranged to send Otto von Corvin, the commander, and another officer on tour of the country to look for the relieving army. Prussian officers courteously escorted these two wherever they wished to go, but it did not take them long to be convinced that the Prussian stories were true—Sigel and his army had fled across the Swiss border, throwing down their arms, two weeks previously, and had forgotten, or been unable, to get word into Rastatt. Corvin had to report to his staff that except in distant Hungary, Rastatt was the only place in Europe where the revolutionary flag still waved.

Surrender was therefore dictated. The officers expected no mercy for themselves, but they requested and believed that their men should be treated leniently. In the negotiations they pointed out to the Prussian officers that the rebel rank and file were mostly Badish soldiers who were fighting for the constitution which they had been sworn to defend, and that the Grand Duke's proclamation and promise of amnesty had never reached their ears, probably because Prussia was unwilling for so many democrats to escape. The Prussian negotiators seemed to promise clemency, although their formal demand was for unconditional surrender. This was unwillingly agreed to, and the Rastatt garrison laid down their arms on the glacis and marched out of the fortress—straight into courtsmartial. The promise of leniency uttered by a Prussian general had not, it seemed, been signed by him, and Prussia was determined to execute as traitors any of her subjects who had resisted her arms. To his own subjects the Grand Duke might have been kinder had his ally allowed it, but Prussian army men sat as judges in the Baden courts-martial also, and from their sentences there was no appeal. The Prince of Prussia, who had commanded the attack, and who turned his back on the defeated army when it marched past him, deliberately separated himself from any appeals for mercy. The soldiers who had to carry out these death sentences, however, came away pale and shaken from executing most of the fighting democrats left in Germany.

A few bold souls escaped. Otto von Corvin, a subject of Saxony, had his death sentence commuted to six years in a common prison, even though he had been in charge of the military defense of Rastatt, because one Prussian sergeant (soon afterwards removed from the duty of sitting on the bench of a court-martial) had voted to spare his life. Carl Schurz hid in a sewer in Rastatt and finally got out unnoticed and managed to cross the Rhine.

No one who stayed in Germany was safe. Hunting for suspects went on for months, even years. Heine in October 1849 depicted the German people starting nervously in their enjoyment of nature or of home on hearing shots that killed their friends. Boerner, the Berlin student who was in such ecstasy in March, 1848, felt now as if he and his friends were on an old wreck in the darkness of night with the sea all around them. All the liberal parties were killed, together with the innocence and idealism of 1848.

Even the conservatives smiled at the irony of a reaction which brought back the worst mistakes of the old regime. When the Confederate Diet reopened in 1850, it reintroduced press censorship, with rigid control over each separate state; and it devoted an unusual amount of attention to the school system. In Prussia Friedrich Froebel's kindergartens were forbidden, for they were said to spread atheism and socialism, and Froebel's sister had advocated the advancement of women. Primary schools were taken over by the church, and special attention was given to teachers' loyalty. Teachers, in fact, were turned into black-uniformed masters, while the children were stultified with the deliberate hope that as adults they would feel politically incompetent. They were led to believe that parliamentary systems were a weakening form which let amateurs into government, while in their efficient monarchy they had a distinctively German type of state. The intellectuals too were harnessed to the Germanic ideal. The wonderful system of the German university which, since it practiced academic freedom, protected itself by picking very carefully the men who were to speak freely, began to be worked out. Instead of applying a property qualification to voting, this was now used, subtly, on professorships. After 1848 the techniques of controlling society by terror, flattery, and well-placed inefficiency developed rapidly. Most liberal movements were either killed or maimed, and only the uncompromising members of the Communist League, few as they were, were left as an opposition force. Marx considered this one of the gains of the revolutionary period.

One of the most famous prisoners after the third Baden revolution was Gottfried Kinkel, who had been a professor of art at the University of Bonn, almost the first man to secure university status for his subject. He married a woman whom he had saved from drowning in the Rhine, and before 1848 their soirées were famous for mixing princes, workers, artists, and middle class persons without distinction. When the revolution broke in Berlin, Kinkel led the parade of Bonn students to celebrate, and later he attended the democratic congress at Berlin, but he saw no fighting until he enlisted as a private in the 1849 struggles over the constitution. He had, however, forwarded to Struve a plan for organizing the revolt of the Rhineland, and it was this unburned piece of paper which earned for Kinkel his sentence in a civil prison. Such a sentence involved loss of civil rights and the chance to read and study during his term, and it shocked the conscience of all Germany that one of its learned men should be forced to labor with his hands in ignominy.

By February 1850, the government was ready to bring Kinkel from prison to Cologne, where he was to be tried, along with several other persons, including Carl Schurz *in absentia*, for an additional crime, that of having participated in the armed revolt. And here, haggard from the physical and mental strains of prison, he made such a powerful speech about the duty to defend democracy that the people who were in the courtroom thundered cheers and the court voted acquittal. This, however, did not exonerate Kinkel himself from his former sentence, and he was sent back to a prison near Berlin. In order to free him, young Carl Schurz traveled to Prussia on a false passport and finally succeeded in finding a jailer who thought Kinkel's sentence so shameful that he agreed to let the prisoner down by a rope to the street, where Schurz met him with a carriage and carried him off to England. Kinkel, unhappily, became conceited after the revolution and never justified the bright promise of his early years. But Carl Schurz, who "long before he had ever seen America, bore the spirit of the New World about with him in his heart," became the greatest of all the citizens America won from the struggles of 1848 in Europe.

Revolution in some form struck nearly every state in Germany either in 1848 or in 1849. In Bavaria it took an unusual character because the King's mistress, Lola Montez, had for a year or two been working for the liberal cause, and she was so unpopular that the Bavarian revolt was a demand for a return to the reactionary Catholic policy of her enemies.

Bavaria, anyway, seemed happier than most European countries, less pushed toward change. Land was held on easy tenure, the government expenses were small, there was full employment, and the King was patriarchal. Even the evils of priestcraft were checked by the kindly Bavarian spirit.

King Ludwig I was an art patron who had made Munich a famous capital by skimping on everything else. He bought no winter overcoats for himself and he underpaid all his civil servants. Lola's first interference in politics was to beg for higher salaries for teachers.

When the Catholic ministry, headed by Karl von Abel, refused to grant her citizenship, she was instrumental in bringing in the first protestant prime minister in Bavarian history, a man who set about reforming the administration of justice and improving the university curriculum, which could conveniently be done by dismissing the professors who had stood up for Abel.

The King swore his friendship with Lola was purely platonic. ("That makes his folly all the greater," commented the Prussian foreign minister.) Their companionship was seemingly devoted to reading Thomas à Kempis aloud to each other; and the King wrote poetry for her which he did not hesitate to publish. Though the Queen herself received Lola, solid Munich citizens were furious.

At the university, which became the center of trouble, a special student corps, the Alemannia, was formed to defend Lola by some students who were expelled from the Palatia corps for drinking with her and letting her try on their corps hat. All other students hated the Alemannia and petitioned to have it disbanded, a move which led to such an outbreak on February 9, 1848, that Lola had to find refuge in a church. The enraged King ordered the university closed, but he failed to realize how many Munich citizens lived off the spendings of the students. People whose business would have been spoiled forced him to reopen the school and dissolve the Alemannia.

Meanwhile, on February 12, Lola fled. But Munich was too aroused to be pacified by such a sacrifice. On March 6 the King granted a free press and responsibility of cabinet ministers, and promised to have the army sworn to the almost defunct Bavarian constitution. But cries for an immediate assembly kept coming. Rather than face this demand, the heartbroken King abdicated—on March 16—and Bavaria returned to its earlier, peaceful, conservative ways.

In the nineteenth century Lola Montez was universally excoriated. Metternich, exiled at the same time, congratulated himself that he did not have to ride to England on the same boat; and nowhere, save in her lover's lyrics or her own forthright letters to the London *Times*, did she find any apologist. The twentieth century has been more liberal, often inclined to idealize her because of her courage, affection, and liberalism. Unfortunately, she was uneducated, so her liberalism was half-baked; she was ambitious, having freely announced her intention of catching a king some years before her advent in Munich; and as for her courage, it too often showed itself with a riding whip, or by drinking champagne from her balcony when her students were howling in the streets. She forsook Europe for the gold coast of California, and died eventually in America, penniless and allegedly contrite.

Of all the 1848-1849 uprisings in Germany, possibly the best known is the one in Saxony for the simple reason that it involved Richard Wagner.

The government of the kingdom of Saxony was essentially as tyrannous as any other in Germany, but Leipzig, the biggest city in the kingdom, happened to be the center of the book trade, and therefore the home of an unusual number of intellectuals. By an unspoken agreement these literati did not oppose or criticize the Saxon regime but used Leipzig as a center to attack other German states, while the local authorities let them alone. It was an uneasy compromise. Saxony maintained many inhabitants it would have liked to be rid of were it not for the fear of hurting trade.

The death of Robert Blum, who had been a bookseller as well as theater cashier in Leipzig, before a firing squad in Vienna not only deprived Saxony of one of its great stabilizers but it made the common people feel betrayed and restless. During 1848 they had been fairly quiet, largely because of Blum's eloquence; but when the King of Saxony tried to keep the Saxon Diet from discussing the Frankfurt constitution—which Robert Blum had been working so hard for—and when on April 28 he ordered the Diet dissolved, the people were ready to rise. It was commonly believed that the King had promised to accept the Frankfurt constitution, indeed even had the proclamation to that effect in the press, when his mind was changed for him by Frederick William of Prussia. For it was on this date that Prussia offered military support to any German king who needed it in order to resist the common danger of the constitution.

The Saxon Diet did not separate, on April 30, without a loud cheer for the constitution; and on May 2 the Leipzig militia also voted for it unanimously.

Now Wagner was at that time conductor of the royal orchestra in Dresden, the capital, and he was dissatisfied with his position because it did not allow him time enough for creative work. It was, he tells us, his despair over art which led him into politics, and his pamphlet, *Art and Revolution*, which he wrote the following summer in Switzerland, is full of an account of the commercialism and sordid taste which were an artist's milieu in nineteenth-century Europe, a milieu, he said, only revolution could purify. "My business is to make a revolution wherever I go," he stated at one point. Still he feared the masses. He had worked with the party of progress not only because it was the party of the future but because it was the one which needed to be controlled—or so he said in a letter to his superior at court.

However, he did not make the Saxon revolution. He simply enjoyed it.

There was one other famous figure who had been haunting Europe during its year of revolutions and who here in Dresden got at last the chance to run one—Michael Bakunin. Bakunin was a Russian who was totally indifferent to the problems of German unity and the constitution; in fact, he felt that parliamentary democracy did not represent the people at all, a novel point of view for that period. His enemy was the Czar—and in so far as he had an ideal, it was to use a revolutionary Germany against that fountainhead of evil. But mostly he just loved the sound of battle against authority. In 1847 he wrote to Herwegh, "I wait upon my, or, if you prefer, our common wife—the Revolution. Only then shall we become happy; that is to say: we ourselves will be, if the whole earth is in flames."[2] Upon news of the first outbreak in Paris he had rushed to that city and earned from Caussidière the quip, "On the first day of a revolution he is a perfect treasure; on the second he ought to be shot." As soon as things calmed down, Flocon was instructed to give him money to get to Poland, where he and the French hoped he would find more excitement. Apparently he just happened to be in Dresden in the spring of 1849, though some people said it was because he had a nose to smell out coming trouble. Stephan Born (who had moved from Berlin to Leipzig to edit the new workers' paper which his clubs had set up) describes how Bakunin used to make Russian punch for his friends, with his coat off, his sleeves rolled up, his great lion's head sweating over the blue flames from the rum which seemed like the fires of hell. Rather than use water he extinguished his fire with Rhine wine, and the resulting concoction had the quickest effect of any alcohol that Born had ever tasted.

Bakunin was present at Wagner's last concert in Dresden, on April 1, of course at the risk of his life, for he was understandably wanted by several sets of police. Wagner conducted Beethoven's Ninth Symphony, a work which he had been the first to perform and for the recognition of which he had struggled hard. After it was over, Bakunin walked up to Wagner and remarked that when everything else was destroyed in the flames of the future, that work of art must be preserved, even at the cost of their lives.

On May 3 the citizens of Dresden stormed the arsenal, or tried to. Troops were called out, and also the militia, which had often been used to quell riots before. Wagner had just resigned from the latter force because he was pleased neither with "the standing army" nor "the recumbent militia." On this third of May, despite his bad opinion of them, the militia stood up and took the side of the people, even though their efforts were ineffective since the authorities had

---

[2] Quoted in Klein, *Der Vorkampf*, 98.

deprived them of ammunition. When the troops fired on the unarmed crowd, the people could reply only with stones. Many civilians were killed but the arsenal did not fall. That night the first barricades were erected, and the next day, May 4, Wagner, on his own initiative had posters printed for distribution to the army asking, "Are you with us against the foreign troops?" For what made the Saxon civilians really frantic, and they hoped it might incense their soldiers, too, was the thought of the Prussian army coming toward them. The appeal failed, because the Saxon troops had been issued too much wine to respond, though later in the fight whenever one was captured he was immediately released by the civilians on the theory that he did not really want to fight against his brothers, and in no case apparently did one of them break his parole.

On this same day, the King having fled at the behest of his cabinet who were afraid he might yield, a provisional government was formed in Dresden. Its inauguration was a ceremony swearing the people to defend the Frankfurt Constitution, amid bell-ringing and more barricade-building. And in order to delay the Prussian arrival, citizens tore up as much railroad track as they could.

The provisional government consisted of a triumvirate, no one of whom knew much about the conduct of revolutions, so they leaned heavily on Bakunin. He organized everything—he deployed men, arranged for their relief, scoured the cafés for Polish officers and attended to a thousand details in his sleepless days and nights. Wagner's job, so far as he had any, was supervising the convoys that brought in provisions and reinforcements from the countryside, which was enthusiastic in its support of the city people. In fact, before the battle was over, help and militia were streaming in from all parts of Germany, all the men who wanted desperately one more chance to fight for their precious Frankfurt constitution.

The Prussian forces kept growing in number too, and by May 9 the defenders were worn out. Their eyelids were red, their voices strained. Bakunin proposed blowing up the town hall where the stores of powder were kept, and themselves with it, as one last gesture of defiance; but the provisional government more cautiously ordered the powder to be removed, and the church bells to ring the signal for retreat, three times three. It was the wild intention of the defenders to retreat to Chemnitz or Freiberg and carry on the fight from there. Peasants provided wagons and shelter as they tried to move their forces across the countryside, but nothing could prevent the rapid evaporation of their fighting effectives, and soon the provisional government itself was captured. Wagner escaped to Switzerland, where he became "entirely an artist" again. Stephan Born also was lucky enough to reach Switzerland, where he became a professor.

Four years later the Saxon government was still trying insurgents from this rebellion, and they deemed it clemency to commute a death sentence to life imprisonment. Bakunin was tried in these courts but he was turned over to the Czarist police and exiled to Siberia, whence he escaped around the world in time for the next batch of European revolutions, in 1870.

PART III · THE AUSTRIAN EMPIRE

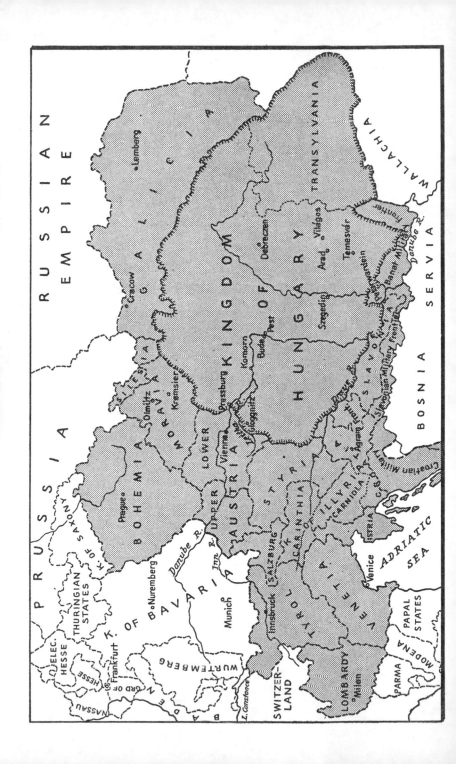

X

The China of Europe

ACCORDING to what little Western Europe knew of the Austrian Empire in the early nineteenth century, it was supposed to be as impenetrable and reactionary as China, to which it was occasionally compared. Its only European rival in absolutism was Russia, and even Russia did not have so many dissatisfied races, classes, and nationalities. When the citizens of Vienna revolted in 1848, they thought they were copying the Paris of that year, yet they would have had to skip two revolutions and go back to the France of 1789 to duplicate the social conditions they wished to change. At the same time, so many new drives had come into being in the nineteenth century, such as nationalism, that after they had won their social reforms, they began to wonder if those were what they had wanted after all, and they did not quite know what to ask for next. There was, indeed, no single system of either politics or ethics that would embrace the many divergent wishes of the subjects of the Empire.

At the beginning of 1848, Ferdinand, the absolute emperor, was feebleminded, epileptic, physically impotent.

Some wit said that the governmental machine had been wound up like a clock by Ferdinand's father, Francis, and in the thirteen years since his death it had not completely run down. Francis had been dubious about allowing Ferdinand to sit on the throne, but he did not feel that he, of all rulers, could upset the principle of legitimacy. So on his deathbed, he entrusted his son to the care of his friend and chief minister, the famous Prince Clemens Metternich, who promised Francis never to abandon Ferdinand.

It might have seemed intolerable to a nation of thirty-eight millions to be under the absolute rule of a half-wit, but as a matter of fact the new emperor was very popular. "Der Gütige" he was called by his loyal Viennese, who trusted his friendliness and adopted the legend that he was the victim of his bad advisers. He was indeed watched by his friends and family as if by jailers, because they knew he would sign anything anybody asked—though it was easy to govern, he remarked, the hard job was writing one's name—and whatever he signed was law. Several times during the revolutionary days various groups were able to break through his chaperonage and come away with his incontestable, though painfully lettered, signature on their documents. Before the revolution, the court was more concerned with keeping Ferdinand out of trouble than with governing Austria, and they were always afraid that he would surrender privileges which his successor would regret. While a mentally competent king might make concessions to his people, they felt, the trustees of an incompetent one ought not to give away a single unnecessary tittle, or allow him to do so. There could be no worse attitude with which to face a revolution.

Under old Emperor Francis things had been different. Though he was not popular, and would never have been called *gütig*, he was a demon for work, and kept his country going almost singlehanded. By seven every morning he was at his desk, having heard Mass, ready to read the reports which his spies and secret police had prepared for him—including copies they had made of the diplomatic pouches of foreign envoys and even private letters of his family and high officials. Then he was ready to meet them. He had no cabinet, only separate offices for war, justice, administration, and foreign affairs, and he wrote instructions to each department separately, so that no one but himself knew what the results of one department's act would be on another. Things were made even worse by the etiquette of absolutism which forbade an Imperial and Royal Majesty to give reasons for his decisions. To explain might have been a step in the direction of democracy—does a German father explain commands to his children? Therefore, the bureaus had no way of knowing whether their plans were vetoed for big or little reasons, for policy or for technicalities—and they had no basis at all for revising their arrangements or for making later decisions.

The safety valve of this regime lay in the right of every subject, however humble, to appeal directly to the throne, either in writing or at special weekly audiences. No grievance or injustice, no favor, was too small to be worthy His Majesty's attention—a conscript wishing to be relieved of service could explain his case, or a landlord who wished to buy a few square yards of ground from his tenant (since the land laws forbade the diminution of peasant holdings). It had been very hard to like Francis in spite of his conscientiousness, for he was cold, indifferent to art, science, indeed, any form of enthusiasm; opposed to industry, opposed to machinery because hard work seemed healthier for the minds and bodies of his subjects. He refused to allow steam railroads to be laid down in his territory, though a few rails were laid for horse-drawn vehicles which could carry steam after his death.

Naturally, poor Ferdinand could not hope to keep up his father's pace. Under his regime the departments of government kept moving like animals whose brains have been removed— -the police, the army, the censorship officials. Even Metternich and the governing arch-dukes stuck to their own duties. Metternich, the Minister of Foreign Affairs, and Count Francis Kolowrat, the Minister of Finance, the two most powerful men at court, hated each other to the point of not speaking. What they had to say to each other they wrote. Thus those who had power at their disposal were at cross purposes and there was no one in the whole Empire to take final responsibility.

Of course, it was said that Metternich was the real power behind the throne, and perhaps he might have been more of one in 1848 if he had not been seventy-three years old, getting deaf and talkative, more and more inclined to live in the past, hashing over to his listeners stories of the great days when he had outwitted Napoleon. For forty years he had been the most important person in Austria, but he had the temperament of a diplomat rather than a statesman. His greatness lay in weighing advantages, devising compromises, holding down and covering up the new passions of the nineteenth century.

To his contemporary opponents burning with their new zeal for freedom, Metternich seemed the incarnation of evil. Everything they stood for he opposed and they had the same trouble attacking him that true believers always have with cynics—for Metternich had a refined dislike of abstract principles, principles which so often lead to violence, though he had a well-thought-out *Weltanschauung* of his own. He wanted to keep peace in Europe and to hold Austria together, and he knew what his excited enemies forgot—that nationalism would break up his conglomerate empire, and that democracy was more of an intoxicant than its lumbering old form would stand. Modern historians, on the other hand, are apt to like Metternich, for they see the agonies that came out of nationalism and the weakness that sometimes followed democracy. Also, they fall victims to his personal charm. His real faults were great, for he lacked compassion, but his sense of irony kept him from seeming nasty and often made him appear quite as clever as his twentieth-century judges.

Yet, even by his own pragmatic standards, he failed to meet what he saw coming. He had as much power as anyone in the monarchy, and more brains; therefore it is more his fault than anyone else's that 1848 found the people he had governed "emasculated and demoralized, ignorant both of their rights and their duties," in the words of the American Chargé d'Affaires. Furthermore, in the circles in which he moved he left no honest and able successor. At his departure, the men left at court lacked firmness, kindness, honesty or even knowledge, qualities any one of which would have saved the country unbearable bloodshed and financial disorder. Even a little of Metternich's irony might have helped, but this he was unable to transmit any more than his long view, suave manners, and great ability.

There was, however, one person in imperial circles who knew what she wanted, and that was the Archduchess Sophia, sometimes called "the only man at court." She was the wife of Ferdinand's brother and heir, a prince who, though not quite so deplorable as the Emperor, was still so subnormal that even Sophia did not look forward to his accession to the throne. All her hopes were centered in her sons, especially her eldest, Francis Joseph, who was to turn eighteen in September 1848. (Later in life she had a great part in getting her second son, Maximilian, crowned as Emperor of Mexico, a prodigious and ill-considered venture which shows again what strength lay in her maternal determination.) In early 1848 she was already wondering how soon she could hoist her Franzi to the throne of Austria and even consulted Metternich, though not her own husband, on the possibility of getting Ferdinand to abdicate and her husband to renounce his rights. Metternich told her she would have to wait at least until Francis Joseph came of age. From her point of view the revolution, in March, broke just six months too soon.

Sophia's passionate desire made her seek help from any quarter, and for that reason she played with the Viennese liberals. She remembered that her father, the King of Bavaria, had given a constitution to his people without curtailing his own will, so she felt that in Vienna a few gracious concessions would increase her popularity without cutting off Franzi's future power. Perhaps the reform she looked forward to the most was the resignation of Metternich,

who did not enjoy her temperament and who besides had sworn to
look after the interests of poor Ferdinand. When the revolution
arrived and could not be stopped, Sophia's bitterness was overwhelming, but until that time the liberal party counted her their
friend at court.

Beneath this pinnacle at the top of society the Empire's 38,000,-
000 subjects were arranged in varicolored striations. They were
set off from each other by race and by class, and at the time we are
speaking of both sets of division seemed more important to a man's
life than they ever had before. Hapsburg territory had grown
slowly, and in the main peacefully, through centuries when religion
or dynastic connections seemed more vital than did race, for land
had come easily under the sway of the ruler who bore the title of
emperor. Though the Holy Roman Empire had died under Napoleon, the Austrian monarch was still, in 1848, the only emperor
in Europe (though his title was aped later by the sovereigns of
Germany, France, and England). He ruled over eight kingdoms,
including Lombardy, Hungary, and Bohemia, and eight other territories bearing such less pretentious titles as duchy or grand duchy.

The German-speaking Viennese knew little of the non-German
provinces. Galicia, they knew, was completely under military control, especially since the Polish revolt of 1846; Bohemia was half-
Germanized; the groans of Lombardy seemed only part of the
habitual and fruitless emotionalism of an Italy divided among many
corrupt rulers. As for Hungary—if Austria was like China, Hungary was like Tibet. Hardly anyone except the Magyars themselves
realized the vigor of their local political life or the determination
rising among Hungarians to revivify their ancient constitution.
Yet all these lands had their own pride, their own history, in some
cases their own religion to which they were far more deeply attached
than to any possible conception of Austria as a nation. The Hapsburgs would even have it so; their best trick in mastering the country
seemed to be that they could use one faction to trump the other.
The late Emperor Francis remarked, "My peoples are strange to
each other and that is all right. They do not get the same sickness
at the same time. . . . From their antipathy will be born order, and
from the mutual hatred, general peace." In 1848 they all got sick,
yet as the Emperor had foretold, not with the same sickness. The

currents of the year—democracy, liberalism, nationalism—were so various that nearly every Hapsburg subject was touched by one of them. Yet, out of their antipathy was born again a certain sort of order, a certain uneasy peace. Francis in his narrow view had been right.

If the Vienna of 1847 cared little about the other parts of the Empire, it defined sharply the class divisions inside its own walls. At the top were the nobles who considered themselves the only group worth noticing. The human race starts with barons, said one of them. Then there were the big businessmen who wanted to buy their way into the human race; the little businessmen; the poor but proud intellectuals; the students who were still poorer and still prouder; and the workers who were poor and had always been very, very humble.

The philosophy of the Hapsburgs was like that of a tyrannical father who is ruthless to his adolescent children even though he may indulge his babies. Austrian intellectuals were kept under daily supervision, but the peasants were given a gentle if unimaginative justice, while in the cities amusement prices were kept low by law. Vienna was accounted the gayest capital in Europe, where Styrian capons and Strauss waltzes were supposed to keep the burghers from thinking about the adventures which were opening up to their brothers in France and the Rhineland under the capitalistic system.

In a large and satisfied family, the dust kicked up by a few obstreperous members is particularly noticeable. The classes in Austria whose grievances might possibly become vocal—and the class revolt which started in Vienna was separate from the nationality revolts such as broke out in the rest of the Empire—were the industrialists who felt cramped by absolutism, that section of the middle class which was not siphoned off into the bureaucracy,[1] the new class of factory workers about whom the regime had hardly begun to think, and the students and intellectuals.

The nineteenth century opened up so many new ways to make money that Austrian industrialists could not help wanting to share in the profits. As is always the case, government was slow to catch

[1] Of the twelve million non-peasant subjects of the Empire, it was figured three-fifths had some vested interest in the maintenance of the existing government—they were either nobles whose privileges were protected, served in the army, were members of the enormous bureaucracy, lived on pensions, or were members of the clergy whose revenues were guaranteed.

up with technology (is this not a common criticism of our twentieth century?)—in this case extremely hostile to free enterprise. The Empire was protected by a tariff so high that it practically cut off all competing imports, and there was a system of licensing small businesses so that there would not be more tailors, butchers, or leather workers than the market could support. Both of these measures were designed to protect industry, but the new liberalism was against them. And, incidentally, the licensing system made it easy for the government to control any outspoken tradesman either by revoking his license or by sending him a nearby competitor.

Businessmen wanted elbow room. They wanted a government that would give them sound finance, that would build roads, railroads, and encourage commerce. Instead of this, every step they took was tangled up by the bureaucrats and studied by spies.

It was not very easy to grumble in Metternich's Austria, but in the 1840's the upper middle classes found a few vents. One was in the provincial assemblies, or Estates. Money was being made in Austria, but there were relatively few opportunities for investment. So many big bankers and railway men bought land in the country and earned the right to sit in the Estates.

Now as in other countries, the Austrian Estates were a holdover from ancient times for which recent monarchs had little use. Their job was to "consider" but not to disapprove measures of the crown, especially financial measures, which meant that practically their office was limited to apportioning the taxes in their own districts (there was no "Estates General" or "United Diet" in Hapsburg territory), or to regulating the internal local affairs.[2] Under Emperor Francis, at a time of famine, the estates of one province ventured to petition the crown for a temporary lowering of the tariff on wheat. The Emperor punished such effrontery by refusing relief to that province even after he came around to helping the others.

[2] The public debt doubled in nominal value, quadrupled in effective value between 1815 and 1840, during twenty-five years of peace. This was contrary to all nineteenth-century theories of sound finance—but matters were handled with such secrecy that no one knew exactly how weak or how strong the central bank was. European liberals made a great point of the weakness of Austrian finance—but only in the first weeks of 1848, and then among the little people, not the big, did a movement start to turn paper into coin all over the Empire.

It was known that government security prices were kept up artificially at great expense to the state, but to the enrichment of some individuals, just as the state kept the ownership of one unprofitable railroad, while the lines that were making money were turned over to private enterprise.

During the 1840's, the Estates of Lower Austria, the province containing Vienna, met periodically in that city and, perhaps as a symptom of a new age coming, discussed rather freely such questions as agricultural credit, representation in their body for towns instead of just landowning nobility, and even their right to advise on new laws.

The government, less ferocious than in Francis' day, watched all these doings with the utmost suspicion. Newspapers were never allowed to report the debates, and the members were given the attention of personal spies. A certain Baron Doblhoff was under special surveillance. Though a baron he was willing to talk to members of the middle class, and used to give parties for the members of the Estates to which businessmen and professors were invited. It was the first time in Vienna that the two classes had ever met on terms of social equality. Doblhoff's body servant received orders to spy on all his mail, note all his visitors, and listen to his conversation. The servant, who was an old soldier, broke down under this assignment and confessed to his master. Being a nobleman, Doblhoff had the courage to demand angrily an explanation from the authorities, but all the satisfaction he could get was to learn that an archduke, one of the governing council, had personally ordered this information.

For informal discussion, the lawyers, businessmen, professors and even a few civil servants in Vienna founded a reading club. The police granted a charter to this group once in 1842 when Metternich was on vacation, and though he disapproved of it he did not break it up when he came back. Instead, the police kept lists of members (many people were afraid to belong since it might damage their careers) and lists of the books in their library. Nevertheless, all prominent foreigners who visited Vienna were welcomed by this group and pumped for news, ideas, and literature. The club's opinions were decidedly independent. When the United States Consul proposed a toast to Metternich at one meeting, he was met with stony silence.

It was when they tried to reach beyond their own circle that they were frustrated. They gave one public lecture—on prisons—and met with such a popular ovation that they were forbidden to hold any more. Their next attempt was to establish a soup kitchen in the depression of 1847 (in this way they were acting like the Democratic Club in Berlin) and though they were not actually forbidden to do so, their efforts could not begin to reach the tremendous poverty of the capital city.

For the situation of the factory workers was so miserable that— as the American Chargé d'Affaires put it—any change at all would be a change for the better. The United States, he smugly added, had never known a class so degraded and he believed that the western frontier would prevent the formation of one for centuries to come. By opposing railroads and steam engines, the Hapsburgs tried to prevent the formation of a class they instinctively felt would be dangerous, but in spite of their preferences there were 469 locomotives, 76 steamboats, and 469 stationary steam engines within their domain. Vienna became a center of machine making, at first repairing machines imported from England, then copying them. But the handcraftsmen did not enjoy being turned into mass producers. They hated their machines and they hated big shops with a raw hatred devoid of social theory. Apparently, the ideas of the French working class never got through to them, and they joined the revolution because they were hungry and angry, not because they wanted socialism.

Of course, there were no trade unions in Vienna, and as late as 1835 the simple efforts of a few printers' apprentices to form a club to make a sick-benefits pool was forbidden on the grounds it was not needed. By 1842 a second effort was successful and the club had 500 members in 1847—but of course this was almost nothing in comparison with the clubs, newspapers, and free discussion which workers enjoyed in Paris or Berlin. The Viennese workers acted instinctively with such perfect revolutionary form that Karl Marx had great hopes of them and spent a week in Vienna in September 1848 at the end of the revolutionary summer. But when he met them he was discouraged by their intellectual backwardness and decided they were not ready for the social revolution after all.

The 1847 depression was no kinder to Austria than to other countries. Even in 1846 there was an alarming increase of robbery, murder, and beggary, and factory girls began hanging around the glacis which separated the inner city from the suburbs, carrying benches and pillows with them to make prostitution easier. By the winter of 1847 casual travelers could feel that gayety had been killed in Vienna. A grim story passed around of a widow who killed one child and fed him to his brothers and sisters, at the same time that a banker gave a dinner featuring strawberries which cost £1 apiece. As prices rose from the bad harvest, a factory worker could not even keep his family in potatoes on his average wages—while the numbers of shoemakers, cabinetmakers, and tailors who were forced out of business by the commercial panic only added to the press of people looking for factory work. The suburbs of Vienna in 1847 were filled with people so dirty that their rags stuck to their bodies. Their houses were small and smelly, with wet walls and broken windowpanes, and were filled with broken furniture. Even the servant girls and apprentices who lived in the homes of their employers were commonly given cold kitchens or unheated attics to sleep in, and they lived more like slaves than the factory workers, for they were underfed, overworked, forced to carry heavy loads of wood and water, and paid practically nothing.

When the authorities had to raise the official price of bread and meat in 1847, this decree seemed so explosive that the garrison was strengthened at the same time.

The Hapsburgs dreaded the workers as if they were eight-year-old children, careless and destructive maybe, but not a real threat to authority. The intellectuals, however, were like fifteen-year-olds, burning with dangerous curiosity and a still more dangerous feeling that their time of submission was nearly over. But the rulers believed fatuously that they could keep bad thoughts away.

Therefore, every single book, paper, or even advertisement printed inside the Empire had to be approved by the censor. In Vienna, twelve men were able to handle this work, which shows how little printing went on. (In 1839 less than six per cent of the books in the catalogue of the Leipzig book fair were Austrian, though Austria was the biggest German state.) If the subject concerned the army, church, or high politics, it had to have a second scrutiny from the institution covered, or the ministry.

The importation of foreign books was so strictly watched that even the Academy of Sciences had difficulty getting books from the outside world. Whenever a traveler entered the realm with a dangerous book in his baggage, customs officials sealed it.

All kinds of subjects were forbidden—criticism of the state theater equally with discussion of state policy. In Mozart's "Don Juan" the chorus "Let Freedom Live" had to be changed to "Let Pleasure Live"; while Rossini's march for the newly elected Pope,

Pius IX, could not be played in 1846 because His Holiness was thought of as a liberal. A history of the Napoleonic War might state that the French advanced but not that the Austrians retreated. And since one censor felt it a slight upon the great ally Russia to read that the Cossacks rode *small* horses, the passage was altered to read that the Cossacks rode horses. Even such a simple joke as, "What is the way into your bedroom, miss?" "Through church, sir," suggested an affront to religion to one literal-minded official."

It was much easier to smuggle than to print something in Austria, so a great deal of effort went into getting news from abroad. Some of the frontier officials winked at book importation, and Viennese booksellers were always running risks far greater than any profit they could hope to make in their clever and heroic schemes to spread forbidden wares. (Their only public effort was rebuffed. In 1845 they ventured a petition for the relaxation of censorship which Metternich refused to accept, saying that the right of private citizens to petition was not recognized and that he did not know what a committee was in Austria.) As soon as a private citizen got his hands on a forbidden piece of literature, it was the duty of no particular official to inquire how he got it, so in intellectual circles it was quite safe and fashionable to quote from the *Grenzboten* and assume that everyone present had read it. The *Grenzboten*, or *News From The Border*, was considered one of the best papers in all Germany, though it was specially angled for Viennese eyes by some young Austrian editors in Leipzig. As for the *Allgemeine Zeitung*, the leading German paper, its prestige was such that officials hardly dared to forbid it to come into the country even when its news was contradicted by the official Vienna press, so that a few lucky Viennese could learn something about Europe in their cafés.[3]

Austrians who were determined to express themselves usually managed to get their books printed in Germany, particularly in

---

[3] Another possible source of news for Vienna might have been from cities within the Empire like Prague or Budapest, for the censorship was lighter everywhere than in the capital. Prague published the only paper in the realm that carried a decent amount of world news. (It made a particular feature, for one thing, of the miseries of Ireland, which everybody but the censor understood to mean Bohemia itself, where the agrarian problem, as well as the sense of foreign domination, were similar.) And one young Viennese looking back later said that he and his friends could have listened to free words coming out of Pest, for Kossuth was writing there during most of the 1840's—but before 1848 Hungary seemed too far away from Vienna. Viennese ears were cocked to the West.

Leipzig where a regular colony of Austrian expatriates wrote for the contraband trade. This began back in the reign of Francis when a professor at Vienna got his manuscript back from the Austrian censor with such absurd and extensive suggestions, that he took the book to Germany and had the whole thing printed, censor's marginalia and all. Later on Metternich hired special spies to keep track of the Austrian thinkers in Leipzig.

Austria had no martyrs before 1848, which was the reproach cast against her by a Germany boasting that historian Dahlmann preferred to lose his chair, that poet Arndt and journalist Struve chose prison and poet Herwegh, exile, rather than change the words they had written. But even the most supercilious Germans had to admit that by the late 1840's the Austrian intellect had revived.

The censorship of mails was even more bumbling, picayune, and rigid than that of books. Clerks worked all night to open, read, and copy letters of diplomats and bankers, archdukes and suspected liberals. Using very thin hot knives, they cut through sealing wax and in the case of important suspects like Mazzini, they kept a forged seal on hand. If the process took too much time sometimes, the date on the letter would be moved up to conceal the delay. Even private couriers of foreign governments were bribed. When the Prussian diplomatic pouch reached the Austrian border, it was met by officials who operated on it in the coach itself while the horses galloped at high speed toward Vienna. Next morning the Prussian envoy and Metternich in the Hofburg read the same dispatch at the same time.

Highest rates of pay went to code breakers in this service, but all concerned were well paid—and incessantly watched by the police. No public acknowledgment of their services could ever be made and they all had to pretend to be doing something else.

The police were ready to watch anybody, of course, as witness the case of Baron Doblhoff. They gathered their information from mistresses, waiters, visitors to brothels, needy nobles and even, it was charged with some show of evidence, from the Jesuit confessors who were supposed to pay unto Caesar this price for the privilege of operating in the country. (The Jesuits had been expelled by Emperor Joseph, recalled by Francis who wanted their conservative influence, and were currently the anathema of liberals. Schuselka, a leader of the Austrian colony in Leipzig, considered them the worst single evil of the Austrian state, especially because of their throttle hold on secondary education.)

With all their snooping, the police were more of a nuisance to the public than a prop to the regime. Intrigued by all the small points of their detective work, they overlooked important currents of opinion, and in 1848 proved even more helpless than their Paris prototypes.

For in spite of everything, political thought was loosening up, especially at the University of Vienna. A student caught reading a forbidden book was not only supposed to be expelled, he was forbidden to matriculate at any other school. Yet, the nine fraternities founded between 1843 and 1847 busily circulated Dahlmann's studies of constitutions and the works of Rousseau. Professors' morals and ideas were constantly checked, and the rules stated that they might not treat as controversial any subject not so treated in the prescribed books—yet they invited students to their homes to discuss the new ideas in small groups, and lent the contents of their illicit libraries unstintedly to their student friends. In public lectures students cocked their ears for double meanings, and were as pleased by a hint of freedom as a modern burlesque audience is by an allusion to sex. By 1846 enthusiasm was so strong that the police decided it would be wiser not to prosecute when Professor Hye publicly compared to murder the destruction of a small state by a large one—a very pointed reference to the recent absorption of the tiny republic of Cracow, the last vestige of free Poland, by Austria.

There were about two thousand students at the university, many of them sons of peasants, many of them desperately poor. Some of them lived in unheated rooms on bread and water—and there was a famous case of one who had no lodging at all, only the sky in summer and some farmer's haystack in winter. Others came from the middle classes, but there were no aristocrats. The Austrian nobility were either taught at home or attended the Theresanium, a special college to train diplomats and army officers, requiring for admission that a boy be a baron or better.

The university must have been alive, or else the students would not have taken over the revolution as they did in 1848.[4] Especially

───

[4] Though one graduate complained that the system of regular examinations at the

the medical school was famous, partly because Metternich loved science and failed to realize the connections between science and the modern spirit. It was, therefore, left the freest of any college in the university and attracted students from other countries who brought with them the taste of liberalism. For another thing the clinical work in the Vienna hospitals gave the medical professors a fine chance to teach students individually and discuss social conditions which showed up there at their worst.

Foreign students as a general thing were not encouraged any more than Austrian subjects were allowed to study abroad. In most cases certificates from a non-Austrian university were invalid. Only the Saxons of Transylvania, the eastern tip of the Empire, were issued passports to study in other German universities, for their ancestors had been induced to colonize the East, centuries before, by promises that their ties with the home country should never be cut off.

The police tried to watch extra-curricular activities as carefully as the contents of lectures, but they had a hard time keeping up with the students. Gymnastics and mountain climbing were officially dangerous, of course, because they were part of the German nationalist program. Old Jahn had started his *Turnverein* movement in Germany after the Napoleonic wars with a double purpose, and when Hans Kudlich as a student joined one of these gymnastic groups in Vienna, he said he could actually feel his German sentiments growing strong with his muscles and his will.

The student fraternities, when they came along in the 1840's, were even more dangerous than the gymnastic groups, for the boys not only climbed mountains and read books together, but kept up correspondence with students in other German universities. The University of Vienna was passionately pro-German.[5]

Most startling of all the students' activities were their efforts to reach the workers. They began to make friends with the working class systematically in the years before 1848, going into their homes and taverns, trying to help them to an understanding of their problems.

---

end of every semester, prescribed by the rules, prevented the formation of truly creative or deeply educated men.

[5] When Schuselka, the most famous Austrian pamphleteer, went into exile in 1842 before the first fraternity was formed at Vienna, and ran into his first student society at Jena, he wept for his lost student days at Vienna where he had never had that much fun or that much sense of purpose.

Thus, when 1848 rolled around, all kinds of people had begun to talk about reform, from Archduchess Sophia down through the estates, the businessmen, the university, and even those workers whom the students and the reading society had been able to reach. Nobody had acted, however, and no one quite realized how different action would be from words.

Vienna, they were all sure, was to lead the Empire. If they could only get a constitution, like France, and reforms like France, then Austria would move ahead like France and become the same sort of country. The reformers were German in blood, from the Archduchess down to the students, and they all assumed they were being generous in offering to get for other races the same liberties they were asking for themselves. Thus, in Prague, in the first flush of revolutionary excitement, Germans and Czechs worked out a common platform. Yet, it was only a few days before that the two races had split hopelessly because the Czechs went on to demand autonomy, to the Germans' great surprise and chagrin.

The truth was, four great races were coming into national self-consciousness under the Hapsburg dominion. Germans were the governing race, but there were important bodies of Hungarians and Italians who did not want to be governed by Germans any more, and half the Emperor's subjects were Slavs. However, so many of these were peasants, and the rest were divided into such small groups (except in Bohemia) that they could do little more than echo the cries for nationhood which the master races were screaming for loudly.

Vienna was a German city. It felt itself as much a part of Germany as any town on the Rhine. And this put the German population of the Empire in the most difficult position of any of the three master races. At least, the Italians and Hungarians knew what they wanted, independence from Vienna. But the pan-Germans were unwilling to give up either form of possible greatness, the unity of the great German fatherland as the Frankfurt professors saw it, or their own position as the "German soul" of the Austrian Empire whose mission it was to civilize the other races. Without these Germans, Germany would be incomplete (as Hitler reminded them ninety years later when the *Anschluss* was consummated). Without them, too, Austria would fall apart, and they were not ready for that. The dramatist Hebbel described their dilemma vis-à-vis other

Germans as if two people who wanted to kiss each other wanted to turn their backs on each other at the same time.

Their dilemma might have made them sympathetic to the problems of the other races, but instead the German Austrians seem to have ignored them. For one thing they were not encouraged to travel or see Austria first. "Do you think the Empire is a dovecote where everyone can fly around as he pleases?" Hans Kudlich was asked by a police official when he applied for permission to go home for his vacation from the University of Vienna by a slightly longer route than he had taken on the way up. He had been sick and wanted to walk home, with some mountain climbing for his health. But even if they had been allowed to get about more, Austrian Germans would still have learned little from the peoples whom they were, after all, out to teach, not be taught by. Their ears were tuned to Western Germany, where the program of a liberal and united Germany was being broadcast with all the two Gagerns' learning and pathos.

Of course, these liberal mentors copied *their* ideas from France. It took the Frankfurt Assembly a year of storm and stress to decide that the French ideas did not work for their territory, that they preferred power to freedom. In Austria the French ideas filtered through German minds, were at *two* removes from reality.[6] This misconception is what brought drama to the Austrian revolu-

[6] Cribbing of French ideas by Austrian liberals shows up most amusingly in the Austrians' attitude toward Poland and Italy. The French, of course, were strong for Polish and Italian independence. Even though parts of Poland and Italy were under their own emperor, it took a revolution, with the possible threat of having to put their ideas into action, to make the liberals of both Frankfurt and Vienna think up reasons why it would be better for Poles and Lombards to remain subject to the enlightened domination of Germans.

In 1847, Franz Schuselka, a pamphleteer, whose works on Austria, written in exile, were smuggled in and widely read inside that country, described the Austria he would like to see. He called himself *one of the few* who held the entire Empire to be his fatherland, and even he excepted Galicia and Lombardy. His point was that the Slav burden which Austrian Germans were called upon to carry was too heavy. In order to increase the proportion of German-speaking Austrians, he was in favor of giving Galicia to a reconstituted Poland. He also felt that Poland's years of struggle to become a nation entitled her to sympathy. Italians also seemed an unassimilable race; he believed the Hapsburgs would be stronger without Lombardy. (This was, incidentally, Lord Palmerston's opinion, in the British Foreign Office.) Himself a German from Bohemia, Schuselka felt his Czech neighbors would make loyal Austrians, and he would give short shrift to the national aspirations of Croats, Serbs, Roumanians and other groups scattered through the Empire.

But, in 1848, when Schuselka became a member of the liberal Diet, with the power to treat with the various provinces, it occurred to him sharply how dangerous it would be for Lombardy to fall under French influence, or Galicia under Russian.

tion. The radicals went right ahead copying Paris, telling themselves they were fighting the worst absolutism in Europe, the worst
censorship, the most stringent economic controls, until they ran
smack into other problems they had never calculated. These problems came from the peculiar nature of the Austrian Empire; the
doctrinaires could have studied them but did not. The court and
the army always knew they were running an empire; Vienna forgot,
in her struggle against that court and army, that she was not, like
Paris, the only spot of political importance in a homogeneous
country.

XI

Student Government in Vienna

No ONE in Vienna believed that the capital would get through the 1848 epidemic of revolution unscathed as it had the 1830 outbreak. Still, even after they heard about the revolt in Paris, the Viennese could not imagine just how to begin. Early in March they began to crowd the cafés for the sake of a look at a newspaper which might give them a clue for action. Meanwhile, paper money fell thirty per cent and banks which formerly did business through two windows had to open ten to change paper into gold. Meat prices rose again, and a thousand men were added to the secret police force.

Out of this general uneasiness the liberal party began to pluck up courage. The businessmen's association was the first, taking the small dare of asking the government for expansion of credit. (The year 1848 was the last time that business could seem radical.) Everyone watched to see what would happen. The Council of State condemned this action as a matter of routine, but when no one was actually punished, other people's bravery increased.

The best hopes of the liberals up to this point had rested in the Lower Austrian Estates, the provincial assembly which met in Vienna. Its scheduled meeting day was moved up to March 13 to answer the excitement, and everyone prepared to present all grievances to this body in the hope that it could ask for a great deal with impunity. Its own committee, too, was busy preparing a list of modest concessions to beg from the crown.

The idea of a student petition may have begun as a joke in an inn, but it soon got to be the most serious business of the entire university. On March 9 forty men from all the fraternities met, swore an oath of brotherhood, called each other "du," and pledged loyalty to the German fatherland. A group of them, medical and engineering students, met secretly at night after that, posting sentries against police intrusion, and made a draft of a student petition whose main point was abolition of censorship together with freedom of teaching. They worded it carefully and had a sharp debate on whether to provoke the authorities by using the word "liberty."

Since their blood was up, they decided it would be worth it to their own morale to publish this almost unheard word.

To speak of freedom had often cost students of the Empire dear. The least punishment these young men could expect was revocation of their permission to live in Vienna. They must also have remembered those Prague students who, some years before, had been inducted into the army as common soldiers and required to do the most despicable labor, hauling baggage trains. Nor was the regime softening with the times—for in January 1848, the same punishment was given the Milanese students who started the tobacco riots in Lombardy.

In the face of such possibilities, a student meeting was publicly called for Sunday morning, March 12.

The police were worried but wished to act tactfully, so they asked the rector of the university whether he would like their help to rule the meeting. The rector was convinced that if the police came, the meeting would end in a massacre, so he promised instead that he and the other professors would go and try to quiet the young men.

On Sunday morning the students first went to Mass, where they listened to a sermon by their theology professor, Anton Füster. Füster was one of those excitable radicals whom the church has often attracted into its work with young people or into heretical fringes, and almost as often cast out later. Füster was a huge priest of enormous energy, opposed to celibacy of the clergy,[1] tireless in leading the young men whom he idealized and in whose company he spent the happiest hours of his life. The March days were like a shot of adrenalin to his already energetic disposition, so that when the authorities asked him to change his text for this particular Sunday, he told them a sermon could not be altered at the last minute. In church he told his eager hearers that truth would conquer, that better times would come, and he exhorted them to act with courage and to hope. Frantically, the students streamed from church to the Aula, the great hall of the university, where someone read the

[1] There was a strong movement among Austrian clergy to change the dogmas of Rome. In advocating married clergy and the use of the vernacular in church, Füster was not alone. A body of Catholic clergy in Hungary voted for these reforms during the revolution. The danger that the Austrian church might actually secede from Rome was apparently so great that Pope Pius IX believed it would happen if papal troops fought against Austria in the war to free Italy, and this was one of the reasons which kept the papacy at peace during 1848—although moral reasons were probably even stronger in Pius' mind.

petition for freedom. The moment it was finished a great cry for pens rose up and the whole audience crowded around the desk to sign the petition. The professors could not do anything with them except that finally Professor Hye (the one who had spoken out for Cracow two years before) got the students to give the document into his care. He and another professor had to swear to take it that very evening to the Emperor and to report to the Aula at another meeting early the next morning.

Etiquette at the palace had broken down so far that the professors were indeed received that very evening. His Majesty accepted the petition and graciously replied that he would take it under consideration.

The professors realized that to the students this reply was as bad as an outright refusal. The young men knew perfectly well that if they failed to win everything, they would lose everything, and many of them were afraid to sleep in their beds that night. And indeed there was plenty of work to keep them awake. In planning how to meet the crisis, they knew the workers would be their most valuable allies, so a large group of students went to the suburbs and systematically aroused the workers from their beds and tried to form them into a guard for the next day.

For that was the day, Monday the 13th, that the Estates were to meet; and everyone was sure it would be a fateful meeting. The diplomatic corps, eager for a view of Vienna in revolt, collected at the Belgian Legation, conveniently across the street from the *Landhaus*, where the Assembly was to meet. Citizens took what vantage points they could find, ready to gape, to mock, to cheer as their more sanguine friends got ready their petitions. An assembly representing just one small province was not the proper place to dump the problems of an empire, but in default of a better one everyone was counting on it.

Long before eight o'clock in the morning, the university was like a beehive with coming and going. Among the crowd there were many characters who did not commonly show up in that part of town; their appearance now seemed like a presage of bad weather. In the eight o'clock statistics class, the window was opened from the outside and someone hurled a proclamation inside. No one paid any attention to the philosophy class because the doors kept opening and voices called through them, "Get out and go over to the Aula." The redoubtable Füster, teaching logic, tried to make things as interesting as he could, but still he told the class that anyone who felt he must go might depart with his blessing. He assured them the Emperor would listen, and at the mention of the Emperor's name, there was a great hissing and scraping of feet. The physics class was taught by a professor who had taught at Lemberg in Poland, where he had seen his young men led off by soldiers and thrown into prison for revolutionary talk. As he told his Vienna students the story, he wept and they listened, but when the class was over they went out and promptly forgot all about it in the press of excitement.

At nine everyone crowded toward the Aula to hear Professor Hye's report about Sunday's petition. He implored the students to wait for the Emperor's answer before they did anything rash, and tried to show them how much trouble they would make by lawlessness, both for the city and for their own parents who, he said, would be childless and destitute if these boys should be executed or imprisoned. His only answer was a "No" thundered by every voice at once, so imperative that no one who heard it ever forgot it. Then they began to yell "To the *Landhaus*, let us march to the *Landhaus*," and they pressed to the doors and out in a long stream toward the building where the Estates were to meet. A policeman who tried to stand in their way was just picked up and set aside. As they passed, many people trembled at their bravery, many more laughed at them. And many followed along to see what would happen or give them support.

The members of the Estates had been told by the police to wear plain frock coats instead of their usual fancy uniforms, so it was easy for a few non-members to slip inside their hall with them, but naturally, most of the crowd remained outside in the courtyard, moving in and out, looking from above like a sea of heads. They wanted news of how their petition was getting along without even giving the Estates time to call themselves to order.

In the crowd was a young doctor, Adolf Fischhof, who felt as if he could not bear it if this moment slipped by without action. Was there no single soul who dared to speak up? You are no better than the others, he said to himself, so, not knowing exactly what he wished to say, he raised his voice and began, "Gentlemen." Immediately, there were cries for silence and he was raised on the shoulders of some students. People who looked up at him saw a pale handsome face framed in black hair and beard, with something about his far-gazing features and expression of quiet earnestness that showed him unmistakably as the Jew that he was. "Gentlemen," he said again, "This is a great day." And he went on to tell the people that they must force their demands on the Estates, free press first of all —and as he continued he listed most of the other wishes of Austrians, winding up with an appeal for unity in the whole Empire, the wisdom of which no one at the moment appreciated.[2]

Just then a young man came plunging through the mob, joy beaming from his face, waving a paper and crying "Kossuth's speech. Kossuth's speech." The moment was electric. For ten days rumors had been going about town concerning a speech which the great Hungarian had given to his countrymen at the moment when he was inspired by the news of the Paris revolution. Everyone had heard of this speech, but very few had actually read the copies which were smuggled in and translated and passed from hand to hand. Now the mob hushed so that people as far away as possible could hear the magic words. For Kossuth was not afraid to use the word liberty. Hungary was a free country, he said, with an age-old constitution, and he demanded that the Hapsburgs should give her back her ancient rights. But Hungary could never count on her freedom, he insisted, under a king who was at the same time an absolute emperor to the rest of his dominions. Austria must have a constitution, too. (Hungary persisted in this demand right through 1867, when the system of the dual monarchy was set up and Austria then received a constitution at the hands of her sister nation.)

When they heard this part of the speech, the people began yelling in spite of themselves. A constitution—hardly anyone in Vienna had dared to think of such a thing, not even the students.[3] Here

[2] Fischhof was an assistant physician in obstetrics at the Vienna General Hospital at this time, an institution that at times cared for 3,000 patients, but had only 36 physicians on its staff. Fischhof received 40 kreuzers a day, or less than 40 cents.

He had been raised in Hungary, the freest part of the empire, and entered medical school because Jews were excluded from other branches of the university. Fischhof, however, employed his spare time, while a student, in studying politics and history. He even gave up the tutoring job which supported him so as to have more time to read, although he almost starved as a result. In this way he laid the groundwork for a career which earned for him the title "the deepest political thinker of the period" from the great historian of the Hapsburgs, Oscar Jászi. But in 1848 he was only three years out of school.

[3] One reason the students of Vienna were not ready to stress a constitution for

was courage, here was progress, pushing them beyond their dreams. As the young reader drew toward the end of his paper, a voice from a window in the *Landhaus* cried "From the Estates," and a hundred arms passed a piece of paper toward the young man who was standing on a fountain. But the mob would not let him read the news from the Estates until he had finished every last word from Kossuth. Then he opened the new paper and read a somewhat humble request to the Emperor to call a united diet (like Prussia's) to consider reform.

"That's nothing. Tear it up," people yelled, and the Estates' document was torn into a hundred pieces and scattered down on the heads of the crowd. "We want deeds, not words. No wishes, no prayers. We *demand*. We have the right to do it." A young man with dark face and flaming eyes climbed arrogantly on the fountain. "Dismiss the minister everyone hates," he cried. "What's his name? Tell us his name," roared the people below. "Metternich." This sally was met with bravos. Finally the crowd elected twelve representatives to enter the Assembly Hall and chaperon the debate, as in Paris the mob had sent observers to watch deliberations of the first session of the provisional government. Even under the severe eyes of these critics, the Estates could not lose their old habit of respect. Nevertheless, they decided, or were forced, to carry their platform to the Emperor. When this decision reached the crowd, joy broke over every face. A path opened up for the chosen delegates to march through as when the waters of the Red Sea parted for Moses. Even the grenadiers opened their ranks. The committeemen were met along the whole road to the Hofburg with handkerchief wavings and greetings. Some delay was occasioned when the president could not lay hands on a black dress coat appropriate for an audience, but finally the deputation reached the throne of the All-Highest— and received the tidings, already familiar, that their wishes "would be taken under consideration."

All this time the press outside was getting thicker, if that were possible, and the good citizens who hoped for peaceful reforms were

Austria was the fear of upsetting plans for German unity which they so much desired. The Frankfurt Parliament had not yet met, in March 1848, but rumors were plentiful about it, and good German-Austrians were reluctant to push their country into a path of possible separatism. It was, indeed, the constitution given to the whole of the empire in March, 1849, that killed any hope at Frankfurt that part of the Austrian Empire might be included in their German Reich.

considerably surprised to find themselves mingling with a number of those workers from the suburbs whom the students had engaged to come and help them. With sudden shrinking, many burghers felt they would rather keep on with tyranny from above than be caught fighting on the same side as the rabble from the factories.

Ordinarily, the two classes never mixed, for the inner city of Vienna was still surrounded by its ancient walls and moat, and outside was a broad grass-covered glacis which separated it from the suburbs where the workers lived.

During the morning of March 13, the city gates were ordered shut, so that all but a few hundred workmen were successfully kept out of the city. Some students who happened to be shut out too were almost frantic at missing the excitement. One bribed a mail coach to let him hang on an axle and rode inside that way. But even the few workers who got in heartened the radicals and students and terrified the milder citizens to the point where they began shrieking for arms, a national guard to protect property. Up to this point, the national guard had seemed a very radical demand, stemming straight from Paris, but now it became one the government was almost eager to gratify. For the government was losing self-confidence rapidly and hoped the burghers would forget their other wishes in their excitement of being under arms.[4]

For perhaps the first time with misgivings, the Hapsburgs called out their troops. Grenadiers were ordered to the *Landhaus*; they swam through the crowd rather than marched to their places and when the people yelled "Sheath your bayonets," they did so. Apparently, the people did not believe the guns could be loaded, and to convince them that they were, an officer commanded the soldiers

---

[4] In their demand for citizens to bear arms, the 1848 revolutionists were fighting for a right Americans already possessed, one for which the drafters of our Bill of Rights felt it was important enough to amend our Constitution. A hundred years ago it still seemed like a right which gave the common man some hope of power. A regular army could always be counted on to beat the militia, but it could not always be counted on to want to try. The army was still thought of as an instrument of internal repression as much as a defensive force against foreign countries. In Paris the demand had been to widen the class base of the national guard. In Berlin it had been to set one up. In Vienna there may have been a skeleton force already, for Helfert describes the March 13 demand as being to let the guard patrol the inner city. If this were not the case, how were they organized so quickly that they could defend the arsenal that night? Only the students were issued arms, as if the citizens already had them. And if there had never been a guard in Vienna, how would the *générale*, beaten to call them out that day, be recognized?

to put the ramrods in the barrels of their guns and march across the square. The press became tighter and tighter, and a citizen got so close that he was able to burn a grenadier's beard with his cigar and blow smoke in his face. The Archduke Albert, the military commandant of the city, rode by on a horse. People hated him because he would not let them smoke in the streets, so on this disrespectful day only a few hats came off as he rode by, and soon a piece of wood flew by his head and knocked off his eyeglasses. He turned and rode away. From the *Landhaus* people started throwing furniture down on the grenadiers. They were ordered to fire a salvo into the air—and then one aimed lower, right into the crowd. They killed five people and wounded more—the wounds were washed in the same fountain on which the students had climbed to harangue the crowd.

The center of the crowd, by this time, was no longer at the *Landhaus*, but had followed the parade of petitioners toward the Hofburg, the Emperor's palace. The mob hooted at the rows of dragoons and the cannon busily being arranged. Stores around that part of town closed, householders barred their doors, and the frightened cabbies fled, sometimes leaving their horses hitched to their posts. The usual thing happened when the mob began pressing close—an archduke ordered the troops to fire. In this case, however, the soldiers were surprised and hesitated. One cannoneer, later court-martialed, testified that he had refused to fire because the order had not come from his proper superior. The archduke, some said, was in civilian dress and had not been recognized as an officer. After a second most of the soldiers responded to their old discipline, but that moment's delay was to be enough to cause the court to go into a funk.

The people were enraged. They saw the first victim fall, a brilliant eighteen-year-old mathematician; then others were killed and wounded around them, and they grabbed whatever weapons they could find. The workmen had brought crowbars and axes, other citizens threw stones. And the students, outraged, began to cry for arms. They announced that they would storm the arsenal with bare hands at nine that evening, if arms had not been granted to them by that time.

The gentle Ferdinand, like Louis Philippe and Frederick William, could hardly bear the news that his citizens' blood was being shed. He said he would give anything rather than have the fighting go on, and by this time most of his brothers and uncles were ready to agree with him, though not, in their case, out of good nature, but from policy, since many of them believed in reform anyway and all of them were terrified by the scene in front of them.

To the people it was only apparent that their emperor loved them when he announced that civil officials were to handle the crowds, the soldiers were to be used only if these failed, and all the things the Estates had asked for would be granted. His picture was commonly crowned with flowers after this concession.

At the university things were still in a turmoil by late afternoon. Professor Hye had to announce to the students that there was as yet no answer to their petition, and he boldly added that though he had four children, he would stand with them until they got arms as well as a free press. Their fathers and elder brothers were being summoned to the national guard at that very moment—the noise of happy greeting almost drowned the sound of the drum, and whenever an armed citizen appeared he was embraced, whereas a soldier would be insulted. The crowd tried to get one soldier drummer to beat the *générale* for the citizens, and when he said he could not, they broke his drumsticks and the skin on his drum. It did not help matters any when shots were fired from police headquarters on a company of thirty of the newly summoned militia.

All this excitement was, of course, more than the students could stand to watch, and they determined to send their rector and two professors to persuade the authorities to grant them the arms they desired. Everyone at court was too busy to pay much attention to the pleas of mere students at a time when the cabinet was shaking (it was the moment of Metternich's resignation). The rector knew he was being given a run-around, and remembering the stern young faces at the Aula, he forced his way into the reception room of the Archduke Louis (who was Ferdinand's *alter ipse*), and, though he was a stooped and stiff little seventy-year-old, he threw himself on his knees in front of His Royal Highness and implored him to save blood. At this point a second delegation, from the medical school, came to back up the students' wishes, and news that the militia had been fired on arrived at the same moment. That meant the roof was on fire, said someone at court. The dean of the medical school said he would lay his head on the block if the students used their arms for any purpose except to keep order, and he begged Louis to keep him as a hostage for their good behavior. At first Louis said they could be armed the next morning, but the students had named nine that night as their deadline. At 8:20 the court gave in and ordered the arsenal to pass out arms to them that very evening.

To the students praying in the Aula it seemed as if God had mercy, for the arms came. Four corps were left to guard the beloved university buildings; the others marched to the arsenal, and were to come back and relieve the first ones later. The distribution took nearly all night. It was done by torchlight and moonlight, and since everyone in the world wanted arms, the professor who was passing the students through tried to ask questions in Latin, so that common citizens might not get in. This test did not work because the engineering students did not know Latin either, so the professor reframed his questions to ask ones which it would take some sort of a higher education to answer. The students fell upon their weapons, and immediately justified the trust of the dean of the medical school in proving to be the only group that could control the workers. The very first day they kept them from a number of violent acts, including a raid on the Treasury.

Just at the time when the students were winning their arms, their arch enemy, Prince Metternich, quit his office. He had known for a long time that the country suffered from incurable ailments—"I am too old a physician to be deceived"—and the news of Guizot's fall in Paris struck him like the death knell.

Not for a minute, though, did he lose his perfect composure. During the morning of March 13, he had telegraphed Pressburg that by evening all would be quiet. Later on in the day, he appeared at a state conference fastidiously dressed in a green morning coat and brightly colored trousers. Glancing out of the window, he made a comment about the rabble outdoors, and when someone observed that there were many well-dressed people in the street, he said, "If my son were among those people, I would still call them rabble." Towards evening his enemies proposed to his face that he resign. Metternich only bowed courteously, saying that he did not want his term of office to outlast his usefulness to the state, but that he had promised the Emperor's father never to abandon Ferdinand. That remark only sent people scurrying, with the natural bad manners of the court, to get poor Ferdinand to give an official kick to his old servant; it was not hard to do, and with perfect *sang-froid* Prince Metternich withdrew. Let no one think, he gently reminded protesting friends, that the fate of Austria depended on any one man. The country could be lost only if it gave itself up.

Outside the palace the crowds were yelling so fiercely against Metternich that Archduke Louis said he could not be responsible for his life—a fine admission from the very Hapsburg who had served with the great minister as a regent of the Empire for thirteen years. And the state treasury would not even advance him cash for a trip to England. The Prince finally got a loan from his friends, the Rothschilds, and made his way out of Vienna in a common cab. After various adventures, he succeeded in settling in England, from whence he watched the Empire he had held together so long, fall swiftly, though temporarily, to pieces.

When the citizens heard that Metternich had fallen and that they were to have a national guard, lights appeared in every window. In some quarters the mob went around smashing every darkened pane. In itself, this illumination was a sign that times had changed. Ten years back, when the term of military service was reduced to eight years, the citizens wanted to light up their houses to show their pleasure and were forbidden on the theory that it was not their privilege to express either favorable or unfavorable opinions on acts of the crown.

Inside the city gates that night was peaceful rejoicing, but in the suburbs, things were different. After the gates were closed Monday morning, rumors began to spread outside, but very little authentic news came out. Towards the end of the day, some men wearing white scarves came out and told the workers the concessions that had been made, but these had very little effect on men who were having their first chance in years to get even with their bosses. So while the city burned lamps and candles, the workers made their illumination by setting fire to all the toll houses, where duties on food entering the city were collected, and by knocking down the gas lights on the glacis. Flames rushed out of breaks in the pipe making a terrifying ring of fire. The danger grew when the whole stock of a liquor warehouse was allowed to run out in the streets and catch fire. Then the workers rushed into their factories and shops and began to destroy the machinery, which they believed took away the jobs they had been brought up to do. Police noticed how little private pilfering went on in all this violence. Revenge was the workers' motive, and they protected the property of employers who had been good to them. Particularly, the workers on the Vienna-Gloggnitz railroad, special friends of the students, defended both the tracks and the shops. In other shops, so much blood was up that it took even the students several days to restore order.

A number of employers were ruined by this violence; a lot of workers found shortly that they had destroyed their own livelihoods. All of this was to make trouble a few months later. But, also, in the first flush of March goodwill, many employers settled long-term grievances. The directors of the Vienna-Gloggnitz railroad reduced the working day in their shops to ten hours, in gratitude, they said, and most other big plants followed suit. Others gave wage increases.

On the next day, Tuesday, March 14, the press was declared free. Men wearing white ribbons paraded the city to announce the fact, for white meant both a free press and constitutionalism in all the 1848 period. Soon the bookstores dragged into the open all their stocks of forbidden books. By the 16th boys were hawking pictures and poems of the revolutionary events.

On the 14th also, the national guard began enrolling 40,000 men, who were soon patrolling the streets. The only place left in the hands of regular troops was the palace, for the Hapsburgs apparently lacked that dramatic confidence which allowed Hohenzollern Frederick William to entrust himself to his citizens' protection. Ferdinand would have been just as safe. The grateful Viennese referred to him as "our Ferdy," and told each other that he was only doing what he had always wanted to do, now that his bad advisers were out of the way.

As for the students, they wept for joy over their guns and set about organizing their famous Academic Legion. The jobs they set themselves were to defend the university, patrol the suburbs and watch the city gates, for they were afraid the gates would be shut on them again. One group went out to the shops of the Vienna-Gloggnitz railroad to announce all the good news to their friends there, and the black sooty workers let out such a yell as had never been heard in those yards before. "We did not have hands enough to press all the hands that were reached out to us," said one of the students later.

The students at the gates finished the destruction of the customs houses which the workers' fires had begun. Then, before anyone could stop them, they attacked the Liguorian convent and drove out the monks.[5] "Just to have lived through those days is enough for one lifetime," declared a member of the Academic Legion twenty-five years later.

On March 15, Kossuth himself appeared in the city, to press his demands for a separate ministry for Hungary and a constitution for Austria. The Emperor, whose advisers had completely lost their nerve, gave in to everything. The Hungarians who had come with Kossuth to help Vienna fight for liberty found nothing left to do but dance in the streets; and as for the man who wrote "Constitution" on a banner and carried it through the streets, women kissed his clothes, mothers held their children up so that they would always remember the sight. In two days Austria seemed to have been jerked from the most backward of European nations to the most advanced.

While the people were rejoicing because they had won more than they had ever hoped to ask for, the men left at court were grinding their teeth because they had given more than they had ever meant to give. At first they went into a panic which Radowitz, then in Vienna on a mission from the King of Prussia, satirized when writing to his master, for he was ignorant of the agonies which Frederick William was undergoing on these same March days. For centuries the imperial household had lived so far from their subjects that now they had no way to guess what these subjects would ask for next or how far they would go. Even the famous spy system did not work. They were scared for their lives, their power and their property; in injured innocence one aristocrat could lament the passing "of our good life which hurt no one and gave livelihood to many"; in outraged self-righteousness another, who helped Metternich to escape and wanted to draw a moral in a British journal, could hope "that

[5] In 1830, Emperor Francis had allowed the Jesuit and Liguorian orders to return officially to his dominions, whence they had been expelled in the previous century, because they fitted in with his ideas of conservatism. Radicals considered them the worst evil in Austria, because of their venality, their encouragement of superstition and the throttle hold they had on education. They not only ran practically all the high schools (when they took over Hans Kudlich's school, they stopped the boys from singing German chorales and forbade nude bathing in the river, two old and joyous customs), but even university students had upon occasion to procure certificates that they had attended mass and confession. There was quite an active black market in such certificates.

in England every man who possesses even the smallest income will stand with the government."

The sterner spirits collected themselves. Prince Alfred von Windischgrätz, the military commander of Vienna after Archduke Albert retired, had advised firing with heavy guns on the mob on Monday. By Thursday he was still ready to break out with his soldiers in the face of the armed citizenry and the Emperor's promise of peace. Balked in this, he stored up his fury. Prague, Vienna, and Budapest were to feel its force within a year, but his first move was to drill an army. Though the liberals at Vienna kept asking the government what Windischgrätz's maneuvers could be for, they never got an answer until the army was turned against themselves.

Meanwhile the Archduchess Sophia, who had been considered a friend of reform, became the revolution's most dangerous enemy. "I could have borne the loss of one of my children," this fierce matriarch declared, "more easily than I can the ignominy of submitting to a mass of students. In the future, the shame of the past will seem simply incredible." And in March 1848, she began writing to her friends in the Russian Court for help, thus instinctively following the policy which a year later was to save the Empire, the dynasty, and absolutism in Austria.

The party which won the victory in March had more pressing dangers to meet than a vague and secret court hostility. The liberal leaders had to rush into jobs for which they had no preparation; they did not even have an educated rank and file behind them. Yet, nothing in the confident way they took over the government foretold their slow heartbreak on realizing that those trained for power, like Windischgrätz and Sophia, still knew how to win at that game.

With victory in their hands, the students became by all odds the most conspicuous, colorful, and popular group in Vienna. The Academic Legion adopted a uniform of black felt hats with ostrich plumes, blue coats with shining buttons, black-red-gold sashes in token of their German patriotism, bright steel-handled swords which the wearers took pains to hang low enough so that they clanked along the pavement, light gray trousers, and to top everything, silver gray cloaks lined with scarlet. No wonder these young men were the admiration of the student world. For the first time in history, an Austrian government let delegates from Vienna go to one of the congresses of students from all German universities, and in this summer of 1848 they even paid their way out of public funds. The girls of Eisenach where the congress met would hardly dance with anyone except these Viennese and the students from other places envied them not only their dancing partners, but their chance to take such a serious part in world affairs.

For back in Vienna, the Aula soon became the center of all revolutionary activity. Student committees sat there to deliberate on every measure the government brought up; they also handled grievances for their friends, the workers, and incidentally ran the university and their own legion. Students ate, drank, and slept in the Aula and had dates with girls there. By September most of the portraits in the Aula had their faces cut out, with monkey faces put in the holes, or else mustaches were added to embellish ancient dignitaries.

The first day after the revolution the professors took up a collection among themselves to provide bread, cheese, and beer for everyone in the Aula. After that Dr. Füster, the priest whose sermon gave so much momentum to the revolution, took over the job of keeping the university stocked with food and drink. Young men kept coming in at all hours, exhausted by their patrol duties in the city. Many of the students had always been poor, and even some of the boys from rich families had to ask for relief now; their parents were unsympathetic with the duties of running a revolution. It was very common for fathers to refuse to pay for the uniform of the Academic Legion. Füster, however, was able to get a substantial contribution from the big bankers, Rothschild and Sina; he was touched when at the same time a group of workers came to him and offered to contribute a kreuzer each out of their daily wages to help maintain their student friends. In order not to hurt their feelings, Füster accepted a lump sum from these workers, but he told them the daily levy would not be needed.

The Academic Legion was organized almost overnight as an autonomous branch of the national guard. Corps of law, medical, philosophical, polytechnic and art students were formed and the total grew to nearly 5,000. True, there were only 2,000 matriculated at the university, but all graduates and teachers were admitted to the Legion, and gradually there was an infiltration of such dubiously intellectual craftsmen as house painters, barbers, actors, and clerks, who by fall had somewhat spoiled the show.

Dr. Füster became the chaplain and spiritual leader of the Legion, and his sermons became more inflammatory than ever. One of his first duties was to preach the funeral sermon of the students who had been killed on the streets on March 13. As before, his superiors tried to stop him without success. Was not one man who fell for freedom worth more than a bishop or emperor? he said to their faces. In full clerical dress he proceeded to conduct the service. During the course of it he saw the Rabbi, also in full regalia, near the bodies of the dead Jewish students. Füster went to him and had him march at his side in the funeral procession.

There was, in fact, neither anti-Semitism nor class prejudice in the Legion. The students succeeded eventually in having the special tax on Jews who wanted to live in Vienna lifted, and they stood loyally, if a bit paternalistically, behind every need of their worker friends. It was an era of general good feeling. Füster, who had to spend the later years of his life in exile for his part in the revolution, said that in his last hour he would forget the bitterness of death in remembering those wonderful young men, that beautiful time which he lived through in Vienna.

May was the month of intoxication. Women, too, considered it a spree and Schuselka, the middle-aged radical returned from exile, was shocked to find that his young friends extended fraternization to girls.

Even their touchiest emotion, nationalism, they managed to keep on a high plane at the beginning, though it was here that the first rift came between student and student. The Legion wore the German colors and was immensely proud of its feat of hanging them on the tower of St. Stephen's Cathedral on April 2. They even planted the black-red-gold banner in the Emperor's hand, and when poor Ferdinand appeared waving them, he was greeted with more fervor than ever before in his life. (It was the same concession to the people that Frederick William of Prussia made at the same time, and in both cases the black-red-gold band was hailed equally as a guarantee of constitutional reform and as a pledge toward unification of Germany.) To other races the Vienna students stressed the brotherhood of peoples and during the summer the Aula exchanged flags—for that was the ceremony—with French, Hungarian, Polish,

Croat, Slovene, and Serb students. But the Czech students at Vienna protested that the capital of the Austrian Empire had no right to consider itself exclusively German and they made so much trouble, that they were finally given twenty-four hours to leave town.

However, student affairs were bound to seem insignificant to young men who felt called upon to run an empire. After Metternich departed there was no one at the Hofburg brave or smart enough to form a cabinet, though a succession of men made the attempt. Ferdinand was now pledged to govern in the constitutional manner, but since there was as yet no constitution no one had any idea what the ministers' powers should be. Nevertheless, the students followed them like bloodhounds to be sure no government officials got away with anything the Aula did not like.

The first tangle between students and the administration came over the freedom of the press. The three newspapers which had been published in Vienna before March quickly grew to a hundred. Like Paris, the city was flooded with reading matter, much of it so wild that educated citizens who were used to the quiet innuendos which had passed the censor quickly became disgusted. All shades of opinions and venom came to light. (However, one critic, looking back, said that its only fault was political scurrility. He said that in 1848 the press had not yet sunk to the obscenity which made it impossible to let growing daughters read newspapers in the 1870's.)[6]

The honest liberals in charge of the new government tried to curb the press by requiring a guarantee which each paper must pay in advance. Also, each paper was required to publish official bulletins and retract libels.

The students saw in this only the return of the straitjacket and were so angry that only one paper, the official *Gazette*, dared to show the prescribed stamp. A copy of the law was burned in front

[6] The most interesting newspaper man in Vienna was Edward Warrens, who had been a journalist in America and as a reward for his services in Polk's election campaign had been appointed Consul at Trieste. While he was there, the governor, Count Stadion, the brightest of the Austrian bureaucrats, noticed his ability. In 1848, when the government seemed to have no organ to express its opinions, Stadion brought Warrens to Vienna to run a paper which would favor the policy of a centralized Austrian monarchy. The paper was immensely successful because of Warren's American style of short sentences and snappy comparisons. There is no way of telling how much it influenced public opinion, of course, but later in the year, Count Stadion was commissioned to draw up the constitution for the centralized monarchy which was promulgated by Emperor Francis Joseph in March 1849.

of the university, and the government hastily retracted the decree.[7]

After the ill fate of the press decree the new ministry was still rash enough to frame a constitution. The cabinet, in April, consisted of six men who had never previously exchanged opinions. They might well have worked out something on a sound basis in time, for they all wanted to put over the reforms which liberals had been talking about before March, but they were in a hurry. When they came out with a neat and fairly liberal document at the end of April, it met with an even ruder reception than the press decree. It satisfied the members of the Reading Club who had been talking for ten years, but it did not please the groups who had just found their tongues.

The most glaring omission was that it did not specify who should have the vote. The ministry tried to meet this with a special decree which would have let everyone vote but servants and factory workers; this was probably further than the new cabinet wished to go and seemed like the limit for any monarchical government in 1848. (The French after all were setting up a republic.) But it was enough to enrage the students that their allies the workers should be left out, so they began to organize battalions of workers with hoes and shovels to protest. On May 15 a parade streamed past the Ministry from two-thirty in the afternoon until midnight, carrying a "storm petition" which asked for a constitutional assembly elected by universal suffrage. When the army told the ministers privately that it could not guarantee their safety, the government gave in a second time.

At this point the imperial family became terrified to find their subjects so bold and their ministers so pusillanimous. The day after the storm petition, they set out as if for an afternoon's drive, but when they were well outside the city they ordered their coachman to drive on to Innsbruck. Here they settled for the summer, surrounded by loyal peasants who had never heard of constitutions, and here they began to rally their generals behind them—Prince Windischgrätz, old Field Marshal Radetzky in Italy, and the Croatian

[7] One of the things the students insisted on was that trials for the offence of abusing the press should be public and be held with a jury—a complete innovation in Austria. The first of these cases occurred in August, when the editor of the *Student Courier* was imprisoned because he printed an editorial in favor of a republic. At the trial, which was attended by thousands of people, the jury acquitted him and the joyous crowd pulled him to his office in a carriage from which the horses were unhitched.

Baron Jellačič. These were the men who would win their empire back for them while ministers and students prattled of reform. The radicals of Vienna mocked at the likeness between the fleeing Ferdinand and Louis XVI, forgetting that Louis was brought back to Paris as a prisoner.

As a matter of fact most of the Viennese were ashamed that their Emperor had not been happy in his revolutionized capital. "Our Ferdy has left us," they said, and sent a petition signed by 80,000 to beg him to return. Ferdinand and the men he obeyed were in no hurry and their stay in Innsbruck lasted three months. During this time Prince Windischgrätz proved his mettle by shooting down the revolution in Prague. During the same interval Radetzky was winning Lombardy back from her war of independence and Jellačič was secretly urged to attack rebelling Hungary. Therefore, when the revolutionary government in Vienna peremptorily insisted that Ferdinand be brought back to his capital, the Archduchess Sophia's tears were no longer tears of despair. She would repay the temporary humiliation of that August day by setting her son over Austria for a reign of nearly seventy years.

To go back to the students in May. They had now made enemies of the foreign students, had twice humiliated the new liberal government, had driven the court away from Vienna and incurred the odium of thousands of citizens who loved the Emperor. They had even had a sharp fight with their old friends in the Reading Club over the expulsion of a radical agitator.[8] The government received

---

[8] The agitator was named Dr. Anton Schütte. In the eyes of the propertied citizens, like the Reading Club members, he was the most dangerous influence in Vienna because he kept haranguing the workers on liberty. He was a Westphalian who had been traveling around Germany for some months and liked Vienna better than any other place he saw because the spirit of liberty was most alive there. His extreme unconventionality, not to say radicalism, from the pan-German point of view, shows up in the fact that he did not like to see German youths sacrificed on the field of battle for a few miles of territory in Schleswig-Holstein or elsewhere. He felt that Dahlmann and Arndt, both such well-known liberals, discredited themselves as leaders of Germany because they urged wars of aggression upon the Frankfurt Parliament. This aspect of his opinions had, naturally, not come to light in April 1848, or the students might not have defended him so warmly. At that point they knew him as a friend of liberal ideas and generous to their worker comrades. The liberal government, however, backed warmly by the influential Reading Club, expelled him from Vienna and gave him a police escort to the border so as to be sure he really left the country. He managed to return to Vienna before the October battle there, and after the city was conquered, he was one of the people whom Windischgrätz insisted on condemning to death. However, he escaped and published his diary of the October days.

so many complaints about these wild young men, including many from the boys' own parents, that they risked a third showdown and decreed that the university be closed and the Academic Legion disbanded.

In giving this order the government completely miscalculated its strength, as the prime minister admitted afterwards. Füster's students kept the university open by force while the national guard (angry because the government had not kept its promise to retire all the troops and let the guard patrol the city) and 30,000 workers thronged to the young men's assistance. In the machine shops of the Vienna-Gloggnitz railroad men dropped their tools and started to tear up the rails to prevent more troops being sent for. Printing shops cast musketry balls that day instead of type.

When news spread that the Legion was threatened, people began tearing up the pavement of Vienna—the best and cleanest in all Europe, consisting mainly of foot-square blocks of granite. In some places they pulled up every other stone and set it on its neighbor to make a surface impossible for cavalry to traverse. In other parts they made conventional barricades as high as the second stories, often sealing inhabitants inside their houses. Women helped beside the men in the actual building, as well as giving their customary offerings of bread, cheese, beer, and coffee to the builders.

Füster climbed over these barricades to tell the gentlemen of the cabinet what they were doubtless beginning to realize—that the students would rather be torn limb from limb than dissolve their Legion.

The result of all this activity was a bloodless victory for the radical democratic party. The ministry gave in for the third fatal time—fatal as far as their authority was concerned. The Legion and the university were both to be kept running, and the troops were to be evacuated after turning over thirty-six cannon to the national guard. On Füster's advice, the students maintained a few barricades near the university until the cannon to defend it were actually delivered to them.

Lectures at the university were livelier than ever. For example, a course in constitutional politics was given that spring for the first time, and Füster was able to give a course on pedagogy for which permission had always been refused before. But storm petitions and barricades proved too much for most professors' nerves. In March even the old reactionaries had been sweet to the students—many professors marched with the Legion, others sympathized with its actions. Now one by one the faculty abandoned them, until by fall the Academic Legion had the support of no professor except the unquenchable Füster.

On June 10 the government finally succeeded in suspending lectures at the university, hoping that the out-of-town students would go home for the vacation. In this hope the government was deceived. The students now had all their time free to devote to politics, while the citizens of Vienna, both rich and poor, united to help house and feed the young men. It seems to have been gladly done in most cases, though the boys were doubtless prepared to back up their demands with force—and some citizens complained that the Legion requisitioned not only their food but their daughters.

The attachment between students and workers flowered during the summer. The workers let themselves be led by the students, for whom they often said they were willing to give their lives. "If one of our men falls it is no matter, but for one of the fine young student gentlemen, to whom we owe our freedom, it would be a great pity." The students in return for this generosity spent a large part of their time taking care of the workers; one 20-year-old law student was even called the workers' king, because he could do anything with them and spent day and night thinking up plans to help them.

A committee of students took over the work of labor arbitration, remonstrating with unfair employers, reasoning with excited workmen. They won such respect for their justice that appeals came from all the nearby cities and villages begging the Aula to settle their disputes. The students enjoyed cutting through red tape and soon became the terror of local tyrants and fussy bureaucrats.

The medical students at the same time arranged to take care of sick workers, both prescribing for them and arranging for better medical service with established doctors. Law students helped with legal advice and fights in court, and showed the workers how to draft petitions. Still other students took up collections for needy cases.

From March until August, a young doctor said, there was no distinction between classes in the minds of the students. They treated workers and bourgeoisie with perfect equality. Perhaps because it was so unusual for anyone from the upper classes to treat the workers as friends, the students could not recognize that their attitude also was touched with patronage. "We expect you to help us keep order, which we all need so badly. . . . You must go about your business as usual and prove we are right in saying you want to be good, well-behaved people," declared a student manifesto to the workers. Füster, too, was talking down to the workers when he thundered at them: "Do you think we have thrown our lords and nobles to let ourselves be ruled by you? Then you are much mistaken. Do you expect us to be intimidated by you? There again you are wrong. . . . You are mostly fine, sensible people. Why do you let yourselves be led by a few hotheads?"

No one remembers any more who these hotheads were—voices that tried to make the workers ask for more than the students wanted to give them. In April a radical newspaper man dared to tell the workers of Vienna that they must fight for what the workers in Paris had won, even if it cost as much blood as the great French Revolution of sixty years before. For this remark, his was called the first voice of hate raised in the general euphoria. Undaunted, he began to plan for a workers' *putsch*; he was, therefore, arrested with the connivance of the Aula itself. From then on no paper bothered to print enough news about the workers' movement in Paris to influence events in Vienna, a policy which the editors could doubtless justify by the excuse that they were giving the readers what they wanted. In the May petitions a few groups seem to have come out for full employment, or "the right to work," but their voices were drowned in the shouting for political reform.

All classes in Vienna were much more interested in politics than economics (perhaps because the industrial revolution was not well advanced there) and when finally a workers' club was formed, it came out for democracy, not for socialism. In fact, the handicraft system was still so strong that many workers distrusted the freedom which was supposed to go with the new liberal economic system of laissez-faire, and would have preferred going back to the various forms of protection which they had inherited from the middle ages instead of forward to an economic democracy which they could not understand.

Naturally, this disdain for economic theory did not prevent certain practical problems from arising, chiefly because the unemployment which had been so bad in 1847 was made still worse by the revolution and the departure of the court. There were shops where not a single item was sold for weeks after March 13. In April the police tried to evict from the city all unemployed servants and apprentices, but within a few days most of them had filtered back into town again.

These conditions almost automatically led to what respectable citizens called a reign of terror. The police were demoralized, partly because they did not know just what part of their former duties was now taken over by the national guard and the Academic Legion—both jealous patrollers—and partly because of the destruction of the secret police system. (During the summer it was arranged that two citizens must stay as watchers in every police station to guard against abuses. Such an attitude naturally made the police as jumpy as they had formerly made the citizens.) Therefore, there was not only a crime wave, but a period when any well-dressed person was likely to be insulted in the streets. The lower classes were trying out how far the new freedom would go.

To meet this situation the national guard, students, and the city council set up a committee of safety, shortly after their decisive triumph in May. It consisted of 234 members, and though there were no workers in it, since workers were not admitted to the national guard, the workers on the whole trusted it and allowed themselves to be led back toward order. Dr. Fischhof, for his "first free word" on March 13, was chosen chairman and under his leadership ("he always spoke from the soul and to the soul") the committee kept a course not so radical as the Aula's, not so conservative as the ministry's. Throughout the summer it was responsible for all public order and safety in the city.

Immediately their hardest problem was unemployment. Though they lacked theories, their practical opinion was that a worker looking for work ought to be provided with either work or money. So they tried to provide jobs by clearing the channel of the Danube and repairing roads, offering a daily wage of 25 kreuzers (roughly 12 cents a day). They sternly forbade child labor under twelve, but for children over that age, and for women, they offered work at 20 kreuzers.

Immediately they ran into most of the same troubles as the national workshops of Paris. Yet the Vienna committee's handling of

the program in their city was so pragmatic they might have succeeded better than the Paris workshops if, as in Paris, they had not
run into ministerial hostility.

As in Paris, workers flocked to the city from villages and the
countryside looking for easy money. The committee arranged to
pay out-of-towners' expenses to get back home.

As in Paris, employers complained that their workers deserted
them for the easier labor of public works. The committee made it a
condition of hiring that a man must not refuse private employment.

As in Paris, the army began to recruit among these workers, for
Austria was just entering a war with Italy. This infuriated the
workers who attacked the recruiting stations, saying that if there
was enough money to send them to Italy there was plenty to keep
them in Vienna. The committee took the workers' part in this issue
and advised them not to enlist.

Likewise, when the Minister of Public Works announced that the
pay might be reduced by five kreuzers a day, the committee of safety
opposed the measure with all its force. On the other hand, when
an agitator raised the demand for an increase in wages and for
being paid on rainy days and Sundays, Fischhof had him locked up.

As in Paris, the ministry had all respectable citizens on its side.
And, indeed, the direction of the public works of Vienna must have
been incredibly bad—a far cry from Emile Thomas' military discipline in Paris. The projects in Vienna were supervised by young
technical students who proved unable to keep the workers from
drinking and playing cards instead of working. If a worker even
tried to work hard, he was threatened by his fellows. The ministry
calculated that it cost fourteen times as much to lift a clod of earth
by these workers as by regularly employed ones.

By August the workers had grown so wild that they would not
listen even to their erstwhile student friends. In order to make them
listen, the committee of safety planned a demonstration early in
August, for which they drew up the national guard with its cannon,
on the glacis, and with this as a background they had student
orators expound the horrors of civil war.

If this show had any good effects, however, they were lost when
on August 18 the Minister of Public Works announced definitely
that pay for women and children on public works would be reduced
to 15 kreuzers, with the general expectation that a cut for men

would follow. The committee of safety could not do anything to stop this move because the ministry had the funds and was bent on coming to a showdown.

The workers were only too willing to fall in with their game. On the 23 of August they put on a farcical funeral of the Minister of Public Works. He was shown riding a donkey, choking to death on one of his five-kreuzer pieces, and was eventually buried with appropriate rites.

The ministry was furious (for such *lèse-majesté* is taken hard in countries used to absolutism), and pretended to be even more furious than it was. It ordered out the all too willing national guard, which fired into the mob of unarmed workers, killing eighteen and wounding several hundred. Respectable Vienna celebrated this victory by crowning the bloody bayonets with flowers; instead, it should have congratulated itself that the affair did not turn into something like the June days in Paris, which were caused by a similar effort to shut down the public works.

But the workers of Vienna were not merely unable to rule half the city, as the Paris workers did. Apparently, they could not make any sort of counterattack whatever, but just let themselves be shot at. Only when the students led them could the workers show their power, and the students were aloof during this battle, partly because they were taken by surprise and partly because they did not want to get into a civil war. Two months later, when the Hapsburgs sent their army to conquer the city, the students again got the workers to cooperate with the national guard as if there had never been a split in their ranks.

While all this was going on, the Constitutional Assembly met at Vienna. It had two important effects on events in the city. In the first place the ministry was supposed to be responsible to this body and at the same time the committee of safety was willing to resign its powers to the Assembly—so that people hoped that at last there would be a single, reasonable, legal authority to take charge of all the tangled affairs of the country. What came as a surprise to the Viennese was that the Assembly, representing the provinces, could not settle down to the job of solving the problems of a single city, even though the citizens of that city felt that their troubles were so important.

Delegates came to this Assembly from all the Empire except Hungary (which had its own Diet) and the Italian provinces (which were in revolt at the time of the elections). Everyone, including workers and peasants, had been urged to vote.[9]

This was the first time the German top dogs had had to meet the rest of the Empire in its full legal proportion, and the effect on them was of surprise and chagrin. About a quarter of the nearly 400 members turned out to be peasants, and although the peasants in each precinct chose their representatives cannily, as they picked cows in a market, even the cleverest peasants made a startling impression in Vienna. Some of them did not know how to use either combs or handkerchiefs. Ten of them piled into an inn and requested two rooms. When they were told that there were but two beds to a room they replied they did not need beds, just some straw on the floor. But their chief handicap as legislators was that they did not understand German. One whole bloc from Galicia was completely subject to Count Francis Stadion. This gentleman, the ablest bureaucrat the Empire could boast, was summoned to be Governor of Galicia after the Polish uprising of 1846, and it was largely because he knew when to make concessions that this province was quiet during 1848. In April 1848, for instance, he abolished feudal dues and the hated labor service there; and thus it was that whenever a motion came up for a vote in the Assembly, his rows of grateful peasants, not having understood a word of the debate, would signify that they wished to vote "like Mr. Stadion."

However, the main division in the Assembly turned out to be more along national than class lines. The left was still provided by the Viennese liberals who engineered the revolution, but it was hardly an ultra-radical left. Dr. Fischhof and even Chaplain Füster were far from being republicans.

This left always called the Czech party "the right" in the Assembly. The Czechs opposed them at every turn for national reasons, even though they shared some of the same political ideals. The right, therefore, was no more extreme than the left. What the Czechs wanted was a federalized empire with Bohemia "a nation" and they used to infuriate the German party by calling the Ger-

[9] These groups had a chance at the same time to vote for the Frankfurt Assembly, but only those precincts that wished took part in this election. Most non-German-speaking districts did not do so, and that was why Austria was so badly under-represented at Frankfurt.

mans who lived in Bohemia "colonists." Being the most sophisticated of the Slavic peoples, the Czechs felt their best chance of getting what they wanted was by sticking to the Emperor, and when revolutionary fever got too high in Vienna (in October), they prudently withdrew from the Assembly, earning thereby from the German liberals the title of "traitors."[10]

When a distinguished Czech scholar, Francis Palacky (who had written a monumental history of the Bohemian people), was called to the Ministry of Education, the Pan-German disciples were furious. They felt it was their job to support culture from the Rhine to the Black Sea and they refused to believe a Slav could do it. For the first time they began to comment on the cleverness of Prussia in trying to Germanize her Polish provinces. This feeling made them turn toward a policy of centralizing the empire; at this time many even of the liberal Germans began to support the war in Italy, for national honor and the national exchequer both gained new importance in their eyes. (Lombardy and Venetia contributed a third of the revenue of the Imperial treasury.)[11]

In the mess of disagreement in which this parliament opened, there was, luckily, one deputy, the youngest in the house, who knew just what he wanted. His name was Hans Kudlich, he was a peasant's son, and he was determined that the first job of the Assembly should be to free the peasants.

Kudlich was born in a peasant's cottage in Silesia, and he knew both the hardships and the mitigations of the peasant's lot. His father was comfortably fixed for one of his class; in fact, he held

[10] The Czechs were called traitors from 1848 until the end of the Empire in 1918. In the war of 1914 to 1918, they were the only group of Hapsburg subjects who were disloyal enough to go over to the Allies, and they earned bitter hatred from more faithful racial groups on this account.

Racial hatred was apparently as strong in 1848 as later. Even the usually genial Füster allowed himself to write of the Czech delegates: "I never saw such repulsive faces, such ugly heads; each, with rare exceptions, was branded with a devilish expression of treachery." He then went on to say that their conduct in the Assembly was like that of Judas, for they sold freedom to the Ministry. Füster was sorry he had had to sit in the Assembly because it forced him to witness so much wickedness.

The bare fact was that the Czechs were given over to their *idée fixe*, and wearied everybody with their constant talk about their "nation."

[11] It should be stated in fairness that a few members of the left stuck to their earlier principles that Italy had a right to be free, and they refused to let the Assembly's vote of thanks to Fieldmarshal Radetzky be unanimous after that officer won the war in Italy.

twice as much land as was allowed for one in his station, but the authorities always winked at the discrepancy. When the time came to educate Hans, his family had to get permission from the landlord before the boy could go to a nearby town to high school and later to Vienna to the university, but tuition was free to one of his class. His parents paid his board in produce from their land, and he never had a decent coat on his back, but poverty was never allowed to keep him back.[12]

Free education was only one of many reasons which made the twenty-six million peasants of the Empire feel that the Emperor was their best friend. Whatever exemptions and liberties they had seemed to come from the crown, ever since Maria Theresa had limited the amount of feudal dues they must pay, and her son Joseph had officially abolished serfdom. At the time the revolution broke, a peasant was legally free to sell his land; therefore he was not bound to the soil and not a serf, although whoever bought that land was still obliged to pay to his landlord not only a share of his crop, but a certain number of days of work every year. This was called the robot. One peasant who was asked during the revolution what a constitution was, replied, "not to pay the robot." The burdens were indeed heavy. Counting a tithe for the church, a peasant often had to give up more than half his income, and there is one documented case where seventy per cent of a certain peasant's time and harvest were taken away from him. But since these dues were paid over to their landlords, and since it was from the landlords that they obtained justice, often at the whipping post, or permission to marry, or, like Kudlich, to go to school, most of the peasants' resentment turned against the landlords rather than the government.

Kudlich tells how his neighbors considered themselves much better off than the Prussian peasants they saw just across the

[12] Common schools were free and compulsory throughout the Empire. In fact, a priest was not supposed to marry anyone who could not produce a certificate that he or she had attended school from the ages of five to thirteen. In this, Austria was ahead of much of Western Europe, including England. The drawbacks in the system are familiar—that the teachers were the worst paid of all public servants, so poor that they were often actually hungry; and secondly, that a commission in Vienna, run by the clergy, prescribed every page and every answer to be studied. (History, interestingly enough, was a required subject in high schools for free students like Kudlich, but not for students who paid.) No time was allowed for exercise or pleasure, and the total result was that the schools were admired from a distance by those who appreciated how they raised the bottom level, yet constantly excoriated by intellectuals whose minds were almost stultified by them.

border, because Prussia's enlightened despotism set up regulations that were much more oppressive than those of the rather easy-going Austrian system. Austria allowed farmers to keep on with their age-old fertilizing methods, primitive and half-hearted, and with their inefficient animal breeding, to the point where the Empire had to import a good part of the agricultural goods it needed. In 1866 the peasants in Kudlich's village learned to respect the Prussians for the first time, after the Austrian defeat at Königgratz. They did not realize that Prussia's intelligent interference in agricultural methods had helped turn the kingdom into the first-class military power it was, but they noticed how pleasant these well-disciplined German soldiers were when Prussian troops were quartered in their village. Even though they were enemies they made better guests than the regiments of their own Emperor, Croats, Italians, or Hungarians, who had been billeted in their huts as long as they could remember. It was one of the peasants' duties to quarter soldiers, and Kudlich was used to having eleven or twelve loud, dirty, drunken men in his cottage, with their horses in the yard, off and on during his boyhood.

By 1848 Kudlich had worked his way through the University of Vienna, and he realized more keenly than anyone else in the city that of all the reforms needed in the Empire, freeing the peasants was the most important. Apparently no one else in Vienna agreed with him, for on March 13, he was in the crowd around the Landhaus pressing for reforms, and he cried "Robot, Robot" at the top of his lungs, but the urban ears around him seemed perfectly deaf.

In the Assembly he fared somewhat better, because of the country-wide representation. It was hard to get the members to pass any laws because they acted during their first weeks together as if there had never been a parliament anywhere in the world before, and they went to unnecessary trouble to set up all the arrangements. In fact, Kudlich was the only person who succeeded in getting an important vote out of them. When he proposed his grand measure, that all feudal dues should be abolished in Austria, it was met with cheers.

Though the gain was so largely an economic one, the debates in the Assembly had apparently foreseen only political results. Possibly politics seemed like a more noble subject for oratory, too. In any case the hall rang with cries for freedom, not prosperity; the speakers denounced not hunger, but slavery.

The only big issue was whether the landlords should receive an indemnity for their losses. Peasant delegates were opposed to this. "The whips that came down on our tired heads and bodies must be the compensation of our masters," they said. But the members of the Ministry were adamant that the landlords should be repaid, and so it was finally voted.[13]

Even Engels admitted that Austria was quiet for decades after 1848 because the peasants were now satisfied. Kudlich tells of a typical neighbor of his who owned, in 1848, two horses, a poor cow, and a poor farm. When Kudlich went back to see him in 1872 (returning from America whither he had fled after the revolution's collapse), the man was the proud owner of four horses and ten cows. At the same time his landlady was more prosperous than she had been under the old system.

Once this excitement was over the Assembly settled down to its proper job of constitution-making—a long, slow process which took until March. Long before that time Vienna grew impatient.

The tensions were increasing all summer long. The students grew more and more arrogant, especially after they succeeded in forcing the Emperor back to Vienna, the government more and more determined to reassert its authority, the workers more and more discontented as they found even a revolution did not fill their pots with chicken. Many of their employers began to take back the concessions they had made in March, and even the public works projects were reduced by half. The small shopkeepers and clerks became more and more worried about their money; their fears crystallized around one of those perennial schemes to make everybody rich that

[13] The official decree which emerged from imperial headquarters eight months after the Assembly voted it in August, stated that there should be no indemnity for *political* feudal rights, such as the power of the landlord to maintain courts and prisons. The new law naturally freed them from the expense of keeping a force of lawyers and jailers. The *economic* losses, consisting of the share of the crop and the free labor they had been entitled to, were to be paid for at two-thirds of their nominal value. Half of this sum was to be paid by the peasant and half by the province in which the land lay. The sum due was capitalized at roughly twenty times the annual value of the goods and services, and averaged 350 florins (or $175) for each peasant holding. Jerome Blum has shown that in this form it was a measure which was highly satisfactory to most of the noble landlords. In the 18th century, these nobles had feared ruin if the robot were abolished, but by 1848 most of them had become convinced of the inefficiency of the system and the need of real reform, particularly because they needed agricultural credit for larger scale farming.

For their part, the peasants were so sure that revolution meant abolition of the system that they spontaneously stopped giving feudal dues and services in the spring of 1848, and in this they were supported by several official decrees pertaining to separate provinces, months before Kudlich's law.

flooded half Vienna that summer. A little hunchbacked watchmaker named Swoboda floated stock for a credit union which was to lend money to small shipwrecked businesses so that they would be able to offer employment again. Some officials like Baron Doblhoff took shares in this scheme so that it acquired a specious air of government backing, and when the shares began to fall thousands of people felt cheated. Swoboda asked the cabinet, and then the Emperor personally to guarantee his securities, but was refused.

When rioting broke out in the middle of September because of these strains, the Assembly stepped in to checkmate both the radicals and the conservatives. Their first step was to vote a credit of two million florins which was to be used to support business in general, and also to redeem the Swoboda shares at twenty per cent of par. This sensible act made people trust the Assembly's authority. At the same time it refused to let the government use troops against the students, even after the Minister of War himself came to tell the Assembly of a student plot which he had mysteriously heard about.

This student plot was pure fabrication on the part of the government, but the conservatives had reached the point where they wanted to stir up a riot in order to be able to use force to suppress it. They did not want to conciliate the students or the Swoboda victims any more than they had the public works employees. William H. Stiles, the American Chargé d'Affaires at Vienna, said that the government suffered from indecision and duplicity, pursuing a policy of shifts, makeshifts, and hesitations. They were faithful to no one of the promises they made, he said, but were weak, timid, false, intriguing, and deceitful. They were constantly yielding to threats, never to reason; they maligned the students to get the troops back into the city and provoked the workers so as to get the glory of overcoming communism. Thus they kept continually justifying the suspicions of the revolutionary party.

In those September days the light-hearted students used to ask their beloved Füster why he was never merry any more. He could not make them see the dangers he saw—that Prince Windischgrätz's army in the north was nearly through its maneuvers, that the Minister of War, Count Latour, was growing bolder every day, urged by the people at court, and that Vienna was becoming isolated from the rest of the Empire.

XII

The Hapsburgs' Return

EARLY in October the news spread around that Count Latour had ordered the Richter battalion of grenadiers, long quartered in Vienna, to leave the city and join Baron Jellačič in his fight against Hungary.

Ever since Hungary had won its independent administration in March, the court party had been trying to win this part of the Empire back, and they were delighted when the Croatians rose under Jellačič against the passionately nationalistic Magyars. Latour had been secretly sending supplies to Jellačič for some weeks, but as soon as he openly ordered reinforcements, the people of Vienna objected.

On October 5 a deputation from the Vienna national guard begged Latour to keep the grenadiers at home. But at the same time they plied the grenadiers with money, wine, women, and propaganda, not to obey the orders to march against Hungary. Then the guards began cutting up railway tracks and destroying a bridge over which the grenadiers would have to march, and they induced the grenadiers themselves to guard it against repair.

Latour, who was both brave and inflexible, told the deputation waiting on him that he could positively not countermand the orders of a mutinous corps without vitiating military discipline in the whole army.

Unluckily for himself, the Count was already the bête noire of the radical party. For weeks the students had been inciting the people against him, and the only thing that kept him in office was his own sense of duty to the Emperor. By keeping hold of the War Ministry through all the changes of the rest of the cabinet, the court had an outpost which served it well, for Latour was able to get supplies to Radetzky in Italy as well as to Jellačič in Hungary, and he was even in touch with Russia, since the idea of getting help from the Czar was always in the back of the Hapsburgs' minds.

Latour was from a French emigrant family, and so had no feeling for any special race in the Austrian Empire, and he had a tremendous contempt for parliaments. When he had to appear before the Assembly, he acted like an enraged tiger in a cage; he never scrupled to deceive it. In addition to telling them about his imaginary student rising, he swore that he had no official relations with Jellačič. This was just before some Hungarian shepherds intercepted a message from that general acknowledging the receipt of military stores from the War Ministry.

When the crisis of sending the grenadiers came, the students and their friends saw that it would be a good chance to maneuver their enemy out of office and began inciting the workers and the national guard to that end.

Shooting broke out about noon on October 6. A party of radical national guards attacked a group of loyal ones and followed them right into St. Stephen's Cathedral where the leader of the loyalists was killed on the steps of the altar. Meanwhile, some railway workers, armed with six-foot iron bars, went after the troops in the city and persuaded many of them to go over to the insurgent side.

This was the biggest challenge the Assembly had yet met, far more serious than the riots in September; but they had gained some experience in quieting those, and clamored to meet and handle this one. When their Slavic president refused to call a session, it was another sign to the Viennese of Slavic treachery. Finally, under a vice president, the members came together anyway and went into permanent session. Their first step was to send out groups of their members to various parts of the city to try to quiet the people. These men tore white curtains from the windows and wrote with coal on them, "Assembly Member," which they used as scarves to identify themselves as peacemakers in the tumult. One of these commissions succeeded in saving the imperial palace and the national bank from the mob, while another waited on Latour, who contemptuously told them their fears were greatly exaggerated.

In view of the fact that a lynch mob was threatening the Ministry of War this time, crying "Hang Latour" the Count's *sang-froid* was amazing. At four o'clock, when the angry crowd was about to burst open the gate, Latour ordered the troops guarding the building to cease fire and the gate to be opened. He himself hid in a closet, while friends pushed furniture against the door and spread paper around the office to make it look to oncoming crowds as if the room had already been searched. If the Count had only stayed in his hiding place he might have been safe. Instead of this he let himself be talked into coming out to parley with some Assembly members who had been sent out specifically to save his life. First, however, they demanded that he resign—and, realizing the situation was hopeless, he wrote down the words they dictated, stating that he resigned, but adding, "with His Majesty's consent." The gentlemen of the Assembly pointed out that to make such a proviso was highly dangerous, but they had reached the limits of Latour's conscience. As a servant of the crown, he insisted he could do no other way. So, escorted by twenty armed national guards that the Assembly sent to guard him, and accompanied by four Assembly members, he made his way down the staircase into the face of the mob. The people were wild. Pulling off his defenders, who tried to put their bodies between him and the crowd, they hit at Latour with hammers, thrust at him with bayonets and iron pipes. After he was dead, forty-three big wounds were counted on his corpse. Not content with this, they stripped him and strung him up to a lamp post, and sang and shrieked beneath his body while women dipped their handkerchiefs in his blood. All his clothes were torn up for souvenirs.

This was the crime which seemed to justify any length of repression when the Hapsburgs got back into full power. They held it over the students, the workers and the Assembly alike. The murder was undoubtedly committed by working men who testified that they had been incited by the students. The students, however, had never meant to use such violence. As for the Assembly, they tried hard to prevent the attack, yet the thanks which the Hapsburgs gave to Dr. Joseph Goldmark, the member who had shielded Latour's body with his own head and arms as long as he had strength was condemnation to death. (He escaped, and became a respected American citizen.)

However, thousands of good people believed from then on that the revolution had proved to be wickedness incarnate, and they ceased to give it their moral support. The Czech deputies were the first to wash their hands—they marched out of the Assembly in a body. The horrified members who remained felt that it was up to them to save the city as far as it could be saved, so they kept on with their heroic efforts to restore order.

By evening the mob had turned from the War Ministry to the

arsenal, which was defended by eight hundred soldiers and was almost impregnable. The Assembly ordered the national guard to take it over before it was pillaged, and at ten in the evening the guard began to bombard the arsenal with the cannon which they had been given earlier in the summer. The balls had no effect on the sturdy old building but Congreve rockets set it on fire, to the great alarm of sensible fighters on both sides because of the ammunition stored inside. While the hard-pressed garrison worked like mad to keep the fires from spreading, the mob outside, heedless of the danger of an explosion which would kill them all, wildly refused to let fire engines come up. With both sides half crazy, it was no easy matter for the Assembly's delegates with their white scarves to get through the lines to parley with the commandant. Risking their lives they pushed through the firing line and, once inside the building, persuaded the commandant to surrender.

To whom, however, should they turn over their charge? Hans Kudlich spent the whole night trying to scrape up enough members of the Academic Legion to keep order in the arsenal and finally had to take in a mere sixty men to replace the eight hundred regulars who marched out.

The minute firing ceased, the mob ran into the still burning building to get arms. The only people who could bother to run the fire engines were some boys from twelve to fifteen—their older brothers were ransacking the stores of arms, emerging with anything that struck their fancy. Ancient suits of armor, gilded helmets, Turkish scimitars shone in the torchlight. Muskets often fell into the hands of young boys. Someone put on the coat of mail that had belonged to the ancient Bohemian Princess Libussa, and another trophy was the shirt in which Gustavus Adolphus had received his death wound.

After such a night it took nerve for the Assembly to petition the Emperor for an amnesty, but they did so, trying to persuade His Majesty that if he had had a truly popular ministry instead of a man like Latour who was kept in office against the people's will, the outbreak would not have occurred. To soften the imperial heart further, they voted the budget he had asked for, twenty million florins instead of the mere six million they had allowed him in August. From now on the Assembly worked incessantly to keep peace, but at the same time it began to provide for the defense of the city in case troops should be sent against it. The meetings never adjourned, and the leaders were on duty uninterruptedly; Schuselka, for one, slept on a bench in the Assembly Hall with a pile of proclamations for a pillow, and saw his home only four times during the rest of the month.

For a while it seemed as if peace might still be won, for the Emperor, according to his custom, granted everything the Assembly asked for, including a promise not to make war against Hungary. Then on the same day he fled from the city for a second time, away to his Moravian province where he could not be kept as a hostage. Here his advisers could keep in touch with Prince Windischgrätz, whose summer maneuvers were finished by this time; and with Baron Jellačič, who was already near Vienna with his Croatian regiments. Back in Vienna the Assembly took great comfort in the scraps of paper he had left them and kept the illusion for many days that the Emperor meant to assure them that law and right were on their side. They did not recognize the characteristic caution of the Hapsburgs, which would never break completely with the liberal party until victory for the other side was absolutely certain.

Even when Windischgrätz and Jellačič moved into view, the Viennese could hardly believe that these troops were going to be used against them. With their brains they armed themselves and prepared for a siege, but with their hearts they sent petition after petition to the court, explaining that the whole trouble came from misunderstanding. Thus it produced a sensation when on October 11 the city council announced that it would provide for the families of any men who died fighting in the city's defense. The next day the Minister of the Interior himself confirmed a young playwright-journalist named Messenhauser as head of the national guard of Vienna, charged with the protection of the city. Was the guard, then, commissioned by one department of the government, supposed to clash with the imperial army?

Messenhauser proved to be a better newspaper man than commander. He was at his best in the news-letters he posted over the city every day, telling the citizens of the progress of the battle, but he neglected such elementary precautions as confiscating the telegraph.

Not only was the guard commissioned officially but the Assembly also kept getting assurances from headquarters that their course was legal and approved. On October 19 the Emperor wrote of his gratitude to the parliament for keeping anarchy away, and he implied that it was the only body with authority to declare martial law. Yet on October 20 a hasty cab dashed from street corner to street corner in Vienna, stopping just long enough at each one to post a decree from Windischgrätz's camp, three miles south of the city, putting the whole city under martial law. Two days later the Assembly was dissolved, and soon thereafter the national guard and the Academic Legion. At last the citizens began to see that the 100,000 soldiers camped nearby were there for business.

Field Marshal Alfred Prince Windischgrätz was momentarily the most powerful person in the Empire. He was as much disgusted as anybody with the doubletalk which the court was passing out, and he finally made the court and the cabinet promise that in the future he must give his consent before they made any important decisions. And they could tell that his own decisions were sure to be harsh. Long before he had been famous as author of the dictum that no man existed for him who was not at least a baron. Now, if the Assembly wanted to abolish the title "by the Grace of God," he muttered, they must hear of the grace of cannon fire. Already, in this year of revolution, he had suppressed an outbreak at Prague, where his wife had been killed in the shooting, and he had no intention of showing mercy to refractory Vienna.

The Assembly rose to his challenge by declaring his proclamations illegal, and then it called up all the men in the city for military duty. The only exceptions were for Assembly members, members of the city council, and foreigners. Rich men were somewhat dismayed to find for the first time that they could not buy themselves out of this unpleasant duty, but the Assembly insisted it was just that all citizens should share equally in the defense, and they also pointed out that this measure would protect the upper classes against resentment from below. To enlist the workers they offered pay of 25 kreuzers a day; until then service in the guard had been unpaid.

About this time, toward the end of the month, a small, white-haired Pole reach Vienna and offered his services to the city's armed forces. He was Joseph Bem, a veteran of many insurrections in his native land, who now, in 1848, looked around to see where he could be of most use in the revolutionary struggle and picked Vienna. He was soon in charge of the defense, superintending every barricade, visiting all parts of the city secretly and inspecting everything— in the last days of the siege he did not even take the hour every day which was needed to dress his years-old unhealed wound. In addition to his talent for detail, he knew just when to punish, when to praise, and when to joke with his men. They all adored him and paid him back in the incredible courage they showed when he gave them orders such as, "You will not surrender this position until it can't be held any longer—and not even then."

The Academic Legion had fallen off sadly in numbers by fall, from about 5,000 to about 1,000. Some students had gone to fight in Hungary, some to study in Germany, many had been driven to their homes by poverty. However, Füster stoutly maintained that the best fifth was left, and the university led the defense in many lines. Chemistry laboratories were turned over to the making of powder; spies were examined by law students; and the technical students were in charge of all the artillery, as well as distributing munitions and supplies among the various defenders. The students also kept watch at several observation posts, the most spectacular being on top of the tower of St. Stephen's Cathedral, where they installed a telescope and kept signalling news of army movements with flags in the daytime and by lights at night. They still kept up the numerous charities of the summer, taking care of wounded soldiers and the poor, and leading the workers in battle. All the time they kept coming back to the university to relax. The lecture rooms were spread with straw where tired students could sleep with their weapons beside them, while from the rector's chair in the Aula a girl distributed cigars and poppy seed cakes.

One of the students' most incongruous friends at this period was Baron Kraus, the imperial finance minister. He was a short, fat, pale old gentleman, with the eyes of a saint, always smiling and easy. Whenever the students needed money he gave them a small sum, on condition they would leave the bank unharmed. Week after week he would travel back and forth from Vienna to the court at Olmütz, with his fat brief case under his arm, accompanied by no secretary or servant, undeterred by the battle, holding things together in a way no one else tried to do. Windischgrätz protested. Kraus blandly answered, "The money I give the students goes more into canteens than into armaments. I tell them to be good boys, and mostly they are." Windischgrätz, who had no sense of humor, threatened to keep Kraus a prisoner. "You could not do me a greater service, Prince. Do you think it is fun to let myself be bombarded by you in Vienna?"

As the battle closed in, with troops sniping at the suburbs, all classes in Vienna united to protect their city. Everyone seemed to understand that they were fighting to make the Emperor stand behind the illusory promises he had made them. Even the workers forgot their hatreds, and did not take advantage of the fact that 20,000 rich citizens had fled town the day after the imperial family left. For instance, the Rothschilds abandoned their mansion, and when their manager stole back into town in a milk cart, disguised as a milk dealer, he found nearly everything in the big house exactly as they had left it. The people even respected the property of Metternich and Windischgrätz. Everyone commented on how much the working class had learned since March, when they had gone wild in destroying the factory machines.

Solidarity showed itself in the efforts of both sexes as well as of all classes. Ladies, properly speaking, disappeared from the streets, so that one shocked observer noticed that when you saw a female figure it might at first look as if it belonged to the upper class, but when it came nearer you could see that it was really one of those who believed in "emancipation," or even "communism." Most people admired the way the women came out to dig up pavement, and the children built barricades of manure, stones, and furniture. Barricades soon rose higher than they had in May—and passersby showed their friendliness by leaving an offering as they went through, or paid a tip to be helped across, so that the defenders of each barrier had a little cash.

By night the patrols that kept watch on the walls and bastions showed the same fraternity. Crowded around the watchfires were legionnaires in high, plumed Calabrian hats and workers in blouses. When they had a chance they exchanged bullets with the enemy as gaily as if they were bread pills, and in intervals between shootings they did Windischgrätz and Jellačič to death in effigy by every known method of execution. Robert Blum, who arrived in Vienna on his mission from the Frankfurt Assembly at the end of October, was delighted to see a revolution carried so *gemütlich* and yet *gründlich,* by which he meant with gaiety on their lips yet earnestness in their souls. The workers, he said, showed an especially wonderful spirit. Blum was invited to become an officer in a special corps of literary men; and although his speechifying annoyed them at first, with his trick of dropping words like beads from a rosary (to allow time for applause) his flat refusal to leave the city convinced them of his earnestness.

As the besieging forces pulled tighter, living became harder. By October 24 milk was scarce, though there was an overabundance of beer and wine. Herds of gray oxen pastured on the glacis, since their owners were unable to send them out to their accustomed fields farther on, and they provided some meat. When the public fountains went dry in some parts of town, it was attributed to the devilish machinations of Windischgrätz, but proved to be due in reality to the fact that no one bothered to keep up the fires which made the steam to pump and filter the Danube water. By the 27th the gas street lighting system broke down also, so the city council ordered all householders to put lamps in their first floor windows at night so as to throw some light into the streets, making a weird and lovely background for the last gruesome days of the siege. And on the 27th also came the first interruption of the postal service.

One great mistake of the revolutionaries was that they expected help from the peasants. Naïvely they believed that since they had given freedom to the peasants, the peasants would back up the city's other desired reforms. Gratitude, however, is like a leaky reservoir, as Hans Kudlich himself, the author of the bill to free the land, found when he went out to recruit. Interest in the revolution was so completely exhausted by this time that he could hardly get a single village youth to volunteer in Vienna's battle. For one thing, it had been easy for the government to make it seem as if the peasants' new freedom were a gift from the Emperor. Few of the workers on the land realized what a battle their own Assembly had fought in their interest. Worse than that, the countrymen took advantage of the occasion to charge the highest prices they could for their produce. Peasant support nearly saved the revolution at Leipzig, and in the case of Vienna it could have made Windischgrätz's campaign difficult if not impossible. Without this support, food became almost impossible to obtain in the city, except by the very rich, who could still get bread, eggs, cheese, salt meat, and fish.

The more sanguine Viennese had counted on help not only from the peasants but from Hungary.

The new separate Hungarian regime was fighting at this time to subdue Jellačič, a Croatian and, therefore, properly an Hungarian subject. In this fight between two parts of the empire, the Austrian government was officially neutral—recruiting for both sides went on in tents next door to each other in Vienna, and the recruits for both sides often drank their recruiting bonus up together before going off to shoot each other down. Secretly, however, Jellačič was armed and supported by the imperial government, and everyone knew by this time of the aid Count Latour had sent him.

By early October the Hungarians had succeeded in chasing Jellačič across the frontier into Austria, quite near Vienna. It was to help him in this plight that Latour had called out the grenadiers on October 6. After Latour's murder had aroused hatred for the Viennese revolution, it became easy for Jellačič to forget that his predicament had been ignominious, and he began to boast that he had given up his campaign in Hungary in order to march to Vienna to restore order there.

The Hungarian army followed Jellačič up to the banks of the Leitha, the river that separated Austria from Hungary, and then encamped. Their army consisted largely of men who had been recruited patriotically as "home defenders," and they feared to lose their amateur status by leaving their own soil.

However, the Hungarians were the natural allies of the revolutionists in Vienna, and they would have been willing to come to the aid of the city if they could be invited officially, so their act would not seem like unprovoked aggression.

Their envoy, Francis Pulszky, came to Vienna sure that it would be easy to find a sponsor, since it was plain to see that the insurgents' position inside Vienna was hopeless without outside support. His first appeal was to the Assembly, which surprised him by declaring that it was incompetent to ask the Hungarian army to cross the border. The Assembly's Slavic sympathies may have had something to do with this attitude for Slavs disliked Magyars but at the same time they were extremely anxious not to cut the cord of legality which bound them to the Emperor. However, they suggested that the city council was the proper agency to negotiate about the city's defense. The municipal governments of Paris, Milan, and

Venice had to take over great responsibilities when revolution over-whelmed the states they were in, but in Vienna the city council, though admitting that the Hungarians were needed, could not bring itself to ask them to come, and hinted to Pulszky that perhaps the national guard would feel like appealing to their brothers in arms. So Pulszky went to interview Messenhauser.

Messenhauser was cordial, and indeed promised to send some powder down the river twenty miles to Pressburg— but as for guns, Messenhauser said that he would be denounced as a traitor if he were caught sending guns out of the city, even the guns which Hungary had bought in England and which were sitting at that moment in Vienna, impounded in the customs house. Pulszky was disgusted, but even in his disgust he admitted to himself that his own side had been just as stiff-necked to insist on a legal summons in the first place.

While the Hungarians dallied, Windischgrätz and Jellačič pre-pared to close in on the city. As in all countries in 1848, the citizens hoped that the army would refuse to fight, and they sent out an appeal to Jellačič's camp dealing with the brotherhood of man and Natural Right. The stalwart Croatian replied, "The Emperor's orders define my Right. I come to Vienna to set up order." Imperial officers naturally could not be brothers to the rest of mankind. Jellačič let his troops act exactly as if they were in enemy territory, and his scarlet-cloaked border regiments that had seen service only on the Turkish frontier, had no idea of any other kind of warfare. Each man of them had won his first weapon from the Turk; thus their knowledge of close-range fighting beat anything the Viennese ever dreamed of. These soldiers used to make sport of the Viennese during the siege, parading openly to draw fire from the barricades and then laughing as the balls missed because of poor marksman-ship. When one duelled with a student, he played around till he was tired, then slit the student's throat with one masterful cut.

Up to this point Windischgrätz was merely organizing his siege. When he was ready he gave the city forty-eight hours to surrender peacefully, before he began to bombard it in earnest. But Vienna did not consider giving in. Instead the citizens let the armistice ex-pire, and at nine o'clock on the morning of October 26 summoned all of Vienna's defenders to their barricades by bells in all the church towers and trumpets in every street.

By the 28th, the troops had taken most of the suburbs and were pressing against the walls. So many officers of the national guard had deserted by then that all corps were commanded by students, and they had a frightful day. The smoke of powder was so thick the opposing sides could hardly see each other, but an earwitness described the thunder of cannon, the crack of small arms, the ringing of bells, the beating of drums, the blasts of trumpets, the yells of the fighters, the weeping of women and children, the crack of falling houses and the clatter of glass. By night the sky was red with fire. "Whoever received no light from that fearful blaze will remain blind to eternity," prophesied a beaten radical. Croats climbed the barricades like cats, with scimitars in their mouths, and they scaled houses in the rear of the barricades so as to pick off defenders from the inside.

After one such day Messenhauser confessed to the city council that further defense was impossible. The national guard was for giving up the struggle at once, but the workers' corps angrily wished to stick to the last barricade. The students threatened to make Messenhauser resign and give the command to someone still willing to assume it, but Messenhauser retorted that his appointment came from the Assembly and was confirmed by the ministry, and he would not resign on the protests of mere students. So he posted the last of his famous daily placards, announcing surrender and the plans for laying down individual arms.

That night the workers took over the city. Tearing up the placards, they forced those who had laid down their arms to take them up again. They cried they were betrayed, and when the news was flashed down from St. Stephen's tower that the Hungarian army was advancing, they could not be restrained.

And indeed the Hungarians had chosen this moment at long last to move, for Kossuth had come up to join his soldiers and he overrode the timid generals who would not violate the frontier. Ignorant of Messenhauser's surrender, he sat on a hilltop, roasting potatoes and bacon over a signal fire, and the next morning gave the order to attack.

Inside the city Messenhauser did not tell anyone of the Hungarian move, although he received a formal announcement of it, for he felt bound by the terms he signed with Windischgrätz. But the students who kept watch in St. Stephen's tower heard the firing, and between tantalizing drifts of fog they thought they discerned a battle. So on October 31, while Messenhauser's white-flagged deputation went out to give the city up, St. Stephen's bells once more called the people to arms. The troops marching up to the glacis to take over the city were met with a hot fire of bullets.

Windischgrätz boiled with anger. He had no difficulty in routing the Hungarian army completely. Then he gave orders that Vienna should be bombarded. The bombardment sounded like twenty thunderstorms, while the last defenders were no more than a child talking back. The copper roof of the Augustine Church melted and shone too brightly to look upon. When finally troops marched in a second time to take the beaten city, they knocked down or shot down anyone with arms, without waiting to question if he bore them willingly or had been forced to carry them by the workers' patrols. In vain the city council pleaded that they could not restrain the students in this last impetuosity. Windischgrätz demanded twelve student hostages to be turned over to him, and decreed death penalties for Bem (who, however, escaped.[1]) Messenhauser, Robert Blum, and a few journalists.

The Croats marched in, quiet as cats, with none of the noise and clang of an ordinary army. Their beautiful scarlet cloaks, clasped at the neck with a large silver egg which opened into a drinking cup, their variety of Turkish weapons, the warrior women who marched at their sides, all made such a sight as Vienna had not seen for centuries. Europe's most urbane capital did not know what manner of men inhabited the edges of the Empire. Unfortunately, it was one of the historical privileges of the Seressan soldiers to plunder. When they found the Emperor, whom they thought they were coming to save, was not in the city, they began to loot it like a Turkish frontier village, though they stole with no sense of value. They would sell a gold watch for a few florins, or even think they had the best of the bargain if someone gave them a few pieces of real silver money for a banknote worth a hundred florins.

---

[1] Bem escaped on a simple pass and rode over to the Hungarian lines in a cab. Many romantic tales described how he left Vienna in an Austrian general's uniform, or in a coffin, but he actually wore civil dress with a top hat. At first he refused to give up his saber, whereupon a friend took it away and hurled it through a window. Some years later it was found. In Hungary Bem fought even more brilliantly than in Vienna, and completely conquered Transylvania.

On November 1 cynics noted a remarkable change in Vienna's exterior. The population in their haste to make ready for the imperial troops threw their arms out of windows in order not to be caught with them, and guns littered the streets. Suddenly everyone cut off his long hair and shaved his beard—for these had been signs of democratic sympathy. Calabrian hats made way for the "tasteless cylinder" or stovepipe; for the first time in months people dared to wear gloves. The coffee houses were crowded, but only the old conservative papers could be read in them. And the crowds quickly learned to say "Hurrah" in many languages—the Hungarian *Eljen*, the Croatian *Zivio*, the Italian *Evviva*,—for from now on during five whole years of martial law, Vienna was policed by soldiers that could not speak German.

Military retribution went swiftly ahead. Blum was shot; Messenhauser was allowed to give the command to fire at his own execution. Every house was searched three times, for men, arms, and forbidden literature, and the police were especially curious about girls' rooms, where many students were unearthed, some in women's clothes. In the end only a handful were executed. Nine students and about two hundred other people were sentenced to military service; and the university was reopened in February. But the promise to reconstitute the national guard was never kept.

Most Viennese were probably tired of anarchy, as they called their experience, and from now on would prefer order, even if it was harsh and the taxes came high. After 1848 the police were just as anti-liberal and a good deal less good-natured than they had been under Metternich. For calling Francis Joseph a rogue, one young man received a sentence of a year in prison and three years in the army. And on the anniversary of the glorious days of March, the police were ordered to arrest anyone in mourning—lest he mourn the revolution—and even anyone with a "doubtful" expression on his face.

A few people saw the silver lining in all this, Karl Marx for one. He was inordinately proud that Germans had given to the world such an example of revolutionary resistance, and said he would not exchange the whole national stand of Hungary for this demonstration of "our own people" in Vienna.

In another spirit, Leopold von Gerlach, the most reactionary friend of the King of Prussia, mused on the strange ways of provi-

dence: "Up to now (God) has done much more through enemies
than through friends in his kingdom and to the establishment of his
order. He has saved Poland through the madness of the Poles, so
that she fell under German mastery; in the Danish affair, he has
compelled the King, through England and Russia, to take an independent position; he broke the Frankfurt Parliament through the
murder of Auerswald and Lichnowsky; Austria came to its knees
through the murder of . . . Latour. . . ."[2]

Gerlach might have gone on to note with more satisfaction that
by late 1848 the Lord was apparently tired of working through
his enemies, such as England and the Aula. At that time he raised
up a friend for the Hapsburgs, a true statesman in the person of
Prince Felix zu Schwarzenberg.

The Schwarzenbergs, like so many of the high nobility, had been
a sovereign family until 1806, holding enormous estates in Bohemia
directly from the Emperor. Thus Prince Felix grew up in a high
social circle—his sister married Prince Windischgrätz, and was
killed by the revolution in Prague in June 1848. Felix, however,
was a second son, and therefore assumed that his career would be
the army. After a period in this service Metternich decided to make
a diplomat out of him instead, so he was sent abroad and given
every chance to study foreign relations. For years it seemed as if
Schwarzenberg's successes were going to be entirely among women;
in his succession of love affairs, the most famous was that with Lady
Jane Ellenborough, who abandoned her English husband, followed
Schwarzenberg to Paris, bore him a daughter, and was divorced by
her husband after a sensational trial in the House of Lords. It was
in the last years of his life that he discovered that work could hold
an equal excitement; before he died, in 1852, he remarked, "If only
I had worked harder!"

January 1848 found him occupying the not-too-grand post of
Austrian envoy at Naples. As the spring advanced, Naples seemed
about to join the rest of the Italian states in a war against Austria
to free Lombardy, so Schwarzenberg demanded his passports and
went north to the camp where Field Marshal Radetzky was defending that province. He was wounded in battle and decorated for
bravery. But Radetzky like Metternich before him wisely chose to
use Schwarzenberg's diplomatic talents rather than his military

[2] Leopold von Gerlach, *Denkwürdigkeiten*, Berlin, 1891. p. 230.

ones. Radetzky was a stout old defender of the Hapsburgs, and he was disgusted when he received orders to treat with the Italians instead of fighting them. The court were so terrified that they were ready to throw away Lombardy as a sop to the god of revolution, but their field marshal who had defended Lombardy for years intended to keep on doing so. He therefore ignored the command to treat, and sent Schwarzenberg to Innsbruck, where the court was established when it fled from Vienna, to wangle 25,000 reinforcements instead of a capitulation. And in this mission the Prince was successful. These reinforcements were to be partly recruited among the public works employees in Vienna, and this action was one of the workers' grievances. It seemed to Radetzky that if the government could maintain them in Vienna, it could maintain them in Italy.

With this help the old marshal quickly reconquered Lombardy and installed Schwarzenberg as military governor of Milan. The Prince, however, had tasted his oats, and he decided to go to Vienna, though he had not been ordered by the court or invited by the ministry. Like many great men, Louis Napoleon for one instance, he owed part of his success to his perfect sense of the right time and place.

His most devoted subordinate in the capital describes how he sat in his room one late September day, wishing that his master would come to straighten out the Empire: "The door opened suddenly. An officer bearing the uniform of a general appeared on the threshold. In the half-dark of the room, I did not recognize him at first, but his appearance made a tremor go through me. It was a man of tall stature, slender, holding himself very straight. Hair cut short and not too abundant and already graying failed to cover perfectly a comparatively small head. The pale and noble face with a high straight forehead, chiselled one would say in marble, would have produced by its immobility the feeling of calm if the speaking eyes, the gaze sweet and severe at the same time did not reveal ardent passions, strongly held in when necessary by an iron will. Now I see who it is, and a sharp joy floods my heart, the joy of the sailor who is in danger of sinking and sees the lifeboat. Oh, it is indeed he. Oh, my darling Austria, you will not perish. For weeks . . . I have been waiting for him with growing anguish and now I see him before me here in my room. It was Prince Felix zu Schwarzenberg."[3]

[3] J. A. von Hübner, *Une Année de ma Vie*, Paris, 1891. p. 318.

The Prince acted for a few weeks as if he were in no hurry to accept a cabinet post, particularly under someone else, and this bluff worked, for during October he was asked to be prime minister. When he took the job, one of his conditions was that Ferdinand must abdicate and young Francis Joseph take the throne.

When Vienna fell to the arms of Windischgrätz, the new prime minister's brother-in-law, the time seemed ripe for the change of rulers. Ferdinand and his stupid brother, the legal heir, were both persuaded by their wives to renounce their rights to the throne, leaving it open for Francis Joseph, now turned eighteen and an appealing candidate by reason of his youth, bearing, and well-known courage.

The abdication took place at Olmütz, the Moravian town where the court was sitting out the revolution, early in December in the presence of the imperial family and a few councilors. Ferdinand had a fit of stubbornness at the last minute and had to be pushed by a lady-in-waiting into the chamber where the ceremony was to take place. Still, after he had dutifully read the paper handed to him—in which he gave his health as the reason for the step—and his nephew sank on one knee before him, Ferdinand said, "God bless you. Bear yourself bravely, God will protect you. It is done gladly." Francis Joseph's remark on the subject was, "My youth is over." And indeed it was. From that time until his death in 1916, his destiny was tragic.

Schwarzenberg made him open his reign with a lie. His first manifesto rang with promises of free institutions, liberty to all his subjects, and particularly interest in the constitution at which the Assembly was still plugging away. After the days of October in Vienna, the members had been reconvened in the little Czech village of Kremsier, not far up the March River from Olmütz where the court was. The tone which Francis Joseph's manifesto should take was the subject of sharp debate in the council meetings just before the abdication. Windischgrätz took the honest, if angry, position that Ferdinand's withdrawal should be based on grounds of condemning the revolution, and that Francis Joseph should indicate at once that he would stand no more of such nonsense from his peoples. But most of the rather able cabinet[4] agreed with the prime

⁴ Schwarzenberg called good administrators to his cabinet, men like Count Stadion, the enlightened governor of Galicia; Baron Kraus, the good old finance minister who smoothed the students' feelings so well during the siege; and Alexander Bach, the

minister that the new Emperor should sound liberal at first, though they were fully determined that he should soon turn away from any appearance of democratic leanings.

As for Francis Joseph himself, someone has suggested that probably he never thought of these manifestoes as lies. He was an exceedingly matter-of-fact young man, like the run of nineteenth-century monarchs, infinitely more conscientious and less successful than many kings of earlier days. He was a soldier first, who conceived that his primary duty to his state was a military one. And his heart was hard like his grandfather's—he showed his attitude toward his subjects by hanging his official audience chamber with pictures of the bloody repression of the revolution of 1848.

In Schwarzenberg's opinion the first duty of his government should be to stamp out the Constitutional Assembly, which, he said, was born of an immature population under such conditions that no prominent, propertied, or experienced members were elected. The Prince's opinion on this matter was colored by the fact that he had been beaten in the election for the Assembly members by one of his own peasants, a fellow named Keim, and his first move against the Assembly was the petty one of ordering this man's arrest. Keim's only offence was that during the Christmas holidays he had talked freely and disrespectfully over his wine cups in his native village, and his fellow assembly members absolutely refused to give him up to the prime minister's justice. This independent attitude naturally did nothing to sweeten Schwarzenberg's feelings.

On the other hand, Schwarzenberg was almost equally contemptuous toward Prince Windischgrätz's wish to organize Austria again on old feudal lines. He told his brother-in-law severely that there were not twelve men of their own class in the whole empire that had enough brains or energy to serve usefully in a house of lords, and for this opinion Windischgrätz called Schwarzenberg a "communist."

In fact he was opposed to liberties and privileges of all subjects, of whatever class; for a house of lords, especially a stupid house of lords, could hamper an able government as much as a popular as-

erstwhile liberal lawyer who came into office in the spring of 1848 as a "barricade minister." Bach hung on through many changes of cabinet, and carried out long after Schwarzenberg was dead his policies of centralization, Germanization, a strict police and Jesuitical education.

sembly. He wanted the Empire to be united and controlled, and he concluded that force must be the basis of power. For this reason he always wore his military uniform in office. He it was who quipped that the Empire was saved in 1848 by three undisciplined soldiers, Windischgrätz, who conquered Vienna in the face of the Emperor's concessions to the city, Radetzky, who refused to surrender Lombardy when he was told to do so, and Jellačič, who was technically a Hungarian subject and who disobeyed orders which labeled him a traitor in order to uphold the larger interest of the Empire.

In foreign affairs Schwarzenberg wanted to reestablish Austria as a strong power. He was interested neither in peace as such, like Metternich, nor in a German federation. It was particularly to show his spite for the Frankfurt Parliament that he ordered Robert Blum to be shot in spite of the plea of his parliamentary inviolability. He believed—and the events of 1848 seemed to bear him out—that a *Mitteleuropa* was only possible by repressing hard *both* nationality and freedom.

To handle the Austrian Constitutional Assembly required more finesse. This Assembly was the only visible sign in Austria proper that there had been a revolution there. So Schwarzenberg traveled to Kremsier and made his first speech as a constitutional minister, a speech in which he pledged his cabinet "sincerely and without reserve" to constitutional monarchy, with "free development" of different parts of the monarchy.

Buoyed up by these promises and the hope that always attends the start of a new reign, the Assembly worked with new zeal at its constitution. The Slav members, including the Czechs, came back in triumph, and the German faction, having been defeated at the barricades, was no longer so arrogant, so both parties were more willing to compromise. If they had shown as much good will six months earlier, they might have gotten their document ratified before having Schwarzenberg to impede them. Though the Slavs still wanted decentralization with power given to the provinces, and the Germans still wanted a strong central state, they now worked out a brilliant solution of the difference. The draft of the constitution provided for local self-government in small areas, towns, and villages, with substantial provincial autonomy at the same time. The independence of the villages would guarantee minority rights, so that a German village in Bohemia, for instance, would not be compelled to hold school in Czech, and these small localities could also act as a prop to the central government against excessive nationalism in the provinces.

Most liberal Austrians since 1848 have felt that the Kremsier constitution was a triumph of democracy, showing that the people could work together "with good will in uncommon measure," even when just emerging from repression. Though this constitution was never tried out, it seems likely that the peoples of Austria could have welded a free and united country better than their rulers ever did.[5]

The progress made at Kremsier only alarmed Schwarzenberg, who was afraid public opinion would get ahead of him and the new constitution would be too popular to ignore. Therefore, on January 20 he told his cabinet he was going to dissolve the Assembly for good and all. He only waited for a military success in Hungary, which he thought could not be long coming.

Not knowing this, the members of the committee which drafted the constitution planned a fete. On March 2 they dressed themselves up in the new white-red-gold tricolor which was intended to symbolize the new Austria, and proudly marched into the Bishop's Palace at Kremsier, where the other members of the Assembly awaited them. The committee announced that their draft was completed. The Assembly thereupon decided to take a vacation, and reassemble on March 15 so as to vote the new constitution on the anniversary of its promise.

Meanwhile, the committee prepared to mail copies out to their constituents all over the country.

Schwarzenberg realized he must act quickly. He told the post office to confiscate the documents in the mails, and sent Count Stadion to Kremsier with orders to forbid the Assembly to reassemble. Stadion arrived, and after conferring with the members who supported the government, he became convinced that it would be a great mistake to dissolve the parliament, so he hurried back to Olmütz. He arrived at three in the morning, and was so excited that he took a candle and burst into Minister Bach's bedroom, waking him up to tell him his news. Bach was alarmed. Apparently

---

[5] Their bill of rights was largely drawn from the constitution of the state of Texas, then recently admitted into our union. "All power comes from the people," the constitution said, but suffrage was to be on the basis of tax-paying, so that workers and peasants would be cut out.

Stadion's nerves were giving way, and indeed that day proved almost the end of his public service.

The next day the Assembly was dissolved by telegraph, with a message from the young Emperor that its meetings "put off public confidence."

It was part of Schwarzenberg's plan to arrest the most prominent liberal leaders. He may even have picked Kremsier as a site for the meetings because it was a small walled town with only three narrow gates, so that it could easily be turned into a trap. This plan was foiled because Stadion had issued warnings. Most of the members who were in danger escaped. Füster was waked by his servant and helped to escape by friends. For many miles the Austrian police kept on his track by asking whether people had noticed his bundle of white laundry, but an underground railway of democrats passed him across the border before the police quite caught up with him. He was afterward formally expelled from the church.

Kudlich had noted beforehand how he could jump from the roof of his room to the city wall, and from there scramble down a tree and escape into the countryside. This plan he carried out.

As for Fischhof, he was too proud to leave. For his courage he was imprisoned and not released until the following December.

In that age of constitutions it seemed hardly respectable to go back to a completely constitutionless regime, so Francis Joseph copied the King of Prussia and promulgated one which had been worked up mainly by Stadion. Schwarzenberg was indifferent to its details, since he did not intend to be tied by it and only wanted to get it out quickly enough to take the place of the parliamentary one. It was therefore published on March 4. Schwarzenberg's only other care was that it should include the entire Empire, even Hungary. This was one way of thumbing his nose both at Hungary itself and at the Frankfurt Parliament, which was this very March agonizing over whether to include any part of the Austrian Empire in its new German Reich. Stadion's constitution led immediately to the offering of the German crown to the King of Prussia, because it took away all hope that German Austria might be loosened from the rest of the Empire and united with other German states.

With Kremsier and Frankfurt both eliminated, Schwarzenberg

considered his own constitution a scrap of paper, and abrogated it formally as soon as he could—in 1852.

This was no great loss to Francis Joseph's subjects. For though his constitution, and the bill of rights which he announced before the constitution proper, both looked amenable on paper, careful reading showed that every single right was limited. Thus, the people had the right of freely publishing opinions, even in print—but a law would suppress abuses of the press. The right of free petition was granted, but only from lawfully recognized groups. The right of free assembly was also to be regulated by law—and so on down the line, until at the last it was stated that the constitution of Hungary should be maintained, although the parts of it not in harmony with the imperial one should be void.

But Hungary is a story of its own. In March 1849, the Hungarians were by no means ready to accept limits to their cherished constitution, the most valuable part of which maintained their separateness. Especially were they unyielding to a young monarch they regarded as an upstart, since he gave no indication of wishing to place the sacred crown of St. Stephen on his head, or of swearing to maintain Hungary's age-old liberties.

XIII

The Modernization of Hungary

WITHIN the Austrian Empire, in 1848, Hungary was in much the position of the southern states of America. Both were agricultural, economically backward areas. In both, the upper, enfranchised classes were ingrown and passionately political. Both of them were to fight unsuccessful wars of independence and win romantic reputations as defenders of a Lost Cause.

The Kingdom of Hungary, which made up slightly more than half of the territory of the Empire, stretched for trackless miles to the east of the River Leitha. In all the kingdom there were only 2,000 miles of roads. Elsewhere, a traveler riding over the plains in a cart could tell when he was approaching a big town at night by the extra bumpiness where many ruts came together. Since only three or four regular stagecoach routes operated, travelers were rare. Those who did penetrate the country before 1848 reported customs almost as outlandish as in Asia—the lavish old-fashioned hospitality at the manor houses, where to stay less than three days was an insult to the host; thirty-six course meals (meat cost a penny a pound); robbers in Robin Hood style; gypsies with their music; the service of peasant carts made of willow which carried one along to the next stop, for it was part of the work the peasant owed in return for his land to provide transportation for travelers and government officials.

The nobles who could afford it lived in Vienna most of the year, where they could speak German and enjoy being in a center of culture. These gentlemen must have given a wrong impression to their friends at the court, because it was the constant assumption at Vienna from the eighteenth century until 1866 that the Hungarian constitution was moribund and could be tactfully set aside in favor of centralized administration from the capital.

No one outside Hungary itself dreamed, apparently, that the new nineteenth-century nationalism was going to act like a blast of fresh air on coals of independence whose glow the Magyar race had never quite allowed to die from the days when they were a proud and separate kingdom.

The Sacred Crown of St. Stephen was delivered by an angel, so it was said, to the Pope, who allowed Stephen to be crowned King of Hungary with it in 1001. The monarchy in those early days was elective. The kings of Hungary were not only chosen by the Diet, they were responsible to it; they could not initiate tax bills, but they had the right of veto.

Six centuries later, Hungary agreed to let its crown be hereditary in the Hapsburg family. When Hungary first chose an Austrian archduke, in the hope of getting protection against the Turks, the long struggle between Austrian absolutism and Hungarian liberty began. Each new emperor had to go to Hungary for a separate coronation as king of that country, and before the crown of St. Stephen was placed upon his head, he had to swear to respect the ancient privileges of the Diet. One emperor, free-thinking Joseph, had refused to undergo this ceremony and as a result he was not listed among the official kings of Hungary, and had a hard time getting his measures enforced there. His successors bent to custom and took the oath again, but hoped in their hearts that the ancient constitution of Hungary would gradually fall into disuse as had happened in Bohemia. The privileges it enshrined seemed like relics of the Middle Ages, which must sooner or later succumb to the more modern force of absolutism.

Yet of all the peoples and nations engaged in revolution in 1848, Hungary was the single one which kept its demands strictly on a legal basis. If the Hapsburgs had had any respect for their oaths, Hungary could have used its ancient constitution as a neat springboard from which to leap over absolutism into the still more modern camp of democratic, constitutional states like England and France.

After Hungary's brilliant and pathetic war in 1849, it became fashionable to compare British and Magyar institutions. In no other continental country were local politics so lively and responsible as in Hungary. Before 1848, however, no one noticed the likeness. The Hungarian county assemblies met, argued, voted amid the indifference of the rest of the world.

The Austrian bureaucrats, at least, ought to have known what to expect in 1848 from the struggle they had in 1826 trying to get greater taxes and larger levies of recruits out of Hungary. These two matters were specifically the prerogative of the Hungarian Diet at Pressburg, but Vienna made one of its periodical decisions that it would be easier to rule Hungary by the same decrees as the other provinces and that the Magyar constitution could not withstand a determined administrative policy. The King took care not to summon the Diet at this crisis and simply decreed new taxes and levies. The energetic Hungarians immediately took the matter up in the assemblies of each county; eight of these assemblies refused to authorize collection of the increased taxes.[1] At the same time, ten counties refused to send the recruits. In other counties soldiers summoned the assemblies by force, keeping the members in session until they had voted right. Angry county officials thereupon destroyed the records and hid their seals; Kossuth made his first political speech in one of the assemblies at this period. Baron Eötvös, who was to become the 1848 Minister of Education, was not spoken to at school by the other boys because his grandfather was one of the commissioners appointed by Vienna to force through the imperial decrees; this old gentleman's wife left him for the same reason.

Eventually the Diet had to be summoned and placated, and Vienna went back to its old policy of using the dietal decrees which suited the Hofburg and of stalling others by delays and legal quibbles, arts in which the Vienna government was a past master.

Politics was the great diversion of the Magyar race. German residents of Hungarian cities, and Slavic peasants, who could vote for their own village officers though not for the Diet, did not share in the passion which caused any two Hungarians to discuss candidates and issues the moment they met. Election Day was the biggest event of the year for them. For weeks beforehand young men of each party electioneered through the countryside with gypsy bands and liquor. On the eve of the voting, the whole gentry of the county met at the court house, where the young danced, the old talked politics all night long. In the morning, they voted by acclamation, each party in a separate courtyard to forestall violence. They voted for their county administrator—one of the least well-thought-of efforts of the central government was to supplant these officials with men appointed from Vienna—and for their Diet representatives. The lat-

---

[1] The increase in taxes came by reason of a new requirement that taxes be paid in silver, not paper—someone figured that there was not enough silver in the whole kingdom to pay the tax required.

ter were sent to Pressburg instructed in their votes, and could be recalled for disobeying their constituents. Even after the Diet had passed an act, it could be thrashed out again on the floors of the county assemblies, which had the power to refuse to admit any act they deemed unconstitutional.

All free men in Hungary were classed as "nobles," even though some had enormous estates while some were scarcely better off than peasants. The theory of the Magyar state, from the days of the conquest, was that every Hungarian was free and equal; his voice helped choose the king in the old days, and had never lost its say on financial matters even in modern times. Western feudalism with its system of vassals and sub-vassals was transplanted to Hungary so late that it never took root. To an extraordinary degree for the nineteenth century, every Hungarian felt himself as good as every other Hungarian—though, unfortunately, much better than the peasants who were mostly Slavs, and unfree. The so-called nobles were protected from arbitrary arrest and from corporal punishment, and they had a great tradition of free speech which went with their right to vote. And they had the extraordinary right of not paying any taxes. Taxes had been paid by peasants in the Middle Ages, while the nobility offered personal military service, so that to pay a tax came to seem the act of a menial. Free men did not even pay tolls on roads or bridges; thus, toll-collectors would open up their gates for anyone dressed like a gentleman, or who acted as if he were not in the habit of paying, while closing them down for peasants or Jewish peddlers until the fare was paid.[2]

One person in fourteen was classed as a noble in Hungary, contrasting with the Austrian archduchies where there was one noble out of 353. In Bohemia, where the nobility had been killed off during the Hussite wars, there was only one noble out of 828. Someone figured out that England had only one voter in 24 at the same time; even the United States had only one voter in eight. These figures may have been rough guesses, but even so they make the Hungarian electoral base look handsome.

Nor was it particularly difficult to become a noble. Dr. Tkalac,

[2] The *titled* nobility of Hungary, the four princes, 99 counts and 88 barons were all created by Austria in an effort to win leading families to her side. These came to sit in a separate chamber in the Diet, and formed just the conservative vetoing power the Hapsburgs needed to control a province which had a diet.

who was a Croatian and therefore a Hungarian subject though not a Magyar, tells how in the village where his grandfather was born every person was "noble." This right was very old, being granted by an act of the crown in reward for some spectacular military service performed by the village centuries before. These nobles all did the work of peasants; however, if one of them took up handwork or business he was considered to have lost his nobility. Tkalac's father went into the river boat business early in the nineteenth century, carrying cargoes of wheat and hides up and down the Croatian rivers, and though he became rich at this job, he lost his nobility. To become personally free again, all he had to do was to buy a house in a small city, for burghers enjoyed some of the immunities of the nobility. But his landlord back in the village where his brothers still worked tried to force them to do the labor of serfs, asserting that they, too, had lost their nobility. The rich brother was able to save them by buying town houses for each of them. Education was another way of rising socially, for doctors, lawyers, and professors enjoyed practically the same rights as the nobility, even though they had no tie to the land.

Not only was the Hungarian upper class large and politically active, its lower class was relatively well off and loyal. The labor service due for the use of land was less than in some parts of the Empire (two days a week instead of three as in Galicia), and peasants had a few political rights such as voting for their own village officers. Though legally they might be flogged or imprisoned at the will of their landlords, actually there was nowhere the social split that in Galicia, for instance, had been used by Vienna to incite the peasants to a civil war against their landlords. The feelings of friendliness and solidarity that led all upperclass Hungarians to call each other "cousin" made lord and peasant address each other with such endearing epithets as "my soul." This affection could be expressed in real social services, too.[3] Baroness Pulszky tells how in the famine of 1847, she cut down heavily on her own table and worked every day with the assistance of village women to distribute

[3] When the writer visited a small Hungarian village in 1930, it was a striking fact that her young hostess, when making introductions, frequently knew only the first names of the people she had been playing with all summer. Affectionate informality was still the keynote of social life—in great distinction to more western countries in Europe.

soup to 500 people, who might be peasants, or gypsies—anyone who showed up.

In the period before 1848, the outstanding Hungarian was, undoubtedly, Count Stephen Széchenyi, who spent his handsome fortune and considerable talents to build up modern institutions in his country. He traveled extensively in Western Europe and in England, where he was well-known and got most of his ideas; but it was easier for the west to understand the practical changes he wrought than the psychological ones which were just as important in his eyes. Wishing to force his country to become both proud and rich, he appealed to every motive among his countrymen—public spirit, private gain, patriotism, the wish to be in fashion, the spirit of fun, the sense of *noblesse oblige*.

He first struck the public eye in 1825 by offering to give a year's income to help endow an academy for the Hungarian language. This, interestingly enough, seemed the prime step toward making a modern nation, and it was largely owing to his efforts that Hungarian came back to the lips of his countrymen. The gentry had been gradually forgetting it, talking German in Vienna, often using Slovak to their peasants, and, odd as it seems, Latin in their Diet. In some parts Latin was a general language of communication. Dr. Tkalac remembered his Croatian mother using it in her household (though this was more unusual in a woman than a man)—and other observers reported the strange effect of hearing a nineteenth-century peasant greet his landlord, "Bonum matutinum, domine." Széchenyi raged at this decay of his mother tongue. His appeals succeeded so well that in 1847, for the first time in history, the Diet members spoke Hungarian, even though it still came haltingly to some lords' tongues.

The Count's next project was to make his fellow nobles as public-spirited as the British, so he hit upon the ingenious first step of starting horse racing. This not only led to an interest in animal breeding, but gave the nobles a chance to come together in healthy rivalry; in time his Casino or clubhouse in Pest became the most important center in the land for informal discussion.

Public spirit and national pride were all very well, but Széchenyi realized that his country was like an unfilled sack which would easily topple over. He wanted to fill it with such solid prosperity that it would stand of itself. So he started a commercial steamboat line on the Danube. Many people ridiculed him and said, as they were saying at the same time of the Mississippi, that the Danube was unsuited to such traffic because of shallow sandbanks and drifting course. The only navigation up to that time had been by boats pulled from the shore by horses or peasants, and the shallows were so wide that the rope sometimes had to be a mile long.

This interest in profit and business shocked many nobles who believed their class should be above sordid gain. When they heard they would be expected to pay toll on the new suspension bridge Széchenyi projected across the Danube between Pest and Buda, they called him a traitor to his class. But in fact this new bridge was a perfect example of Széchenyi's technique. Since it would be the longest suspension bridge in the world, all Hungary could be proud of it. At the same time, it would be of immense economic advantage to the country, for until that time only a bridge of 47 boats connected Hungary's biggest city, Pest, with the fortress Buda across the river. The boats had to be taken out in winter, so then no vehicle could cross the Danube at all unless the ice happened to be thick enough. The new bridge would speed up traffic across the river and also navigation up and down it. But Széchenyi was deliberately trying to break down aristocratic prejudice, too. Once the nobles paid a toll, however small, they could not complain so self-righteously about ordinary taxes, and Hungary could never become a modern state until the wealth of the upper class was taxable.

In the same spirit he wrote his great book on credit. Hungary had the highest interest rates in all Europe, partly because the law of entail prevented landowners from mortgaging their estates. (Unless a property was offered to all possible relatives when it was sold, and they declined to buy it, any one of them had the right to buy it back within thirty years for the purchase price plus a sum for improvements. After the expiration of thirty years, any heir of the family could force its resale to him on the same terms, even if he or his father had refused to buy it when it was first up for sale.) It was thus almost impossible to raise capital for agricultural or other improvements. "We need credit," cried Széchenyi (and by that time he was so well known that everyone read his book) and he intended by that cry to include both senses of the word—money and faith in each other.

By 1839 Széchenyi had come to seem something like a patriarch, as he courteously greeted passengers on the Danube steamboat, and made friends with Metternich. In truth he was only forty-eight years old. Like most reformers he was able to excite only one generation, and younger men became impatient as the count grew conservative. He urged his countrymen to stick to the possible, and younger patriots were already dreaming of what seemed impossible—to make Hungary free, not merely rich.

Their new leader was only eleven years younger than the count—Louis Kossuth, the most conspicuous newspaperman of Hungary. In the early thirties Kossuth, a bright young lawyer, had been sent to the Diet, when it was finally summoned to see about the long withheld taxes and recruits. He was not an elected member, but a count's deputy. It was customary for members of the hereditary upper house to send substitutes; these deputies, not being titled, sat with the lower house, but, not being elected, they had no vote in it. Most clever youths managed to find excuses to hang around the Diet—both gallery and floor were always full of them. Kossuth's distinction came from the fact that he wrote such brilliant letters back to his employer that other people wanted to copy them. Soon Kossuth was editing the equivalent of the *Congressional Record*. Because Austria disapproved printing Diet debates, he tried at first to lithograph his material. When even that was forbidden, Kossuth arranged to dictate his material to a large group of young men who made handwritten copies of his words to be sent to every county in the land.

Perhaps it was the intoxication of speaking aloud, but as he dictated these reports, Kossuth could not resist the temptation of making his friends' speeches sound better, and his enemies' worse than they had on the floor. Kossuth's gift for language was so great that he was later able to enthrall audiences in England and America with the English he had learned by reading Shakespeare in prison. In his own tongue, to his own countrymen, he seemed an oracle. When the Diet closed in 1835, he dictated a "Farewell to My Readers" which made the copyists stand up and cheer. His message of freedom excited liberals in every county; for the first time the country had a single voice, and it began to count its wrongs in unison, to remember its traditions, to make plans for a greater future.

With the Diet no longer in session, Kossuth went to Pest and began editing news from the county assemblies for the other ones to read, the first time there had been any systematic communication between counties. This was so distasteful to Austria that Kossuth was thrown into prison, quasi-legally since as a noble he was immune to arbitrary arrest, where he improved his hours reading Shakespeare and the French socialist, Lamennais. When he was released in 1840, the government surprisingly let him go back to newspaper work and he edited the first liberal paper of Hungary. Vienna, meanwhile, took care that his words were not allowed to circulate in other parts of the Empire.

In 1847, when the Diet was called, the whole nation felt the time was ripe for something momentous. Széchenyi, though he had long sat in his hereditary seat in the upper house, now ran for the lower in order to be able more effectively to oppose Kossuth. Kossuth also was running for the first time. His election demonstration at Pest was bright with gypsy bands and tricolor banners, green, white, and red. When he was declared elected and had to take the customary oath not to accept a job or favor from the Austrian government for six years, he altered the words to say "never." Kossuth admired Széchenyi, but he was certain the time had come for less indirect methods. Kossuth had been trained as a lawyer and wanted a frontal attack by the Diet to free the peasant lands. This he considered the primary job ahead. He believed that this nation of noblemen could never be great until it was turned into a real democracy; even as a very young man Kossuth had taken the trouble to call the peasants he handled by the plural or polite form of "you," and reading Lamennais in prison had only stimulated his sense of justice. In appealing to his politically-minded nation for a political solution, Kossuth was far more in the Hungarian tradition than Count Széchenyi with his talk of profits, capital, and free trade.

The Diet opened in November. Everyone was present, it seemed— titled lords, deputies, and all their numberless hangers-on. The entire diplomatic corps was invited to sail down the river from Vienna to hear the King (Ferdinand was not Emperor in his Hungarian dominions) address the Diet in its national language. His well-coached little speech was a thundering success.

Members of the Diet, and indeed nearly all Hungarians present, wore their national costume, a frock coat of brilliant color, heavily embroidered, with sabers at their sides, knee boots, velvet buttons and plumed fur caps. Prince Esterhazy's outfit had diamond buttons, its seams were of pearls. (The maintenance of this eyestopper was a tax on the entire family, for it is said to have shed $30,000 in jewels at each wearing.) Talent as well as wealth was present, and anyone in proper costume, whether elected or not, was admitted to the floor of the house. Those in conventional or western dress had to sit in the galleries, which were also crowded. On the floor everyone knew everyone else—from college days, from the Casino, from former Diet meetings. And they were all determined as never before to do something about their oppressed country.

After choosing as palatine, or viceroy, Archduke Stephen, an amiable young Hapsburg who had been brought up in Hungary and was not illiberal, the Diet set to the work Kossuth doled out to it. For Kossuth became the accepted leader of all debate after he won his first point; this was to persuade the chamber to work on a general program of reform instead of talking humbly to the King about specific grievances. Such rude disregard of convention shocked the upper house, but they were forced by public opinion to pass some of the reforms suggested even before the fateful news that Paris had revolted reached Pressburg on February 29.

The chain reaction set off in Paris was quickly utilized in Hungary to press at once for the complete reform program. Word went about that Kossuth was preparing his greatest speech, and on March 3, when he rose in the Diet, the galleries were packed as they had been at the opening. His listeners were not disappointed. They heard their leader demand that the Kingdom of Hungary should have a separate and responsible ministry, a separate national army, and separate well-audited finances. This was the first statement of the dream which Hungary kept in her heart until 1867, when Francis Deák succeeded in creating the Dual Monarchy.

Kossuth went further. He warned his friends that unless the other parts of the Empire were also given constitutions, Hungary's would not be safe. This was the spark that jumped the frontier, this was the oration read in Vienna, giving courage to the sober Reading Club there, inflaming the already ardent students on March 13.

When they heard that Vienna, too, was in revolt, the young men of Pressburg were so delighted that some hundreds of them went up the river, along with Kossuth and the Palatine, hoping to help with the fighting while the leaders pressed their demands on the collapsing regime. The party arrived at nightfall, and finding the street battle won and no places to sleep, they danced in the streets all night long.

No city liked to miss its revolution in those days. Pest, the biggest city in Hungary and its natural capital, was determined on its share of excitement and glory, even though there was no very satisfactory authority on the scene to revolt against. (The Diet sat in Pressburg, originally to keep out of the way of the conquering Turks; it had stayed there because the town was conveniently close to Vienna.) On March 15 a group of young men went around Pest's schools and university halls to pull crowds of students out into the streets. One of them composed a poem for the occasion, which they carried around to a printing shop to be printed. The proprietor objected that it had not been passed by the censor, and somewhat coyly suggested he could not print it unless he were "constrained." The boys cheerfully asked him what that would involve, and got the answer that if they laid hands on his presses, that would be constraint. This was easily done—a few light hands on the presses and the typesetters went gaily to work on their first uncensored assignment. The poem was printed, along with twelve revolutionary "points," the usual demands of free press, militia, and so on. The sheets were snatched from the press and read to the mob outside; as each verse of the poem, exhorting Magyars to great deeds, ended with the refrain, "We swear," the crowd speedily took up the chorus and intoned it. The double eagle of Austria was broken off public buildings. A committee of public safety was set up; likewise the militia was organized. When certain citizens refused to serve in the same company with Jews, many young revolutionaries hastened to enroll themselves voluntarily in the special Jewish companies.

They were also so spontaneously friendly to Serbs and Rumanians (who reciprocally supported their aims) that Kossuth felt he had to check this over-brotherly feeling in his Magyars, and refused admittance to the delegates from Pest who came to tell him about their activities. Thus the revolution in Pest was stymied. The authorities met the enthusiasts with such patience that one nonplussed young man stammered out, "Brothers, the difference between a revolution and ordinary times is supposed to be that in a revolution prudent heads are not listened to." Hungary was the only country where the prudent heads—at Pressburg, not Pest—were gathered together, prepared to exploit whatever opportunities Viennese dynamite might open for them.

So on March 15 the Diet, scarcely allowing itself time to eat, debated and quickly passed the enormous amount of legislation which Kossuth demanded.

They voted, like every assembly in Europe, for a free press and a national guard. Like the Austrian Assembly, they voted to abolish feudalism promising landlords an indemnity to make up to them partially for the loss of their peasants' services. And they imitated the French Estates of 1789 in agreeing that nobles should be taxed. The Diet, let it be remembered, consisted entirely of noblemen—in voting to tax themselves they were moved partly by public spirit, partly by enlightened self-interest, and partly because of the fear of peasant uprisings—a fear which Kossuth was not loathe to exploit in his oratory. This was exactly the same mixture of motives which persuaded their French prototypes.

In reorganizing their government, the Diet voted that from now on it should meet at Pest, and that sessions should be held every year. For the new Diet, they ordered elections in which a large number of citizens who had never voted before could take part. Their culminating decision was Kossuth's main point, namely, that Hungary should have a cabinet separate from the rest of the Empire, responsible to her own Diet.

Just as the nation was getting ready to celebrate the birth of this new regime, the staggering news came from Vienna that the Emperor was going to hold the power of war and finance for his whole territory under the single administration at Vienna.

Ferdinand's new Austrian advisers, even though they were liberals, were unwilling to preside at the dissolution of His Majesty's Empire. But to Kossuth and to Hungary, power over their own troops, sworn to their constitution, and over the spending of money, were the very crux of their expectations. These were the same questions about which the county assemblies had rebelled twenty years before.

Austrian finances had not only meant taxation without representation (for only one-sixth of the taxes paid by Hungarians were direct ones approved by the Diet; the other money came from a levy on salt and tobacco, and customs duties), but Austria had also misused the taxing power to keep Hungarian industry crippled by regulating the customs duties between the two halves of the Empire. Worse still, Austria had tried to influence Hungarian politics. In allocating funds, Vienna noticeably passed over counties with outspoken liberal deputies—sometimes such counties were never given permission to build a bridge or a road even with their own money.

When Hungarians heard that the Emperor wished to deny them their right of handling their own money, the check to enthusiasm might have been serious. Luckily, Archduke Stephen, the Palatine, agreed to hurry to Vienna to try to get the complete Hungarian program approved by his imperial cousins. Stephen offered to resign if his mission failed—and indeed in two days he was back with the powers of war and finance in his pocket. The crust of perfect legality had still not been broken. Perhaps Vienna gave in because Milan and Prague were seething, too, for as soon as these cities were subdued, Pest was to find out that imperial promises could lie, but for the moment none dreamed that His Royal and Apostolic Majesty was acting in bad faith.

Armed with confidence, and with a large number of royal signatures on various new laws, Hungarian leaders began to organize the new modern country which they had dreamed about. Kossuth never let them forget that their first responsibility was toward the peasants, so they declared that April 2 would be Emancipation Day.

In each village the people assembled on that day to listen to the proclamation which declared the land exempt from all feudal dues; peasants and lords celebrated their new equality with services in all the churches, and then with dancing. Count Charles Leiningen, a cousin of Queen Victoria who had married an Hungarian heiress, wrote his wife in detail how the change would affect their estate. He figured that the free labor and the share of the crops to which they had been entitled had been worth 8,500 florins a year; besides the loss of this sum, they would have to pay wages for all work in future. These losses, however, would be almost compensated by the fact that other nobles would have to pay tolls and ferry dues, presumably on Leiningen lands and mills, which would bring in nearly as much cash as they had lost. The Leiningens could afford to be very cheerful; if the government ever paid the promised indemnity (the terms of the law left such payment to "the national honor") they would be very well off indeed. At the moment, however, there was no money for repairs. As for his peasants, Leiningen believed that they did not feel any better off under the new order, not having recognized injustice in the old; he was sure they would not use their new freedom to rise against landlords like himself with whom they had always been on excellent terms.

The job of forming the new Hungarian Ministry was given to Count Louis Batthyanyi, an extremely prepossessing nobleman of forty years, handsome, with a look which observers commonly compared to an eagle's. He had been rather poorly educated by a flibbertigibbet mother, so that his own natural intelligence came out only after he became a young officer and was stationed in Venice. His soul responded to the art of that beautiful city, and since garrison duty left him plenty of time to himself, his studies progressed from art to language, from language to science, and from science to politics. The last interest naturally drew him into Kossuth's circle, and he became both the sponsor and the disciple of that magnetic orator. With his help, Kossuth was elected to the Diet. However, by the time Batthyanyi was called to form a cabinet, he began to see that Kossuth was no easy bird to handle. It was impossible to leave the national hero out of the ministry, for he would be more dangerous outside than in, and the only thing to do seemed to be to give him the least dangerous portfolio.

Kossuth was known to want the Interior, which would give him control of the press, the elections, and county administration. This seemed far too much power for a gentleman whose limits were unknown, so Batthyanyi offered him Finance. Though Kossuth had no training in this field, he loyally accepted the job in spite of friends who advised him to object.

Indeed, someone with great ability was sorely needed to run the treasury. Austria sent orders to all its officials to hurry any gold and silver they collected right to Vienna; so Kossuth's first move was to stop the export of bullion and to steady the bank of Pest. He then put into effect the new law taxing everybody—on land, income, and personal property; he also taxed rich absentees three times the amount of indirect taxes they would probably have had to pay if they had stayed in the country.

Kossuth's first big fight with the Vienna treasury came from his refusal to pay interest on a quarter of the imperial debt, an amount which Viennese financiers allocated as Hungary's fair share. They based their estimate on the fact that a fourth of the revenue of the imperial treasury had come from Hungary. But to take over this obligation would have meant ruin to Kossuth's precarious situation, for he found his treasury almost empty and immediately had to adopt a budget calling for three times as much expense as the revenue he had in sight. Therefore, he rationalized his refusal with great oratorical bitterness, pointing out that the Diet had never approved the constant loans with which the Hapsburgs for years had regularized their financial position, and furthermore, that none of the money had ever been used to build even one road or one school inside the borders of Hungary. Thus he made it seem a point of national honor for Hungary to leave Austria holding the mortgage papers.

Count Széchenyi was another member of the new cabinet, the Minister of Public Works, for he could not be left out any more than Kossuth, notwithstanding the fact that the two heroes were at sword's points. In fact, the Count's main motive in joining the government was to block Kossuth. Széchenyi was a free trader, being an Anglomaniac and an agriculturist, whereas one of Kossuth's main interests was to support infant Hungarian industries. (For years the tariff wall between Austria and Hungary had been rigged to keep Hungary in the condition of an agricultural colony.) The Count reproached himself for the number of times he let himself be outwitted in debate, for he was not so quick as Kossuth; in time he developed a real persecution complex and had to be confined to an asylum.

The only other figure of note in the cabinet was the Minister of Justice, Francis Deák, distinguished more for being the successful hero of 1867 (when Hungary won for good and all her right to separate administration in the Dual Monarchy) than for his part in 1848. He was a tall, stout, cheerful moderate who withdrew from public affairs when the country seemed to be going wild under Kossuth and held his fire for nearly twenty years.

Though the Hungarian cabinet was able, far abler than the gentlemen who were called to power in such quick succession in the Vienna cabinet, they never enjoyed the confidence of their king—and a king is a vital part of a constitutional monarchy. Whenever Batthyanyi tried to see his sovereign, he was physically kept out of the royal presence, for none of the people who ordered Ferdinand about, like Sophia or Minister Bach, had any sympathy for Magyar nationalism. Lacking even the passive cooperation of the crown, the Pest government was stymied.

They went ahead, nevertheless, with elections to the new Diet, which would meet at Pest. Suffrage was liberal, though by no means universal, since there was a small property qualification (except for those impoverished nobles who had always voted) and a quasi-religious one, Jews being excluded.

However, in order to be a member of the new Diet, it was necessary to speak Hungarian! And this was Hungary's undoing.

Schuselka said that nationalism was at once the hobby horse and the war horse of his era. The passion for the national language seems childish, but for that reason it was all the more easily exploited by the Viennese war office. When it came to dealing with their Slavic subjects, the leaders of Pest ceased to be statesmen and began to act like small boys in a tough game of war. The hobby horse quickly turned into the war horse.

A century afterward, seeing what trouble the East of Europe made for itself by cultivating racial passions, it seems as if the liberal movement of 1848 would have done better if it could have separated itself from nationalism. To the eyes of the most liberal men of that period, however, nationalism was holy. Schuselka specifically apologized for the rivalry and bloodshed on the fringes of the national movement, but, nevertheless, he believed that the eighteenth century's vague cosmopolitanism was over for good and that the new spirit was healthier.

Metternich would have seen the irony in turning the national hopes of the Serbs and Croats against the national hopes of the Magyars. It was a game he had played in a minor way for years. But Metternich had left the Hofburg; when the Archduchess Sophia wept and threw her arms about the neck of the Croatian Colonel Jellačič, begging him to save the Empire for her son, her passion was innocent of subtlety. She was too scared and angry to consider philosophy of government any more than the dangers of gossip about the impetuosity of her appeal.

The southern Slavs in Hungary were ideal for Sophia's purposes. Croatia and its neighboring provinces were a part of the Kingdom of Hungary that had no reason to be loyal; their fierce border soldiers were rather trained to exclusive devotion to the military hierarchy. Yet national or pan-Slavic feelings were beginning to stir also, and these could be dished up unadorned by all the embarrassing liberal demands that stirred up the rest of the world. It was true that Croatian traditions of independence had been moribund for centuries, but they were not beyond revival by interested parties, either Illyrian nationalists or Viennese officials. Croatia had the historic right to have its own Diet, at Agram, which elected three deputies to the Diet of Pressburg, and they also chose the *Ban*, or viceroy, of their "kingdom." Croatia also enjoyed a tax rate half that in Hungary proper, as well as an exemption from the quartering of troops, because of the hazards of living near the Turkish border. These material privileges backed up pan-Slavic feelings which were already encouraged (said alarmists) by Moscow gold, or at least agents from St. Petersburg. Ideal pan-Slavism, said our German friend Schuselka, was a dream of generous hearts (like later Russian dreams) ; but actual pan-Slavism was the greatest danger in all Europe.

To the Slavs themselves the intellectual appeal of nationality was just beginning to be evident. Many of them were peasants, poor and ill-educated, talking their ancient dialects without realizing that a few intellectuals were making supreme efforts to revive these languages as literary ones. Nonetheless, the literary revival paved the way for a political one, in which field it was easier to win converts among the people, until Slavic nationalism became the source of wars for the next eighty years. Freedom for them meant freedom for their countries, for they were far behind other nations in their demands for personal liberty (except for the Czech branch of the family), and their fierce belligerence was more unmitigated than that of other countries.

Dr. Tkalac was one of the intellectuals who tried to make his countrymen proud of being Slavic, yet as late as 1840, when he was in his twenties, he had never read a Slavic book. The reason was there were none, though he spent most of his schoolboy allowance getting books, allowed and forbidden, from booksellers in Pest and Vienna. He remembered that at this early age the idea of nationality seemed limiting to him, for he wanted to claim all Europe in his heritage.

Since history officially stopped with the French Revolution in his school, Tkalac spent a large part of his adolescence trying to find out what had happened in the world since then. One of his exciting discoveries came at thirteen, when he learned that steam-boats were now crossing the Atlantic. And he would not have had any idea what a locomotive looked like if he had not happened to acquire an English-made handkerchief printed with a picture of one. This treasure greatly increased his prestige among the other boys. One day the Count of Chambord, the French Bourbon pretender, passed through his village, and from him Tkalac learned that the French had had a second revolution in 1830. After this he was determined to learn more, so he began to sneak into cafés in order to peruse newspapers. (No private family would have thought of subscribing in those days.) Cafés were strictly out of bounds for all schoolboys, but even though Tkalac once saw one of his teachers there, he was not betrayed to the headmaster. When he started to buy books on his own, along with Goethe and Voltaire he had no difficulty in purchasing the most fiercely banned critiques of the Austrian monarchy. Thus he found out how well organized book smuggling was, and he also learned that the local censor at Agram was neither bright nor vigilant.

He may have used this information when he joined the excited group of young men who were running the only newspaper in Croatia. It was written in the new, literary "Illyrian" language, and Hungarians who were contemptuous of Croat culture declared that it had only 450 subscribers. Nevertheless, permission to license it would never have been obtained in Pest if Metternich and Kolowrat had not expressly favored it.

An Illyrian party was accordingly not hard to form. (Illyrian was a word coined to cover a medley of provinces and dialects in and about Croatia.) To distinguish themselves from Hungarians with their time-honored costume, Illyrians adopted a special dress of their own, wine-colored jacket with red embroidery, corn-flower blue hose and red hat. The Magyars naturally laughed at such sincere flattery. The Illyrians mustered what arguments they could to prove that their territory had always been a nation; Hungarian historians countered that it never had been one. The Illyrians raised their red-white-and-blue tricolor and tried various tricks to make sure that the Magyar party (mostly country gentry in that part) would not take part in elections to the Diet, while a pamphlet entitled "Shall We Become Magyars?" appeared with Vienna's tongue-in-cheek approval, and only after furious representations from Pest was it belatedly suppressed.

Thus in 1848, when Hungary took over complete management of her own affairs, party lines were already drawn in Croatia. Sure that Hungary's guarantee of constitutional rights would not extend to their specifically national demands, the Slavic party chose to rely on the doubtful indulgence of the Hapsburgs. (Tkalac reported that a certain servility toward the Germans had crept into his erstwhile proud people since 1815, when German-speaking bureaucrats had been sent in from Vienna—the native ones having all been tainted by the French rule under Napoleon—and the road to advancement for the first time seemed to be through these officials.)

The chosen bone to pick, by common consent between Hungary and Croatia, was the one of language. ("I cannot make out," said Nassau Senior, "the precise nature of the quarrel. . . . The demand of the Hungarians that the Magyar language should be spoken in the Diet does not seem a sufficient ground for civil war.") In 1844 the Hungarian Diet had given non-Hungarian-speaking members six years to learn the language and required Hungarian to be taught in all the higher schools. Tkalac remembered the boys hated it worse than Greek, and made joyful bonfires of the textbooks. In his Croatian school German was the language of instruction, although Croat and Latin were the languages he heard at home.

When Count Batthyanyi had proposed to the Diet of 1847 that Croats be allowed to use their own tongue on the floor, his suggestion was ironically described as excessively generous by his party, and voted down. After they had won their separate Hungarian ministry in 1848, Kossuth and his colleagues were in no mood to be more open-handed; their persistent attitude was that civil liberties ought to suffice for everybody, and they threw the entire blame for Slavic discontent on machinations from Vienna. At the same time, they were so intent on Magyarizing their country, that not once did they consider asking any Slav to join their cabinet. Twenty years later, when Hungary again became separate, they would still deny legal and political rights to their Slavic subjects.

This attitude may have been natural, inasmuch as the Magyars were an island of six million persons in the sea of Slavs. They readily believed that the Slavs were out to massacre them, but they looked down on the Slavs at the same time that they were terrified. In this way they felt that pan-Germanism was their natural ally, for Germans were also in continual conflict with Slavic peoples, and bore like the Magyars the burden of civilization in the East. (Hungarian appeals for sympathy from England and America were based on a totally different line—the picture of Hungary fighting for the same rights Anglo-Saxons had cherished since Magna Carta. Both propaganda angles were highly successful.)

For their part the pan-Germans were most sympathetic. The Frankfurt Assembly, as one example, was extremely favorable to Magyar independence, realizing that if Hungary became a separate kingdom, even under a Hapsburg king, this would almost automatically ensure that German Austrians would be free to join their blood brothers in some sort of German empire. Logically such a point of view ought to make Frankfurt smile on Polish and Italian claims for independence, but consistency was no more a virtue of statesmen then than now. The discrepancy only shows how complicated were the crosscurrents of the period.

Even Karl Marx, good German that he was, noted that Slavs always supported despotism, and since he felt that Slavic countries were unsuited to industrialism, he deplored any revolutions they made.

In Vienna, all this time, there was cool disregard of Germanism as well as Magyarism. If Francis Joseph was to have an empire, idealism of any sort must give way to practical considerations.

It is easy to see that Austria's trouble was that the nationality principle, so eagerly taken up by the common people everywhere, would divide Austria while it would unify Germany. The small German princes were against nationalism and resisted their subjects because they feared being deprived of their power if their lands should be absorbed; the Austrian Emperor was against it for the opposite reason. He had to unify his state instead of letting it disintegrate either into separate nations or a loose federal union. If the Germans in Austria had succeeded in going over to greater Germany in 1848, the Poles, Hungarians, and Italians would have been freed; contrariwise, if these races had won the freedom they each fought for in 1846 or 1848, it would have thrown the German provinces into the lap of Germany.

The truth was the Austrian Empire was not suited to any sort of state the nineteenth century had in mind. Even a federal system like the United States—had it been well enough understood in Europe to be a model—would have met difficulties in the close confusion of races and languages along the Danube. Each race, beginning with the Germans, wanted complete national sovereignty in the territory even if it hurt minority groups. Even the solution which the Kremsier parliament worked out so democratically for the Austrian half of the Empire would probably not have worked if they had tried to apply it to the territory beyond the Leitha, where Hungary began.

Though it would be difficult to work out the policy which the Hapsburgs should have followed when disintegration threatened, what they actually did was almost the worst possible. They acted throughout the crisis as if the whole country were as much their personal property as the castles they lived in. If they had any political theory at all, it was to remind themselves that the Congress of Vienna had set up Austria as the guardian of legitimacy for all of Europe, a bulwark against French revolutionary principles compounded of liberalism and nationalism. If these two forces could be used against each other, it seemed only sensible politics to do so. Thus, while the revolution at Vienna was proceeding as a class revolt, the Hapsburgs were able to use the nationalistic Croats against it. In the same spirit they had made a class war of peasants to extinguish the Polish national revolt of 1846.

In the Hungarian case, to inflame Slavic hatred into civil war seemed the natural thing for the rulers to do. By setting a Croatian to catch a Magyar, they managed to keep on top of the heap themselves. Slavs and Hapsburgs made a ring of enemies to squeeze Hungary to death while her friends outside, Germans and Anglo-Saxons, exhausted themselves in eloquence.

It was not surprising in itself that the March days of 1848 turned up a hero for Croatia as they did everywhere else in Europe. Croatia, however, was the only place where a professional military man was raised by popular demand. At Agram the Croatian Diet acclaimed as their *Ban*, or governor, Baron Joseph Jellačič, who until that moment had been a colonel of a frontier regiment.

Jellačič was one of those officers who are adored by their men. Handsome in a dapper military way, though bald and short, with a black mustache and fiery eyes, active, gallant, poetic, humane, he abolished corporal punishment in his regiment and is said never even to have rebuked a soldier. A famous story told how once when his troops were lined up for parade in zero weather and the reviewing general kept them waiting for an hour while he drank in a tavern, Jellačič coolly ordered them back to their barracks. The troops returned such care with devotion based partly on superstitious joy that bullets never hit him even in the thick of battle, partly on his constant good humor in defeat as in victory. As a young officer he served under Radetzky in Italy; since 1841 he had been on the Turkish frontier, putting it in perfect military order.

The military frontier was a very special part of the Empire, and Jellačič owed much of his importance to the fact that he commanded here. It was a strip a thousand miles long, twenty to sixty broad, which was owned by the crown (the original owners having been driven out by war and disease), and enjoyed in common by the inhabitants. This was a place where the theories of Louis Blanc and Proudhon were really tried out, said cynical conservatives. In this whole area there was no civil authority, no right of emigration, no right of young men to become artisans, merchants, or students unless they were physically unfit for service. It was a seminary for soldiers. The line of the border was defended by posts so close together that one could see the next, each one occupied by six to eight men at a time. Every man was supposed to spend one week out of four in the post, the rest in the fields; whenever war drew the men to fight elsewhere, women and boys took over the posts, as happened in 1848.

It was said that the entire frontier of Serbia and Dalmatia could be alarmed in an hour and a half, and within four hours 200,-000 soldiers could be mobilized.

The border was a useful instrument to prevent smuggling, for tobacco, coffee, salt, and sugar cost only half as much in the Turkish provinces as within the Austrian Empire; and it also kept the plague out of Hungary. There was never another epidemic after the border organization was complete, though formerly plague had entered Hungary on an average of every twenty years.

This was the home of those border troops who so astonished Vienna when they marched up the butcher road (along which swine and cattle were driven to the city in peace time) to the October siege in 1848. Even in Hungary nothing like them had been seen for centuries, with their wide dirty white linen trousers tied at the ankle, their red or yellow sashes carrying Turkish swords, their long, hooded red cloaks, their wagons pulled by ponies, the handsome women who went along to cook goulash and dance at their campfires—women who were dead shots like their brothers. At home these soldiers got no pay, just their living from the communal land, but outside their own territory, they were not only paid at the rate of other soldiers of the Emperor, but also enjoyed the unique privilege of keeping what booty they could pick up. Goods acquired this way were the only private property they ever saw.

Few civilian visitors were allowed at the frontier, but one who visited somewhat before the revolution doubted that conditions were more oppressive here than under the old-fashioned county governments of Hungary. As he put it, the main difference was that officers instead of landlords took the *jus primae noctis*. Nevertheless, in 1848 the inhabitants of the little towns in the area appealed to the new government at Pest for city government and civil rights.

It was Count Batthyanyi's first great mistake that he did not insist that this area should be incorporated into the new kingdom of Hungary. On this subject Vienna was intractable—a sign that the War Office there never lost its grip like other government offices, for it realized that the military frontier could always be used to strangle Hungary. Batthyanyi, on the other hand, failed to understand its importance, and did not even inform the Diet that he left the frontier to Vienna. Not until the border soldiers poured into Hungary did the government of that country see what had been done.

As for Jellačič's politics, he may have been interested at first in Croatian independence, though his convictions can never have been solid. As soon as Archduchess Sophia wept on his shoulder he became the slave of the dynasty even if his military allegiance had not been theirs already. He speedily adapted himself to court life—a lady who saw him in Vienna after the revolution was over noticed that his manners, though polished, showed too much assurance to be pleasing, and she summed him up as the perfect type of counterfeit chivalry. The last judgment was not entirely fair. That his chivalry was not altogether counterfeit was proved when he became one of two generals in Windischgrätz's council of war to urge clemency toward Vienna when it lay conquered in October.

For freedom, other than that which he proclaimed with his sword, he had no use. Six times he was invited to confer with the Hungarian Ministry, from whom, technically, he should have taken orders, but he went only once. On that occasion Batthyanyi met him appeasingly, asking him what the Croatian demands were, and whether they could not be reconciled. Jellačič forgot the list of liberties acclaimed by his own Diet at Agram—a free press, Croatian autonomy with a responsible ministry, abolition of feudalism—and nonchalantly told the Count that Croatia's first demand was the centralization of the war and finance ministries of the whole Empire in Vienna! His second demand was another point on which the new Hungary was sore—Jellačič had the nerve to ask Hungary to take over part of the imperial debt. And his third point was the old one of equality of the Hungarian and Croatian languages. Jellačič's tone indicated that he knew his remarks were meaningless, and seeing no hope of compromise with a stooge of the court party, Batthyanyi stood up. "We shall meet on the Drave," he said, naming the river that divided Croatia from Hungary. "On the Danube, rather," said Jellačič, rattling his saber. Batthyanyi went out, and to the Hungarian Chargé d'Affaires who remained, Jellačič said, "*You* may have no duty or responsibility. But I owe all that I have and am to my Emperor; he educated me, the coat I wear is his; whatever may follow it is my duty to save him."[4]

The Emperor was obviously finding his friends again—but Batthyanyi was still his minister, and as a minister he resolved to get rid of the insubordinate Jellačič. His coup was spectacular, though it proved empty. The Count managed to penetrate into Ferdinand's presence during one of the rare moments when that feeble-minded monarch was unchaperoned. He was thus able to obtain the royal signature on a document which branded Jellačič as a traitor and suspended him in his office as *Ban*.

Jellačič read this news in a newspaper on his way home from Vienna, but he acted as if he never felt the charge of dishonor, and nonchalantly refused to submit. When he got back to Agram he failed to dissolve the Diet there, as he had been commanded, and kept on with his preparations for war. Batthyanyi tried to have

[4] F. Pulszky, 135.

him impeached, but it was said that the imperial officer sent to do the job was stopped by private letters from Sophia and the governing archdukes.

Batthyanyi's touching faith in his scraps of paper ought to have faltered at this point, yet in June 1848, when Jellačič was levying all the manpower of Croatia, the Pest government refused to accept enlistments for the Hungarian army beyond the 10,000 men who had been voted in May.

News trickled into Pest all summer that Jellačič was getting money and supplies from Vienna. Count Latour at the war ministry sent him guns billed as "pontoons," and then had the cheek to charge these supplies to the Hungarian treasury under Kossuth. Likewise Fieldmarshal Radetzky in Italy found a legion of Croats to spare for service in their home province although the Hungarians that he ordered home somehow got lost on the way.

Meanwhile, the newly elected Hungarian Diet was taking charge of the nation's affairs. It was far more businesslike than the 1847 Diet. Now nearly all the deputies appeared in European-style frock coats and only one or two peasant members wore costumes which brought back to mind the gorgeousness of the preceding year. The broader suffrage did not uncover new names of distinction; just as in France the old center party became the new right, while the old left ran the country.

Naturally, the question of Croatia soon came to the top of the pile of urgent business. On July 11 Kossuth devoted to it one of his most famous speeches. Beginning with an account of Hungarian generosity to the Croats, who benefited by all the freedoms enjoyed by the rest of the kingdom, Kossuth went on to say that he could not understand a nation revolting because it was given too many liberties, fighting to go back under the old yoke of absolutism. His listeners cheered. But when he went on to ask for 200,000 men and all the money the country could give, the Diet rose to its feet and shouted, "We give it, we give it." No other vote was needed. Kossuth wept as he told them that with such a spirit, Hell itself could not conquer Hungary.

In building up its army the government could not but remember the large number of Hungarians serving in Italy under Marshal Radetzky. These men were urgently needed at home for self-defense, and at the same time liberals were pointing out that it was a shame for Hungarian soldiers to serve in a campaign against Italian liberty. Kossuth's position was somewhat delicate. He remarked privately that as a man he would prefer the Italian provinces of Austria to be free, but as a minister of the crown he could not advocate this policy. He was pledged to defense of the Empire, and besides, if Hungary proved its loyalty by supporting the war, there was reason to hope the King would more readily sign their bills for domestic reform. So it was voted, by 236 to 36, to support the imperial armies in Italy provided that the reconquered provinces should be given a constitution. By this corkscrew logic Kossuth satisfied his conscience, but he showed himself up once for all as an Hungarian nationalist, not a European statesman.

After all this support, His Majesty proved disillusioningly ungrateful. The minute Radetzky's armies were successful in Italy, the court began to accuse Hungary of forcing unseasonable concessions. Bills were left unsigned, appeals to call off Jellačič unanswered; recruiting offices in Vienna accepted enlistments for Hungary and Croatia indifferently. Even the Vienna Assembly refused to receive a deputation from its sister body, the Hungarian Diet.

On September 4 all pretense was given up and Jellačič was able to brandish a letter from his Emperor restoring him to all his rights as *Ban*, with personal assurance from His Majesty that the Baron had never been a traitor. By that time he was all encamped on the Drave, ready to march across Hungary to the Danube.

On September 9 the Hungarian cabinet tried to force a decision by calling on the monarch in person, and demanding that Jellačič be withdrawn. Ferdinand's hand trembled as he read haltingly the short reply prepared for him by his private advisers, worded so that the deputation realized there was nothing to hope any longer from the court or the sovereign. They left in silence, and on their way back to their boat some of them took red feathers from the hands of Vienna radicals and stuck them in their hats—a sign of defiance.

Back in Pest there was only one thing for them to do in proper constitutional form—resign. When this happened, Kossuth was given such an ovation that, in terror lest he might take over the government, the Palatine put Batthyanyi back in power with instructions to form a cabinet leaving Kossuth outside. Given Kossuth's popularity, this cabinet was bound to fall, and indeed it lasted only a few days.

Meanwhile, the country was invaded. Jellačič crossed the Drave on September 11, and, pillaging and plundering, made his way across Hungary nearly to Pest. He swore that he had no orders from the Emperor, he swore that he came as a friend to the Hungarian people, but he could not keep his booty-loving men in hand even with a thousand floggings a day. (Evidently, he had abandoned his ban on corporal punishment.)

To defend their capital, Hungarians rose in a mass. Pest was defended by peasants and by national guards; men and women, workers and nobles labored together on the fortifications, gentlemen boasting of their blisters. Jellačič expected to find no artillery resistance because Hungarians had never been allowed to study that branch of military science, but to his surprise he was met with hot cannon fire. The engineering students of the university had spent the month of September studying under Bohemian artillerists and made such a good corps that Austrian observers believed the guns must be served by French gunners.

Recoiling, weak and dizzy, from Pest, the Croatian commander asked for a two-day truce during which time neither side was to move troops; then he used this period to flee with his army toward Vienna. By forced marches he got across the Leitha and encamped outside Vienna just in time to observe the Vienna revolution—in fact, it was when Latour ordered reinforcements for him that the Count was lynched and the revolution began. But this sequence of events did not prevent Jellačič later from claiming credit for his gallant rush to the defense of the city.

Slav against Magyar

THE CROATIAN invasion of Hungary made peculiarly difficult circumstances for those of her leaders who worshipped legality and up to this point had stuck to it at great cost.

Here was a country with no legal government, since the monarch could not be persuaded to appoint ministers who were acceptable to the Diet. Meanwhile, the land was being invaded by an army composed of its own most feared and hated minority. It made no difference that this minority claimed to be fighting for the right of autonomy, just as Hungary herself had done, for in this case Hungarian statesmen clung to the bitter letter of the old laws which annexed Croatia to Hungary in the Middle Ages. What did matter was that the invaders were almost savages, and that they were being egged on by the King.

Desperately, the Diet voted to put matters in the hands of Kossuth, as president of a committee of defense. From this moment he was the actual head of the country, though for some months to come he kept up the fiction of acting in the name of the King.

Austria, however, now began to feel free to throw off the mask of constitutionalism. When the Archduke Stephen resigned as Hungarian Palatine, Vienna sent in Count Lamberg as an imperial commissioner to dissolve the Diet. This gentleman had hardly reached Pest on September 28 when he was murdered, dragged from his carriage, and torn into bits. Though the Hungarian government was in no way responsible, yet this event, like the murders of Lichnowsky in Frankfurt and Latour in Vienna, all occurring within a month of each other, seemed to put the revolution beyond the pale of decent society. So many rich families left Pest that the sailing of steamboats for Pressburg had to be forbidden, and many members even of the cabinet fled. Francis Deák went to live on his property, Count Batthyányi entered the ranks to fight for his country as a common soldier.

On October 3, Hungarians heard that the invading Jellačič had been named civil and military governor of Hungary, and that he had ordered the Diet dissolved and the whole country put under martial law. Their answer, as we have seen, was to chase him right out of the country, until he landed in front of Vienna.

When they came to their own frontier, the Hungarian army came to a halt and waited there foolishly for the revolutionaries of Vienna to invite them across. Finally, having delayed until Windischgrätz had forced a capitulation upon the city, Kossuth gave his ill-timed order for the Hungarians to attack.

Just before the battle, Kossuth drew up his officers and read to them a proclamation from Windischgrätz, ordering all imperial officers serving Hungary to report to his camp. Less than half responded to this call. The others were held to Hungary by Kossuth's oratory, or perhaps by the general mix-up of the situation. For while the Emperor's right hand had issued a proclamation declaring every Hungarian a rebel on October 16, on October 17 his left hand had confirmed the commissions of the Hungarian minister of war. In such circumstances an honorable soldier would have a hard time choosing among his various obligations.

The battle near Vienna not only marked the fact that Hungary was now willing to fight against Austria, and was no longer merely suppressing a Slavic rebellion, but it was distinguished by the rise of the most important figure in the Hungarian war, except Kossuth —Arthur Görgey. In the battle the raw Hungarian troops were smartly defeated, but Görgey, a young and almost unknown officer, rallied the soldiers to prevent a total rout so effectively that he was raised to the rank of general on the field of battle by Kossuth.

Görgey was of noble blood, but poor. As a schoolboy he suffered because his allowance would not encompass fruit, his schoolmates' usual treat. Preferring to steal rather than to beg, he robbed nearby orchards. Later, in the army, he found that position depended upon wealth; particularly in Prince Windischgrätz's command in Bohemia, where Görgey served as a lieutenant, young officers were encouraged to make an extravagant splash. Even though the Prince offered him personal help, Görgey could not stand favors, and, unable to live on his pay, he resigned and went to study chemistry at Prague. Here he lived on twopence a day in a garret. He married a poor governess and returned to Hungary to manage his aunt's estate, where he was when the revolution broke out.

His own ambition was to become a professor of chemistry at Pest, and he offered his services to Kossuth first as a chemist. No one, not even himself, suspected that he was a strategical genius, but because of his military training, he was given a commission. Up to the time of the battle of Vienna, he was known chiefly as the man who had court-martialed and hanged two wealthy counts who were accused of being spies for Jellačič. (Copies of Jellačič's proclamations were found concealed in the lining of their trunks.) This sentence undoubtedly gratified Görgey's peculiar resentment against the aristocracy; at the same time it labeled him as one officer to whom the road back to Windischgrätz's camp was not open. His loyalty to Hungary seemed certain.

In view of this judgment it is ironical that within a year he was universally branded as a traitor. He was not a traitor in the vulgar sense, but the fact that he did not care a fig for Hungary in his heart, or for any other ideal, produced the same result. Contemptuousness was outstanding among his expressed feelings. He sneered, openly or privately, at Kossuth and the government of Hungary, at the common people, at the militia, at his own soldiers, and even at himself.

His officers, nevertheless, adored him. By refusing to serve under anyone else they made him practically independent of the government, and the most powerful person in Hungary. He was a soldier's soldier, strong and squarely built, one who wore old uniforms full of holes and disdained to polish his boots, while he sat with his noncommissioned officers at table so that he could carry on fine points of their training there. He loved joking, though his dirty, blasphemous stories showed a bitterness toward love and religion which shocked his more idealistic admirers. He was able to appear cool at conferences, particularly by his trick of taking snuff at the right moment, but his temper was bad, and once he hit a lieutenant with his saber. The boy's comrades forced him to apologize.

Gratitude is the most insupportable of all emotions to such a temperament, an acute contemporary remarked. It was easy for Görgey to refuse the honors and decorations which the government tried to heap upon him, to refuse even a pension for his wife, who, he said, could easily become a governess again. He had sneered at wealth and position so long in others that he enjoyed showing that he could be consistent when they were applied to himself, especially as it was a way of insulting Kossuth. However, few at the time saw that these actions were a concealed expression of a bitter hatred, and the general became all the more popular for his lack of ostentation and his rough and ready manners.

That Görgey had an army to train was the result of Kossuth's barnstorming. Five years later, when the revolution was lost and the country under martial law, an English visitor (to whom people were not afraid to talk) observed that every peasant and every noble he met had seen Kossuth personally and remembered the days when they answered his call as the most glorious of their lives. It is hard to see how one man could have reached so many places.

Women were almost more ready to serve than men. Poor Kossuth was at a loss to know what to do when two female regiments threatened to march upon him, but he sent one group to the hospitals, which were in charge of his sister, and set another to make cartridges. This suited most but not all of the female recruits. Many stories went around of women in the ranks, while two at least reached the rank of captain before they were discovered.

Jews, too, supported the nation. It was one of the first times in modern history when Jews fought for the country they lived in, and admiring contemporaries noted that they lost money and gained courage in this experience.

If volunteers failed to fill the quota for a county, it was filled first by 19-year-old conscripts, then 20-year-olds, and so on. This force of "Home Defenders" (Honveds) was enlisted for four years and given higher pay than the regular army, but any soldier could become a home defender if he wished. They wore dark blue trousers, red-trimmed short Hungarian coats, and black shakos. This body of infantry was supported by the famous hussars or cavalry, the newly trained artillery and the national guards whom Görgey would have liked to send home in spite of their valiant work as guerrillas.

All men between twenty and fifty (with the interesting exceptions of domestic servants and owners of a certain amount of property) were to serve in the national guard. Each one owed a six week term of service. Since many family men disliked this interruption of their home life, any unit of the guards could select one-third of its number to serve three times as long, and these were called the mobile guard, who were to be ready for action at three days' notice. Their chief assignment was interrupting the enemy's line of communication, and they were instructed to retire from open battle.

Now that he was fighting Austria, Kossuth reversed his former stand and appealed to Hungarian soldiers abroad to return home. Most of these were in Italy, where old Marshal Radetzky knew even better than Kossuth how to make soldiers loyal; and in order to make it harder to desert, Austria dismounted Hungarian cavalry. Still, a certain number of deserters, on foot, trickled across the border to serve their own country.

When Windischgrätz, victorious at Vienna in October, marched toward Pest in December, the government had to flee to a small city called Debreczen, carrying with it all their military stores and the invaluable banknote press. No one wanted to touch Austrian money after Kossuth notes, backed by the national iron mines, became available.

Hardly ever was a city so well guarded as that little capital. No stranger could approach for miles around but what wind of his coming would precede him. Every peasant was a spy, every cottage had a boy ready to leap upon a horse and carry a message. Signal fires blazed at night across the marshes, while river fishermen devised light bridges of casks which moved troops and messengers swiftly across the network of rivers. (At first the Austrians sneered at these inventions, but before the end of the campaign, they adopted them in preference to their own heavy pontoons.) And whenever Austrian soldiers approached a village, all provisions mysteriously disappeared, while the returning Hungarians found lavish feasts.

The government at Debreczen was run in a simple personal way which everyone could understand. Kossuth lived plainly, saving only one hour a day to play with his children, the rest of the time being available to visitors of any rank in the order in which they arrived. For his audiences he dressed simply in a black coat, but he kept two pistols in plain sight. In the Diet he reserved no special seat for himself. But still his magic voice was more successful in getting out recruits than gypsy music or all the girls who danced with patriotic volunteers.

Only a Kossuth could have kept the nation together at all during that winter, for the Austrian armies kept advancing and advancing until free Hungary was merely eight or ten unoccupied counties. Resistance seemed as hopeless as American resistance in the winter of Valley Forge. Yet, from the little center of Debreczen, Hungarian armies cleared the whole country again by spring.

In fact Hungarian spirits rose with every Austrian insult. When young Francis Joseph mounted the imperial throne in December, he made no special mention of his position as King of Hungary and gave no indication that he intended to take the oath which went with the crown of St. Stephen. This was in line with Schwarzenberg's unitary policy, to treat all parts of the Empire the same, but it was a red flag to the Hungarian Diet, which promptly declared the abdication of Ferdinand was null and void. No one but themselves, they said, could dispose of the Hungarian throne except when a king died and passed it on to a legal heir. Francis Joseph was a usurper, and from that moment Hungary had no legal king and the army was sworn to the Diet.

When Windischgrätz marched across the land, mouthing offers of pardon to those who wished to submit to the Emperor, Magyars laughed in his face and got ready to resist to the end. But they could not keep his forces out of Pest. On January 4, 1849, the last planks were laid down on Count Széchenyi's famed suspension bridge and Austrian conquerors, in single file, were the first to use what should have been the pride of new Hungary.

The Prince Field Marshal's vengeance in Pest showed what the rest of the country could expect if the Austrian army conquered. He searched every household, threatened death to anyone who knowingly or unknowingly harbored arms, and he even court-martialed post office officials who had handled letters or goods which furthered the rebellion. Against the Jews he was particularly fierce; it pleased the anti-Semitism of that day to fine the whole Jewish community because some members gave excellent service as spies to the Hungarian rebels.

Already, however, Hungarian forces were winning back their land. The first victories were won by little white-haired Bem, fresh from his escape from Vienna, who had been sent by Kossuth to fight in Transylvania. This province, almost as big as Hungary proper, was separated from it in 1526—a long time back, but not too long for Magyar memories. Its political reunion with Hungary was one of the triumphs of the revolution and was described as "the child returned to its mother's breast." Now Bem, with barely 7,000 troops, all untrained and badly armed, beat not only the regular Austrian garrison forces stationed there, but also some Russian reinforcements which the Austrian general had begged to come across the border. Besides the military, Bem had to contend with pro-German sections of the population, which included cities full of Saxons who had been settled in Transylvania centuries before but who still kept their German affections.

By midwinter Görgey, too, was beginning to rally his forces and he soon entered upon an equally astonishing series of victories against the Austrians in the west, which drove them clear back behind their own frontier by April.

Görgey, who could not bring himself to say a good word about anybody, even his own soldiers in their moment of victory, attributed his success to Windischgrätz's mistakes and the poor care which the Austrian army was given. The unfortunate invading soldiers had a bad enough time, indeed, for they dared not light fires in the fields, and their bread was often frozen. When they rose from sleeping on the bare ground, their clothes and beards were often hanging with icicles. Görgey, however, was not in a position to exploit this situation since he never had more than one day's supply of food and could not follow up his victories, and this failure, naturally, he attributed to Kossuth's poor management.

Görgey's second gesture of defiance against Kossuth's government was less subtle than refusing decorations, yet Kossuth failed to read it as a warning. The general issued a proclamation to the effect that his army was fighting for the 1848 constitution, and for the abdicated Ferdinand as king. This action kept his conservative officers together, for it held them to the oaths they had taken when they were commissioned and seemed to protect them from fighting for independence or any more radical reforms. Nevertheless, it was an impossible line to hold, for Ferdinand was gone, and young Francis Joseph was trying to foist a new constitution on them which would merge Hungary into the rest of his domains.

The news of this constitution, promulgated on March 4, 1849, was slow to get across the fighting lines and did not reach Debreczen until late in April. A few days afterwards the Diet declared Hungary's independence of the Hapsburgs.

This was Kossuth's answer to Görgey as well as to Francis Joseph. Probably he never imagined that Görgey would fail to follow the government in the case of such provocation from Austria.

The Hungarian Declaration of Independence was based on the American one, and when Kossuth read it in his thunderous tones, his listeners trembled at its curses and shouted at its promises. The ceremony took place in a plain protestant church where the Diet met in Debreczen. The three centuries of Hapsburg rule, stated the document, had been three centuries of uninterrupted suffering for Hungary, during which time no single prince had advanced liberty, but many had curtailed it. Hungary had not rebelled, had not broken its allegiance, did not ask concessions; the nation would have been satisfied with the rights every king had sworn to in a sacred oath. Now, when their very existence as a nation was to be taken away from them, Hungarians refused to submit any longer.

The Diet enthusiastically voted to accept this declaration, and made Kossuth the "governor" of the new state. No one knew what political form it would take—whether they would make a republic or offer the crown to some other prince—but for the time being Kossuth was practically a dictator. His four months of power were unenviable. Not only was his military force more or less openly hostile to his civil government, but within each sphere his generals distrusted each other and his cabinet members likewise.

For example, the man who took Kossuth's old job of finance minister was an Austrophile who kept all the bullion of the country ready to turn over to Vienna. He would not coin money for Hungary, and in the printing of paper notes he slowed up the process of manufacture by ordering that even notes of small denominations must be printed in two colors. In July Kossuth wrote to Bem that the twenty hand presses owned by the government would take thirty-three days to print the sum of money needed for the Transylvanian campaign—therefore, Bem must not look for it quickly.

Far more serious than this disloyalty, of course, was Görgey's. Görgey was by this time commander-in-chief, and, at the same time, he was the natural candidate for minister of war. Though Kossuth thought this was too much responsibility for one man, it proved to be almost impossible to get rid of Görgey in either capacity. In the army, he had the devoted loyalty of so many officers that they would not serve under another general, while at Debreczen, even while he swore loyalty to the new regime, he was busy plotting with the peace party in the Diet to undermine it. He urged officers loyal to him to run for the Diet, and by talking undermined confidence in

Kossuth and in the military prospects of the nation. Görgey naturally thought Kossuth even stupider than usual to allow such intrigues, but he had no scruples about exploiting the situation.

One reason why Kossuth failed to see what was happening was that he got along much better with people in the mass than individually. He knew the last nuance of playing on the hearts of a mob, to extract from them unbelievable sacrifice. His power to call out men and resources in the emergency was remarkable, but this was only the first test of the people's devotion, which proved to be unshakable even in the disastrous years to come. Kossuth played the part that Mazzini took in Italy, though he never shared Mazzini's broad view of Europe and humanity, and was totally without Mazzini's warm wit and affection in personal relationships. Most people who worked closely with Kossuth became estranged from him. Perhaps the silly pretentiousness that made him so obnoxious in his years of exile, when he wished to be treated as a sovereign, had begun to make his vision cloudy during his months as governor. In any case, his misreading of Görgey's character was the most fatal of many cases in which he put people to bad use.

Someone who meant to praise Kossuth's unworldliness said that if he had had a servant who was unable to clean his boots, Kossuth would never think of superseding him, but would clean them himself. (This in a world when cleaning boots was *never* done by gentlemen. The greatest hardship of Wagner's early years of poverty in Paris, when he took a boarder, was that Wilhelmina Wagner had to clean the boarder's boots. Of course, it never occurred to Richard to lend her a hand.)

However amiable this characteristic may have been in a household, by carrying it into politics, Kossuth ended up attending to far too many details himself, and continuing in office many incompetent subordinates. Francis Deák, who had the best intellect among Hungarian leaders of 1848, believed that Hungary was sacrificed needlessly to Kossuth's bad judgment.

Görgey, who did not like anybody, found Kossuth even more antipathetic than most. Kossuth was forever mouthing platitudes that positively gagged Görgey, and Kossuth was always hopeful, while Görgey was cynical. Kossuth fought for victory, and the best Görgey hoped for was a glorious defeat.

At one brief moment in the war Kossuth put a general named

Dembinski over Görgey—it was an effort to hold Görgey down. Görgey flatly disobeyed this superior. Afterwards Görgey remarked that if he had been Dembinski he would have shot any officer so insubordinate. He added that if he had been commander he would not have given orders that required to be disobeyed. How must such a man have felt towards one who could not fire a bootblack? Kossuth could not understand how Görgey "could live for anything besides Hungary and freedom" at a moment when Görgey, by his own admission, was just stopping to ask himself whether the *Austrian* monarchy could survive if Hungary became separate.

This disagreement was particularly sad because by May the whole land was free except for the fortress of Buda, across the river from Pest. Görgey had the choice of taking time to capture it or of pursuing his enemy quickly toward Vienna. The proper military answer was to chase the Austrians, but politically Buda seemed important to many patriotic Hungarians, and also, for different reasons to Görgey himself, who realized that the possession of Buda would give him a better bargaining position, when it came to making peace with the Austrians, than Vienna would. Hungarian soil would then be entirely free, whereas Austria would only be enraged if he attempted to attack its capital.

Thus they spent three weeks besieging the fortress, which was on a rock rising several hundred feet sheer above the Danube. Görgey's men had to scale it on ladders, and every time a man was hit, his body knocked off all the men below him on the ladder. But the Hungarians were roused to fury by a gratuitous bombardment of Pest on the part of the Austrian commander within the fort, so they attacked boldly and finally won. All Hungary went wild in celebration of this last great victory. Görgey's own message to Debreczen, in Caesarian style, was "Hurrah, Buda. Görgey."

Political delight rarely makes up for military failure. The army Görgey refused to follow up was notorious for its stolidity in defeat, and it soon reformed and turned around, so that by midsummer, Görgey was again in retreat from the Austrians.

In that dazzling summer of independence, when success was so close, prodigies were performed all over Hungary. The nation's boundaries were closed so that exports and imports were impossible, and the country was without gold, medicine, or arms. Yet recruits kept pouring into the army, villages smelted their churchbells, and chemists extracted sulphur from copper ore, and manufactured salt-petre. Popular confidence was so great that the paper money never depreciated until news circulated that Russian troops were coming to help the Austrians, and then it fell only five or ten per cent. Kossuth, to be sure, threatened to court-martial some merchants who refused to take it at the end of June.

Desperately Kossuth turned for help to other countries. He sent a romantic young countess, disguised as a peasant, across the lines to Vienna in a wicker cart to beg for intercession by the United States Chargé d'Affaires. This gentleman, though full of good will, could do nothing to help. To England Kossuth sent his ablest propagandist, Francis Pulszky, who pleaded the advantages that would open up to Britain if trade with Hungary could be carried on without the Austrian tariff wall. Popular sympathy in both England and America reached a fervent glow such as has rarely been equaled, but neither government was moved to help. Lord Palmerston, the foreign secretary at London, would have liked free institutions in Hungary, but he was convinced that the balance of power required a strong united monarchy on the Danube as a barrier against Russia. As the affairs of Hungary became more desperate, the Magyars, rather than go back under Austria, prepared to offer their crown to a Russian Grand Duke, or even to the Sultan of Turkey.

Austria, too, was desperate, but luckily for her she had a friend in need. One of the astute moves of the old Emperor Francis had been to charge young Czar Nicholas of Russia to watch over his family, particularly the helpless Ferdinand. Nicholas, kneeling, had given his promise while the Emperor blessed him. Now, a dozen years later, he could fulfill that oath.

Russia was the single European country in 1848 that was untouched by ferment. Nicholas I, Czar since 1825, was more successful than his brother monarchs in imposing his single will upon his people. Behind an iron curtain his subjects suffered the evils both of civilization and of barbarism, and they entirely lacked strength to revolt—but Herzen prophesied that when they did they would abandoned all scruples and keep no respect whatever for any institutions that were worth preserving.[1]

[1] A French cliché of 1848 showed the popular view of various nations' roles in that period. France was a nation of artists and soldiers. She was the heart of Europe. Germany, the savant, unable to make war, represented the head; and Russia was the arm. Her mission was to keep order.

Nicholas was another of those nineteenth-century rulers, like Frederick William, Francis Joseph and Pius IX, to whom power was more of an obligation than a pleasure. His face was severe and misanthropic, his smile complacent, never gay, his words and movements were cadenced as if he had a roll of music before him at all times. The observer who noted these details added that you felt as if his heart were closed, as if the barrier were inaccessible. In order to fulfill his duty he put back the hated secret police and the censorship which his predecessor had abolished, and his control over his courtiers went to the length of commanding them to cut their beards, for beards were a sign of democratic sympathies in Western Europe, though in Russia they had been merely a common fashion.

When 1848 brought revolution to all his brother monarchs, Nicholas I felt that his duty was to help them. Although he was disgusted with Frederick William IV for his efforts at reform in calling the Prussian United Diet in 1847, and at the time remarked sadly, "We were three, now we are two," Nicholas was in 1848 willing to help the repentant King of Prussia if need be. As for France, though he had hated Louis Philippe, he was disappointed that nobody invaded revolutionary France so that he could join in a fight against the republic.

In 1849 all this frustrated good will expended itself on Francis Joseph; his sentimentality yearned toward this boy, "called so young to tread such a thorny path," as Nicholas put it.

His personal feeling was buttressed by several strong political reasons for Russia to support Austria. For one thing, there was the fear that revolution would be stimulated in his own Polish provinces. There was also the wish to avenge the Russian army corps which had tried to help the Austrian forces in Transylvania and had been so ignominiously driven out of the country by Bem in January 1849. And there was a pan-Slavic motive, too. According to a Russian pamphlet which the Czarist government approved, Hungary hates Russia because Russia is able to restring the beads on the Slavic chain which Hungary keeps trying to break. Or, as Iranyi, the Hungarian pamphleteer, put it more grandly: "The Czar did not want to see established, at the gates of his Empire, a free state whose moral grandeur and material prosperity might have excited among his subjects comparative ideas and dangerous hopes."

At the same time Russia did not want a united Germany, and if

Francis Joseph failed to get help from Russia, Prussia was the only other state to which he could turn. Prussia's price would surely be that Austria should let Prussia go ahead with plans for German hegemony.

The objections the Czar met among his officials were chiefly financial, though there was also doubt whether some of his younger officers were not already beginning to be revolutionary and might not get still more ideas in Hungary. Russian finances were not in such bad shape as Austrian, but there was sure to be resentment among landowners if taxes were raised for an expeditionary force. However, Austria's first appeal was precisely for money, not men. In December 1848, shortly after he had taken office, Prince Schwarzenberg realized that he could not carry on affairs without a substantial loan, and this the Russian finance minister at first refused in spite of the Czar's personal wishes. Finally, when the dangers of Austrian collapse were pointed out, he was persuaded to exchange forty million francs' worth of French five per cent securities for an equal nominal value of the Austrian state debt, and this improvement in backing pulled the Austrian treasury through.

In a few months Schwarzenberg realized he would need soldiers, too. True, he could have pulled men out of Italy to fight in Hungary, but though Italy was beaten, Schwarzenberg wanted to leave Radetzky's army strong enough to keep Lombardy and Venetia quiet. The price of this policy was the humiliation of requesting troops from a foreign power to beat the masterly strategy of Görgey.

The Austrian request, backed by a personal letter from Francis Joseph and sentimental appeals from Sophia that the Czar could not allow her dear boy to lose part of his heritage, went to St. Petersburg just before news of the Hungarian declaration of independence; therefore, it was not a result of this act. The Czar agreed to help, and a meeting of the two monarchs took place in Warsaw on May 21 to map strategy and to decorate each other's ministers with their best orders in diamonds. Nicholas is said to have admired the "charming and interesting face, the profound and severe expression" of his young kinsman, though there was no great warmth of feeling between the two cold-hearted rulers.

Schwarzenberg came out of the negotiations with what he needed, not only diamonds, but 140,000 men, and all without having given any promises in return except that Polish prisoners were to be turned over to Russia. Austria was not even required to pay the interest on the sum Russia expended on the expedition, though its transportation and feeding, as well as hospital care, were to be borne by the Vienna treasury. Nicholas was too proud to ask a re-ward for doing his plain duty, though four years later he may have reflected bitterly on Hapsburg ingratitude when Russia lost the Crimean War because of Francis Joseph's unwillingness to return the favor.

Schwarzenberg, now safe in Italy, and with an ally against Hungary, was free to follow up his policy of force in every corner of the Empire. His mood was reflected in his picking General Haynau to carry the Austrian troops into battle again against Görgey's Hungarians. Haynau was an able officer but he had an odious reputation for cruelty to civilians, which would have made any prime minister who cared about the feelings of his conquered subjects hesitate to employ him in a civil war. Hungarians heard with horror of how this "Hyena of Brescia" had allowed his Croat soldiers to plunder that city in Italy, burning prisoners alive while their wives were forced to watch, making men eat the flesh of their wives and children. Haynau's tears were only for his own side, for when his army re-lieved the fortress of Temesvar in Hungary, where the garrison and citizens had eaten their horses, water was seen coursing down the nine inch mustaches of the old Hyena.

Under his leadership Austrian troops made a good beginning to-ward conquering Hungary before the Russians arrived on the scene. The young Emperor came out to see the fighting and made a perma-nent impression on his army by leading a column of troops across a burning bridge—a feat for which his cousin, the Czar, sent him the third class (out of four) of the Russian Military Order of St. George.

Plundering open cities as no European army had done for cen-turies, inciting the racial hatreds of the peasants, paying five florins for each bound Hungarian soldier, the imperial army moved across the country.

By July this movement swept the Magyar seat of government back once more, this time the south, to the small city of Szegedin. A perfect stream of wagons, carts, and cabs filled the roads, bearing all those who clung to Hungary's last hope as well as those who wanted to be in a strategic place from which to escape across the border into Turkey. When Kossuth arrived he made a last pathetically hopeful speech in the great square, telling the citizens that their town would have the glory of sending freedom out to the rest of Hungary and to Europe. The Diet met here for eight distracted days, during which they made a frantic appeal to the submerged Roumanian population of Transylvania, a racial group whom they had hitherto ignored and, for a crowning gesture, to please Kossuth, granted emancipation to the Jews.

Görgey, meanwhile, indifferent to this civilian chatter, was busy finding out what terms he could make with the Russians. By surrendering to them instead of to the Austrian army he could fling a last defiance at Francis Joseph, and he also hoped that Russia would protect his officers from the wrath of Schwarzenberg. The Russian officers to whom he talked, seemed, indeed, to hold out the promise that all Görgey's officers could pass over to the Russian service and win commissions from the Czar.

Kossuth was still full of plans to save everything. Could not the army, still unbeaten though retreating, go to the great plains where innumerable waterways and bad roads would keep all enemies at bay for years? The Russians would succumb to malaria if they stayed on even a month or two longer. Would not England, would not America eventually be forced by public opinion to help Hungary's just cause? The army's courage was as great as ever, the people were crazy with devotion. It took a good deal of Görgey's sober talk to convince Kossuth that Hungary's best hope was for the commander-in-chief to make military terms with the enemy.

To get a free hand, Görgey had to insist on Kossuth's resignation, whereupon Kossuth, always exalted, offered to kill himself. This was a shock for which the general was unprepared, and he had to change his tactics and implore Kossuth not to die, to spare himself for a greater future. In his memoirs Görgey tells us his real reason was to keep Kossuth from becoming a martyr whose memory would keep alive forever the dream of Hungarian independence. The flattery worked, however, and Kossuth merely resigned, on August 11, leaving all power in Görgey's hands. The governor's fulsome proclamation expressed the hope that Görgey would love the fatherland as much as he, but that in guarding its destiny, he would be more fortunate.

Possibly Görgey would have liked the crown of martyrdom he was so anxious to keep from Kossuth, for he seemed to court death in his last battles. Uniformed in red and gold, instead of his usual torn field coat, flaunting a white heron's feather, he led the charge in person. Still he was fighting for glory, rather than for victory which he did not really desire.

On August 13, in accordance with plans made with Russian officers, he drew up his 160,000 soldiers on the field of Világos and announced to them that they were surrendered. The reaction of the troops was heartbreaking. Some wept, some begged their beloved general to lead them into any kind of combat, some threatened mutiny. Görgey, scornfully impassive, said he would shoot anyone who disobeyed. Then he surveyed the scene while the infantry kissed their muskets and piled them in pyramids, the artillerymen spoke to their hundred and forty-four guns as if bidding goodbye to old friends, while they arranged them evenly behind the infantry, the cavalry dismounted and hung their swords on their pummels. Some of them shot their horses rather than let them be taken, and a few galloped away to the great plains before they could be caught—perhaps to join the robber band of General Rosza Sandor, who was not caught until 1857. Six mortal hours this process took, and then Russian officers marched the men away and took charge of the arms.

After the surrender at Világos, the flag of free Hungary still flew over two great fortresses, Komorn, guarding the northern end of the Danube, and Petarwardein at the south. In Komorn, General Klapka refused to surrender his garrison at Görgey's orders, and sent two of his best scouts by different routes to Petarwardein, telling the commander there that the two of them could hold out indefinitely and that they should do so, not only for themselves but for the entire country. He suggested that they should demand a free amnesty for all who had fought for Hungary, redemption at par of Kossuth's paper money, and certain other guarantees against confiscation of property. This bold scheme fell through because the scouts were captured, and the commander of Petarwardein, believing false tales that Komorn had surrendered, capitulated.

Komorn was one of the romantic spots of Hungary. It was a fortress that had never been conquered by force of arms, and when it was first besieged in the spring of 1849, it had been heroically relieved by Richard Guyon, an Englishman in the Hungarian service. This officer first tried to get inside disguised as a Jewish peddler with a yellowed jacket, tobacco-covered beard, and a packet of matches, needles, and shoe blacking. When this scheme did not work, Guyon made a second, successful attempt as a hussar in Austrian uniform. Now, in the summer, General George Klapka held it while the Austrians swept past in their pursuit of Görgey, and actually used it as a recruiting and training center for Hungary, while all the territory around was subject to Austria. One sally into the countryside netted him 2,000 cattle and 18 cannon, and he also enlisted over 5,000 young men whom he brought into the fortress to train. This sort of exploit naturally made him feel optimistic about holding out.

With the fall of Petarwardein, however, Klapka realized he would have to give in sooner or later. He gave up the idea of making terms for the whole country, but for his own garrison he won the only honorable conditions of any surrendered corps of Hungarians. His men were to leave with their guns in their hands and be free to return to their homes or to ask for passports to leave the country.

In spite of these honors of war, the Komorn soldiers were in as great despair as Görgey's at giving up, and many of them felt they could no longer bear to live in their defeated country. Hundreds of them applied for exit visas, but they found that every country refused to receive them except England and America, to which distant points many of them lacked means to travel.

The lucky ones who were going to America were treated with marked respect, even by the haughty Austrian officials who filled out their papers. Only one thing marred the happiness of these emigrants—they found their papers were stamped "No return." This was a violation of their terms, but there was no one to defend their rights. Each man had to decide whether to move across the waters with no hope of seeing his homeland again, or to stay and suffer whatever punishments might be meted out to keep Hungary in order.

The rest of their countrymen suffered far more than the Komorn soldiers. Many of Görgey's army were pressed into the Austrian service, mixed up in other regiments so that the tradition of a Hungarian army should die. Stories told, instead, how the memory lasted. A common soldier was flogged for crying "Hurrah for Kossuth," and the regulations required that he should thank the officer who whipped him. This the soldier refused to do, so he was given twenty-five more stripes. He still refused his thanks. The third time he grumbled out the required words, but added, "My back belongs to the Emperor, but my heart to Kossuth."

Hungarian officers received insults even more degrading than the men in the ranks. The Russians proved completely unable or unwilling to fulfill Görgey's hopes of saving the honor and careers of his officers, although the Czar himself stipulated that Görgey himself must be spared. Görgey asserts that this was a surprise to him; in any case he lived on, safe if unhonored, for sixty years in a remote part of the Austrian Empire. The other officers were given up without protest to Francis Joseph's vengeance, and it was a terrible one. Four hundred and ninety were court-martialed, 386 went to prison, some of the officers were degraded to the ranks so that the unusual spectacle might be seen of an Esterhazy and a Batthyanyi serving as privates. And thirteen were executed, mostly hanged, at Arad.

The thirteen of Arad become part of popular history; even in the twentieth century their names could still rouse a public meeting to fury. Among them was Count Charles Leiningen, whose observations on the emancipation of his serfs were so temperate. He was a cousin of Queen Victoria, of a family so noble that he was classed socially as a member of a reigning house, although his family's small principality had been taken away in 1806. Count Charles was a blond giant of a man, with blue eyes and yellow hair, who was drawn into the war through his Hungarian marriage. The irony of his fate was that he hated nothing more than fighting against Austria, for he had gone into the army only to quell the Croat rebellion. Admiration of Görgey and the fact that there was no very honorable point at which to withdraw held him in service. None of these facts prevented his hanging by the neck on October 6. The execution was held up until one day after Komorn fell, for if these men had died earlier it might have delayed the surrender. Hungarian women went into mourning for years, and many of them wore iron bracelets with the initials of the thirteen arranged in a way to make a mystic promise of retribution.

The hangman's work did not stop with the military. Count Louis Batthyanyi, though loyalist scruples had made him resign his royal ministry months before the end, was sentenced to die on the same October 6. He had to be shot instead, finally, because he cut his throat with a razor the night before in his prison and his neck was not strong enough to stand the strain of the rope. A hundred and fourteen other death sentences were carried out, and seventy-five more were issued against men who fled the country.

Women were stripped and flogged for speaking for rebels. One noble lady was made to sweep the streets of Temesvar, and in another town a university professor's daughter was publicly whipped for turning her back on the Emperor as he entered the city. The most famous case was described by the victim herself before she went insane: "I am not aware that any of us committed any fault. I was suddenly, without a previous trial or examination, taken from my husband and children. I was dragged into a square formed by the troops, and, in the presence of the population which had been accustomed to honor me, not because I was the lady of the manor, but because the whole tenor of my life deserved it, *I was flogged with rods*. You see I can write the words without dying of shame; but my husband took his own life. Deprived of all other weapons, he shot himself with a small cannon."[2]

Haynau announced that he would burn whole towns at the first sign of insubordination; he decreed death for anyone of whatever age or sex who should wear a revolutionary emblem or insult an Austrian soldier. Jewish fortunes were systematically ruined, but indeed all merchants suffered from the ruling that Austrian officers might pass Kossuth's paper notes, while Hungarian subjects might not. In a final frenzy, Haynau announced that he would enlist all males who had taken part in the rebellion, and actually enrolled 50,000 soldiers before someone convinced him that this policy would strip the country of its entire manpower and there would be no one left to work the land.

His Apostolic Majesty, Francis Joseph, nineteen years old and newly come to the throne, granted audiences to the wives and mothers of his victims, but listened unmoved to their tears and prayers. Even the Czar interceded for kinder treatment toward the beaten subjects, but the young Emperor, advised doubtless by Schwarzenberg, only said that though he might like to pardon, his duty caused him to act otherwise.

[2] Quoted from Stiles, *Austria in 1848-1849*. II, 810.

Kossuth and his cabinet and that part of the army which was in southern Hungary, and therefore was not surrendered with Görgey, fled to Turkey. They met for the last time on Hungarian soil on August 17, in a poor farmhouse. Everyone laughed when they discovered that Kossuth had lugged the crown jewels thus far in his retreat. A republican jeeringly tried on the Crown of St. Stephen, whereupon the unhappy Kossuth hurriedly took it out and buried it so that it would rest in Hungarian soil. Then he and Generals Bem and Guyon and several thousand soldiers marched across the frontier on a fine late summer's day, their hearts too heavy to notice the beauty of the scenery or the weather.

In Turkey they were received by one of the most civilized rulers of Europe. The Sultan announced that according to his religion anyone who asks for mercy is bound to get it. Though Russia and Austria ground their bayonets in rage and threatened war, he positively refused to hand Kossuth or his friends over. In this policy he was shortly supported by Britain, which sent a fleet through the Dardanelles as a gesture of support, contrary to international regulations, but the Sultan's grand gesture came before he was certain that he would have this backing.

The refugees were all piled in concentration camps, because Russia declared that if they were allowed to escape, she would consider it a cause for war. Nevertheless, numbers of internees were lured away by both sides until September 1851, when those who remained were all released. On one side, Austria finding force of no avail, promised an amnesty to any soldiers who would return. Many were drawn home by this promise, and many of these found to their sorrow that the amnesty did not include exemption from military service in the imperial forces. On the other side, Turkey, needing soldiers, and officers particularly, offered commissions to any Hungarian officers who would embrace Mohammedanism. Bem took up this offer with alacrity. Declaring that his religion had always been enmity to Russia and that the Sultan was necessarily Russia's enemy, he took the fez and ended his days in the Turkish service. General Guyon also received a Turkish commission, without, however, renouncing his Christianity. He used to order Bibles from the London Bible Society to distribute to the peasants on his Hungarian estate, and would never have given up his religion.

In America Kossuth's lost cause became a national mania. A

gentleman who spoke against Hungary was declared unfit to teach at Harvard and could not get his appointment there confirmed. In Congress enthusiasm was so lively that in 1851 the American government sent a man-of-war to carry Kossuth out of Turkey. When the hero arrived in the United States, his reception was like nothing since Lafayette's famous tour; he made 600 speeches, all cheered to the echo, and collected a large but unspecified sum of money which he said he would use to equip another army to free his fatherland.

In Britain, where public opinion was also aroused, the foreign secretary, Lord Palmerston, officially advised Prince Schwarzenberg that generosity to the rebels could no longer endanger the Empire (which Palmerston had been almost as anxious to keep together as Schwarzenberg himself) and he therefore urged a policy of humanity. The Prince, suaver than Palmerston, icily replied that since the imperial government did not offer Her Majesty's government advice about how to handle Ireland, it expected a reciprocal forbearance about Hungary.

In the worst of the old days, Hungary had never known a repression such as was meted out to it now. In Metternich's time Hungary had been ignored and neglected, robbed and dealt with unjustly; but police spies, passports, and even the efficiency of German bureaucrats swarming into every county were something new. The Magyars had always enjoyed the right to grumble and to vote; and both were now denied them.

As in the rest of the Empire, the serfs were legally freed in Hungary. It was the single permanent accomplishment of the revolution. But in Hungary the average indemnity set on a farm was twice that in other places, one way of punishing the rebels. Besides, the ex-serfs were not now allowed to vote, and since they had enjoyed that privilege for two years under the Hungarian rule, they disliked giving it up. In 1850, when the census was taken, so many persons of Slavic origin inscribed themselves as Magyars, to show their sympathy with the Hungarian cause, that the imperial authorities took another census under military auspices in which every inducement was made to discourage registration as Magyar—and still there were better than two million more people who called themselves Magyars than there had ever been before. The figures went from five to seven million.

And was Croatia's loyalty recognized? Were its demands for autonomy or freedom granted after it had fought so well for the Emperor? Jellačič, who had been raised to power because Croatia wanted to be free to use its own language and self-governing institutions, this same Jellačič, now published to his province the constitution that merged them into the rest of the Empire. German was to be the official language everywhere, in Croatia as in Hungary; there was no autonomy anywhere; and, in fact, the complaint in Croatia was that it received as a reward no more and no less than Hungary received as a punishment.

That was just the way to govern, according to the gentlemen now in the Hofburg, and their convictions were as solid as their enemies'. One of Schwarzenberg's friends quoted the Hungarian declaration of independence and remarked that the document spoke truth, only the sides should be reversed. There had indeed been a conflict of sacred interests with treason, freedom with despotism, civilization with anarchy. Society was indeed defending itself against everything that threatened its destruction, but society in Austrian eyes meant legitimacy, absolutism, force.

Hungary was bitterly, passionately resentful. Countess Karolyi, whose husband was one of those executed by command of Francis Joseph, voiced the public venom in a famous curse beginning, "May Heaven and Hell blast his happiness." But there were still statesmen as well as widows of statesmen in this parliamentary country. Francis Deák, who retired early enough in 1848 to save his skin, had not lost his hopes. In the next decade an Austrian official remarked, "Deák cannot demand after so many accomplished facts that we should begin affairs all over again."

"Why not?" said Deák. "If a man has buttoned one button of his coat wrong, it must be undone again from the top."

"The button might be cut off."

"Then the coat could never be buttoned right at all."[3]

---

[3] Forster, *Francis Deák*. (London, 1880.)

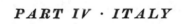

PART IV · ITALY

SWITZERLAND TYROL CARINTHIA

S A R D I N I A (PIEDMONT)

LOMBARDY

VENETIA

ISTRIA

Trieste

Novara

Brescia
Peschiera ★
Custozza
Mantua ★

Verona

★Legnago

Venice

Pola

Turin

PARMA

MODENA

Ferrara

Genoa

Nice

LUCCA

Florence

Leghorn

TUSCANY

PAPAL

STATES

ADRIATIC

CORSICA
(Fr.)

Civita
Vecchia
Rome

Pontecorvo
Benevento

Gaeta
Naples

TYRRHENIAN

SEA

SARDINIA

KINGDOM OF THE TWO SICILIES
(NAPLES)

CALABRIA

M E D I T E R R A N E A N

SICILY

SEA

★ = Fortress

SEA

Fort
Malghera

Railroad Bridge

Grand Canal

R.R. Station

St. Mark's Square

Arsenal

VENICE

ITALY IN 1848

XV

Italy: Each after His Own Image

In 1848 Italy, like Germany, was divided into many small states, all of them ruled by absolute princes, and most of them hopelessly inefficient, corrupt, and reactionary. There was the Kingdom of Naples in the south; then came the papal states across central Italy, and north of them four small duchies and the Kingdom of Piedmont. The richest provinces of the peninsula, Lombardy and Venetia, were part of the Austrian Empire, and thus governed from Vienna.

Sometimes it seemed as if most of the rest of Italy was governed from Vienna, too, for an Austrian army had put down a revolution in 1821 in Naples, and the other princes knew that they could always count on Austrian help in suppressing disorder but would meet with Austrian opposition if they tried to introduce any form of progress into their regimes.

Italians, a race whose proudest political tradition was one of republican city-states, were left without a voice in their own affairs in the mid-nineteenth century.

In habit and attitude, however, they were the most democratic people in Europe, except possibly for the Swiss. Travelers often noted that the aristocracy treated the lower classes with a courtesy totally unknown among the Germans. Mazzini remembered his parents' uniform politeness to every class as one of the major influences in his growing up; and the earliest recollection of Marquis Massimo d'Azeglio, a Piedmontese aristocrat, was that his mother made him kneel down right in a public park to beg the pardon of a servant whom he had struck. The boy remembered that the servant drew back completely nonplussed by such a scene. Yet, in general the workers responded with a kind of easy friendliness and self-respect which made them seem like real people, not, as in so much of Europe, set apart as "the brute part of the population." Perhaps an important factor in this spirit came from the fact that property was not monopolized by any single class in Italy. Cavour noted this fact with great satisfaction—that common people as well as the aristocracy owned their bit of land.

For another thing, the women of Italy were a tremendous force in public life. The biographies and especially the autobiographies of the Italian leaders of this period are full of the unusual respect and gratitude which these men show to their mothers, and often to their wives and daughters. Mazzini's mother supported him in years of exile with understanding and with all the material means she could muster; his lifelong attachment for Giuditta Sidoli was an intellectual passion as well as an emotional one. Among the many sorrows of his personal life she was one of the rare pleasures. In 1848, with revolutions on every side, he yet found time to go back to Giuditta after fifteen years of exile with more joy, he says, than may be imagined. The Marquis d'Azeglio, again, excoriates the foolish passions of his youth; his first wife died early, and his second separated from him, though he never ceased writing her urbane and informative letters about his work and interests. Yet he also tells us that once in his life he found an affection which never failed him, to which he could always turn with confidence, and which made him feel lucky to have known it. Garibaldi, of course, had his Anita, the one real heroine of 1848, the Brazilian whom he snatched from the arms of another man, a girl who learned how to ride through the jungles, to shoot, sail in his ships, and to nurse and to bear children at his side. As for Manin, the only emotion that could rival his love for Venice was his tenderness for his invalid daughter. Countless nights he spent at her bedside, trying to assuage her pain, and when he was in prison the hardest thing for him to bear was the idea that he could no longer help her and might even cause her extra suffering by his plight. What comparable stories are told about their contemporaries in other countries? Lamartine and Louis Blanc, Robert Blum (with his *echt deutsch* family), Georg Herwegh (with his warrior Emma a pale caricature of Anita Garibaldi), Fischhof and Kossuth, spent their lives and energies without the strength that comes from a society where men are matched with women to whom they feel equal. Of all the 1848 revolutionists Mazzini alone tells his comrades that there are no qualifications to women's equality. Politically as in other ways they should be on a level with men.

This feeling came, not from women tied to their homes, but from women free and responsible in public affairs. The London *Times* correspondent told his readers that it was hard for Englishmen to allow for the freedom of manners which Italian women enjoyed, coupled with perfect respectability. The Marchioness Constance d'Azeglio was a good example of what he meant. She was married to Massimo's brother and moved socially among the important men of Turin, yet she took her job of teaching in her school for poor children so seriously that she was often too tired to go to parties in the evening. The Princess Belgiojoso, in something the same manner, introduced not only schools but a recreation hall and a housing project on her estates in Lombardy, and later on edited newspapers in Milan—this although she confessed once that she could not cook an egg, hem a handkerchief, or even order a meal, and that since she had never touched money she could not make herself imagine what a five-franc piece meant. The *Times* man commented acidly that whenever English women emulated the Italians' public activities, their hearts always became entangled in private attachments. The only non-Italian women who managed to have an influence worth mentioning on the political life of 1848 were those like George Sand and Lola Montez who had broken away from all the ties of home.

There were no fiercer patriots than these Italian women. They nurtured their sons to serve Italy well or to die for her gladly. No one impressed the English economist Cobden more, on his tour of Italy, than the Neapolitan lady who told him she would give the blood of her four sons to see Austria expelled from the land; and when the crisis came this spirit did not fail. Giuditta Sidoli sent her son to fight in Rome under Mazzini, and in Venice Theresa Manin blessed her 16-year-old Giorgio when he followed his father to capture the arsenal, though she scarcely expected to see either of them alive again.

The Italian universities, too, were democratic in spirit, and for those who had gone beyond university years, there were professional societies. One of these was founded by the most brilliant young man in Piedmont, Count Camillo Cavour, who was stuck with the job of managing his father's estates. Cavour turned his magnificent head for business at once to the problem of making the land pay, and one of his steps was to organize a society for agricultural improvement. The members moved from a study of such problems as chemical fertilizer to the problem of credit and banking, from there to railroads and steamboats, and from there to international trade and tariffs. Nearly every problem besetting the Kingdom of Piedmont, except that of a constitution, came to seem a natural concern for the Agricultural Society.

Political democrats, concerned only with rights of suffrage, saw nothing in Cavour's movement but a sidetracking of the main issue, for much the same reasons as made Kossuth's party vilify Széchenyi in Hungary. The leader of the Piedmont democratic party went so far as to list progress along with Jesuits and censorship as the three great evils of the country, like only to the plague, and this sentiment made Cavour so unpopular that he was kept out of office for years beyond 1848. Nevertheless, in ways that the political democrats could never measure, the Agricultural Society did more for democracy than a constitution. It brought large and small landowners together, a very desirable mixture of classes, and it taught these men to meet their problems in common, to discuss them in parliamentary form, and to consider the needs of the nation as a whole. Political democracy was bound to come to a country that had learned how to use it so well.

Out of these cities and homes and schools grew an extraordinary group of young men ready to devote their lives to the service of their country. Their first aim was to get the Austrians out of Lombardy, and their second to reform the governments of Italy.

If the Austrian police had wanted to name the single man of whose machinations they were most in awe, they would very likely have picked Joseph Mazzini, in their minds a terrifying image of fanaticism.

Mazzini, they told each other and the world, was at the head of the most extreme republican revolutionary societies in every country—Young Italy, Young Germany, Young Europe—a network which extended to Constantinople and New York. The objects of this society were to destroy the peace of the continent by murder and anarchy. Horrid tales were told of the fearful oaths, the relentless purpose, the stocks of arms of these bloodthirsty patriots, and indeed there were enough martyrs who hurled themselves against the bastions of order to give color to the belief that Mazzini enjoyed throwing other men's lives away.

Mazzini was perhaps proud of his reputation as Public Enemy Number One, so long as iniquity was the basis of European public law. It made him sick to see men forced to think in one way and act in another, bending to power which they hated and despised. He wanted men to become apostles, "fragments of the living truth," and because he made his followers feel that they were just that, he won the sort of devotion against which police power is helpless. He gave you eyes to see and ears to hear, said one of his followers, and you would leave your father and mother to follow him who seemed to have come to overthrow the whole wretched fabric of falsehoods that held mankind in bondage.

Even in little ways he was more than the equal of the men governments sent to catch him. At the time of his first arrest, in 1831, he tells us he had on his person enough for three convictions— rifle bullets, a letter in cipher relating to secret society affairs, a history of the recent July revolution in Paris printed on tricolor paper, the formula for a secret society oath, and a sword cane. Before the police could use these objects against him he had gotten rid of every one. Later on, in Marseilles, he outwitted two policemen; one he talked into letting him go, the other he walked right past in the uniform of a national guard while the man arrested someone else.

Mazzini was born in Genoa and was therefore a Piedmontese subject, although Genoa was the least loyal city in the domains of the King of Sardinia. His father was a doctor, his mother one of those fierce Italian souls whose faith and hope were all bound up in her son. He grew up to be quiet and melancholy, always dressing in black in mourning for his country, and addicted to long solitary walks. These alone were enough to draw unfavorable notice from the police. Mazzini wanted to be a writer, but he found himself unable to write because he did not have a country. He did not feel, with Wagner, that art is itself revolutionary, but rather that a revolution was a prerequisite for art in those days. Therefore, he gave himself over to the long, thankless, sometimes bloody task of creating a united Italy. Since the republic was the ideal form of government, he resolved Italy must also be republican.

His ideas were so unwelcome in Piedmont that he had to leave the country, and he spent the early 1830's in Marseilles. Here he and his friends edited a paper which they exported to Italy in marked barrels of pumice stone and pitch. Across the border other friends took good care to buy the marked barrels, and they distributed Mazzini's propaganda far and wide. Mazzinians everywhere were soon organized into Young Italy, a purified secret political society, made of men under forty who would pledge themselves to carry on both education and insurrection for a democratic Italy.

In exile Mazzini, who had already formed his ideals, formed his character. For a while he was happily in love with a young widow, Giuditta Sidoli. They lived together for over a year and even, apparently, had a child who subsequently died. Giuditta, however, was torn with love for her other children, living in Italy with their paternal grandfather, who would not let her see them because of her radical ideas. When she decided to go back to where she could at least steal glimpses of them, Mazzini was left alone. Added to this was the fact that an armed expedition he had planned to conquer Savoy was a laughable failure. The unhappy Mazzini fell into an agony of doubt about himself and his beliefs which lasted all one winter. Then on a spring morning he woke up, composed, "retempered like steel," with an unshakable, if arid, religion, that did not save his soul one atom of unhappiness, yet kept him alive and working.

Hounded out of France, then out of Switzerland, Mazzini betook himself in 1837 to the only country that did not care what he said and was strong enough to maintain his right to say it—England. He arrived lonely, embittered, and with all a Latin's repugnance for the outward forms of British life, but at least he was free and safe. Gradually his work brought him into contact with the sort of Englishmen who could appreciate his originality and friendliness. They never quite got used to him; even Carlyle, one of his best friends, touches his description of Mazzini with a slight condescension:

"A small, square-headed, bright-eyed, swift, yet still Ligurian figure, beautiful and merciful and fierce, as grand a little man . . . as has ever come before me. True as steel, the word, the thought of him pure and limpid as water, by nature a little lyrical poet, with plenty of quiet fun in him, too, and wild emotion. . . ."

English women were inclined to be complete hero worshipers of Mazzini, and a goodly number of them married his followers, contributing their bit to Italian history and letters. These ladies, not knowing of Giuditta and of Mazzini's complete faithfulness to her, imagined that his heart was given over to Italy and that there could be no competition with such an idol. Therefore they surrounded him with warm platonic friendship which did a lot toward reviving his enjoyment of life. He was always affectionate and to these ladies he poured out his high spirits, his wit, his interest in small human affairs, his penetrating comments on their interests and his.

Most political refugees spent their time in dreaming of past glory or planning future seizures of power. Mazzini was one of the few who could work wherever he was at whatever needed to be done. Thus, though he never gave up for a day his concern for Italy, he also started a school in London for Italian workers and their children. His aim was to teach them to think as workers, so that the next revolution would not be lost in purely political reform. Mazzini was far from advocating the class struggle; he never wanted the workers to rise against their masters, only to rise with them in such force that afterwards their just demands for social reform would be impressed on the community. Though he was sometimes domineering with friends, and always doctrinaire in his views, he had far more real faith in the people than most self-styled democrats in the 1848 period. And to do him justice, he was one of those natural leaders for whom such faith is perfectly justified; when he took charge the people followed with angelic simplicity. Even when he lectured them sternly to think about their duties rather than their rights they adored him.

While he was in London he also kept up a tremendous correspondence. He encouraged Garibaldi in South America to fight for liberty, and he proclaimed through England and Italy that an Italian hero was fighting brilliantly on the Rio Plata. Thanks to this word, half the young men of Piedmont kept Garibaldi's picture in their vest pockets.

Austrian censors kept such a strict watch on Mazzini's mail— with a forged copy of his seal to help them—that they even copied his love letters to Giuditta. Thus we know about them. But the real scandal of Mazzini's mail came when he found out that the British government, too, opened his private letters and passed on information to foreign governments. Mazzini noticed first that his letters arrived later than they should—by the small amount of two hours— and then he discovered that the postmarks had been altered. To prove his suspicions he enclosed hairs or poppy seeds within, and when these were lost he knew. There was a huge scandal in Parliament on this subject and as a result the principle that British mail should be inviolable was established. Yet Mazzini never quite overcame the suspicion among Italians that the disclosures which had been made had led to the capture of a small band of men, led by the Bandiera brothers, who landed in Calabria and tried to start the revolution, and who were subsequently shot, to the horror of the civilized world.

Such events had sharply reduced Mazzini's popularity in Italy in the years just before 1848. There was a recoil of feeling against Young Italy and its heartbreaking sacrifices. Mazzini believed that the blood of patriots would be the seed of the nation, but there was no evidence that the fanatical young men who had rushed into the arms of the police at his behest, and had been shot, tortured or exiled for their pains, would yield any fruit.

While Mazzini was out of Italy, conspiring from exile to make his republic, inside the country a number of men decided that conspiracies endangered their work almost as much as foreign domination. In the Roman states the republicans threatened to start another outbreak whenever the sick old Pope, Gregory XVI, should die; and to try to quiet them, the moderate men sent Massimo d'Azeglio to tour the secret network of Mazzini's followers with a message to stay quiet for the time being.

D'Azeglio started out in September 1845. He was rather surprised to be given such an assignment, for until that day he had taken no part in politics, either secretly or openly. Of course, that was one reason for choosing him: the police had no suspicion of him.

He had grown up in Piedmont, the plainest and most old-fashioned corner of Italy; the correct career for him would have been the army, which indeed he joined at fifteen, living, he tells us, the life of an absolute rake. Then, at twenty he suddenly reformed and announced to his horrified family that he was going to Rome to study painting. His father would not quite forbid it, but he offered his son the same allowance to live on in Rome as he had received for spending money while he lived at home. The threat of poverty did not deter Massimo, who added to his family's horror by the announcement that he hoped before very long to sell some of his pictures. The idea that a marquis could accept money for something he made with his hands was enough to ostracize him from all the aristocracy in Turin. Once in Rome, however, Massimo forgot his noble birth as far as possible and settled in small lodgings which cost, with board and laundry, 15 scudi (about $15) a month. Since his allowance was around 25 scudi, and six went for the rent of a studio, he had only four scudi for the all-important purchases of paint, canvas, and instruction. He was far too poor to buy clothes. In the summer he used to go to the country to paint landscapes and often had to sleep on straw and sometimes butcher his own meat to save expense. He could have gone into the best society in Rome, of course, but he found social life so rotten that he went out very little except to see a countess with whom he was in love. Whenever he sold a picture and his finances looked up, he bought a horse, for he was a passionate horseman, but he could never keep one for long.

He lived this way for ten years, and then, at thirty, went home. Finding Turin unbearably provincial, he moved to Milan, for in this bigger city he found the life he wanted. He had grown comfort-loving and enjoyed the wealth and ease of this Lombard capital, but he also found more intellectual activity there than in any city in the rest of Italy. It was true that he lived under Austrian rule, and every step reminded him how much he suffered through Austria—but for another ten years he was content to let his hatred simmer while he painted and wrote novels. He married the daughter of Manzoni, the great novelist whose *I Promessi Sposi* was not only already recognized as a great work of art but in the Italy of that time was usually interpreted as symbolizing the plight of Italy. Their country was the promised bride, held from them by a tyrant.

D'Azeglio followed in his father-in-law's footsteps so well that the official at the Austrian bureau of censorship told him his second novel ought certainly to be forbidden, for its historical romance was nothing but an incitement to his readers. But, continued the official, being an Italian himself he would not forbid the book; and he hoped this leniency would convince d'Azeglio that the Austrian states were the best-governed ones in Italy.

Naturally, no Austrian kindness could soften d'Azeglio's opinions, and in 1845 he was delighted to be able to perform a service for Italy and against Austria by making the tour of the secret network.

He went from town to town on this journey, and in each he was given the name of just one man at the next stop—the person who was entrusted with the job of forwarding confidential news, letters, and people. He must never ask for this person at the inn, but had to loiter around town, asking indirect questions until he found the right person, then he must speak without suspicious talk until they could withdraw to a safe place.

This underground organization was called the *trafila*—literally, the wire-drawing plate, only in this case the wires were revolutionaries. It functioned so well for many years that the police never discovered a single link.

In his assignment, d'Azeglio tells us the first part was easy, persuading the patriots along the *trafila* not to revolt. They were already tired of Mazzini's cloak-and-dagger tactics, and quite willing to believe that a new pope might be more liberal and that their country needed a long, quiet period of preparation before it could make the single united effort that would be needed to drive out the Austrians.

It was the second part of d'Azeglio's job that was hard, for when they asked him to whom shall we turn now, he had to answer: Your hope lies in Charles Albert, King of Piedmont. Everywhere he met the reply, Charles Albert is a reactionary; he will not give his people a constitution; his police are as cruel as the Austrians; he even married an Austrian; he is bound to Metternich.

Then d'Azeglio had to show them that even if Charles Albert was a bad hope he was their only possible one. The House of Savoy was the single native dynasty among all the ruling families of Italy; Piedmont alone of the eight states had a strong army. And, insisted d'Azeglio, it will take an army, it will take more than citizens shooting out of windows, to drive the Austrians back behind the Alps. Furthermore, he went on, granted that Charles Albert's views are reactionary, granted that his character is untrustworthy, still he cannot fail to help you because of what is in it for him—the iron crown of Lombardy. Ask a thief to become an honest man and I grant you you have little assurance of success, but ask him to help you in a robbery and I do not see how he can fail you. By this simple metaphor, d'Azeglio tells us, he made many converts.

Charles Albert, all this while, knew nothing of d'Azeglio's none too flattering propaganda in his behalf, and d'Azeglio honestly did not know whether His Majesty would be pleased. The King had been a mystery for years, keeping his thoughts so well to himself that even his intimates could not have agreed on what they really were. So when d'Azeglio asked to tell him about his tour through central Italy, it was with great trepidation.

The audience was granted for six in the morning, well before dawn. The streets of Turin were still dark as d'Azeglio went up to the palace, but it was abustle and ablaze with light. He was ushered into a room with two gilt seats covered with green silk, embroidered in a large white pattern which caused his artist's soul to shrink from touching it. The King, however, politely asked him to sit down, and seemed so interested in what d'Azeglio had to tell him that the Marquis had to keep repeating to himself, "Massimo, do not trust him." When he was through telling the King that a large part of Italy could easily be made to follow his banner, Charles Albert looked him in the face and said, "Tell your friends to stay quiet and avoid a rising, for nothing can be done at present; but let them be certain that when the time comes, my life, my sons' lives, my sword, my treasury, my army shall all be expended for the Italian cause."[1]

D'Azeglio's heart was in a tumult as he repeated what he was to tell his friends—to be sure the statement was for the record—for a great hope hung over him with outspread wings. So he described it. Then, as he prepared to bow himself out, the King gave him a kiss so cold that it brought back icy waves of distrust. When he wrote to his friends, in cipher, a letter which he knew would reach every intellectual in Italy, he told of Charles Albert's promise and added, "These are his words, but God alone knows his heart."

Although d'Azeglio could not be sure, Charles Albert was perfectly sincere, and afterwards, when he had given tragic proofs of his devotion to the Italian cause, d'Azeglio reproached himself for his lack of faith in 1845.

Several stars would have to be in conjunction before a propitious day would come to strike for Italian freedom, and Charles Albert was the first one to swing into place.

Even if the men who read d'Azeglio's letter believed that Charles Albert was their star, they could not hope that the other ones would rise so soon. In fact d'Azeglio and his friends would rather have had twenty years of "moderation and activity" (that was the phrase with which d'Azeglio ended his letters to political friends) than the

[1] D'Azeglio, *Recollections.*

sudden gathering of forces which brought war, revolution, and apparent disaster to Italy within three years.

D'Azeglio was by this time thick in politics, and from historical novels he turned to writing political tracts. Knowing that he would not be allowed to live under Austrian rule much longer, he arranged his affairs in Milan so that he could leave them for a long period. His first pamphlet had to be printed in Tuscany—even Piedmont would not allow it—and though the king for whom he worked so hard allowed d'Azeglio to settle in Turin, he would not receive him at court after he had become an open reformer.

Italians wanted to expand in so many directions that nobody could have said at which point their inflexible institutions galled the most.

They believed in those days that all their country needed to become immensely prosperous were a few modern improvements. As soon as the Suez Canal is put through, they said, Italy will again be an international thoroughfare as before the discovery of how to sail around Africa. They wanted to be ready for this event, yet their political system almost negated the advantages of steam power. For instance, a boat on the Po had to stop for five customs inspections, and its cargo was subject to five sets of duties; sometimes a train's required stops took more time than the journey itself. And Pope Gregory during his reign refused to let a railroad cross his dominions at all. Likewise it was hard to sell a book in Genoa that had been printed at Florence. States were not only too small to provide markets for the industry they might develop, but they were run so lumberingly and corruptly that it was hard for a businessman or anyone else to get his rights in court.

Progress, then, depended largely on reforming the governments, and reform depended largely on the question of getting Austria out. So long as Austria was in Lombardy, Metternich would feel free to put out fires in his neighbors' houses before his own should catch, as he expressed it. Independence, in turn, seemed to depend on united action, since none doubted that if all Italians joined in a common cause they could drive the barbarians beyond the Alps.

To further these aims which every patriot had at heart, the young moderates kept up a tremendous correspondence. Their letters show what affection united men from Milan to Rome and from Florence to Naples—they outdo each other in the protests of friendship and in the endearing diminutives in which Italian is so rich. The writers show how much joy they get out of each other's activities, and they constantly assume that their friends will understand and agree with them.

Even better than letters were chances to talk things over. In 1839 these men organized the first of an annual series of scientific conventions, begun perhaps for an exchange of knowledge, but soon turning toward what was most on their hearts. "Volcanoes" made a most interesting subject in 1846; and in 1847 they investigated the "potato disease." Since in Italian vernacular a "potato" is a German (just as in English he may be called a "kraut"), the possibilities of this discussion were endless.

These young men were bent on economic, social, and moral improvement all at one time. The many economic needs of their country were no more important than various others—or rather, as Cavour put it, "Those who see nothing in the progress of industry except material things have small minds." Like the French reformers they were horrified by the poverty which capitalism had brought to British workers, and they were determined to raise the level of their own lower class by schools, public health work, industrial health, and by writing a literature consciously adapted to their interests.

If there was one principle on which all the Italian reformers found a common ground—Mazzini and the republicans as well as his bitter enemies, d'Azeglio and the constitutionists—it was to agree with Cavour that "fraternal love is the principal strength of modern society."

In 1846 it looked as if Italy were in for a slow period of education by her moderate reformers, looking to the House of Savoy and the Piedmont army as the ultimate means of unifying the country. In the long run this is what happened, but not until Mazzini had had his stormy day. If, in history, his genius makes any one of theirs seem pale, at the time they despised him and vilified him. When his revolution, carrying Italy to new hopes, failed in greater despair than ever, the moderates picked up the pieces and never admitted what they owed to Mazzini's work in preparing people's souls.

As for Mazzini, he was nauseated and furious at the limited aims and slow caution of the moderate men, and his most particular enmity went to their hero, Charles Albert. In 1831, when that monarch took the throne, Mazzini wrote a famous letter, "telling him all that his own heart should have told him."

"God created in six days the physical universe; France in three days has created the moral universe, and, like God, reposes. . . . Rise, then, and like God, bring forth a world from this chaos."[2] This was not the kind of religion Charles Albert could understand, nor did Mazzini expect him to—he wrote the letter to show the prince up. As Mazzini's secret societies began to make headway in his kingdom, particularly in his precious army, Charles Albert exiled Mazzini and set the police on the trail of all republicans. Some of them were tortured, and after his best friend committed suicide in a Piedmont prison, Mazzini's hatred of the King was implacable.

Yet the dream of Charles Albert's life was to free Italy, too, and like Mazzini, he was convinced that he could do it without any foreign aid, though he might have won a French alliance or English backing. Mazzini wanted a European war, but not intervention, just so that Italy would have a chance to do for itself. Charles Albert's proud motto was that Italy will do for itself anyway. A decade later, studying his failure, his son Victor Emmanuel and Cavour accepted Napoleon III's help, at the price of ceding Savoy to France—and succeeded.

Since Italy could not be freed without a war, Charles Albert consciously and hopefully looked forward to war as an instrument of his national policy. And knowing that war, when it came, must be waged in a totalitarian spirit, the King was unwilling to grant libertarian reforms. Though he did an immense amount to improve Piedmont's administration, and still more for the army, he always sought to keep responsibility centered in his own hands, much like Frederick William of Prussia. Liberty, at least in the common opinion of the day, would loosen discipline in the army; democracy, by the same token, would drain the public treasury and ruin honest administration; while no one knew what crazy schemes might be concocted by amateur legislators.

Since his hostility to reform was obvious and his hostility to Austria was veiled, he was usually set down as one more enemy to Italian progress. This is why d'Azeglio on his first mission around the

[2] Quoted from Flagg. I, 301.

country had such a hard time convincing liberals to follow the King of Piedmont.

This lack of confidence hurt Charles Albert inwardly but he was supported by a clear conscience and was utterly unable to change his devious introversion in order to win love or popularity. His soul was solitary, and one of his friends said that pessimism put unhealable black patches on it. To forget the agonies of his spirit, he inflicted agonies on his body; he fasted and wore haircloth and spent long hours in prayer. One of his most trusted advisers was a nun, one whose convent dowry he had paid, and who soon began to have mystical dreams about his mission of freeing Italy.

As a result of his regimen, by 1848 he was aged and thin, with emaciated hands and a pale, gloomy face. Yet, those who came close to him were always moved by the sweetness and depth in his expression and admired his quiet dignity.

Most of Charles Albert's friends believed that he had been given his throne only after making a promise to Metternich that he would never grant a constitution to his people. Whether this was true or not, the door against political reforms seemed tightly shut in Piedmont. Censorship to keep ideas standard was as strict as in Austria. One might refer to a country but not a nation; to institutions but not to a constitution, even in speaking of England or France; and as for the words liberty or liberal, they were quite forbidden.

An artist and a progressive like d'Azeglio would always find Turin a hard place to live in, and indeed that wayward son touched off the quality of the place neatly:

"As in some countries a standard measure or scales are set up in the market-place, by which to test the upright dealing of everyone, it might have seemed as if God had only gone to the expense of one set of brains for the whole nobility of Turin, and placed it at court in the throne room, where each might go and supply himself with the ideas he required."[3]

Meanwhile, another star had risen for Italy. In June 1846, Gregory died and the new pope, Pius IX gave an immediate gauge of good intentions to his people by an amnesty of political prisoners.

The news reached the Roman population on a warm summer

[3] D'Azeglio, *Recollections*. I, 324.

evening, when large numbers of them were already on the streets.
The new ruler's gentle heart was distressed, they learned, that so
many Roman families were not united; he would let their prisoners
and exiles come home. With a single impulse, the crowd began to
move toward the palace and they waited under his balcony till he
came out to bless them. Three times the crowd moved on and three
times the square filled up and the benediction had to be given again.

Every house was illuminated, and even the jails, where political
prisoners gave themselves great banquets and embraced their guards
as they marched out. Seven hundred men were returned, pardoned,
and when they had had time to gather together, they flocked to receive the sacrament from the Pope whose grace had blessed them.
Not one prisoner, and only one or two exiles, refused to sign the oath
of allegiance that was required.

There were, however, at least two people who went on record to
deplore the Pope's attitude. Metternich remarked dryly that God
does not grant amnesties, and added that a liberalizing pope would
surely undermine his own temporal power. Mazzini was more bitter,
and more incoherent:

"If ever there has been a moment in which I could achieve a
heroic-mad thing and walk there with a few companions like the
Bandiera for the simple aim of saying: 'We scorn your forgiveness
and despise you; take our life for it,' it is now."[4]

What he meant was that an amnesty was a cheap way of buying
popularity. Also, it upset Mazzini's strategy when princes gave
spontaneous concessions; what he preferred was that the people
should become conscious of their strength by forcing reforms, and
that when the princes failed, as fail they would, they should be
shown up as inadequate. Therefore, he told his followers to exaggerate in the popular mind the expectation of what the Pope
might give and to build up their hatred of the foreign oppressor by
attributing anything the Pope did not do to Austrian influence. To
help along in the work of exposing the Pope, Mazzini wrote him a
letter, urging him to shed the shackles of an outworn church and
head up a new religion of humanity. In moments like these Mazzini
appears at his most preposterous, whether on the face of the document or in the motives behind it. Two years later, however, when

[4] Quoted from Richards, *Mazzini's Letters to an English Family*, p. 38.

Mazzini had his strut upon the stage of power, his actions rather redeemed his words.

Pius, in the past, had been noted for his quiet charities. As Bishop of Imola he seemed to like to help people without getting credit for it. He was also known in his young days as a famous revivalist preacher, capable of such stunts as illustrating the fires of hell in a darkened church with a thigh bone steeped in spirits. People who met him socially found him handsome, easy, with good taste and a good vocabulary. He never expected to become Pope but when he went to the Conclave of Cardinals that was to elect one, he carried with him the books of Gioberti, Balbo, and d'Azeglio dealing with Italian reform to present to the new pontiff, whoever he might be.

Yet, when Alexander Herzen searched his face for traces of thought in 1847, he found only inertia mingled with bonhomie. (He would also have said here was a man incapable of persecution— later on, Herzen apologized for having been mistaken about this.) Someone else described the Pope's intellectual processes by saying that liberal ideas filtered into his head like snow blowing in around the cracks in a closed window.

These liberal ideas at first, and the agitation of the aroused public later on, made Pius give concession after concession during the eighteen months before the revolution broke loose. First, he created a council of state, designed to draw the best lay minds in the Roman state into consultation about affairs of government. The council of state ran into immediate and significant difficulties; something like the United Diets of Prussia, the new body assumed the right to draft a program, when the sovereign had expected it to advise merely on the matters he brought before it. This, however, was known only in literate circles. To the mobs of Rome, as to the other peoples of Italy, panting for a breath of liberty, the council of state was the gift of one who loved freedom and who was going to bring in a new era.

At this point the Pope might have been inclined to stop for a while ("Let me be a tortoise so long as I am not a crab."), but the men who wanted to push reform dared not stop before they had a civic guard. The moderates wanted one as a police force, the radicals as a weapon against Austria. These leaders made a fine art of handling crowds, with the result that clubs, banquets, and street meetings flattered or intimidated the pontiff into granting the militia in July 1847.

Instead of appeasing the people, concessions only whetted their demands. Riots with great banners, saying "Holy Father, trust the people," did not make Pius trust them; but as other princes in Italy were granting constitutions in early 1848, the Pope had to give one, too—a conservative model.

The gratitude of Italians was beyond belief. Theirs was the only country where the legitimate rulers seemed to be on the side of freedom. In France, Germany, Austria, the first requisite to reform was to overpower the monarchs, or at least to overrule the royal unwillingness to make concessions; happy Italy suddenly saw itself being led toward liberty and independence by crowned heads. Surely after reform would come a crusade to free Lombardy.

For a long time Charles Albert had governed unobtrusively through reactionaries who were friendly to Austria—this was part of his smoke screen. But to win support for a national war against Austria, he had to cultivate the very men who were demanding a constitution.

In the fall of 1847, inspired partly by the Pope, he threw his first reforms into Austria's teeth—no constitution (indeed the King hoped a constitution was as far off as ever) but extensive revision of the press law and the police system. Old Radetzky, the Austrian marshal, crouching in Milan read the sign aright, and expected war in the spring.

In January 1848, the Piedmontese army, which was already dreaming furious dreams of war, was increased. At the same time Turin merchants signed a petition to the King, begging him to use their lives and fortunes to help the Lombard brothers. Robert d'Azeglio was one of the men who collected signatures, and he found that even bankers, usually so hard, signed this document with the best grace, while storekeepers ran to him to be sure their names would not be left out.

Among his subjects the King had never been so popular; nevertheless he did not want his people to rejoice, and he ordered police to break up a crowd singing Rossini's new hymn for Pius IX. Charles Albert was afraid of his people, afraid that they did not know what was best for them, and afraid above all that they would interfere in his war. To d'Azeglio he said, "I want freedom for Italy and for that reason will never grant a constitution."

The King was alone in this opinion of his, bred by his mysticism —and the person who pointed out the error of his ways was Cavour. This was the first political deed of the man who eventually brought genius to the moderate party of Italy. In 1847 he moved into public life by starting a newspaper in Turin, using the new freedom of the press. He found the job of organizing a paper at least as hard as organizing a province—though he was still a gentleman journalist, with office hours from 10 to 2 daily. (The contemporary, more professional, editor of the London *Times* was at his desk from early morning until long past midnight every day.)

Cavour did not believe that even the threat of war justified postponing the constitution, and he persuaded a meeting of journalists to petition the crown for it, early in 1848. It was stupid, he told them, to ask for petty reforms; they ought to come out for their full program at once.

As for Charles Albert, he would almost rather have abdicated than grant a constitution at such a juncture. Yet his patriotism overcame his repugnance, and on February 13 he announced that he would give one to his country, providing for a legislature of two houses and a civic guard; in order to show the poor in his cities, and his peasants, that he was trying to do something to help all his people, he lowered the price of salt in the same proclamation.

When this news reached the people in the streets of Turin, many of them wept. It became a common sight to see people who did not know each other kiss. Bells rang, so that peasants in the countryside thought it must be an invasion and they hurried for their arms. Across the border in Milan, the news of a constitution in Piedmont caused men to take off their hats, while the cries of joy they meant to utter stuck in their throats for tears. Every seat in the theaters was full that night, with the ladies wearing white and blue, the colors of Savoy.

It was carnival time, and instead of the usual costumes ladies took up black velvet riding habits with the skirts looped up over tricolor petticoats, while the feathers on gentlemen's Calabrian hats grew so tall that they obscured the gaslights in the streets and their spurs tore holes in ladies' silk dresses. The Duke of Savoy, Charles

Albert's eldest son, the future King Victor Emmanuel, sported a peasant costume.

On February 27 Massimo d'Azeglio used his artist's talents to organize a huge procession, including every rank and trade, the students, the butchers, the journalists—and a group of Lombards who marched in silence and in mourning. This fete was to show the King the gratitude and trust of his people, but as Charles Albert viewed the procession he was pale and drawn, in fact, so lifeless that someone said that he took the place of the corpses which were carried at the head of the revolutions in Paris and Berlin.

If this sad monarch received any comfort that month, it was to hear the news of Louis Philippe's fall—for at least that showed Charles Albert that the reforms he granted so hesitatingly had been absolutely necessary. Piedmont was one of the few spots in Europe where the race toward revolution seemed to have been beaten. Yet, the new Piedmont constitution was copied from the very one under which Louis Philippe fell.

On March 4 the constitution was formally promulgated, and a few days later its ardent advocate, Cesare Balbo, was asked to be Prime Minister. The two pleasures in life, Balbo had said, were making love and making war; now that he was at the head of a reformed Piedmont, no one doubted that war was imminent.

The effect of the reforms on his kingdom was exactly what Charles Albert had foreseen. People began talking politics instead of strategy—too much energy went into reorganizing the government at once. Yet enthusiasm was at a new pitch. Italians everywhere flocked to fight under a man whom they were already calling the first king of united Italy.

XVI

Milan's Five Glorious Days

WHEN the Congress of Vienna offered Austria the Italian provinces of Lombardy and Venetia, with the idea that Austria could then keep order in the rest of the peninsula, Emperor Francis was far from enthusiastic. The bribe was great, however, and furthermore the Emperor had a sense of public obligation; for Italy had been greatly stimulated by its liberalizing Napoleonic administration, and a strong hand would be needed to suppress French ideas there.

Emperor Francis had selected the ablest officer in his army to command the Austrian troops in Italy. In the person of Field Marshal Count Joseph Radetzky, Italian nationalism met the force of an idea as strong as its own. If he had had no more sense of duty than the civilian officials of the Empire, the Italians could have chased him out and kept him out. Radetzky, however, had personal convictions, and convictions are either dangerous or lucky in a soldier. He had been sent to hang on to Lombardy and Venice in the name of the Emperor—and in so hanging on he was certain that he was defending the future interests of all Germany, of Prussia and Bavaria as well as Austria. He was also sure the Empire had a mission. Until nationalism had played out its game and the Hapsburg lands were dismembered in 1918, no one quite realized the values which belonged to their unwilling union. In Radetzky's mind, along with its old-fashioned loyalty, the tragic consequences of the split-up were adumbrated.

For the Italian nationalists he had no sympathy whatsoever, remarking that three days of blood would quiet them into thirty years of peace—and he was eager to prove his point. When Metternich issued specific orders tending to help the Empire slide through as painlessly as possible whatever crisis might be coming, the field marshal obeyed. But when, in 1847, a legal justification occurred to occupy the city of Ferrara (in the papal states, just across the border from Lombardy) Radetzky seized it without giving Metternich a chance to say no. His soldiers swept through the streets with their artillery matches alight—and though this act was based on a treaty right, it inflamed all Italy.

Even if Radetzky had a fierce impatience with Italian patriots he had real sympathy with the peasants, just as he had with the common soldiers who came from that class. While the Italians were carrying on about constitutions and reform, Radetzky's weather eye was on the harvest. He knew that another year of poor crops after the disastrous year of 1846 would make food very scarce and the country harder than ever to police. At one time Radetzky carried his interest in the peasantry so far that he proposed giving them more political rights, so they would be a counterweight to the "communism" he felt rising among the city workers—but the Hapsburg viceroy laughed at the marshal and told him to stop talking like a revolutionary.

When the battle came Radetzky's faith in the country people was justified. They took rather little interest in the revolution of their countrymen, and eased the Austrian army's path by their friendliness.

In 1848 Radetzky was 81 years old, and the greatest commander of the age. He was a stout, short, old gentleman, cordial, full of bonhomie, with a clean-shaven face which reddened happily every time he laughed. He had been a poor boy, an orphan, whose military education was taken care of by the government; he joined the army in 1785, and by 1813 had risen to the general staff, where his planning was a great factor in the defeat of Napoleon in the battle of Leipzig.

While he was away at the wars his wife ran up so many debts that he was faced with the choice of disowning her publicly or of surrendering his entire property and having half his salary withheld. He chose the latter course, though it meant that he had to live in the provinces, and at 66, as he retired from some unimportant post, he wrote his memoirs as if his life were over. If it had not been for troublous times, he said later, he would never have made up the seventeen years he lost in his career. As it was, two years after his retirement, in 1834, Emperor Francis called him back and asked him to take command of the Austrian forces in Italy. Radetzky pleaded that both his debts and his years were great, whereupon the Emperor said, "If I take care of your debts, I trust you to handle your years."

Indeed the old Field Marshal took his years lightly, for he had an illegitimate child born in Milan as late as 1846, when he was 79. His legitimate children were not much good except for one daughter in Pressburg to whom he often sent presents of Italian silk for herself and her children. As for his sons, he once thanked a priest warmly for thrashing them.

As a commander his genius was at least half a matter of the training he gave his army. He knew that his brains would have to make up for exasperating economies at Vienna—for he could never get either as many men or as much money he thought necessary. Therefore the officers he could afford were practiced in the hardest kind of maneuvers, so they learned how to take infantry, cavalry, or artillery over any kind of terrain. Even the notorious Haynau, whom civilians called the hyena, bowed to Radetzky's discipline. He was made to take part in war games, and Haynau lost because of not using Radetzky's modern tactics—an outcome which caused childish joy for the old marshal. Radetzky's forces also learned to get their provisions out on time, to keep their equipment perfect—and if ever the commander was angry it was over mistakes which caused the common soldiers to suffer.

Within the army there was unusual camaraderie from general down to private, of a sort that soldiers of other countries envied. Radetzky spoke to at least a hundred privates every day. He knew five languages (by no means usual among officers, for many boasted that they could not speak the language of the men in their command) and he knew the soldiers' hearts by instinct. Once he saw a soldier without the little sprig of greenery which the Austrian army wore on days of victory. To cover the soldier's embarrassment the field marshal took the twig from his own cap and gave half of it to the man. By touches such as these, and by sending comforts to his men who had been taken prisoner, Radetzky won every man in his command. It was far more effective than political propaganda.

The army, to be sure, had its own methods for breaking political ties—methods with which Radetzky in his years as chief of staff may have had a good deal to do. An empire that was to be held together more by force than by affection had to train a different sort of army from that of a single national state. This army had no patriotic allegiance and no tradition of great national victories, but it made up for these by being impervious to civilian ideas and traditionally unmoved by defeat.

Instead of having love of home appealed to, each soldier was deliberately sent for training to a part of the Empire where he knew neither the language nor the people. Lombards were sent to Hungary, Silesians to Croatia, and there, remote from home, soldiers learned their special military esprit de corps. Radetzky, to be sure, had a large number of Italians serving under him, but that was because they were raw recruits, and when trouble came in 1848 these boys deserted in droves. In great contrast were the Hungarians serving in Italy at the time, who had had time to be seasoned by absence from home. Most of the Magyars were deaf to Kossuth's appeals to come back and fight for their own country.

Because they would be cut off from all domestic ties, mothers hated to have their sons go into military service. Under Ferdinand's rule the term was reduced from fourteen years to eight, but even eight was plenty to ruin a man for civilian life. Kudlich said that in his Silesian village to lose a son to the army was considered worse than to have him die, since he was sure to come back, if at all, spoiled for work and a drunkard. Kudlich's own family were so eager to keep his brother at home that they paid a doctor 300 florins (nearly $150) to make him look scrofulous. After the army doctor turned him down it was months before the poor boy was presentable again, but they all felt it was worth it.

Common soldiers were paid roughly four cents a day, out of which they had to buy everything but their clothes, quarters, and bread. Even meat was not supplied to them. Corporal punishment was universal. Though not unknown in other armies (considering that only the 1848 revolution abolished flogging in the French navy) still the number and publicity of military whippings throughout Austria were noted by all foreigners. Within view of the emperor's palace in Vienna were two barracks where Sunday mornings were given over to this unsabbath-like duty; while Mass was being sung in nearby churches, soldiers were stripped and given 25 lashes by corporals specially trained to inflict as much pain with as little vital damage as possible.

One extra and characteristic precaution was taken to insure the unity of the Empire. Each province was taught only one branch of the service so that none of them would be prepared to wage war separately. Bohemians made up the infantry, Hungarians the cavalry, Austrians the artillery. Italians provided a regiment of light horse. This policy shows why the Austrians had so confidently expected no artillery resistance from Hungary.

When the revolution broke in 1848, Radetzky met the crisis for which he had prepared for fourteen years, and he was delighted to prove his tactics and his convictions in battle. He was sick and tired like other people of the inefficient civilian bureaucracy in Lombardy — he wanted to show everybody that the sword could be quicker, cleaner, and in the long run kinder.

In working up their case against Austria, Italians were handicapped by the fact that Lombardy, though under the hated foreign rule, was the richest and almost the freest section of all Italy. This in part was a result of good soil, and in part came only from the fact that the other states were corrupt and tyrannical. Nevertheless it made an embarrassing point for Italian apologists to get around.

The Lombard plains looked almost like a single highly cultivated garden, with a magnificent irrigation system which watered mulberries, vines, and wheat at once. The land was rich enough to support the densest population in Europe; at the same time communication was easy because of a network of fine roads. All these things owed nothing to Austria, said the pro-Italians. Even the roads, they insisted with exaggeration, were built during the twenty-year French Napoleonic rule. Or, if these propagandists allowed that Austria had used the period since 1815 to increase Lombard prosperity, then it was just to get more out of the country in taxes. Three times what the French had taken out of the country every year went now to Vienna, so that one-third of the revenue of the whole Empire came from its Italian provinces, Lombardy and Venetia, although only one-sixth of the population lived there.

As for administration, it was universally admitted to be cheaper and more honest than that of neighboring states. Elementary schools reached more of the children—68 per cent of the boys and 42 per cent of the girls—and the penal code was both mild and firm.

Even in the control of thought, Austrian censorship at Milan was lighter and more sensible than either Italian censorship at Rome or Austrian censorship at Vienna. Milan was, indeed, the liveliest and most intellectual city in Italy. There had been martyrs, notably the poet Silvio Pellico, who was kept for years in a cold dungeon in Bohemia while the Emperor Francis read daily reports on how he behaved and issued orders as to how many cups of coffee or books he might be allowed. After his release in 1830 Pellico published *My Prisons*, intending to show how even in prison the love of God and human kindness can sustain the soul, and because of this religious appeal the book became famous all over the world. In Italy, however, readers were more angered by news of Austrian brutality than moved by Pellico's faith. But in 1848 there had been no spectacular recent persecutions.

Anyone determined to find fault with this enlightened despotism—and all Italian patriots were—could criticize the slowness with which the huge machinery of state turned over. For instance, when a fire engine broke down in the city of Venice, authorization for another had to come from Vienna; during this delay a bad fire broke out. The slow deterioration of Austrian affairs which occurred all over the Empire when the idiotic Ferdinand came to the throne seemed more startling in Lombardy, which had formerly been the best-governed province. Italian patriots also complained that the famous school system taught a rigid loyalty to Austria, and that the 36,-000 "Germans" in the civil service prevented a fair share of good government jobs going to natives, although there was no systematic effort to keep Italians out of government positions. Hundreds of little things kept adding to Italian restiveness.

"The Austrian government levied immoderate taxes . . . it forced on us shoals of foreigners, avowed functionaries and secret spies, eating our substance, administering our affairs, judging our rights, without knowing either our language or our customs; it imposed on us foreign laws . . . and an intricate system of proceeding in criminal cases, in which there was nothing true or solemn except the prison and the pillory, the executioner and the gallows . . . it forbade the development of our commerce and industry, to favor the interests of other provinces . . . it enslaved religion and even public benev-olence . . . it subjected the liberal arts to the most vexatious re-strictions; it persecuted and entrapped 'our most distinguished men, and raised to honor slavish understandings . . . and threw the patriot into the same prison with the assassin."[1]

[1] Quoted from Stiles, *Austria in 1848-1849.* i, 186.

There was, however, a body of men in Lombardy whose duty was to bring grievances before the government, at least in theory—for in 33 years these "congregations" had never ventured to mutter one single word of complaint. The congregations were given to Lombardy and Venice to make them willing to exchange French for Austrian rule in 1815; the members were elected by the people but had to be approved by the crown; and until 1847 their actual work had never gone beyond supervising roads and schools.

In December 1847, however, a brave though modest member of the central congregation of Lombardy, a lawyer by the name of Giambattista Nazari, startled his colleagues by presenting a petition listing the country's grievances and proposing a committee of inquiry.

The administration was furious and tartly told Nazari he should have warned them of his action. Nazari countered that he would hate to show lack of respect for the government, yet if they had told him to keep quiet, he would have been constrained to disobey. In his petition he stressed economic complaints and never mentioned political rights. Nor did he breathe a hint of any wish other than to cause the Hapsburgs to be adored, and this, Nazari insisted, could only happen if the rulers understood the needs of the country. In spite of his mildness, his gesture was grand enough to bring to his door a shower of calling cards from great Italian families who had never met him socially before.

At this critical hour Vienna did what it could to offer Radetzky belated help. He received a large reinforcement in December 1847 and put his army on a war footing, canceling all leaves. When his peasant boys grumbled, Radetzky blamed their extra duty on the conspiracies of the upper classes, thus trying to create discord between Italians. In early 1848 Radetzky heard that Rothschild had granted a secret loan to be used for further reinforcements to his army, and at the same time Metternich stirred around to see if reforms could be made—but it was too late for that.

That same winter Italians began to withdraw from their Austrian social contacts. Only six ladies attended the Vicereine's ball that autumn, and the ones who stayed at home were delighted to hear that she wept with rage. Radetzky complained to his daughter that there were no parties at the garrison any more. "We Germans are very uncomfortable," he told her, for living in Milan suddenly became harder than living in a conquered enemy town. The same Italians who had trained their sons to speak German in order to give them a better chance in the civil service now pretended that they could not understand the language.

The Milanese adopted velvet suits, since silk was a local product. In cafés the young men who undertook to read newspapers aloud used the chance to improvise many fine radical opinions. Next door to the Viceroy's villa in a small Swiss village was a printing press, whose incendiary products were packed into trunks by Sunday excursionists from Milan, and distributed to their countrymen from an inn just outside the walls of the city. Disassembled arms were smuggled in from Piedmont—100 English rifles that winter—and nearly every courtyard and garden in Milan had holes to bury ammunition which the patriots were careless about concealing.

Then a professor at the university told the Milanese the story of the Boston tea party, and he urged that his fellow citizens copy American tactics. He thought they might stop using tobacco or playing the imperial lottery, for the tobacco monopoly brought in millions of lire to the imperial treasury, and the lottery was even more profitable. In answer the Milanese agreed to give up these pleasures beginning on New Year's Day, 1848.

For the first two days of the year things stayed fairly quiet, and Radetzky's impatience grew when he perceived that the citizens' boycott was a success. To provoke trouble, on January 3, every Austrian soldier was issued six cigars and a ration of brandy. Until this moment their manners had been impeccably correct, but now they swaggered around in groups of twenty or more, blowing smoke in civilians' faces and sometimes flaunting two cigars at once. Finally a civilian snatched a cigar from a soldier, and the fight for which both sides were spoiling was on. The results were tragic. Infantry cut down civilians, cavalry trampled them. At the end of the day there were 61 dead, including six children under eight and five old people over sixty. A man in a café who tried to shield his little girl with his own body was cut down along with the child. Soldiers fell on a group of workingmen coming out of a factory and tried to force them to smoke; the workmen refused and some of them were killed. Hospitals, which incidentally had been warned to get beds ready, were crowded with wounded.

Radetzky may have been pleased with this result. At any rate he refused for a whole week the civilian governor's request to hold his soldiers in their barracks. All the time he told the Milanese proletariát that the nobility started all the trouble—it was the work of a small party only.

Even though you call us twice a party, said the Marquis Massimo d'Azeglio in his report to the civilized world on the massacre, we will answer three times, "We are a nation, a nation, a nation." Austrian civilization, he said, is an illusion as long as such things can happen under her rule. A treaty might give Austria the power to withhold civil rights, but no treaty gave her the right to murder. To prove to the common people that they were not a separate party, Milanese nobles raised a subscription for the wounded and for the families of the dead. Fifty-two gentlemen took the unusual step of soliciting from door to door to give the lie to the Austrian assertions and show that Italians of all classes were united.

From that time until March the Milanese led their Austrian masters a dizzy dance. One day all patriots appeared with their hat bands buckled in front. When the bureaucracy caught on to this and passed an ordinance forbidding it, the same gentlemen came out the next day with the beaver fur of their hats brushed against the nap, and next another unusual fashion, and then another. Ladies too seemed under the sway of some powerful organization which told them what to do. Often La Scala was empty, except for the rows of white-coated Austrian officers, but on the night when Milan heard that the King of Naples had granted a constitution to his people, every great lady attended the performance in a gala gown. On the same day the poorer classes of people celebrated by eating Neapolitan spaghetti. "Here is a police far stronger than our own," complained a harassed Austrian who could not keep up with such tactics.

Some explosion would have come soon to any city so tense with feeling. As it happened, the news of the Vienna revolution reached Milanese patriots just as they were wondering what sort of a demonstration to make; as soon as they heard it Milan's date was moved up to March 18.

The night before, many Milanese youths took the sacrament. Afterwards, with glowing faces, they pulled out their strange and rusty assortment of hidden arms, even though their first orders were only to form a procession.

"Men to the street, women to the windows," was the cry, and 15,000 men answered the call to march to the Austrian government house, while uncounted women waved handkerchiefs and red-white-and-green flags from the casements. At the head of the procession marched Count Gabriel Casati, the Podestà, or mayor of the city, who, as the highest Italian official, made the affair seem as legitimate as possible. Casati was in fact a stickler for legality. Though he sympathized with the Italian cause, he had always cooperated well with the Austrians under whom he had to work, and he showed divided sentiments by sending one son to the army in Piedmont and the other to an Austrian university. On this March 18 he paraded in a formal black suit, but sported a tricolor boutonnière, and an Italian flag was carried beside him.

The formal request of this body of citizens was that the Austrian police should be disbanded and a civic guard be formed by the citizens. The Austrian officials, even while they abolished censorship in imitation of the capital of the Empire, had tried to hide the fact that Vienna had won a national guard. But once this fact leaked out, the citizens' case seemed strong. Casati, for one, was so sure that the demand would be granted that he persuaded the Austrian officials to refrain from asking military protection from Radetzky—a move which, argued the mayor, would lead to certain and needless bloodshed.

The highest Austrian official whom these patriots could find at his office was terrified, and he signed at once the order they asked for, an order to establish a civic guard for all citizens not living by their daily work. In order to guarantee this concession, the Italians kept the official as a hostage.

When Radetzky heard that an Austrian was in custody, he said he would never recognize concessions obtained by force, and he made belated efforts for the military to occupy the important posts of the city.

But by this time the citizens could not be stopped. Barricades began to rise in all the narrow crooked streets which made up the city, so that even when the army captured the city hall, which had been ransacked by the mob, and the cathedral, where officers concealed sharpshooting Croats behind the pinnacles of the Gothic roof, Radetzky was unable to provision his men.

The barricades of Milan were the most fantastic of all the impromptu structures of 1848. Not only viceregal coaches and omnibusses, but sofas and pianos went into them. Rich merchants opened their warehouses and the people carried out bales of silk or coops of hens. Schools were emptied of their benches, churches of their confessionals. Rich citizens and factory workers helped each other in this work while children carried stones and tiles and boiling water to the roofs to hurl on any unlucky Austrian uniform below. Young girls pulled up the two white rows of flagstones which ran down the middle of each street for carriage wheels to pass over. Though a dozen chemists worked night and day to make powder, this item was so scarce that it was rationed out as if it were tobacco. Only men who knew how to shoot were allowed to use it, and they were happy whenever they got enough to charge their guns once or twice. They all felt that they could not afford two shots to kill a single Croat, so the young men shot in turn instead of simultaneously. Astronomers on a tower scanned the countryside with their telescopes and passed news down a wire on a little ring. University students, who were in charge of prisoners and of attacking the gates of the city, were the happiest of all. They hurried along the streets or over the roofs or through windows, intent on their business until they lost all idea of time. When they were hungry they begged a bit of bread at any doorway; if they were wounded all homes were open to them.

Radetzky's highly trained army was not prepared to deal with this sort of an insurrection, where cavalry and artillery were useless and his infantry patrols were all too easily picked off. So he decided to retire his foodless, sleepless troops from the interior of the city and make an iron ring outside from which he might starve the town and bombard it if it refused to come to terms.

One young Austrian diplomat was too gallant to leave with the troops. He was Count Alexander Hübner, whom Metternich had sent in just three weeks before to look the Lombard situation over. Metternich was always hoping for peace; nevertheless his protégé's first question on arrival was how strong was the army. For he could foresee that it would be needed, and even in February he realized that Radetzky had been the victim of economizing.

When the outbreak came, Hübner attended to his own affairs as well as he could, and then hastened to look after the wife of another Austrian who had asked Hübner to see that she came to no harm. When the Count arrived at the home of this young and handsome lady he found her scared and almost servantless. Her houseboy had never come back from an expedition to buy groceries and only the cook was left to provide for their wants. Hübner was too polite to leave while a barricade was run up just outside the door, with Italian women of the neighborhood screaming cheers at the work, and by nightfall he was sealed in and could not get out even if he wanted to. In the only room of the apartment that seemed safe from shots, Hübner and his hostess dragged two separate mattresses and passed the night. Imagine, says Hübner, the situation and believe that these two Austrians were too panicky to do anything indiscreet, for the room was full of smoke and powder while outside were all the sounds of insurrection. At any moment the house might be invaded by Italians, or, what was almost as frightening, by some of their own Croats.

In the apartment above lived a French modiste, and on the top floor a young Swiss woman whose profession Hübner thought it best not to investigate too closely. During the second day, when the fighting seemed to be getting worse and stray bullets might come in any window, Hübner persuaded his hostess to make a blockhouse of mattresses and bring all the inhabitants of the house there for safety. Even the Swiss was invited, though reluctantly. It was agreed that if soldiers came in, all the women should scream to show their sex, since speaking German would do no good if the troops were Croat. At this point the Swiss offered her help, for she spoke many languages, she said, and would be glad to be their interpreter. Hübner's dry verdict was that she was a young person of courage, and he added that she seemed used to assaults.

No Croats came, however (since Radetzky had ordered them out of the city), so the ladies in Hübner's company set themselves to making Italian cockades, and they tied huge tricolor ribbons to their balcony.

During the first two days of the insurrection the Italian patriots acted on the theory that he who brings down an Austrian can do no wrong, and each man went his own way. As individuals they had made a notable beginning but might never have achieved enough direction to complete their job if a university professor, Carlo Cattaneo, had not joined the revolt and organized a defense committee because he was furious at Casati's wish to compromise with the Austrians. Cattaneo was a republican, and he informed Radetzky that there was a split between the citizens and their timid mayor. The citizens, he said, would never give in, even when they had only forty-eight hours' provisions on hand and meat rose to fifty cents a pound, for they believed they might as well starve to death as go back under the Austrian rule.

The men who rallied behind Cattaneo decided first of all that they would never speak in the name of Milan or Lombardy, but would always use the name of Italy, which they were serving. They headed their proclamations, "Italia libera. Viva Pio Nono" showing that at this time they believed the Pope was the natural head of a free Italy.

Though the hasty departure of the white-coated Austrians had left a surplus of munitions in the city, so that the defenders no longer had to ration their shots, the city was completely cut off from the outside world.

In order to communicate with their friends, the Milanese devised little balloons which floated up and out of the city while the Croats shot at them in vain. Wherever they landed they were sure to find friends; some got as far as Piedmont and some were reported in Switzerland. They carried the news that started help pouring toward Milan. If just one city gate is opened, the message read, we shall be free.

Radetzky's forces still patrolled the wall of the city, and against this long thin line a group of students picked the Porta Tosa to attack from within. At this gate houses came close to the wall on both sides, so the enemy was under cross fire. Movable barricades were rolled up toward the gate, and one of the students, Lucius Manara, got close enough to make a dash for the sentry box, waving his tricolor standard. Then his followers beat down the gate itself, which was simply a folding iron door between ornamental pillars. The moment it was open, friends from outside the walls and peasants who had come to help swarmed inside.

Now that food could enter the city and help was pouring in, Radetzky decided to withdraw completely. "It is the most terrible decision of my life," he said privately, though he wrote a bold proclamation to his soldiers telling them not to be downhearted. "You are not conquered, you are not going to be," he said. "I have withdrawn before the enemy, not you." He led them to a group of fortresses in the province of Venetia, and he promised to carry them back to victory another day.

To protect his retreat he covered the city with a heavy cannonade, partly out of anger at stories that one of his sentries had been crucified to a sentry box and that ten had had their eyes put out. These atrocities were nothing compared to what Italians reported of the behavior of the Croat soldiers—a lady's jeweled hand found in a soldier's pocket—and they only show that both sides were thoroughly inflamed.

By this time Hübner had been taken prisoner, leaving his ladies in good care, however, and was kept in protective custody in the home of an elderly couple. He was assigned a small room in this house, where he had to remain except when his custodian took him out for exercise; but a gentleman was a gentleman in those days and his servant was allowed to come in every morning to do up both the Count and his cell. Here he was when the bombardment came. Hübner noticed that there was not a voice on the streets, for everyone fled to the cellars. Artillery did very little damage to the heavy stone houses and strongly barred windows of Milan, and everyone laughingly said the attack would cease at 8:30, Radetzky's bedtime. On this night, however, the old marshal must have lain awake late, for the firing kept up until one o'clock in the morning.

In Milan next day, the citizens cheerfully pulled their possessions back off the barricades, a noble his carriage and a housewife her kitchen table or her featherbed, soaked by this time with rain, and a greengrocer his counter. The only objects not claimed were the Austrian sentry boxes.

Shortly after this Count Hübner, who was still in his genteel confinement, was sent back to the Austrian lines to arrange for exchanging prisoners. As he traveled through Italian cities women held dirty empty plates almost in his face, to show what the Austrians would get if they tried to come back. In one place the mob yanked him out of his carriage and made him walk to the city hall to prove that his mission was genuine, but in spite of the roughness with which he was handled, here it was that Hübner decided that the social order was safe and the disturbance superficial, because no one of the crowd assumed the right to climb into his carriage and use a nobleman's seat. Someone climbed up beside the coachman, and they hung all over the outside of the carriage, but the lower class would not overstep a final line of respect which had been bred for centuries into their bones.

It is hard to imagine the enthusiasm which the events of Milan created in all Italy. That the citizens of a place garrisoned by the Austrian army could rise and chase their oppressors out in five days seemed like a miracle which justified the hopes of Italy's giddiest patriots. As for the sober reformers, they were discredited because the physical battle was so much easier than they had predicted; it seemed the political reconstruction ought to be equally easy.

Plenty of Milanese citizens, however, the rich nobles and prosperous business men, did not share Count Hübner's conviction that this revolution would not become social. These men found rabid republicans and excitable volunteers a poor exchange for the Austrians. Many of them wanted a strong monarch to protect property rights, and a still larger number, men who might have been willing to see a republic, knew that at that juncture they needed a strong army to chase the retreating Austrians.

In the middle of the siege the cry for help had gone out from Milan to Charles Albert, the King of Piedmont. To Mazzini, the republican, in Paris, the news was also borne. Both of these men felt the call of destiny in recent circumstances and both arrived in Lombardy, where they began to struggle against each other for the soul of an Italy barely and precariously free from foreign domination.

XVII

Italy on Her Own

WHEN the news that Milan was in arms reached Turin, it found everyone in the city ready to march across the frontier except the King. Yet Charles Albert hesitated. Being a man who could never make up his mind quickly, he found it difficult to meet a call that did not come just as he had expected it. He could hardly in decency announce that he was marching to annex Lombardy to his kingdom, yet was he to go to Milan in order to proclaim the republic? That would be against both his interest and his honor.

It took Cavour, who had given such a push for the constitution, now to give a final push for war. He ran an editorial on March 22, saying that at such a moment audacity was the true prudence, even to a calculating, cautious temperament like his own. We must fight now, he said, and the sooner we start the better.

The next day Charles Albert marched his troops into Lombardy, offering the people there no political word, but simply the help "which brother expects from brother, friend from friend." He was careful not to say to them, as he did to the courts of Europe, that he moved into a territory left temporarily without a master. "Can you not bear to be your own masters for once in your lives?" the Milanese republicans asked their fellow citizens—but the truth was that a huge majority of the citizens welcomed both the master and the protection of his army.

Only when the Austrians were gone—and gone for good, most people believed—did Italians realize how great were the differences between those who wanted a master and those who did not. Each party found in the other an enemy quite as dangerous as the departed foreigners. To the republicans, Charles Albert seemed a tyrant just as much as the Emperor Ferdinand—after all, both of these monarchs had granted constitutions only within the last six weeks—while many conservative patriots would have preferred order under the double-headed eagle to the license which went with their idea of a republic.

It took a while to sort these opinions out, however, and in the first flush of enthusiasm Italians flocked to Milan, hoping to get in on some of the fighting yet to be done. The news reached Rome, as it had Turin, at a psychological moment.

An Englishwoman living in Rome at the time said that no one who heard Garibaldi's hymn, *Fuori d'Italia lo straniero*, sung with demoniacal passion by a chorus of maddened Italians could fail to understand the times. Reform was forgotten overnight, as 12,000 volunteers left Rome for the front on March 24. Massimo d'Azeglio was one of their officers. Monks carried muskets in this holy war and priests went with the army carrying altars. Adolescent boys were caught up in the excitement and marched away without going home lest their mothers' kisses weaken them. Rich boys, who could have hired carriages, walked with a knapsack, a flag tied to their walking sticks, in order to be democratic.

Before the troops departed, the Pope blessed them and they departed in an ecstasy of national fervor and religious emotion. One of the young men who had been helping the Pope in the midst of his political troubles remarked that it was like paradise to get away from the miry politics of Rome and reach the front. In the first place, military discipline helped to calm his spirit in these disturbing times, and then, he added, war affords the largest and most instructive range of human experience. These days at war were the happiest of his life.

In Milan itself young Manara, the hero of Porta Tosa, took 129 friends and calling them "the army of the Alps" marched out on March 24 to pursue Radetzky. The young men were so excited they took no change of linen nor extra shoes with them. The band grew in a few days to 2,500 by accretions from the "flower and the dregs of society," students and bandits, men in velvet suits or men in peasant costumes. They followed Radetzky, it is true, and once had the pleasure of sitting down to an untouched dinner which had been cooked for the fleeing whitecoats. If Charles Albert had trusted these volunteers he could have used their *élan*—but guerrilla forces were republican, in ideology at least (for Manara was personally a good Charles Albert monarchist) and therefore doubly distrusted by a regular army man like the King.

Even more picturesque was the volunteer legion brought to Milan by the Princess Belgiojoso. This lady had been born of the highest

Milanese aristocracy. She said she had spent her youth like a rat in a library when she was free to do what she chose, and like a doll in the parlor when she was not. However, her intellectual interests caused her to run afoul of the Austrian authorities, and for years she dwelt in ostentatious poverty in Paris. Just before the revolution she had been allowed to return to home and fortune, and she had spent the year 1847 on her Lombard estate giving her property all the most up-to-date improvements. She studied agricultural reform, and sought to increase her peasants' earnings by setting up a glove factory. She also built schools and a housing project with a recreation hall.

At the time of the news of Milan's upheaval, the Princess happened to be in Naples, and in order to get home as quickly as possible, she chartered a steamer. Immediately crowds of young men besieged her with requests that she should carry them with her, and, the boat only holding two hundred, she selected this number and commissioned them herself as if she were a sovereign. When they arrived at Milan they paraded with a huge flag, the Princess in the lead, and then rushed off to seek the foe. Three weeks later, a cynical observer noticed most of them were back on the Milan street corners begging, for the battalion had been provided neither with military direction nor with supplies. As for the Princess, she settled herself in Milan, where with typical flamboyancy she took up the editing not of one journal but of two.

In this maelstrom of an Italy, Mazzini certainly deserved as warm a welcome as any prince, and he got it. When he heard the news of Milan's five days, he was in Paris, working on a new organization to mix for the first time Italian republicans with monarchists pledged to a united country. He left at once—and as he walked across the frontiers into Italy, he plucked the first little Alpine flower he saw and sent it to one of his English hostesses. Then he went on to Milan. A guard recognized him as he entered the city gate, and raised the cry "Viva Mazzini," so that before long his lodgings were surrounded by crowds who called him to his balcony to speak. When 2,000 Italian deserters from the Austrian army marched by, tears filled Mazzini's eyes. The people were sublime, he said, beyond conception, far beyond the people of Paris.

A few days later a group of tailors brought him their demands for higher wages and no Sunday work. Was not this what he had promised a revolution should mean? Mazzini told them, instead, that though their wishes were just it was not a moment to think of anything save Italy. Once the country was free, the first duty of the new state would be to see the workers were not cheated.

Mazzini felt that he had come to Milan not to handle tailors' grievances but to free Italy, and to that end he was willing for the time being to support the conservative Casati's provisional government, to tolerate even Charles Albert's help. The local republicans under Cattaneo, indeed, decided that he had been bought,[1] and turned from him. He was shortly disillusioned with the men in power also, and felt like an exile in his own country. Nevertheless, he stayed on in Milan all summer, hoping for a chance to rouse the sublime energies of the people again. This being the last thing the provisional government wanted, he found himself "disliked, dreaded, suspected, calumniated, threatened."

In July Mazzini was joined by his own most famous proselyte, Giuseppe Garibaldi—and like Mazzini, this hero found himself not too welcome.

Garibaldi always had something simple and heroic about him. As a young sailor in 1833 he first ran into one of Mazzini's men, and he says that Columbus was not happier in the discovery of America than he at finding a man actually engaged in the redemption of Italy. A subtle man would have made distinctions about ways and ends, a weaker one would have faltered or sought his own advantage; Garibaldi had no intellectual or emotional inhibitions, he simply said, "Use me." From that day until long after he had handed Sicily to King Victor Emmanuel in 1860, he used himself for his country, undiscouraged by personal rebuffs or political finagling.

Mazzini's first assignment to this promising recruit had been to conspire in the Piedmontese navy, a job which Garibaldi did very well, but the police uncovered the plot and Garibaldi had to flee with a death penalty on his head. Next he found scope for his talents in South America, where he won a reputation fighting for the republican cause in a revolution against Brazil. He discovered and practiced in these struggles his natural genius for handling men;

---

[1] Cattaneo, although as devoted a republican as Mazzini, was against nationalism. He believed that local autonomy was the best guarantee of individual freedom, and wanted nationalism everywhere to fade away. Mazzini could not tolerate anyone who differed from himself on such a cardinal point in spite of Cattaneo's courage, ability, intelligence, and sincerity.

he learned to extemporize military decisions and to keep a company going in the wildest countryside, two talents which were to baffle the forces opposing him in Europe.

In South America also he picked out his wife Anita, and again he showed the simplicity and permanence of his emotional decisions. "Friendship is the fruit of time," he wrote later, "while love is the very lightning and sometimes born of the storm." One day he looked out from his boat and saw some girls on the shore, and among them he picked out one for himself. When he went ashore, "my heart was beating but for all its agitation I felt resolved. A man invited me to come in. I would have entered even though he had forbidden me. I saw the girl and said to her, 'You must be mine.' "[2] Anita, although she had been married to another man for several years, recognized her destiny. With Garibaldi she fled and lived with him, aboard his boat, or in the tropical forests, or in poverty in Montevideo. Once she had to ride for days to hunt for him. Once she fled through the jungle with her twelve-day-old baby across her saddle.

During the years in South America Garibaldi kept in touch with Mazzini in London, always hoping for the day when he might return to Italy. In October 1847, it seemed as if that day were almost at hand, and he wrote to Pius IX to offer his sword to a Pontiff who "understood the need of the age." After he had dispatched this letter people noticed that his face changed, a light smile played over his features as if he expected good news.

The good news never came, however, Pius being far from able to accept the support of a republican atheist guerrilla. Nor did the money materialize which Mazzini kept promising, for a boat to sail home in. Garibaldi's impatience finally led him to open a subscription in Montevideo to charter a small boat for himself and 56 of his Italian legion. The government of Uruguay gave him two cannon and 800 muskets. They sailed on April 15, 1848, not having heard of any revolution. However, a passing ship gave him the news before he reached Europe, and the joyful men put together a red shirt, half a bed sheet, and a patchwork of green facings ripped out of their uniforms to break out a tricolor.

On June 24 they arrived at Nice, somewhat uncertain whether to land in view of the fact that Garibaldi was still under sentence of death, but the whole population swarmed to greet him, and men who

[2] Garibaldi, *Memoirs*, p. 88.

had read of his exploits from Mazzini's pen flocked to join his standard. The third of July he offered his sword to Charles Albert, much to Mazzini's disgust. "He will not be any longer the Garibaldi whom Italy loves and loved," Mazzini opined.

Charles Albert was naturally no more willing than the Pope to commit himself to a man whose notions of military tactics, let alone a united Italy, were far more violent than the King was prepared to cope with, so he told him insultingly to go to the Adriatic and fight as a corsair.

It was characteristic of Garibaldi that he never gave up, and now he turned to the provisional government of Lombardy for uniforms and permission to pursue the Austrians—he could provide his own arms. They gave him the rank of general, and as for uniforms, they told him he could use a supply which the Austrians had left behind and which their own frock-coated, velvet-breeched volunteers were too proud to wear. In their pride Garibaldi disgustedly foresaw the failure of Italy, and he ordered his own men to don the Austrian linen. Stripped of trimmings, the white coats made the men who wore them look like a regiment of cooks, but did not daunt their will to engage the enemy. Mazzini went with him for a while, carrying a gun given him by an English lady and a huge banner inscribed "God and the People." Military headquarters neglected General Garibaldi, and after some brave attacks on Austrian outposts, he was forced to lead his men across the Swiss border for safety.

Once in Lombardy it did not take Charles Albert long to collect his mind. His second proclamation to the Lombards, a week after the one when he promised aid as from a brother, pointed out that Piedmont was called in by *temporary* governments, with the hint, obviously, that the Lombards should make some more permanent arrangement than Casati's provisional government. Though that government announced at first that it would take no political steps until the war with Austria was over, it was soon beset with difficulties which made it change its mind.

The first difficulty of the provisional government was bankruptcy, a rock on which many a more secure state has foundered. The new administration had abolished many of the most hated Austrian taxes without thinking of any good new quick source of revenue—and meanwhile, it had to feed each man in the Piedmont expeditionary force with twenty ounces of bread daily, nine of meat, nine of rice, lard, salt, and a half bottle of wine.

In addition, their vaunted allies seemed to fall away from the Lombards. The Pope was the first. So early as the end of April he decided that he could not wage war against a Catholic power, and therefore withdrew his troops, which by this time were holding a line between the Piedmont army and Venice. The Kingdom of Naples pulled out, leaving the forces which remained in the war demoralized as well as angry. The rest of us must draw closer together, they said, and unless we give him a strong inducement to take care of us, Charles Albert may be the next one to leave.

The alternative to Charles Albert seemed to be a republic, and there was much terror at the prospect among those who lived by rents and industry. These propertied citizens told each other busily that they needed a king.

Moved by these facts, and in spite of the noisy disapproval of the republican party, Casati and his government arranged for a plebiscite on May 29, to vote whether Lombardy should unite with Piedmont at once, or whether to decide at the end of the war. It was stipulated that if the two lands should merge at once, a constitutional assembly for the whole area would be chosen by universal suffrage.

With all his antipathy to republicans, Charles Albert was evidently in awe of their influence, so that he was willing to make huge concessions if only he could keep his crown. He offered Mazzini, if he would not oppose fusion, a voice in drawing up the new constitution as well as a position in the new cabinet; luckily for the King, Mazzini was haughtily indifferent. "Someone," he said, "should maintain the banner of the future unsullied."

To most Lombards, however, the opportunity to join Piedmont seemed generously given. They need not have worried about Mazzini's influence, for the plebiscite went overwhelmingly in favor of union now.

Political fortunes were so distracting that for weeks no one realized that the military tide had turned. Radetzky had at first retreated to the province of Venetia, into four fortresses called the Quadrilateral, where his position was impregnable. The area he controlled was very small, less than twenty miles from one corner to the next, but here he settled down with his usual calm, never losing either his joviality or his complete confidence in God or his soldiers.

Within a day or two after his reinforcements arrived on May 22, he was ready to show off what he had learned in sixty-six years in service. In this first campaign in which he had ever had full command, neither his logistics nor his imagination failed. He completely baffled the Italians by moving a large body of troops noiselessly one night during a frightful storm, wrapping his soldiers' boots, his horse's hoofs, and his artillery wheels with cloth.

While the Lombards were struggling with their plebiscites, they barely noticed that Radetzky was mopping up the mainland of Venetia. Then he began his march back into Lombardy, prepared for the happiness of laying that province again at his imperial master's feet within a few weeks.

For the first time the Field Marshal was running things in Italy the way he thought they should be run—and then he was almost stopped in his tracks by the nervous Vienna cabinet. With the capital in a tumult over the students in the Aula, and with Hungary breaking loose, the shaky new ministers could not see beyond the Alps, and they ordered Radetzky to make a truce. They were prepared to treat with Charles Albert on the basis of complete autonomy for Lombardy—more than the Italians had asked for in their most far-fetched proposals of reform—or, if that failed, even the complete cession of the province to Piedmont.

When Radetzky received these orders he simply failed to obey. As a trustee of the empire he would show the barricade ministers that the army could ignore them. To Innsbruck he dispatched his aide, Prince Felix zu Schwarzenberg, to tell the Emperor that with only 25,000 more men he could reconquer Lombardy, for he had lost about 20,000 deserters.

In the war office at least, Radetzky had a whole-hearted backer in the person of Count Latour, whose efforts to get reinforcements to Italy all summer long were superhuman. This was one cause of his hatred of the public works projects in Vienna, which employed 20,000 men, or nearly enough to satisfy Radetzky's requirements.

Since even the weakest Austrian cabinet was unwilling to give up Venice, far more important for strategic reasons than Lombardy, Italian patriots were unsatisfied by the offer of Lombardy alone. Charles Albert was secretly tempted by the plum offered him, until, as Mazzini put it, the people rose like a sleeping lion and forbade him to give up his Venetian brothers. Thus the negotiations would have failed from either side.

It took the Italian forces weeks to realize that the Austrian counterattack, begun methodically and unpretentiously, was like a bulldozer. The Piedmontese were buoyed up by their own courage (even Radetzky praised them for this) and by the excellence of their artillery, which steeplechased about the battlefields with the horses at a gallop and the gun carriages rattling after in a way previously unknown. Piedmont's weakness lay in her command, of whom Radetzky is supposed to have said to his gunners, "Spare the enemy generals—they are too useful to our side." More than that, the Italian troops were ill-supplied by their Lombard quartermasters, who were inefficient behind the lines and almost non-existent at the front. In the last great battles the soldiers were left without food for periods as long as three days. Added to this hardship, they often had to sleep on the bare ground; in rainy weather officers slept in their overcoats, and could buy blankets, but the privates had no protection from the mud except what they could get by digging a trench around the spot where they lay, to drain off a little water. The medical service also seems to have been poor; ambulances were bumpy and there was a shortage of amputation instruments. And there was no ice, used for packing wounds, since it came from the Alps. When the diplomatic corps of Turin were invited out to watch the battles, they had to sip warm drinks and forego the sherbets which were ordinarily a staple article of refreshment.

Outside the armed forces, confidence among Italians was sickeningly high. What did they do to help their brothers? asked a young officer. "Nothing, except to crown themselves with flowers, dancing, singing, spouting, and calling each other 'sublime,' 'valorous,' 'invincible.' "[3]

The final battle came in the last week of July, at Custozza, and it was a fatal rout for the Italians. At the end the only order among the fleeing troops was preserved by young Victor Emmanuel, Duke of Savoy, who managed to rally around himself enough troops to protect the flight of the others.

There was nothing to do but fall back on Milan, a city so fed on hopes it could hardly believe that its defenders were coming back

[3] Pasolini, *Memoirs*, p. 90.

defeated. When they heard their city was merely a halfway point, that Charles Albert was about to retire behind his own frontiers, leaving them at the mercy of the Austrians they had chased out themselves in five days, Milanese could only echo Garibaldi's hasty judgment that the King was a traitor. If he would not defend them, his worst enemies the republicans would try.

The frantic Milanese appealed to Mazzini, who advised them to appoint a triumvirate of three competent citizens chosen more for their ability than for their politics; his next advice was to call on every man to fight—a strictly republican way of fighting. Mazzini wrote his own name at the top of the list of volunteers. Barricades rose again, half a million cartridges were distributed, flour and cattle were stored in the city; in fact, Mazzini said that more was accomplished in three days than in three months previously.

When the bedraggled Piedmontese marched in they were received with jeers. The citizens held Charles Albert as a hostage, inside the town, away from his troops, barricaded with his own carriages, and demanded that he make another stand against the enemy.

Moved more by the city's enthusiasm than by threats, and possibly feeling that he had lost a round with the republicans, the King announced that he could not abandon a city fighting so bravely for its liberty. His willingness to fight again earned him a small measure of respect; but his tired soldiers were unable to resist Radetzky. Within three days he had to retire, promise or no promise. Having begged from the Austrians twenty-four hours in which to leave the city and to escort civilians who wished to leave, Charles Albert stayed at the city gate watching while half the population of Milan fled toward Turin.

All day long the refugees streamed along the dusty road. Soldiers threw away their flags to carry children instead, and women were allowed to ride on caissons. In Piedmont, citizens put themselves out to welcome these exiles, although 25,000 extra guests—the number who stayed in Turin all winter—were a severe drain on both public and private purses. When they saw their own soldiers, the citizens were even more shocked, for they looked like mummies after the disastrous campaign, with skin dried out and black, staring eyes.

In Milan, meanwhile, Radetzky took over, and the remaining citizens made the best of a bad bargain. By the time the first Austrian entered the city gates on August 7, every tricolor ribbon, every sign of revolution disappeared, and the people watched the parade with quiet dignity—no cheers, but no insults either. This army was immaculate. Though their shoes were worn, every one was polished till it shone. Every white coat was snowy, though many officers possessed only the one uniform that was on their backs.

When Radetzky moved into his old quarters, he found that all his furniture had been sold, but he hoped to be able to buy it back again—cheaply. One of his servants had thoughtfully saved the clothes which had been at the laundry when he left town, so he had a nice supply of clean linen. But he lost 1,500 florins, buried in his garden by his servant and dug up by an observant neighbor.

The Frankfurt Parliament sent Radetzky congratulations which must have been peculiarly gratifying to his Germanic soul. He replied that he had come back into Lombardy not as a conqueror, not to suppress freedom, but to grant to the province perhaps more freedom than it would know how to use.

At the very first meeting of the cabinet of the fused Kingdom of Piedmont and Lombardy, the members listened to the news which meant that Lombardy would have to go back to Austria.

In his own territory, Charles Albert was safe from invasion because neither France nor Britain would allow it. His danger lay in his own people, who, like the men of Milan, turned from a defeated king to the bright promises of the republican party. The legend grew that Charles Albert was faint-hearted and treacherous, the army bumbling, and only the people themselves invincible. Everyone with a voice in the nation's affairs knew the war would have to be renewed eventually, but the democrats screamed why not now?

The unfortunate King, heartbroken at being misunderstood, yet lacked the nerve to declare himself openly; he particularly hated to reveal to the public the completely demoralized state of the army. The democrats wanted a people's war anyway, which would make the army less important; and they took another democratic step to equalize sacrifices by pushing through the brand new Assembly a capital levy from one-half of one per cent to two per cent—a move which deprived the rich of half of their income (assuming it was 4 per cent), and which confirmed their most despondent expectations of what a republic would be like. With the common voters the move was popular enough, so that elections held in January 1849 were far more to the left than those of 1848.

At the opening of the new Assembly in February 1849, the King, white as a swan, uttered an address in a voice so feeble that scarcely anyone heard it. But in it he told his people that Piedmont could fight.

By this time he may have agreed with Cavour, who believed that even a lost war would be better than no war, since it would clear the air of the democratic vision, and in Cavour's opinion, if it forced Charles Albert to abdicate, the country could make a new start. The situation was so intolerable that an army officer remarked that war and peace were alike impossible, and the country might as well toss a coin and let heads or tails decide.

To make ready for battle the army increased its size, with a furious program of recruiting, training, and supplying arsenals, uniforms, and tents. But nothing could enable Piedmont to catch up with Radetzky in these particulars. Furthermore, democratic discipline slipped into military life, too. For the first time old-time officers began to see soldiers who thought before they obeyed, who considered insubordination a mark of democratic zeal. Many former non-commissioned officers had been given commissions to further the democratic spirit, and many of them lacked not only the bearing of officers, but the ability to keep records.

While old officers grumbled about their new subordinates, the old nobility met the new governing class with an equal sense of shock. "I hardly knew the bourgeoisie," wrote public-spirited Marchioness Constance d'Azeglio, "but I had always supposed it contained capable people who would take part in affairs." Instead they seemed to be throwing the country to the dogs. The republicans cannot stand to hear a bullet whistling over their heads, said Massimo. The only ones who do not want the war will bear its burdens, the poor peasants, who, "knowing exactly how fierce and unequal the battle will be, leave their wives and children without a murmur because it is their duty; and the King will go." Yet the d'Azeglios themselves did not complain, and were willing to sell their diamonds in Paris to help the cause.

On the Austrian side the war was just as popular. When a Piedmontese colonel called at Radetzky's palace one day in March, bearing a letter, the old marshal could not conceal his pleasure. "I know already what you bring me, and I thank you for it," he said. After he had read the dispatch, which gave the necessary eight days' notice for the termination of the armistice, he looked even more satisfied and invited the colonel most cordially to dinner. The colonel declined.

When the news spread, Austrian officers let out a yell of joy, and the troops rushed to decorate their helmets with the green twigs which were a sign of victory. Radetzky's officers had been begging him to grow a beard, to be in military fashion, and now he gave in to them and promised to grow one as soon as he had beaten Piedmont.

At the hour of the expiration of the armistice, Piedmont soldiers looking across the river at Lombardy could perceive no hostile preparations. Eagerly they swarmed to cross the bridge, but the King stopped them, drew his sword and walked over the bridge first himself.

It was the start of a disastrous and pitifully short campaign—not a week long. Charles Albert was always in the thick of the fighting, so that all who saw him realized that he was hoping to die. Bullets always avoided him, and he had to live and watch his army, the pride of his life, hopelessly routed on the field of Novara on March 23. Asked for terms, Radetzky harshly announced that Austria would demand the right to garrison some Piedmontese cities, and that the Crown Prince should be given up as a hostage.

This was the moment Charles Albert realized that he could do nothing more for his country. Having lost everything, even honor, as it seemed to him, he abdicated, leaving his eldest son as the new king, Victor Emmanuel. Charles Albert rode quickly out of Italy, and died a few months later in a Portuguese monastery. He tried to tell his people that his heart was still with them, and he said that he would gladly return to fight as a private in the army of his son if the war should ever be renewed.

On March 24 the young King himself rode out to meet Radetzky to win easier terms for his country. Radetzky's animus against Charles Albert was personal. The marshal fought him as the old enemy of Austria, but more than that the two men were antipathetic types. Toward the new king, however, Radetzky felt a certain measure of tenderness. In 1842 Radetzky had accompanied the

Austrian archduchess who became the bride of Victor Emmanuel, and he was present at the wedding in Turin. Also, Victor Emmanuel was an earthy sort, easier to understand than his father and Radetzky hoped, easier to influence. Therefore, when the two men came face to face, Radetzky dismounted from his horse, even though he was so stiff he had to be lifted, and they embraced. Radetzky made many concessions to the young monarch, promising not to occupy any of his territory. In return the Austrian hoped that Victor Emmanuel would compromise, yielding a promise not to support his father's constitution, but this the young king stubbornly refused to do. He even convinced the old general that if he abandoned the constitution Piedmont would revolt and Austria would have anarchy to deal with instead of a stable government. This logic satisfied Radetzky, who managed affairs his own way in this part of the Empire, though his conduct displeased Schwarzenberg in Vienna, who wanted much stiffer terms.

Victor Emmanuel returned to Turin in the dark of night, so as to avoid a hostile demonstration on the part of his subjects. The next day he took an oath to the constitution his father had granted, but even for this he won no applause from his disillusioned people. It took months for them to find out that he meant what he said, that he was fit and strong.

He was a complete contrast to his father, vulgar and a show-off where Charles Albert had been dignified and retiring, sensible where the old king had been idealistic, short instead of tall, quick to think instead of slow. He was 28, with enormous mustaches, hair that stuck straight out, a turned-up nose—and from his manners he seemed born, as one of his friends said, "to a tent where all is equal, or to a throne where all is allowed." Above other qualities, he had the good sense to use the intelligence of the many able men about him.

The first minister he called to pull the country together was Massimo d'Azeglio. D'Azeglio had refused to serve earlier, when things were going downhill, but now that they were at the bottom he felt it his duty to help his country as well as he could. "Love of country," said he, "means sacrifice, not enjoyment." And then, in one of his history-making phrases, he bluntly told his king that he could not think of any honest kings in history—Victor Emmanuel might as well be the first.

D'Azeglio found a country practically in civil war, bankrupt, with a legislative body which would not cooperate even to the extent of ratifying a treaty of peace with Austria. The King had to dissolve his parliament twice before he could find a body of men which would agree to this elementary step toward stabilizing the country.

The defeat at Custozza in 1848 had given Italy over to the republicans. The defeat at Novara in 1849 gave it back to the moderates. Italy was the only country that did not go back to the conservatives after the revolutionary year.

In Lombardy, meanwhile, Schwarzenberg was inflicting his policy of force. Not lightly did Austria punish revolution. In Milan fifteen men and two women were stripped and publicly flogged, being revived with vinegar if they fainted under the blows. Over 900 were executed in the provinces for possessing arms. Rich patriots had to pay huge fines, and if they refused, their property was confiscated. Any houses where arms were found were burned.

Old Radetzky lived on until 1855, always genial and friendly. Even the Italians seem not to have hated him as much as other Austrians, for he told General Haynau that a guard of 10,000 would not be able to protect that officer's life in Italy after the horrors he committed at Brescia, whereas he, Radetzky, might safely ride in an open coach. Haynau was well advised not to revisit Italy, for when he went to London, in 1852, the workmen at Barclay's brewery—one of the sights of the city because of its use of a mechanical production line—set upon him and beat him up. This act so pleased the foreign office that they could barely conceal their smiles as they explained to the furious Schwarzenberg that there was really nothing Her Majesty's government could do in the way of punishment.

Radetzky, by his victories in 1848, killed Italian independence for only another decade. His real victim was constitutionalism in Austria, which never thereafter got a chance to be tried, and in Hungary. Perhaps his most ironical achievement—since Radetzky was a pan-German at heart—was that from now on, with the Austrian Empire held together, German unity became impossible.

There was one other consequence of the defeat of Novara. It inflamed the French, who in 1848 would have liked nothing better than to fight for their Italian brothers, and who even in 1849 had not cooled their passions to the point of indifference, in spite of

Charles Albert's dislike. Now France, afraid that her little buffer state would be lost, agreed to send an expeditionary force "to occupy some point in Italy" and to guarantee Piedmont's integrity. Louis Napoleon found ample use for this force, though not where the French republicans had expected. He sent it to Rome, where Mazzini was trying out *his* dream of a republic.

XVIII

The Rome of the People

ONE of the ironies of 1848 is the way in which Charles Albert and Pius IX forced each other's hands. The King, who had tried not to yield a constitution because he wanted to save all his strength for a war, had to give one after the papal reforms had caught the imagination of all Italy. The Pope, for his part, wanted only to improve the administration of his own state, yet when war broke out in Lombardy, his people would not let him remain neutral.

As an Italian himself, Pius blessed his young soldiers with a full heart, even though he would not bless their flags. Yet as head of the Church he was the spiritual father to millions of Austrians. Bishops from all parts of the empire lost no time in pointing this out to His Holiness; they recalled to his mind the fact that the Austrian church had been dangerously independent from the time of skeptical Emperor Joseph. To prosecute the war in 1848, they told him, would lead to schism.

But his new lay ministers in Rome, mostly young men who had worked all their lives for the Italian ideal, were in despair at this turn of their sovereign's mind. They knew that their government could not stand if they drew back from the war. It was, after all, an attribute of a sovereign state to be able to wage war. "What can the Pope be afraid of? Is it not the cause of humanity, religion, and the Gospel we are defending?"

Against their remonstrances the Pope issued a statement, on April 30, that as pontiff he could not make war. Rome's answer was a riot. The anger of a people who had been rapturous until this moment was deadly. Their leader, a wine carrier called Ciceruacchio, whose warm heart had almost burst with enthusiasm at the news of the amnesty of 1846 and who had since believed devotedly that he could persuade the Holy Father to trust the people, now turned all his rage against Pius, and persuaded the people that they could not trust the Holy Father.

It was with the greatest difficulty that the moderate men in the government prevented the establishment of a provisional government then and there. Nor were matters improved when the Pope wrote to the Austrian Emperor a few days later, with the suggestion that he might well give up his Italian provinces as a matter of justice and humanity. Such a move pleased neither Austrians nor Italians, and the papacy was left completely friendless. Italians in every city could hardly believe at first that their idol had reneged; as soon as the sad truth became certain they turned against him with a violence which proved that the really important problems to the age were social, not religious. "Porco Pio Nono" is still a word of execration in Italy.

General uneasiness grew as the summer wore along. The Pope could not bear his liberal ministers, he could hardly listen quietly while his prime minister explained a point. As for the unfortunate ministers, of course they knew that the last hope of saving the state depended on their making sensible reforms, yet they were blocked not only by their unsympathetic ruler but by their entrenched subordinates. So many administrative matters turned out to be in the province of the church, and therefore not susceptible of being handled by lay officials, that the cabinet could hardly find a single corner in which to start operations. When the young Minister of Public Works ventured to ask a council of engineers for professional advice, this rash move in the direction of progress and materialism brought angry looks and words from the men in his department. Meanwhile the common people were no better off, possibly worse, as the beginnings of financial reform seemed to make paper money less abundant. Thus the clubs grew stronger and the civic guard mutinous that summer of 1848 in Rome, as in Berlin and Vienna.

In September the Pope called Count Pellegrino Rossi to head up the government.

Rossi had been perhaps the most distinguished of the Italian exiles, for he had been a professor of constitutional law at Paris and a friend of Guizot. Naturalized as a French citizen, and ennobled, he was appointed ambassador to the Holy See, and was therefore living in Rome at the time the revolution broke out. His abilities as well as his studies made him a natural, and indeed admirable, choice for prime minister from the Pope's point of view—even though some of his writings were on the Index. The unfortunate thing was that in this particular summer popularity was more essential than ability. A year earlier, before the people had become confident of their power, or a year later, after they were disillusioned about it, Rossi might have done well. In 1848, though he introduced telegraphs and chairs of political economy, though he reformed the civil service and the hospitals, he never sold himself to the tyrants of the street corners. He scorned them. He was not a democrat. He wanted to give them reforms but not listen to their voices. In his deep-set eyes and compressed lips they read his scorn, and they vowed that he should die.

Rossi knew of their hatred and their threats, but like other victims of the same year, Count Latour and Colonel Marinovich, he was too proud to let them interfere with his duty. On November 15 he drove to the opening of the Assembly, to present a plan of reform which he believed held "the safety of Italy." As he dismounted from his carriage and started quickly through the marble hall leading to the Chamber, the mob pressed in about him, cursing him. Suddenly someone hit him with an umbrella, then, as he turned, another drove a stiletto deftly into his jugular vein. Technically, it was a perfect job—Rossi bled to death within half an hour. Meanwhile someone threw a cloak over the assassin and hurried him away. He was never caught, but there is evidence that he was a son of Ciceruacchio.

Rome celebrated her deliverance from Rossi as she had her great victories. The people were now free to go ahead, since there was no one left to balk them, certainly not their weak Pope. With the frenzy of a lynch mob they shrieked under the windows of Rossi's widow, until all respectable citizens were disgusted and most were terrified, for they had not learned that political passion in 1848 did not spill over into vandalism. Indeed, though public authority was demoralized and government lapsed, there was no more of a crime wave in Rome than there had been in Paris or Vienna.

There was, however, no one to grab the helm. Pius was stupefied by the blow. He seemed to lose interest in public affairs and talked only of the will of God. In vain his young ministers told him he must rouse himself, he must fight. When the mob pulled cannon up to his palace and disarmed his Swiss guards, he offered no resistance but instead quietly disappeared. While the French ambassador called at his palace and kept lights burning in his apartment, Pius slipped out in the dress of a plain priest and fled south in the coach of the Bavarian ambassador.

All Catholic countries offered their hospitality. Cavaignac hoped that he would come to France, Charles Albert to Piedmont, but the Pope (fearing both the French republic and the would-be sovereign of united Italy) chose to go to Naples, and there, surrounded by the most reactionary political and clerical influences, waited to be rescued, while he mused on spiritual things which made him feel at last "like a true Pope."

Instead of making plans for the government in his absence, the Pope washed his hands of Roman affairs. He would not even sign a bill for new treasury notes, to meet the immediate financial crisis, and he required the men who had been loyal to him, the moderates who still had faith in him, to get out of office, leaving in power the republicans. When the Pope finally named a new government it was a government in exile. All of its lay members were titled and it could make no dent at a time when all Italy was turning to democrats.

The men who dared to take charge of the Roman mobs rioting for bread, and of the clubs raining manifestoes, were the ones who dared to give them what they asked for. They abolished the tax on flour, started unemployed artists to restoring the mosaics in churches, promised contracts for making uniforms to unemployed tailors. They also called for a constitutional assembly and federation with the rest of Italy, and they ordered work on the railroads which Pius and Rossi had authorized to go ahead.

This was the nearest thing to a social revolution in 1848 outside of France, and progress did not stop when the Assembly was elected. The Pope called it "abominable, monstrous, illegal, impious, absurd, sacrilegious and outrageous to every law, human and divine," and he excommunicated any person who took part, even to the extent of casting a ballot. Since the people who followed this judgment were primarily the Pope's own party, it threw the election open to the candidates of the clubs "who confounded all classes together," just as if Providence had not decreed that there should be a difference between a shoemaker and a professor. Seventy per cent of the adult males voted (the suffrage was as broad as in France); one cardinal even declared the Pope lacked power to excommunicate for political matters, while the Bishop of Rieti led the election by casting the first vote in his see and then watching whether his clergy followed his example. Most of them did not. In the north of the Papal States Garibaldi's legion marched to the polling places with their voting papers already signed so that their general should be assured a seat in the Assembly. Mazzini was also elected, though he was not in Rome at the time.

This was Mazzini's chance to make Italy into his dream. To romantics a dream, even if a false one, becomes necessary to existence—and thus is built up the lie men live by. In a way Mazzini provided the vital lie for Italy. No nation could live out Mazzini's dream, but by trying, Italy became at least a united nation in the end, and one with a conviction of destiny.

Mazzini's dream began with the republic; it was right, in the first place, he thought, and in the second, it would be the only way to unite the sovereign states of Italy under one government. He wanted a united Italy because it too was "right." A nation would be less materialistic than a federal union, strong, modern, able to fulfill a mission. A nation was a source of energy to its sons, giving scope to artists and statesmen, strong enough to check poverty and tyranny, vital enough to prevent dissipation of that strength into cosmopolitanism. The world-wide view of Goethe and Metternich seemed to men like Mazzini to suck out the strength and joy of belonging to a particular nationality. Allegiance to a larger society oddly enough seemed selfish and materialistic. Italy, in Mazzini's fervid imagination, was the messiah in the new religion which should come to save groups of men as Christ had saved individuals. In a map of Europe in which Germany represented thought and France action, Italy united thought with action, heaven with earth. Suffrage was the rite of the future religion, and it would be exercised by men who thought more of the duties than of the rights of man.

Mazzini hated atheism, and he hated socialism. He once remarked that an atheist could not have a sense of duty, and Garibaldi, who heard him, cried out, "I am an atheist. Have I then no sense of duty?" Mazzini was caught. "Ah," he said. "You imbibed a sense of duty with your mother's milk."[1] As for socialism, Mazzini agreed with Marx that the generation he saw about him had a philosophy of self-interest. God was not in the heart of the century, but while

[1] Holyoake, *By-gones Worth Remembering*, I, 220.

Marx did not want to put him back, Mazzini did. He hated the doctrine of class struggle, mostly because if workers, or anybody, had a loyalty to class which vitiated or superseded their national feelings, it would undermine Mazzini's dearest hopes.

Early in February the Assembly met, and even as the roll was called the Prince of Canino answered, "Long live the Republic," a cue which Garibaldi took up in his turn: "The delay of a minute is a crime. Long live the Republic." The Assembly did not delay. They voted a republic. Rome and Venice were the only places in Europe that dared to carry their revolutions to the limit set by France.

Mazzini's friends had been gathering at Rome ever since the Pope's flight. For a few weeks, however, Mazzini stayed at Florence, where Giuditta lived, and where the citizens were also trying to set up a republic. Now the friends at Rome sent him a telegram—"Rome republic. Come."

Not immediately, but soon, Mazzini came. "Trembling and almost worshiping," he approached Rome on foot, at night, and he tells us that this first sight of the Eternal City "will mingle with my dying thought of God and my best beloved." Faith, love, and now hope were in his soul as he moved toward his greatest opportunity. That very night he took his seat in the Assembly, and he told his colleagues that after the Rome of the Caesars, after the Rome of the Popes, it was now their turn to build the Rome of the People.

Like that other first-class romantic, Frederick William of Prussia, Mazzini believed that the purpose of life was to become better and that the purpose of a nation was to help people become better. Now, for a brief moment, he was to be Frederick William's equal in actual power as he had always been in the ability to dream; all schools of romantic thought had their day in 1848. If Mazzini was the more successful—not in solving economic problems, which never yielded to romantic treatment, but in making the people under his rule better—it was because he flattered and coaxed and inspired his subjects with the century's most intoxicating brew, freedom mixed with nationality, and that nationality the most sophisticated of those then struggling to be born.

Mazzini's title in Rome was that of a member of a triumvirate, though actually he could not have brooked sharing ideas or dividing responsibility for his Roman republic. In spite of the fact that he despised the external trappings of power, the Roman republic was his offering to the world; he could no more compromise in making it as perfect as he knew how than any other artist.

He lived in a small room in the Pope's palace—one small enough to feel at home in—and he was accessible to all comers, high and low. His salary he gave to the hospitals, and he lived on two francs a day, eating in second-class restaurants. After the French besieged the city he lived on bread and raisins. His luxury was a bunch of fresh flowers sent to him every day by an admiring workman; sometimes he sang to himself while playing on his guitar at night. Still, he grew old at this job; nothing is more exhausting than creating one's dream. His eyes became bloodshot, his skin turned orange and his vital juices seemed exhausted. Or, as Margaret Fuller, who was in Rome at the time, put it, holiness purified but somewhat dwarfed the man in him. Later on, after he recovered from the physical strain, Carlyle noted corresponding benefits: "The Roman revolution has made a man of him. He has quite brightened up ever since."

With Mazzini at the helm the republic moved ever more swiftly toward its social goals. The most spectacular decrees concerned the poor, as might be expected. For the peasants the republic confiscated some of the great land holdings of the Church and distributed them in free permanent leasehold in parcels as big as two yoked oxen could plow—the equivalent of forty acres and a mule. Other nations had confiscated church property, but only the Roman republic went on to ensure that this process would not force off the land the men who worked on it.

For the Roman poor, especially for the wretched masses who lived across the Tiber, the republic took over the office of the Holy Inquisition and turned it into apartments for the neediest cases.

Neither of these processes amounted to more than a gesture, for the republic had but five months' existence. Still, they were the kind of gesture that Mazzini wanted to make, gestures that persuaded the poor the republic had something to offer them, that would convince the world to come that the dream had not been empty. As for the right to work, that Mazzini never admitted. It had been a failure in France, and it smacked of socialism. The republic compromised by employing large numbers of men in excavating the Roman Forum.

There were many ways in which Rome took on a glow from the color of her leader. Order was the touchiest point in any republic in those days, and Mazzini got enormous pleasure from explaining that the republic, when new, had no police force and no army, "yet scarcely was the republican principle declared when an incontestable fact was made manifest, i.e., Order. The history of the papal government was made up of disturbances, but not one disturbance has taken place during the republic."[2]

Shortly after he had expounded this doctrine there was, to Mazzini's chagrin, a disturbance. Three men whom the crowd called Jesuits were assaulted and torn to pieces. Mazzini was more hurt than angry, and lectured the people to the effect that everything in Rome should be great. The government, he said, is trying to show Europe that Romans were better than their enemies, that the republic had extinguished sparks of anarchy.

Tolerance, of course, and freedom of the press and secular education all had their share in coloring the republic with enlightenment. The civic guard was opened to all ranks of citizens. Prisoners and the insane were moved out of their dungeons to the better light and air of vacated monasteries.

The weak point of all this system came from the fact that though Mazzini could make men work for him, he could not command money. In fact, he noted with disgust that the same men who would give their lives for a cause would not give up the treasure which might make the sacrifice of life unnecessary. He did not understand that for men of property their fortunes represented a kind of immortality, just as the divine-right kings would risk death or abdicate personally but never sacrifice the substance of power for their dynastics. The devotion with which some men defended their coffers would have been sufficient to save Italy, but they were not capable of spending it for Italy.

Inflation bedeviled the republic all its days, so that if it had not been for the French invasion that came in April the regime would have fallen anyway, and perhaps more quickly. Without money the republic could not activate its own reforms, it could not help the

[2] Farini, *The Roman State from 1815 to 1850*, IV, 91.

poor, while lack of credit nullified the advantages of commercial freedom; but even a bankrupt nation can fight for a while.

Though the republic would have liked to rob St. Peter to pay Paul, there were not enough ecclesiastical resources to keep a young and hungry state going. A forced loan from the upper classes (ranging from 20 to 66 2/3 per cent of their incomes, to be paid back with interest at five per cent) satisfied the poor that the republic demanded sacrifices from everybody, yet it did not yield enough to ease the strain. Printing presses worked overtime and Rome was flooded with notes of small denominations. As inflation spread, the government tried to keep down food prices at least, and threatened to confiscate any stores of food on which the price was raised. The government also forbade hoarding, particularly of oil and grain.

The customary celebration at Easter was held with almost more than usual pomp, in order to show the people that the republic was not hostile to religion. The cross which was always hung at the top of St. Peter's blazoned out this year in red, white, and green lights, and it looked like a chain of jewels about to melt. Mazzini himself, in a frock coat, appeared on the balcony where the Pope used to bless the people, and a priest at his side uttered a blessing on the crowd, for which he was afterwards severely disciplined by the Church. Mazzini thought this was mummery, but his heart almost failed him now when he heard the Latin phrases and saw the crimson rockets and the 1,400 veiled lamps like swirling fires outlining St. Peter's. "It is useless," he is said to have said. "This religion lives and will live for long years on account of the beauty of its form."[3]

Sterner matters required his attention, however. Though Mazzini had not wanted Piedmontese help for his republic, lest Rome receive the same kiss of death as Milan, he would have delighted to heap coals of fire on Charles Albert's head in the shape of a vigorous Roman reinforcement for Piedmont's second attack on Austria. On March 29, 1849, accordingly, the Assembly voted to send troops northward, only to hear the next day that Charles Albert had been completely routed at Novara. This news changed the republic's need from offense to defense. No one knew whether Austria would go on to invade the Roman states, or whether the Neapolitans would press from the south to restore the Pope. The one quarter from which the infant republic expected support was from her sister republic, France—yet within a month a French expeditionary force was attacking her gates.

The policy of President Napoleon in sending an army to Italy was devious. His apologists say that the Prince-President wanted France to have the glory of restoring the Pope added to the gratitude of Roman citizens for maintaining liberal institutions. If such an act of statesmanship were possible it would have given the French government popularity at home and *éclat* abroad, and there were only two things wrong with the plan. First, the Pope was afraid of the French; he was thoroughly anti-constitutional by this time, and wished very much that he could give material concessions to Austria rather than moral concessions to France. After Rome fell and the keys of the city were proffered to him by the French commander, Pius refused to go back to his capital until he could do so without any French strings attached such as accepting liberal government; and he wounded Napoleon's feelings by never admitting publicly that he owed his restoration to France. Napoleon's second miscalculation was to assume that the Roman citizens wanted the Pope back on any terms at all. Men who hauled cardinals' carriages through the streets to burn them, calling them the blood of the poor, were unwilling to have their blood squeezed out again by the ecclesiastical machine.

There was only one strong republican leader left in France after the shambles of 1848, Ledru-Rollin, and he put forth his last effort in trying to make his countrymen ashamed of the attack on Rome. He tried to have the President impeached, and failing in that, he led Paris in another insurrection, on June 13, 1849. Napoleon was prepared for it, and it was a fiasco. Ledru had to flee to England thereafter, and Napoleon had one less enemy in his climb toward empire.

In the spring months of 1849 Rome was the city, as Milan had been in 1848, to which the young, the generous, and the brave repaired. A legion of Lombards, under Lucius Manara (the hero of Porta Tosa in Milan), who had been training in Piedmont all winter, landed at Cività Vecchia, Rome's port, just after the French were established there. "What are you, a Lombard, doing in Rome?" asked the French commander. "And you," retorted Manara, "I presume that you were born in Paris or Lyons?" Eventually the French let the legion march along to Rome, on condition that they would not fight until May 4, by which date the French expected to have conquered the city.

All spring Garibaldi's legion had been kept charily outside of Rome, while their leader came in to Assembly meetings, for no government wanted to be responsible for a force which had been living off the countryside, terrorizing the people. After Charles Albert had surrendered in August 1848, Garibaldi refused to give up his legion and took it to Switzerland. From there, in the fall, he had returned to Italy and collected a new supply of volunteers—peasants, artisans, shopkeepers, and students, and a great group of boys from 14 to 16 who became the regimental pets. Now that Rome needed every soldier, the city called Garibaldi to lead his men inside the walls. They made a great show, Garibaldi on his white horse, with his white poncho, and many of his men, with their long hair and long black plumes in their hats, still showing the sunburn of South America. Staff officers wore the red shirts which Garibaldi was to make famous; before the siege was over these were issued to the men also. The city ordered a group of nuns to leave their convent within an hour, and barracked the legion there.

These defenders arrived none too soon, for the French attack came on April 30. First the Romans tried psychological warfare, placarding the road from Cività Vecchia with a quotation from the French constitution: "France respects foreign nationalities; her might shall never be employed against the liberties of any people." Blind to the irony, the French more than half expected to be welcomed as saviors by the respectable part of the population; they were quite astonished when Garibaldi led an attack against them which sent them reeling back to the seaport. Garibaldi was all for chasing them right into the sea, if possible, but Mazzini restrained him. It was the first open quarrel between the two great republicans. Mazzini's point was that he did not want to offend unnecessarily the only great republic in Europe whose ultimate friendliness he counted on, and to emphasize his good will he set all the French prisoners free except the wounded, who were tenderly nursed. As a final touch, he sent 50,000 cigars to the French troops, each one wrapped in a leaflet proclaiming that France was governed by traitors with criminal designs. Unfortunately there were no republicans in the French army, which was made up of gay and cheerful boys who boasted, "We sleep in a stable, wash on a soup plate, and eat eggs with a corkscrew."[4]

Whatever the motives with which they advanced, the French forces had not been prepared for the sort of resistance they met at Rome. General Oudinot was ordered to occupy the city as a friend. The French had counted on Mazzini's unpopularity, and they imagined they could raise a fifth column among people faithful to the Church, and property owners who feared confiscation. They were always unwilling to believe that the new government actually had a strong hold on all classes—a fact which reactionaries tried to explain away by saying that workmen whose wages were doubled and whose wives strutted about in palaces, amid furniture meant for princesses, would naturally support a government so kindly. Other critics said tartly that most people would support any government that preserved life and property, not realizing that anarchy had been transferred from the streets to men's souls. The republicans' apology was drowned, outside the city walls; no one could hear their plea that they had at last given the people a country to be proud of. This being the case, the French were more impressed with republican bullets than republican propaganda. Oudinot even boasted to Paris that none of his men were prisoners while he avoided mentioning that this was due to Roman courtesy. He settled down in Città Vecchia to await reinforcements while Rome prepared somewhat lazily for defense. The American sculptor, William Wetmore Story, who had been in Berlin the year before, said that it took the Romans three days to build a barricade which would have gone up in an hour in Berlin. During the lull Garibaldi went off to the south to repel a Neapolitan attack. This foray made a great impression on the countryside; mothers told their children that the general ate babies, whereas the worst he actually did was to requisition a convent and allow his men to parade around in monk's clothes, carrying tapers in mock ceremony. When no convent was handy the men bivouacked, astonishing the natives as they lassoed sheep and cattle, and roasted them at great fires. What seemed wildest of all to other soldiers was the lack of military hierarchy. Men who were captains one day would be privates the next, for variety; and the general's cook was a lieutenant. No wonder

[4] Colomb, *Memoirs of Admiral the right honorable Sir Astley Cooper Key*, p. 206.

Manara, who always wore the blue cross of Savoy to remind the Romans that he was not a republican, thought Garibaldi's men "a troop of brigands." Grandiloquently he offered them support in their mad onrush from his "disciplined, proud, silent, gentlemanly regiment."[5]

Having routed the Neapolitans, Garibaldi hankered after a chance at the Austrians who were hovering near Bologna in the north. He told his soldiers to pray for a charge: "Tell the legionnaires to get the idea well into their heads, let them think of a charge with cold steel and of sticking a sharp bayonet into the flank of a cannibal."[6] But these laudable sentiments had to be implemented, if at all, at Rome, for French preparations looked more dangerous and all forces were recalled to the city.

Nevertheless the Prince-President was still prepared to play the game softly if it could be played softly, so in May he sent Ferdinand de Lesseps (whose fame as the man who put through the Suez Canal was still in the future) to make peace in Rome. Lesseps' freedom was hampered by instructions not to recognize the republican government and not to antagonize the Pope; his hope was to find some group of allies within the city. Accordingly, he took pains to talk to men of every rank and party, and he reported in surprise to Paris that the Roman shopkeepers and men of good family, "the classes which defend social order in Paris," were on the side of the Roman republic. Still, Lesseps believed that if he could discount Mazzini's influence he might find a party which would assist the French to enter Rome peacefully and bring back the Pope, and he thought he was succeeding in this effort so well that he sent word to the Roman Assembly, on May 24, that he would not treat with Mazzini. Let them nominate other commissioners. Rome's reply to Lesseps was a threat of assassination and an assurance that if he sent a second letter like the first the bearer would be torn to pieces.

Lesseps, however, conceived it to be his duty to make some sort of agreement. On May 29 he sent an ultimatum to the Assembly offering the protection of the French republic, and the Assembly agreed, with the proviso that the French army would not parade through their city streets. Lesseps agreed to sign this and the people of Rome hailed the alliance with joy.

[5] Quoted in Trevelyan, *Garibaldi's Defence of the Roman Republic*, p. 139.
[6] Quoted from Larg, *Guiseppe Garibaldi*, p. 123.

When Lesseps returned to the French camp, bearing his piece of paper, Oudinot refused even to read it, let alone sign it. Lesseps, confident he was following instructions, signed it himself under Oudinot's nose and determined to return to Paris. But before he could leave Oudinot passed on to him, insolently opened, a message from Paris containing his recall. In France, Lesseps found rumors had spread that he had suffered a sunstroke in Rome and was mentally unbalanced. He came to the angry conclusion that his whole mission was a maneuver on the part of the government to gain time for reinforcing the French army.

One of the glories of Rome during the siege was its hospitals with the inimitable Princess Belgiojoso at their head. This lady had given up journalism in favor of the relief of suffering, for in this work, she said, she was absolutely sure she was doing good, while in other fields it was problematical. Luxurious convents, which had often been inhabited by just a few nuns, were turned over to hospitals, and the Princess quickly mobilized 6,000 Roman women to staff them. She soon found out, she said, that it was usually better to use old toothless nurses instead of young pretty ones, but this policy did not keep her from tending certain cases herself, smoothing brows and, to one dying hero, reading Dickens aloud. Her cases always developed a fever. Had not Heine declared that the Princess was the most beautiful, the best, the most admirable being he had ever met on earth?

Outside of Italy, except to poets, the Princess seemed mad. She seemed mad to Cavaignac when she appeared before him like a phantom, wrapped in a huge black veil, to pour into his hard ears news of the blood and cinders of Milan. And she seemed mad to Henry James, who was led to wonder how in her the love of the thing in itself mixes with the love of all the attitudes and aspects of the thing; he concluded that a social agitator was often queer, a bird "all of whose feathers, even the queerest, take part in his flight."

Many of the Princess's best friends and greatest helpers at this time were members of the colony of rich Americans, though they mostly left before the end of the siege. William Wetmore Story used to carry ice cream around to her when she was too busy to leave her post. Margaret Fuller Ossoli used her New England fortitude as head of one of the hospitals. She had left her baby boarding in the country, and stayed at Rome with her husband, having encouraged him to break away from his family and defend the republic. During the siege the baby's nurse wrote that unless she received a sum of money quickly the child would be abandoned. By that time it was hard to get anything in or out of Rome, but finally Margaret entrusted the money to a doctor, who delivered it. The baby was spared, only to be washed up dead a few months later on the coast of New England when his parents were lost at sea.

Everything in Rome was being readied for an attack on June 4, for the French general had handsomely announced that he would not attack the place before that date. On the night of June 2, when the garrison troops were trying to get a last good night of sleep, they were pulled from their beds by a furious French attack—not against "the place," but against several strategic villas outside the city walls. Rome's defenders roused like their ancestral she-wolf but their success was limited. Garibaldi said he had never seen such butchery. Mazzini, who cared only if the Romans fought bravely, told them, "Yesterday we said to you: Be great. Today we say to you: You are great."

As the siege tightened, during June, the defenders of Rome justified Mazzini's fondest dreams. Soldiers were so eager to fight that they barely took time to sleep or to have their wounds dressed. Taxicab drivers made a regular service of driving out to bring in the wounded. Ciceruacchio spent his days exhorting the workers who dug fortifications, or carrying wine to the soldiers. Life was so inspiring that Garibaldi wrote his wife one hour was worth a century of common existence.

This letter never reached Anita, for she was bored living with her mother-in-law at Nice and scraped up money to join her husband at the war, even though she was pregnant. Garibaldi was surprised to see her, when she arrived on June 26, but he told his companions simply, "Here is my wife. Now we have another good soldier."

Only four days later came the day when the defense could hold out no longer. Garibaldi, his red shirt bloody and dusty, his sword bent so that it would only go halfway into the scabbard, came to tell the Assembly that he could beat back the French for only another hour. Every one of his artillerymen had been killed, so the cannon were manned by soldiers of the line. Manara, the hero of Milan, was killed on this 30th of June, as was Aguyar, the gigantic, handsome, popular Negro who had come from South America, and of whom Garibaldi said that his soul was made to be loved. The general told the deputies that there were three courses open to them, to surrender, to die at their posts, or to flee, the army and the Assembly together, to make a government in exile.

Much to the disgust of both Garibaldi and Mazzini, the Assembly voted neither to die nor to flee. They did not vote exactly to surrender either, but that only meant that they surrendered by default.

This was the moment when Mazzini's sins caught up with him. The vital lie now became a fatal one for him. In all his life he had never been able to tell the truth when he feared the truth would injure his cause. In his youth he arranged with his mother that she would cut off the appeals for money from the end of his letters before his father could read them, and later on, in order to keep his affairs running in exile, he borrowed large sums from his father, which he declared he was investing in a lumber mill. Old Dr. Mazzini was delighted to think that Joseph was settling down, and lent the money with pleasure. The son even victimized his English friends by raising money ostensibly for his workers' school, which he used for revolution. When he dealt with the Roman Assembly, these habits of a lifetime persisted. In his eagerness for the republic to go down in glory, he simply failed to tell the deputies that Ledru-Rollin's insurrection in Paris had failed so miserably that there was no longer any possible hope of help from the French republicans. Instead he read them private letters from friends in Paris which still sounded encouraging.

As soon as the Assembly discovered what he was doing they rebelled. Not a single man supported his plea for a government in exile, and Mazzini resigned. Later on he admitted that he had had too much faith in the Assembly. He trusted them to be Roman-hearted, he said, without intellectual preparation from him. This was only a halfway confession, and one which shows that Mazzini would rather have told them more lies than less, anything to make defeat shine brightly.

Garibaldi was of another temper, and said a republican never gave up. Therefore he offered to lead his legion out of Rome to Venice, which was still fighting for the republican cause. "I offer neither pay, nor quarters, nor provisions; I offer hunger, thirst, forced marches, battles and death. Let him who loves his country in his heart and not with his lips only, follow me."[7]

On July 2, the night before the French troops were to enter the city, Garibaldi's men assembled in Vatican Square. Four thousand foot and 500 cavalry soldiers elected to follow him; among them his wife Anita, pregnant five months, but dressed as a man in the uniform of the legion; Ciceruacchio, who had found in Garibaldi a substitute for his earlier idol Pius; Ugo Bassi, the chaplain, a liberal priest who knew Dante by heart, who had gone to Palermo in the height of the cholera epidemic to nurse the sick and console the dying, and who persuaded himself that the Catholic doctrine led straight to the republic. Garibaldi was ordinarily not fond of priests, but he succumbed to Bassi's charm and declared that their souls were like sisters. When Bassi joined the legion, the general sent him one of his own red shirts, which he wore with a cross on a silver chain, because, said Garibaldi, his men did not like black clothes.

This little force moved with the agility which its leader had learned in South America, and neither the French nor Austrians could catch it. Garibaldi led his men to the Apennines, and there, abandoning their wagons for pack horses, they moved up to the crests, even carrying their dismantled cannon. Having no money they were forced to take what they needed from the countryside, but Garibaldi was capable of shooting a soldier that robbed a poor man's cottage. Instead their preferred source of supplies was monasteries.

On the march Anita showed all her Latin temper. In a convent where she was billeted she refused to be served by monks, but made soldiers bring her food. In the towns, where women ogled her handsome husband, she showed her ferocious jealousy. She was not in the least pretty herself, being brown, with irregular features. In South America she had forced her husband to cut off his beautiful golden hair because other women admired it too much, and on this march she flew into a rage if her José complimented a pretty girl. At times she chased deserters with a whip.

Nevertheless, desertions thinned the band and the Austrians got closer as they reached the Adriatic, so when Garibaldi found himself

[7] Quoted from Trevelyan, *op. cit.*, p. 229.

near the independent little republic of San Marino he decided to cast himself on the citizens' mercy and disband his group in this neutral territory. Even while he was negotiating the enemy appeared, and Anita had to pull a rear guard together and defend the others until they had time to enter the tiny city-state, where they surrendered their arms. Then every man went off to seek his own home.

Garibaldi, who could not stomach the idea of giving himself up, chose two hundred companions for a last effort to reach Venice by sea. First he begged Anita, who was feverish, to stay in San Marino, but all she would do was wail, "You want to leave me." There was nothing to do with such a woman but take her along.

The party finally managed to push off in some small boats, but as Anita grew steadily worse, Garibaldi soon had to carry her ashore, wading through shallow water up the beach to a nearby farmhouse. There she died, refusing a priest, on August 4. The other men who had shared the leader's boat were caught by the Austrians and shot —Ciceruacchio and his two young sons, and Ugo Bassi. To save Garibaldi himself, heartbroken but still determined, Italians made a chain which passed him along from hand to hand until he reached safety and could sail for New York. There is a legend about every one of his stopping places.

Garibaldi's greatest days were still to come, but Mazzini's were over. He wandered for a few days in the streets of Rome to prove to the invaders that the people loved him and that he was no tyrant. Then he escaped with an American passport, but no French visa, on a boat to Marseilles. The story has it that at Leghorn his boat was searched, but the soldiers did not discover Mazzini washing dishes under a steward's cap. The rest of his life he passed in England, reiterating his old ideas.

The French administration in Rome tried to be lenient but their example did not move the Pope any more than their precepts. Pius had done with amnesties and lay government, and came back the next year under an escort of foreign soldiers, after he had made sure that the French would not interfere with his free hand. From that time France kept troops in Rome, and Austria kept them in the rest of the papal states, until they were driven out by Victor Emmanuel twenty years later.

Mazzini summed up the natural reaction of all liberals: "I feel from time to time emotions of rage rising within me at this triumph of brutal force, all throughout the world, over right and justice." He felt that even if the people reacted with daggers, it would be better than what the rulers were doing. "To have to struggle against feelings of hatred, for which we have not been born, is very sad."[8]

[8] Richards, *Mazzini's Letters to an English Family*, p. 132.

XIX

Venice: A Model Republic

SOME time before 1848 a Venetian lawyer, Daniel Manin, decided to attack the Austrian rulers of his city on the subject of quarantine for cholera. There were two schools of opinion at the time, one that cholera was contagious and one that it was not; and since most citizens of Venice clung obstinately to the opinion that it was contagious, the Austrians adopted the other doctrine out of perversity.

Manin drew up a petition on the subject, pointing out that if there was any doubt on the subject the officials ought to act as if the possibility of contagion existed. His hope was that the terror in which his fellow-citizens held the disease would be strong enough to drive out their sickly fear of Austrian authority. He wanted to make his lesson in civic virtue easy, but he could not find a single man willing to risk his name by affixing it to a public petition.

Yet if Austria had done well by any city in the Empire, that city was Venice. It had first come under the Hapsburgs when Napoleon had traded it off for Hapsburg territory on the Rhine, and when the treaty of 1815 stabilized boundaries, Vienna was very glad to keep this part of the bargain. Venice was the key to the Mediterranean, and likewise to the passes in the Alps which gave routes for Germanic drives to east and south. Even the gentlemen in the Frankfurt parliament of 1848 recognized the propriety of Venice as a German city. Austria showed that she knew this elementary fact when she indicated to Charles Albert that she might be willing to negotiate for the separation of Lombardy from the Empire, but Venice she must and would hold.

After 1815 the Austrians busily improved the harbor with huge breakwaters to keep off the storms that swept up the Adriatic, and with deeper channels for ocean-going boats through the shallow sands. Once more the ancient arsenal, long almost deserted, came alive. A two-mile railroad bridge, finished in 1845, gave the island city its first direct contact with terra firma. French engineers were summoned to install gas lights in the city, and to dig artesian wells to provide the city with its first drinkable water other than rain. Many of these were works a small city-state could not have afforded. Economically, Venice needed Austria as much as Austria needed Venice.

Another sign of progress in the city was the new steam flour mill, instigated by the Swedish consul, which could grind three hundred sacks of flour every day. Lack of horsepower on the islands, and of windmills, had previously required all flour to be imported. The steam mill was installed in a huge unused church. Stones from the cloister were used to remodel the church, and the tower made a fine chimney even though the black clouds of smoke coming out looked anachronous. Grain was brought to the door by boat, hoisted to the top of the building, and then allowed to fall of its own weight through three grindings right into sacks at the bottom, the 40-horsepower steam engine simultaneously pumping water, grinding the flour and moving the sacks along. Only one boiler was used at a time, for after boiling seawater for three days each boiler had to be cleaned of salt.

At this period Venice proper contained 125,000 citizens, and more lived on outlying islands. The city was the neatest in Europe, for no horses could be used in a city of gondolas and high-stepped bridges, and the gentle Mediterranean tides cleaned the town almost automatically. Even St. Mark's Square was washed off occasionally when the sirocco winds pushed an inch of water over it.

The Square was lined with coffee houses which served an unusually democratic assortment of citizens—nobles, merchants, literary men, French engineers met there on equal terms to eat ices, listen to the Austrian band concerts and watch the unique spectacle of ladies in ball gowns going on foot to their parties.

From the point of view of the rest of Italy, Venice was certainly not alien but at least a corner of the country relatively untouched by ferment. Manin, who was to lead the Venetian revolution, had never before 1848 read a single word of Mazzini's widely spread polemics, although he had followed d'Azeglio's career with interest. Venetia was a commercial province, not only ignorant of Mazzini's social dogma but lacking the high-spirited nobility of the Lombards, hanging on a word from Charles Albert, and without the passionate religious interest which made Romans hang on a word from their

Pope. Venice was indeed so out of touch with the rest of Italy that the men who steered Italian scientific congresses deliberately planned that the meeting of 1847 should be held there in order to stir up national feeling.

This trick worked very well. The presence of hundreds of distinguished Italians in their city made Venetians suddenly aware how their countrymen were awakening. A particular sensation came when the Prince of Canino paraded the streets in the uniform of the just established civic guard of Rome.

Manin, naturally, found in the congress a magnificent chance to spread the doctrine which he had decided made the subtlest attack, namely, that Austrian laws were good (having been set out in the more liberal days of 1815) but that Austrian officials did not live up to them.

Manin had been asked to prepare a report on charitable institutions for the congress, and he took the occasion to remark that the laws of Venice were the best in Italy. Everyone sat up, including the governor, who looked pleased; a moment later his face fell when Manin went on to explain that they were never enforced. Under the terms of the law, he said, a man has a right to come and ask for work, every time he needs to, and it is supposed to be given him without prejudice to his character or prospects. Yet actually a man out of work needs a police certificate before he can receive aid, and then what he gets is to be thrown into an institution from which there is no way out.

The prize exhibit which Manin dug up in his investigation was a certain Padovini, who was confined to an insane asylum though he was perfectly sane. Padovini had been an orphan, apprenticed to a tailor until his eyes became too bad for him to work. Not blind enough for charity, not strong enough for heavy outdoor work, not old enough for the old folks' home, he could get no help from any agency and began to beg. When this was forbidden him, he raised a frenzied placard saying, "Shame on a government that lets an honest workman starve." For this action he was carried off to an asylum. Once he escaped and made his way as far as Milan, where a kind tailor gave him work—but since he had no passport he could not stay, and eventually had to give himself up and go back to the asylum.

Manin's efforts to have the man turned loose succeeded, and after the revolution the man came and thanked him; but for the time being it seemed as if Manin's reward would be the application of the governor's remark, that Manin ought to be stuck in the asylum in Padovini's place. At least he was soon to land in prison.

When the panic of 1847 hit Venice, the tourist trade was discouraged, no one bought presents for ladies any more, and unemployment rose in spite of heroic efforts by some employers to keep their workers busy. Perhaps these facts helped turn the mind of Venice away from Austrian blessings toward the remarkable benefits which other Italian subjects seemed to be reaping. They were specially stirred when they heard that Nazari had petitioned the Lombard congregations for reforms.

Manin could not bear it if the Venetian congregations did not follow suit, and he implored a friend of his who was a member to get similar action. But the friend refused. Convinced that someone had to act immediately, Manin himself then wrote a public letter to the Venetian body. It took more courage for him even than for Nazari, for Nazari was a member of his congregation with a right to speak, and he had the assured backing of Milan's nobility. There was no nobility in Venice, and the circumstances of Manin's personal life would have made it much harder for him to flee if it should become advisable.

Whether Manin believed that in its increasing distress the Austrian government would be ready to listen to reason or whether he thought that this was the way to expose its unreasonableness, Manin drew up his indictment in terms of touching loyalty. It would be impious to suppose, he said, that the imperial government should give its people sham rights. Rather let the congregations blame themselves that they had never fulfilled their duty of letting the administration know how unhappy the people were.

Manin's hope at this time was that the Venetian provinces might win a separate administration like Hungary's, with an Italian army and a constitutional viceroy who would guarantee the usual liberal rights of jury trial, free press, and a civic guard.

As news of Manin's gratuitous advice reached the Austrian authorities, they were anything but pleased. Since all their training led toward suspicion rather than generosity, they could not believe that all of Manin's activity was in the open; and they rushed to arrest him, in January 1848, with the expectation of finding proofs of secret conspiracy. Manin was in bed when the police arrived; he begged their pardon for rising and dressing in their presence, and then, as they fumbled through his desk, he directed them to the papers they would find most interesting. Meanwhile Manin's wife served coffee, which the officials drank shamefacedly before they took Manin away in a covered gondola. His *sang-froid* never failed him, though he had to clench his fists to control himself when a guard put hands into his pockets.

Later on when Manin became president of Venice he was able to read the testimony of his trial, which of course was conducted in secret. He was touched to find that not only his friends, but even his political enemies swore that he was honest, brave, patriotic, and devoted to duty; and that if he were to be jailed, he was no more guilty than they themselves, though they had often differed. There was in fact no evidence to condemn him; nevertheless his judge had received strict orders from the governor not to let him go, so he was kept in prison while his case was carried to Vienna. Manin himself expected to be freed any day; meanwhile he used his time in prison, his first free moments in years, to think about Italy, its unification, and the place Venice might hold in it.

Though he was kept in jail on the charge that he disturbed public opinion, his imprisonment disturbed public opinion more drastically than anything he had ever said. When the people found out where his cell was, it became a custom for men to take off their hats as they passed by in the street. At the same time offers of help poured in on his family, which had been dependent on his daily work. Lawyers in the city divided out his work, and a prosperous tailor named Toffoli put his entire substance at the disposal of Signora Manin and her two children.

News of the Milan tobacco riots did nothing to quiet the Venetian population. By common understanding they gave up the carnival that year to send money to Milan's wounded. Women no longer dressed up, men wore informal black gloves instead of formal white ones, except for one famous performance at the theater when a dancer danced the *Sicilienne* just after the kingdom of Naples gave a constitution to Sicily. On that occasion a red, a green, and a white bouquet were hurled at the performer. When she picked them up together, the house rang with applause.

The stupid Austrians could think of nothing better than to forbid green, red, and white bouquets. At the next performance, the dancer was pelted with Austrian black-and-yellow bouquets and received an equal ovation when she scornfully refused to touch them.

In church as well as in the theater Venetians found their national feelings quickening. In March a priest dared to tell them that love for Italy was rising to new life "pure as morning light, warm as summer sun, fruitful as dew . . . impatient as love."

On March 17 an Austrian Lloyd steamer, bearing the Vienna mails, sailed into Venice from Trieste. Even before the mail could be carried ashore a French businessman on board leaned over the side of the boat and shouted to the gondolas which had swarmed out to meet it that there had been a revolution in Vienna. The gondolas sped back into town with the news, so that before the governor knew what had happened people began hurrying from the small crooked alleys, up and down the high bridges, toward the great square in front of St. Mark's. When soldiers blocked the Rialto bridge across the Grand Canal, gondolas arranged themselves instantly to make a bridge of boats for the crowd to pass over.

As the people swept past Manin's prison they set up a cry to free him, and soon they overran the prison and unlocked Manin's cell. Manin had no idea what had happened, but, always a legalist, he refused to leave his cell until he had received a signed release from the judge. He was still disheveled when this arrived; his admirers carried him out to the great square with a boot on one foot and a slipper on the other, and demanded an oration. He had to begin by confessing that he did not know how he happened to be freed; what he did know was that this moment must be seized, so he went on like Lincoln to tell the people that there were times when insurrection was not only a right but a duty.

This was too much for Count Palffy, the governor, who had been looking forward to being the first constitutional governor of Venice. He listened benignly to Manin's speech until he heard about the insurrection. Then he remembered who he was and suddenly banged his window shut.

Manin was carried home to his adoring family while Venice gave itself over to rejoicing. People embraced. They even embraced Austrians, for Manin had told them all races were their brothers. Yet already they were thinking as Italians. A poor boy had only to shout "Evviva l'Italia" for a rich man to throw him a coin, and within two hours the cafés around the square had changed their names from royal ones to Café Manin, or L'Italia. The greatest miracle of all was to look up and see Italian tricolors floating high on the three great flagpoles in front of St. Mark's. Soldiers came to clear the square and haul down the banners, the mob fled into cafés, breaking glass tables and mirrors. But whenever they looked up, there on the central mast still waved the flag of Italy. An Italian sailor had cut the cords so that all that day the Austrians could not get the reproachful tricolor down. As night fell, St. Mark's bell began to peal, without Austrian sanction, and well into the night it carried to the shimmering Adriatic with its foreign ships, and over the monuments of Venice's proud history, the recollection of her greatness.

The first thought in Manin's busy mind during that day and the next was that Venice must have a civic guard. An armed people, in Venice as in Vienna, would have a guarantee that they could keep their rights. Part of Manin's alarm came from the fear that the proletariat would get out of hand. He expected frankly that they would have to be kept down, and he thought it would better be by Italian arms than by Austrian.

The government's first instinct was to refuse the guard, but as commotion increased, the administration, which could not keep Manin in prison nor even haul down a flag, naturally found they could not keep arms from the citizens. On March 19 Palffy said two hundred citizens might make a civic guard. By five that evening three thousand guards had wound around their arms white scarves, sewed up by their womenfolk of handkerchiefs or towels, and were patrolling the streets.

Everyone in Venice was happy during the next few days except Manin. No one seemed to feel that there was any more work to be done, and Manin could not get even his best friends to agree with him on a next step. He refused to go into the new city government which the Austrians sanctioned because he wanted to have a free hand. Should his party raise the cry "Viva la Repubblica" or "Viva Rainier"? he asked his friends. Rainier was the Hapsburg viceroy who might be installed as a constitutional king. Having posed this question, Manin went off to sleep for an hour, leaving his friends to argue. They woke him up to tell him that they favored Rainier.

In complete anguish Manin sent them away, not willing that they should know he would go ahead with plans for a republic anyway; and as he lay still there came to him like a revelation, "Viva San Marco." Venetians would follow the cry of St. Mark. Their history lay in it, and Manin was filled with a new confidence.

His plan was a bold one, to capture the arsenal. If he had the arsenal for the people, it would be easy to expel the foreigners, whereas if it stayed in Austrian hands Manin believed that the enemy could use it to bombard the city. He had thought about this problem a great deal, and in times past had teasingly drawn opinions from his military friends on the tactics to be used.

On March 22, when these thoughts were already in his mind, news came to him that Colonel Marinovich, the head of the arsenal, had been murdered. To Manin this news meant anarchy, unless the civic guard could use the arms in the arsenal and take over the protection of the city—and there was not a moment to be lost.

Marinovich was the only Austrian in Venice who would have been capable of handling the Venetians. Though he was vastly unpopular he had rare efficiency. Before he took command of the arsenal, workers there used to take home something each day from their job —everything from kindling to cook their polenta to furniture for their houses. Under Marinovich's rule, the windows were barred and each employee was searched as he left work—a process which took an hour's time after the regular working hours were over. If something was found on a man he was not only discharged but blacklisted from employment in other jobs. Add to this the fact that Marinovich reduced wages while granting himself a higher salary, and it is possible to see why the arsenal workers were glad to murder him.

The last service which he was able to give to his emperor showed his energy and practical judgment. Foreseeing trouble, he had arranged for the Venetian fleet to be sent across the Adriatic to Pola.

On the fatal 22nd of March this iron officer, after being once rescued from the mob, determined to go back to his office, and was set upon again and killed.

Manin was by himself when he heard the news, and he set out alone to save the situation with hardly a hope of coming back alive. He left his house with his sixteen-year-old son beside him and began to walk toward the arsenal, calling to civic guards as he passed to follow him. They all obeyed, and he arrived at the arsenal door with quite an array of men, who easily forced the gate and filtered inside. The under officials were too demoralized to resist Manin's demand, first for cannon to be turned over to the civic guard; then for the bell to summon the workers, whom Manin harangued; and lastly to open the supply of arms to the citizens.

While Manin was winning the arsenal, a friend of his took over St. Mark's Square. He managed this coup by persuading the Italian soldiers in the military guard to disarm their Austrian officers, and then to turn the cannon around so that they pointed not at the people but at the windows of the governor's palace.

With Palffy thus a prisoner, the city council which Manin had scorned to join took courage from his example and demanded that the Austrians get out. Palffy, cowed by cannon and touched by memories of his beautiful Milanese mistress, resigned his power to the military governor, Count Zichy. For this defection Palffy later served ten years as prisoner in a fortress.

The Venetians then faced Zichy with their terms. He was to leave affairs in the hands of a civil government of Italians, remove all non-Italian troops, deposit their arms inside the city, and leave with all his officers for Trieste by sea.

Zichy replied, "This will mean war."

"Let us have war, then."

"I'll lose my head," said the poor count.

"More heads than yours are at stake," said the inflexible Italians.

Manin was not present at this conference, but he shortly appeared in the square, on his way back from the arsenal, and he climbed up on a table and spoke to the mob. He was a small and sickly man, dressed in a black frock coat, but he had lightning, they said, behind his spectacles and thunder in his voice. He urged his fellow-citizens, now that they were free, to form a republic and thus save themselves the trouble of a second revolution later on. Nor, he took trouble to assure them, would a republic separate them from the rest of Italy; rather their city would become one of those centers around which the rest of Italy could gather. This was the moment when he launched his cry, "Viva San Marco."

The magic that Manin had expected was indeed in those words.

Boys ran up and down the town tearing off every sign of Austrian dominion; even the little metal signs that marked houses insured against fire fell by hundreds into the canal because they bore a double eagle.

Manin was so popular that if the city council had not offered him power, the fishermen and gondoliers would have forced it upon him. On March 23 he moved into the governor's palace and set up his government. He had several able friends beside him in office, among them the good tailor Toffoli who had succored his family when he was in prison, and who played in Venice the same part that Albert, the worker, played in Paris.

Someone asked Manin whether he wanted to be Doge of Venice. "Doge?" he said. "No. My aim is far higher. It is so high I hardly dare tell it to myself—Washington!"[1]

Meanwhile one dreadful mistake had been made before Manin took office. The new government wanted the Venetian fleet back from Pola, where Marinovich's prescience had sent it. Almost all the sailors were Venetians and would have been loyal to the republic. Thus orders were made ready for its return, and entrusted to the captain of the Lloyd steamer, who was instructed to stop at Pola and deliver them before he landed at Trieste.

By bad planning this was the same ship on which Count Palffy and his staff left town. In the middle of the voyage the Austrian passengers waited upon the captain and told him that he would be disloyal to his Austrian owners if he went to Pola. The captain was in great distress, for he knew he could never enter Venice again if he disobeyed the Venetian government, but he found himself powerless—for other passengers appealed to the engineer, "an honorable Englishman" like most engineers throughout Europe in those days, and persuaded him to shut off the engines if the boat went off its ordinary course. The boat accordingly went on to Trieste, and since this was one of the most loyal cities in the Empire, men were soon found to take over the fleet and prevent its returning to Venice. This event was to prove tragic for the newborn republic.

Manin, however, never worried quite as much as he should about the navy, the use of the few boats left in Venice, or the construction of more. The coup at the arsenal was a tour de force on the part of

[1] Manin, I, 153.

a man whose genius was not military but political. As his republic took shape he showed the Venetians the kind of a state he believed they should create, not like Mazzini out of bravado, but in the ordinary course of solving practical political problems as they arose.

Manin's first efforts were to make Venice into a free state. He himself was the son of a converted Jew, and was therefore particularly happy to be able to institute complete civil and religious freedom for all groups in the city. Being a lawyer, he at once reformed justice so there could be no more secret trials like the one he had just been through. He abolished corporal punishment in schools, for Austrian schools had relied on the rod almost as much as the Austrian army, even in the case of girls; and he ordered teachers to emphasize Italian history.

For the working class, for the arsenal workers, the tailors like Toffoli, the fishermen, the government lowered the salt tax—the same measure which in Rome and Turin had been the sign of a new government's good intentions.

Among the democrats of 1848, Manin was an exception. He was the only leader who wanted to be the servant of the people. Mazzini, Kossuth, Louis Blanc all manipulated the people who raised them to power. Manin had the power but not the desire to manipulate them. Several times he forced the Assembly to decide a course of action, after he presented the facts, at moments when they would have been quite willing to leave things up to him. He was so anxious to give even the common people a political education that he himself took time before the elections of January 1849 to visit factories and wharves, exchanging ideas with the workers. But when these same workers crowded around him to give him an ovation he would send them home with disdain. At one point the loyal workers heard that the Assembly was not supporting Manin, so they formed a mob to invade the chamber and force it to do Manin's will. On this occasion Manin met them at the door with a drawn sword, and the words that they might pass into the Assembly only over his dead body. No other figure of 1848 who wielded power so capably laid it down so gladly.

As the Piedmont army chased Radetzky across Lombardy, Venetians felt the same call as other Italians to help. For a while they forgot Manin in their enthusiasm. A day after the Assembly which Manin's government had called into being met, on July 4, 1848, they voted to merge Venetia into Charles Albert's dominions, just like Lombardy. This move, said the famous republican poet Tommaseo, was like a woman's offering her honor to a man who saved her life without its being demanded of her. Manin, too, felt grieved for his three-month-old republic, but he rose in the Assembly (having sternly warned his family not to attend the session if they could not control their emotions) to ask his party to obey the majority will. In March all wanted the republic, he said; now all do not want it. This is a fact. It is also a fact that the enemy is at our doors. I demand from my party, said Manin, from the generous republican party, the sacrifice of giving up their wishes. Let them not worry, for the future would belong to them; let them wait for the all-Italian Assembly at Rome.

Next day Manin resigned from the government he urged his followers to vote for. "I am a republican," he said simply. And he retired to private life, to the law, and to his patrol duties as a private in the civic guard.

On August 7, 1848, royal commissioners arrived from Turin to take over Venice in the name of His Majesty Charles Albert.

The document had hardly been signed when news spread that Charles Albert was fleeing toward his original frontier, abandoning Milan to Radetzky. Venice was in a panic that the same fate might befall her, and in their trouble the citizens began to yell for Manin again. The unfortunate commissioners stated that they would rather be torn limb from limb than give the city back to the Austrians. These words were vain to a crowd passing the word "traitor" from mouth to mouth about the King, and only Manin could quiet them. Like a *deus ex machina* he appeared on the balcony, with the promise that within forty-eight hours the Assembly would meet to elect a new government. "Until then," said Manin, "I will govern."

He showed his energy at once by sending detachments of the civic guard out to defend the forts along the mainland coast, and by sending men to Paris to beg the help of the French Republic.

Not unnaturally the Assembly, when it met two days later, wished Manin to continue his dictatorship, but this he was unwilling to do. He would, however, he said, consent to be a member of a triumvirate, especially if the other members could be men more skilled than he in military science. So they gave him a military and a naval aide.

Manin's reward, and his first moment of real happiness since

March, came when the Assembly roundly turned down the surrender terms proffered by the Austrians. He was proud of his people, and he noted that gaiety had appeared again upon the faces of all his fellow-citizens.

Though he was the epitome of a democrat, the few occasions on which Manin used his dictatorial power were to keep the doctrines which in his opinion had ruined republican France safely away from his beloved Venice. Thus he sent out of the city a certain revolutionary priest, Father Gavazzi, who preached a Christian communism far too radical for any man who, like Manin, wanted to get things done. Manin's letter to Gavazzi was kind, but firm, stating that he knew how easy it was for uneducated artisans to be seduced by theories, and now, when every single citizen was needed to help win the war, he could not run the risk of a division among classes.

All during the winter of 1848-1849, until after the battle of Novara in March, the city of Venice was blockaded by the Austrian navy but not otherwise attacked. The Venetian terra firma had long since been reconquered by Austria. At first even the blockade weighed lightly. Three Austrian frigates were posted in front of the three channels leading from the open sea through the sandbars into the city, claiming as prizes of war not only munitions, but cloth, leather, or provisions.

About this time Prince Schwarzenberg summoned the American Chargé d'Affaires, William Stiles, to his palace in Vienna and berated him about a rumor that an American frigate had made its way into Venice carrying supplies. The Prince went on to say that the imperial navy had orders to sink any ship that did so again. Stiles remarked coolly that although the message was rather irregular, he believed he was at liberty to tell the Austrian government that they could sink an American ship when and if they could catch her.

Blockade-running was easy for a while, and most Venetians assumed that their city could never be conquered. Manin, seeing harder times ahead, laid in all the supplies of wheat and corn he could afford, though not as much as he would have liked because he could never get the city's finances into shape.

Lack of cash was not the fault of anyone in Venice; in fact, it was the glory of the city that rich capitalists seemed as eager to give their substance as the poor. A group of millionaires backed an issue of paper money to the tune of four million florins, and the people, who had never been willing to touch Austrian paper, cheerfully accepted this. Everyone contributed what he could. Thus the theaters pooled their profits to buy a ship. As for Manin himself, he gave up all he had—variously stated as a silver snuffbox, or as two silver dishes, two coffee pots, and a dozen forks and spoons—in either case a sign of the simplicity of his life. General Guglielmo Pepe, the military commander, gave a canvas attributed (though erroneously) to Leonardo, an offering which the republic was too grateful to sell; however, they pledged the ducal palace for a foreign loan.

But since Venice was not economically self-sufficient, none of these efforts could make her so.

After the battle of Novara ended all Italian hopes in the north of Italy, the Venetians, summoned to surrender, again refused all terms, and it became the fashion to wear red ribbons as a sign of resistance at all costs. Manin would not wear one because he disliked such outward and visible marks, but in his heart he was proud of his people, and he spurred on the last works of defense in preparation for the enemy. In the month of March 1849, Manin accepted the title of president from the Venetian republic.

Venice was defended by 21,000 soldiers, two-thirds of them native, and most of the rest volunteers from other parts of Italy. General Pepe, commanding, had disobeyed orders from his sovereign, the King of Naples, in order to get to Venice. Ferdinand of Naples had been caught up like other Italian rulers in the rush to send troops to Milan after the Five Days. By the time they reached Lombardy, Ferdinand repented and sent orders to Pepe to withdraw, whereupon Pepe took his staff and the few troops who would follow him to Venice, where they could still fight for their convictions.

Venice also recruited in Switzerland in the early days of the revolution. Swiss law forbade Swiss citizens to join foreign armies, so the recruiting had to be done with one eye on the police; yet sentiments for a free Italy were so strong that many of the police also closed one eye. They knew too that many Swiss citizens needed the fifty-franc enlistment bonus, having looked for work a long time after the depression of 1847. Recruiting was for two years, with a franc a day pay, very high for soldiers; bread, quarters, uniforms, and arms were free, and a pension was to be given the disabled. The Swiss company at Venice was small but active and devoted, and far steadier than the velvet-clad university battalion, who showed courage but not endurance, who constantly complained of fatigue professional soldiers would not notice, and who, by disobedience to the officers they had elected, had a bad effect on the morale of other troops.

By April nearly the whole population was engaged in some sort of defense work. Three times as many men were employed at the arsenal as had been under Austria; 2,300 worked there, not only in the daytime but also overtime for no extra pay. In the same way sailors began to work at night to build boats, to make up belatedly and in small measure for the lost fleet at Pola. People noticed how eagerly they invented tools and devised ways to make their work easier and quicker. Two 48-pound guns were manufactured in the city, but most of their cannon were 18 or 24-pounders. In order to have powder to charge them, the government offered rewards for deposits of saltpeter which could be recovered out of old casks, or stables. They also encouraged little boats to set out during squalls to bring in provisions from the mainland. Women nursed and made bandages; even the highest-born ladies visited the army hospitals distributing oranges. As for the really rich, their money was alternately coaxed and forced out of them and even the poorest realized that the wealthy had given till it hurt.

None of this island activity disturbed the Austrians as they began pushing earthworks in a long line just beyond the effective range of the cannon of Fort Malghera, which protected the land end of the great railroad bridge and which was the only piece of terra firma still controlled by the Venetians. Six thousand Austrians worked to dig the trenches, protecting themselves by throwing earth in a high mound between them and the fortress. They worked night and day, often waist-deep in the marshy water. Baffled when their cannon could neither hit the mark nor draw fire in return, the garrison at Malghera insisted on making constant sorties, and when their commanding officer tried to stop these as being too wasteful, anger against him ran so high that he had to be retired and given refuge on a French warship.

On May 4 the Austrians' purpose was revealed as they unmasked four batteries and opened fire with a vengeance. Explosive missiles fell inside the fortress all that night at the rate of one a minute. One shattered the china in the cupboard, another cut the chain of the drawbridge. By the next day Radetzky was confident the fortress would be softened up for surrender; three archdukes waited hopefully in his camp to enter the place as the surrender terms were handed to the Venetians. Characteristically the letter was left unsealed, with the idea that the garrison would be seduced by the offer before it could be handed to Manin. During the interval of the truce the Austrians pushed up a second line of earthworks, half as far from the fortress as the first. When, to the besiegers' surprise, the Venetians refused to give up, Radetzky was ready to let go a rain of fire such as had hardly been seen in military history up to that time.

Across the water the citizens of Venice used to gather night after night to see the illuminating fusees, held in the air by parachutes, light up the fortress as bright as day. As for the 2,500 members of the Malghera garrison, there was never a moment's rest for them, even in their supposedly bombproof barracks. Whenever the flash of an enemy mortar was seen a bell rang which gave the inmates a moment to take cover. Between times they fired their own guns—74 cannon and 16 mortars—though so much of the fortification was destroyed that they were often completely exposed in this service. The archdukes grew tired of waiting and went home; one-third of the besiegers were casualties, often to malaria; yet still the fire increased, until on May 24 it reached a climax with 30,000 projectiles fired by the two sides in one day.

With a fifth of the garrison wounded and the fortress being slowly demolished, the Venetians decided the time had come to evacuate. They made their preparations with great secrecy, so that some of the soldiers led out between dusk and midnight on May 25 did not realize where they were going until they were ordered into boats. Cannon were equipped with slow matches, so that they kept on firing for three hours after the last man had left; and the powder magazine was booby-trapped so that inquisitive Austrians handling the abandoned guns set it off and killed themselves.

Years later it was said that any Austrian officer, except for Haynau, would uncover his head if he heard the words, "That man was one of the defenders of Malghera."

As they withdrew to Venice, the defenders blew up five arches of the railroad bridge so that no hostile army could march toward them. Once more Venice, wrapped in her primeval lagoons, felt secure, and on May 31 the Assembly voted again to carry on resistance at all costs. The Venetian sentry showed the common will for independence when he refused to accept an Austrian dispatch curtly addressed to "Lawyer Manin."

After about May 20 the blockade became so tight that the only news entering the city came through dispatches to foreign consuls. No more food could run the blockade, though etiquette allowed foreign ships to donate a part of their medical supplies to the hospitals of the city. Anger ran high against a French captain who refused to give up any of his ice for this purpose.

The city fell back upon the supply of grain which Manin had laid in, but the single steam mill, working day and night, could hardly grind it into flour fast enough to feed the population. Its work was made harder, though never quite stopped, by the 22 shells that fell in and around the mill after the Austrian bombardment began. When the regular engine had to stop for repairs, the Venetians moved in a locomotive from the railroad station; and to supplement steam power they distributed hand flour mills free to any women who would use them. As a matter of fact, said the notice of this offer, it will be a good thing for these women to have something to keep them decently at home instead of out on the streets all day.

Venetians could still remember the siege of 1814, when rolls went from one sou to ten francs apiece, and rich ladies who had private hoards of food distributed it on the streets as a charity, though not in sufficient quantity to prevent some people from starving. Manin was determined to prevent anything like this from happening again, so as a first step, at the end of May he forbade food prices to rise above what they had been in the few days before this decree. To conserve wheat and corn he ordered that they must be mixed half and half with rye, and as the shortage grew worse the proportion changed. Only hospitals had white bread at the end of the siege, and all wine was reserved for convalescents. Bread was the only food for most people; even fish was hard to get, for the fishermen's boats could not be protected. Practically the only meat of the summer came from one successful raid on the mainland which netted 100 oxen; this news was of such transcendent importance that a performance of *William Tell* at the opera was interrupted to spread it.

In June food riots were suppressed; Manin convinced the people that he did not have secret hoards of foods, as the rioters shouted. After this it became extremely bad form for anyone at all to admit that he was hungry.

By July 23 still tighter controls were urgent, so food ration cards were given out. The cards were good for two weeks, but each family could buy only one day's supply at a time to prevent hoarding by those who had money.

Thus Venice, empty-stomached but gay, went to bed on the night of July 29. The winged lion of St. Mark's slept in darkness, the colonnades and the gold and azure walls were invisible; only two small lights burned in front of the mosaic madonna. Then in one moment the horizon become alight and a stream of bombshells fell into the city. People poured out of their houses, partly in dismay, for they had believed they were out of range of the enemy's heaviest artillery, and partly in amazement at the beauty of the scene, as the water reflected the trajectories of balls and rockets.

Military engineers had long known that if they could fire at a higher angle they could shoot farther, but found if they simply sunk the rear end of mobile gun carriages in the earth the recoil proved too destructive. This time the Austrians, firing from Fort Malghera, dismounted their guns and arranged them on heavy beds of timber, put nine pounds of powder behind a 24-pound ball, elevated the barrels to 45 degrees, and had the satisfaction of reaching Venice, a more distant mark than was ever hit before, three and a half miles away. Even so the guns upset with every discharge.

Various other military problems were not quite solved. For instance, fuses on the shells had been calculated for a shorter distance, so they often exploded before they reached their mark. And it was found that red-hot balls, intended to cause fires, fell mostly into the water, far short of unheated ones. Also, when the balls reached the city their force was spent, so they fell merely with their own weight. The British consul was lying in bed on his back when a ball fell through his roof and passed between his legs without causing more than bruises. This was one of 25,000 projectiles that reached the city between July 29 and August 22.

Venetian powder, mostly homemade, was so weak the defenders could not hope to return the fire. They could shoot only a mile.

People soon began to laugh at this effort to subdue them. "What lovely oranges," they would say, or, "Radetzky is throwing us alms." Boys chased the balls and turned them in to the depots as a patriotic offering; it was considered bad form to collect the franc which was the official reward.

To the authorities, mere cheerfulness did not solve the problems of housing the refugees from the half of the islands under fire. Firemen had to be exempted from the civic guard because they were so constantly on duty—there were thirty-six huge fires caused by the bombardment. Manin ordered the ducal palace to be opened for people to sleep in, and shortly commanded the inhabitants of the untouchable part of the city to take in families from the other end whether they knew the people or not. An Assembly committee devoted full time to providing bread, work, and shelter for the evacuees.

Long-range bombing did not exhaust Austrian ingenuity. In August a rumor reached the Venetians that they were going to be attacked by balloons—an idea which struck them as supremely ridiculous. For days beforehand they laughed about the matter— and then, indeed, one day the enemy launched a hundred bomb-carrying balloons. They were supposed to discharge over the harbor and set the boats afire, but the wind changed, blowing them off into the lagoons and even back toward the Austrian lines. That was the end of aerial warfare in those days. A further Austrian project of 25-foot balloons to be attached to a long copper wire, so that they could be detonated electrically, was never put into practice.

After famine and after bombardment came cholera. It struck a city crowded with soldiers and refugees, one without provisions, medicine, or hospital space. In the week of August 16, 1,500 people died of the disease; two-thirds of those stricken. (The epidemic persisted for a week after the surrender, until a huge cold rain stopped it on August 29 as if by magic.)

Hospital conditions, in spite of the wine and white bread and beautiful ladies, had never been good in Venice. The Swiss soldiers complained that the rooms were smelly and dirty, that the doctors carried on bleedings with unnecessary brutality, that the beds were mere pallets of straw. Most soldiers contracted malaria at one time or another during the siege, so that even before the cholera struck the hospitals were full. They received 424 wounded during the six weeks after the fall of Malghera, of whom 55 died, 250 were cured, and 117 were still under treatment when the count was made.

Well into this frightful August the Venetian people were undaunted, indeed so eager to fight that they hurled violence on anyone who suggested capitulation. Nevertheless, on the 6th the Assembly gave Manin power to treat. It seemed to him the thing to do, though he made a heartbroken offer to turn over his office to any man or group who still believed they could save the city.

The next day a group of die-hards gathered around the government palace crying "Away with Manin," and yelling that what the city needed was mass conscription. Calmly Manin descended from his inevitable balcony onto the street, where he ordered a table to be brought to him. Then he reminded his hot-blooded critics that enlistment rolls were always open, and he urged them to sign up. The hot blood chilled rapidly, and the crowd crept sheepishly away, leaving only 18 signatures, and of these only three men were fit for service.

It was a delicate matter to time the surrender, and on August 12, just to gain a few more days, Manin slapped another forced loan of 6 million florins on the city's rich.

On the 13th he reviewed the civic guard, in a last show of the strength and pride of the republic. Tears filled the President's eyes as they passed. "To be forced to give up, with such a people behind me," he cried.

On the 19th, when there was only food for three or four days in the city, Manin asked for formal surrender terms. He was afraid of food riots if he waited longer, and he could not have borne it if his republic's reputation for order had been blemished. The Austrian reply was that the city must surrender unconditionally, but that soldiers who had served in the ranks would be forgiven and that anyone who liked might leave the city freely. A list of forty persons was to be proscribed. On the 23rd, Manin himself patrolled the streets with a white flag to give the news and maintain order. On the 24th he took his family aboard a French war vessel which was to carry them into exile.

Shortly thereafter Radetzky entered as a conqueror, undeterred by the fear of cholera. There were the usual civilian floggings that followed Austrian victory in those days, and beyond forcing circulation of the republican paper money at fifty per cent of its par value, the government did little to support the city's economic life. Two years later Venice seemed like a dead city, her commerce destroyed, since she was no longer a free port, her citizens apathetic, her hopes smothered.

Manin's wife died of cholera before they got to Paris. With his two children Manin lived on in that city, devoting most of his time to nursing his invalid daughter, who had suffered painfully all her life from a nervous disease. In a few years she died, and then in 1857 Manin himself. His last advice to his countrymen, as he followed young Victor Emmanuel's career, was to join Piedmont when they had a second chance.

PART V · CONCLUSION

The Workings of British Justice

DURING the days of 1848 England stood apart, unshaken, apparently unshakable. Her reformers were already in power, and though the radical Chartists caused some propertied spines to shiver, no one ventured to forbid their English right to speak their minds. The nearest thing to a national guard in Britain was the appointment of 15,000 special constables (including Louis Napoleon) for the day of April 10, 1848, when the Chartists were to present a huge petition to Parliament. On the same day came the nearest thing to a barricade: the clerks of the foreign office blocked up their windows with bound volumes of the *Times*. The Chartists were allowed to have a meeting but not a parade, but they accepted this limitation meekly and sent their 500-pound petition to Parliament with a small escort. The Duke of Wellington had soldiers ready in case the petitioners should catch revolutionary fever from across the Channel, but he kept his troops hidden so as not to provoke anger—this in spite of the fact that Frenchmen marveled how a tiny contingent of British soldiers could control a large mob, so unused were British civilians to the handling of guns.

The Prime Minister, Lord John Russell, the champion of the Reform Bill of 1832, said publicly if the people have grievances, by all means let them tell us. English stomachs, commented a German visitor, might be as hungry as German ones but they felt better because they were allowed to grumble.

It was not only the chance to grumble, it was the hope of getting something done. The Reform Bill of 1832, which had extended suffrage and given more power to industrialists, had passed, though after a good deal of difficulty. Its passage gave the Chartists hope that they too might win their demands for manhood suffrage if enough of the Queen's subjects showed that to be their will.

Mazzini looked upon the People's Charter with horror. It hurt him to see a whole class concerned with the principle of happiness instead of moral duty. If they were so concerned, it was the same complaint that Engels made about their so-called betters, for he declared that the English middle class, and most especially the reforming middle class, was so debased that for it nothing existed except for the sake of money.

Most of the famous exiles from the continent landed in England and most of them shared Mazzini's and Engels' dislike of the British. Armies of rank-and-file Germans and Italians fled to Switzerland, and hundreds of young men with their lives before them—Germans, Hungarians, Italians, and Irish—came to America. To England, however, trooped the great names—Louis Philippe, Guizot, Louis Blanc, Caussidière, Ledru-Rollin, Marx, the Prince of Prussia, Kinkel, Metternich, Kossuth, Mazzini. England had the virtues of wealth, which they envied; stability, which they professed to admire; and tolerance, of which they all took advantage.

To find anything like love for England on the part of a foreigner one must turn to Lamartine, who was not an exile. He visited England for strictly private reasons in 1850, and his feelings were not constrained by the necessity of accepting hospitality. It was his first visit in twenty years. In 1830 he had been so dismayed at the expressions of hatred between the classes that he expected a revolution and actually moved all his investments out of Britain. In 1850 he would have felt safe in putting his whole fortune there. In England the spirit was at work for which the continental revolutionaries struggled so hard, the spirit of conciliation of classes, each one eager to render justice to the others, each one contributing by its good will to the common welfare.

To Lamartine, the good will was not the result of England's enlightened legislation; in fact, the laws which made her so famous were but a sign of the good will which had found its first expression in private charity. He made a list of the charities of London, a list going into many hundreds of entries—and he showed how giving charity educated the rich, while receiving the gifts of health and instruction educated the workers.

A hundred years later people do not feel so tender toward charity. Our ideal is of a more impersonal justice, of an industrial society where each man's place is honored and secure. In those days only the rich were honored and secure, and charity was the only way to plow back surplus wealth into the nation, the first easy lesson in social justice, and a more wholesome one than the June massacre in Paris.

The wealth of England stunned all continentals at that time. The masts of sailing ships from every country on the globe crowded the Thames; the shops of Oxford Street, with gilded woodwork and mirrored walls, blazoned at night with so many gas lamps they seemed like fairyland. Even the poor shared in this wealth, in spite of their awful sufferings as victims of the factory system. In England a man who had only potatoes to eat called himself starving, while in parts of Germany a man who had potatoes was well off.

Free speech and good will and wealth—these made England safe. Where wealth was lacking, where there were not even potatoes, and where the good will that came, at least in part, from a common nationality, failed as happened in Ireland, free speech and all the vaunted merits of British government broke down.

Ireland was always a stick the enemies of England could use to beat her with. Whether it was a radical actor in Paris telling Queen Victoria that his social drama dealt with "the Irish of Paris," or whether it was Prince Schwarzenberg begging Lord Palmerston to treat the affairs of Hungary with the same forbearance which His Highness showed toward Her Britannic Majesty's second island, both of them enjoyed pointing to the spot where the British did not live up to their theories.

In 1848 Ireland had just come through the potato famine which had killed off a quarter of her population. The government of the richest kingdom in the world had failed to prevent starvation and fever among part of its own people who lived on a food-producing island, from which, even during the famine years, more than enough grain and meat was exported to keep all its own people healthy. Only the potato crop failed, potatoes on which the Irish peasantry had always nourished themselves while the meat and grain were sent out of the country to pay the landlords' rent. In vain did Irish members of Parliament urge that Irish food should be kept at home by law. In Bohemia and Württemberg, when food was scarce, export of wheat had been forbidden. But England had recently discovered the laws of the market; to withhold rents from the Irish landlords would interfere with the principles of economics. So the meat and grain were shipped off, under armed guard, and the Irish peasants lay back in their hovels or their ditches and starved. Not the £2,000 given for relief by Queen Victoria, nor the £45,000 by the Society of Friends, nor all the public relief, consisting largely of corn meal mush served out from chained ladles to those Irishmen who had proved their need by disposing of their land at forced sales and eating their seed potatoes—not all these put together were enough to save two million Irish lives.

To the young Irish intellectuals, the heartbreaking thing was the passivity with which the peasants met their fate. Italians and Poles would fight their foreign oppressors, and the Irish, who had as good a right as any people in Europe to be free, could hardly be roused. Hunger and disease had killed in them even the instinct which causes the worm to turn against the foot that crushes it. For years, furthermore, they had been taught peaceful agitation by Daniel O'Connell, who had shown them how to value their country, it is true, and roused them for repeal of the Act of Union with Great Britain—but he believed everything should be done without force. Mass meetings, petitions, "repeal rent" paid in penny sums to O'Connell's organization, were his means of agitation.

O'Connell died in 1847, and to bolder new leaders it seemed the time had come to fight. Reliance on moral force had only ended in the death of two millions of their fellow-countrymen, who could have been spared if there had been an Irish Parliament in existence able to close the ports. In the Parliament at London whenever the Irish members said they needed a special law, they were told that all the Queen's dominions must be treated alike, whereas if they said they wanted to be treated the same, that time they were told that Irish problems were a special case.

A group of these young Irish leaders called themselves Young Ireland, in imitation of Mazzini's Young Italy, even though Mazzini would not let the Irish in his league of European peoples. Actually Mazzini was afraid of antagonizing his British supporters, but publicly the high priest of nationality declared that the Irish were not a nation because they had no distinctive moral contribution for humanity. Indifferent to this judgment, Young Ireland acted just like all the other nationalities of Europe, by studying the ancient language and traditions of their island, wearing native dress, and popularizing their history. They also talked a lot of fighting for Irish freedom, though they were sadly lacking in military genius and the ability to rouse their poorer countrymen.

These efforts for a purely nationalistic struggle seemed too thin to John Mitchel, a newspaperman, who told the peasants plainly they should fight for their food supply. That peasants should keep the food they raised to feed their own families first, even if they had to tear up the new-laid railroad lines to prevent its being carried off was so revolutionary a doctrine that Mitchel had to break with his companions and start his own paper to expound it. This happened in February 1848. "Let the man among you that has no gun sell his garment and buy one," Mitchel told his readers.

Thus when the news of the Paris revolution came, Ireland was already divided into two factions, like every European country— those who wanted self-determination and those who wanted social revolution.

To meet this crisis the British government prepared the garrison at Dublin for a siege with a show of force deliberately intended to impress the citizenry. Yet Lord Clarendon, the lord-lieutenant, had the sense to realize that too strict an application of the laws of repression would cause an outbreak, and he made a point of avoiding even the smallest collision. His secret method of defense was to use agents to keep up dissension between the factions of would-be revolters.

Such force and such guile are natural means for a government; they seem almost legitimate. But the British administration in Ireland had another method, a most un-British one of clinching cases. For centuries the English, who had carefully imported the jury system to Ireland, equally carefully packed the jury panels to get the verdicts they desired. After the Catholics had been given political rights in 1829, packing became all the more necessary for being harder to do. When the Tories had been in office, Lord John Russell and his Whigs had expressed their horror of jury-packing in such irretractable language that it was embarrassing to find themselves facing the same issue. In 1848 Lord John Russell was Prime Minister, and he expressed his hope to Lord Clarendon that jury-packing could be kept to a minimum.

Accordingly the Irish courts, called upon in May to try for sedition some of the leaders of Young Ireland headed by a member of Parliament named Smith O'Brien, packed only eleven out of twelve places in the jury and allowed one Repealer to sit in the box. Of course this hung the jury and prevented O'Brien's conviction.

The very day of this acquittal Mitchel, the more dangerous

enemy, was arrested and charged with a brand new crime, created by act of Parliament—"treason felony," for which the punishment was transportation. This time no chances were taken, all the jurymen were carefully picked, and Mitchel was convicted, sentenced, and rushed away to a prison ship and eventually to Tasmania.

Even packing juries was not enough. It could cure the disease but not prevent it, and for that latter purpose, Parliament voted to suspend the Habeas Corpus Act. In July 1848, Smith O'Brien and his friends were known to be planning an insurrection, timed for after the harvest. By suspending habeas corpus, the British forced the Young Irelanders to move before they were ready. Later one of them wondered how this move could have come to them as such a complete surprise.

When the blow struck, O'Brien was already in Tipperary, collecting men with guns, pikes, and pitchforks, but he had trouble holding his little army together because he could not feed them forever out of his own pocket, though he was a wealthy landowner, and he scorned the step taken by guerrillas on the continent, that of paying for provisions with a draft on the new free government. He was much too tender with property for an insurrectionist, for when it was a question of barricading roads, he forbade his men to cut down trees without the owners' consent.

On July 29 a group of 47 police were sent to arrest O'Brien, whom they found in a village behind a barricade manned by 300 men with twenty firearms among them. These gallant defenders chased the police into a strongly built slate farmhouse, owned by a widow McCormick. When the widow appeared among the Irishmen and begged O'Brien to save her six children, all inside the house with the police, O'Brien walked up to the open windows and asked that the children should be passed out. Instead the police fired on their attackers, killing two, and held the children up to the windows to prevent a return of fire. Finally the attackers dragged up a wagon-load of hay to set fire to the house door, but this was too much for O'Brien's tender heart. He stopped the Irishman who was about to shoot into the hay to start the blaze.

Before long another group of constabulary rescued the first detachment, and O'Brien fled into hiding. Of this he soon grew tired, and early in August he went to a railroad station and bought a ticket to Limerick, intending to leave the country. There was a £500 reward for his person, however, and he was easy to spot, a huge, six-foot man, with light hair and dark eyes. A railroad guard turned him in, and he was tried a second time, convicted this time and sentenced to be hanged, drawn, and quartered.

In spite of this ferocious justice, or perhaps because of it, and all the impassioned oratory it inspired, there was an air of unreality about this trial, as about the whole Irish revolution. No one seriously expected the execution to be carried out. Some of the members of the 1848 Whig cabinet had planned insurrection in Birmingham, if the 1832 Reform Bill failed to pass—just what O'Brien attempted in Tipperary in 1848 for the sake of Irish nationality. Documents to prove this were given to the press, and, chagrined as no continental government would have been, the British Whigs commuted the sentence.

The trouble with the Irish rebellion, the reason it never got beyond the siege of a farmhouse, lay partly with the people of Ireland, who were weak from the famine and not military by training. The British government, for its part, was certainly not conciliatory—yet it avoided the silly tactlessness of most continental rulers faced with insurgency. The British were unjust but they were effective; they were hypocritical but not afraid of their own weakness; their sins of omission were as bad for Ireland as cruelty but they were not utterly shameless.

Nevertheless, it was apparent that only in their own country could the British follow through their admirable policy of conciliation of classes. Nationality was a necessary bond. In this failure of the well-intentioned British to provide happiness for an alien race lay the justification of all the struggling nationalities of Europe— not because their rulers were evil, but simply because there are some things that a nation, like an individual, has to do for itself.

XXI

The Revolution of the Spirit

MOST of what the men of 1848 fought for was brought about within a quarter of a century, and the men who accomplished it were most of them specific enemies of the 1848 movement. Thiers ushered in a third French Republic, Bismarck united Germany, and Cavour, Italy. Deák won autonomy for Hungary within a dual monarchy; a Russian czar freed the serfs; and the British manufacturing classes moved toward the freedoms of the People's Charter.

That these things could happen showed that the aims of the revolutionists were not dangerous to the structure of society, only their methods. A person who has power may use his power to create changes, yet violently resist having others take power from him so that they could make the same or better changes. In 1848 what neither the governments nor the moderate leaders could brook was popular agitation and popular control. The historian Trevelyan regrets that 1848 could not have seen successful liberal regimes established before the class struggle became acute as it did later in the century. But in a sense the 1848 revolutions turned into class struggles, and failed because they did. In every country appeared a split between two groups which cooperated at first in the struggle against authority, between the forces typified by Lamartine and those by Louis Blanc, Heinrich von Gagern and Robert Blum, the Reading Club and the Aula in Vienna, between Deák and Kossuth, Cavour and Mazzini. In those countries which, like Hungary and Italy, were struggling against a foreign oppressor, the conflict of nationalities made a screen to hide the conflict of classes. But Deák would not have relished Kossuth's success, nor Cavour Mazzini's.

This is true despite the belief of the leaders of all the parties that the conciliation of classes was the greatest gain that could come from a new government, and despite their hope that by this revolution the class struggle could be avoided. During the generation before 1848 fear of the lower classes was growing, and the men then in power could only bridle the workers with work, as Guizot proposed, or, like Metternich, clamp on a lid which they knew to be temporary. The reformers turned these fears inside out, saying that by kindness the working classes could be won away from the class struggle and given an honored place in society. This doctrine had many intellectual ancestors; in 1848 it was propagated by men like Louis Blanc and Mazzini. Yet this view was not the property of the radical parties alone. Lamartine declared on February 24 that the Second Republic would suspend the frightful misunderstanding that had grown up between classes; Cavour thought that in fusion of classes lay the principal strength of modern society.

When governments with this hopeful ideal took over in 1848 enough violence occurred to make their predecessors' fear of the lower classes seem more and more justifiable. The truth was, violence was present in society as a whole; only very few people were able to perceive this fact and to accept its implications. Karl Vogt, the biologist in the Frankfurt Assembly, saw beyond his contemporaries in this. When he asked himself whence came the brutality that attends every revolution, he noticed a phenomenon that is perennial:

"The brutality which is present in higher circles filters down, and this brutality which above lives only in thoughts, below takes the form of action. I have heard hundreds and hundreds of times expressions like 'The whole bunch ought to be knocked out with grape shot,' 'the agitators deserve to be hanged all together.' . . . Such expressions are mostly used by people who are fanatics of order and who make it their business to preach order and peace."[1]

Vogt made this statement before the full force of the reaction had shown that when the upper classes had a chance to indulge themselves, in the interests of "restoring order," they were quite as capable of actual physical brutality as the men they feared.

A modern psychologist might speculate, where Vogt could not, that unconscious as well as conscious hatreds were bound to pervade any society held together with such rigid and arbitrary bonds as Europe in the mid-nineteenth century. The mass of the people were kept down not only by laws but by customs, by studied arrogance, by pious sanctions. Herzen quotes from a Russian writer who admired the west because everyone born there "learns in his cradle, in his games, in his mother's caresses, notions of duty, justice, law, and

---

[1] Quoted from Petzet, 52.

order." These are the very sources to which psychology today traces repressions. It may have been these same conceptions of duty, law, and order which had hogtied western Europe for centuries. Class hatred had persisted there from the Middle Ages; it is one of the most characteristic features of the twelfth century.[2] What the nineteenth century failed to realize was that merely by overcoming people's conscious hostility, by trying sincerely to conciliate the classes, they could not also overcome the unconscious feelings that were bred into their bones. To speculate further, is it not reasonable to imagine that when new ideas loosened the sanctions which had kept each man in his place, a lot more force was let loose than men realized they had within them?

When hostility that has been repressed is first released into consciousness, there is a moment, for individuals at least, and perhaps also for nations, when it appears to be of uncontrollable violence. Perhaps this is because there exist, at first, no habitual or institutional skills for dealing with it overtly. Thus violence erupted among the lower classes as they began to dare to ask for more equal conditions, a violence which came in good part from the release of their old resentments. At the same time the upper classes, who were just beginning to dare to give more equality, found that this process simultaneously brought to the surface in themselves the fears which they had long kept hidden of the results of lower class resentment.

The great advantage which America had was that its social arrangements to a large measure prevented these hatreds from forming; not completely, but enough to make a startling contrast with Europe in those days.

Another psychological factor took the men of 1848 by surprise. It was noted by Massimo d'Azeglio, although its explanation had to wait for a hundred years—and that was the distinct ambivalence in the human soul toward freedom. It was not only the unexpected violence that shocked people, it was that freedom itself terrified them. This ambivalence has been expounded psychoanalytically by Erich Fromm, in *Escape from Freedom*. He shows that from the time of the Reformation freedom has been a burden, and indeed a threat, for men who are not prepared to accept its responsibilities—and there are many. This quality made every demand for a revolution two-faced, so that men were always retreating as well as moving

[2] See Luchaire, *Social France at the Time of Philip Augustus.*

forward, in spite of themselves. Or, as Massimo d'Azeglio perceived it: "The gift of liberty is like that of a horse, handsome, strong, and high-spirited. In some it arouses a wish to ride; in many others, on the contrary, it increases the desire to walk."[3] A great many people felt more like walking as the year 1848 passed,—all the French who voted for Napoleon, on the ground that he would restore "order," all the Prussians who paid their taxes after their parliament had been dissolved in the very act of telling the citizens not to pay them, all the Hapsburg subjects who in 1849 did not have a chance either to vote for anybody or to support a constitution. All these were people who found that the effort of doing something for themselves was not so rewarding as letting somebody on top do it—especially when it came to the task of overcoming the violence of the lower classes.

When the moderates took fright at the contemplation of their danger, they accused the radicals of trying to destroy order and property.[4] To the radical intellectuals, this was ill-will and insult. They loved order and property and class conciliation as much as anybody, but being somewhat closer to the people than the other leaders they realized that they would not be satisfied with constitutions but would require some social reforms. None of the radicals had a chance to show how far he would go before he was stopped. He was lucky if he was stopped by foreign arms, as Mazzini was, so that his dream could go on. To be halted by civil war such as the June Days of Paris seemed to prove that the radical case was hopeless, or that, as Frederick William put it, soldiers are the only cure for democrats.

After the middle classes had won most of what they wanted, they often voluntarily gave up some of their new privileges so that the lower classes would not have to be given liberties too. They were like the man in the story who was asked what he would like best in the world, provided his worst enemy could have the same thing in double measure—and he answered, *one blind eye*. There was practically no one to say that the cure for democracy was more democracy.

[3] Massimo d'Azeglio, *Recollections*, II, 8.
[4] In the mid-nineteenth century it was probably true that property gave a feeling of responsibility—and men preferred the easier task of holding on to their property and the reins of government than the more difficult one of devising ways to give genuine responsibility to men who did not have property. There again the American continent offered an advantage.

CONCLUSION

This was the situation that Marx saw, and he thought of a brilliantly original answer. Do not minimize class conflict, exaggerate it. Even the most far-reaching concessions of the conciliators would not give workers an equal status in society, and the only way for them to achieve it would be to throw over all the privileged and property-clutching classes, ignoring the soft words of socialists like Louis Blanc as well as the turncoat policies of the Lamartines.

Thus when the 48ers failed they were beaten physically by the terrified conservatives, and also beaten intellectually by the theories of Marx, which made most socialist movements forget the poetical and discredited 1848 fancies.

To the men of 1848, class violence was anathema, but violence between nations was natural and often admirable. The French radical parties would have been as happy to march into Savoy or the Rhineland as the Germans were to march into Schleswig, or the Italians to chase Radetzky. Disarmament was preached only by eccentrics like Karl Vogt and, indeed, Louis Napoleon, neither of them typical of the 1848 spirit.

Marx branded nationality a myth, a verdict which was just as greatly opposed to 1848 ideas as was his doctrine of the class struggle; in fact the two went hand in hand. Loyalty to class, the Marxists maintained, would prevent international wars. But the men who wished to create nations realized that all classes must share in patriotism by having a stake in the nation, and the men who wanted peace between the classes felt that national loyalty was one way to encourage it. Thus the doctrines of struggle between classes and between nations were in inverse ratio. One may ask, of course, whether class is not a myth, whether property, at least the prestige that comes from property, is not a myth, whether ultimate democracy would not surmount all of these mythical obstacles. But the fact remains that the men who wanted democracy a hundred years ago planned to organize it in national units, and that political democracy has not yet succeeded in units any larger. These national blocs made plenty of trouble for the world, but perhaps no more than the class struggle.

The democratic spirit is elusive, and has first to be learned within a much smaller group even than a nation. It involves, first of all, a recognition in each man's soul that all other men are as good as he, at least potentially. Where could that spirit be born in Europe in 1848? Albert, the workingman, was called by his first name all the time he was a member of the French government; Baron Dobl-hoff in Vienna was suspected because he gave parties where the no-bility could meet the middle classes socially for the first time; the King of Prussia could label an assembly of professors "the gutter"; Macaulay could stand up in the House of Commons to say that universal suffrage would destroy civilization and everything that made civilization worth while, the security of property; Sir Strat-ford Canning, Britain's ambassador to Turkey, could tear up Lamartine's proclamations with the remark that he would not live in a Europe run by reds and demagogues; Metternich doubted that society could exist along with freedom of the press; in Vienna an officer threw his shaving water out the window, and the worker whom he drenched was arrested because he complained; Guizot was shocked that anyone could confound the welfare of the lower classes with that of society as a whole. In such a climate of opinion it is not strange that even those men who had the ideal of democracy in their hearts found it was hard to explain to others, and almost as hard to live with themselves.

Democracy also involves the recognition in each man's soul that he is as good as other men, at least potentially. Donelson, the Ameri-can consul at Berlin, believed that a republic could not succeed in Europe while thousands starved and millions lacked the sense of personal independence on which the American system rests. Cavour recognized the same point when he said that the lower classes in the New World would be shocked at the lack of dignity among Euro-pean servants and workmen. Kossuth embarrassed his peasants when he addressed them with the plural or polite form of "you"; the Italian revolutionaries who pulled Count Hübner from his car-riage did not assume the right to sit there in his place; in Italian the very word "democratic" came to mean shabby, so that one would speak of a democratic pair of shoes.

Could a common will emerge from such a society, an agreement of the sort that would guarantee more rights to the majority and would find the minority yielding gracefully? To build such a society the men of 1848 had the right start. With all the weight of custom and prejudice against them they labored to make a world where men would feel more equal, and to make nations within which this feeling could operate. Their mistake was that they miscalculated the barriers—even in their own souls. It was too easy for leaders of the people to become either mass hypnotists, like Held and Robert Blum, or authoritarian improvers. Mazzini, Louis Blanc and Kossuth were all democrats in theory but became autocratic when it came to putting their plans into action. Revelation, after being ousted from religion, as someone remarked at the time, had turned to politics, and every man thought he knew how to govern.

There were a few nuclei of real democratic spirit. Manin in Venice handled his affairs with more of it than any other 48er in power. In some of the guerrilla armies partial democracy worked, as in Garibaldi's, where a man might be a captain one day, a private the next. Democracy was in some of the workers' movements, such as the editorial board of *L'Atelier*, the French workers' paper, or in Born's club for workingmen in Berlin where he said, "We want a club in order to become men." It could be found in some of the universities, like the Aula at Vienna, and in other groups interested in progress such as the Italian scientific and agricultural congresses. It was from the development of such groups as these that democracy could eventually be born again in Europe.

The revolutions, then, seem like a hurling of violence against violence, the struggling of vast incompatibilities to be born together —the incompatibility of freedom for all with power for some; the incompatibility of class solidarity and national solidarity; the demands of race, of privilege, of recently born economic groups, and new intellectual groups to be heard amid all the din.

Yet when the people had a chance to express themselves quietly on these subjects they accomplished a good deal more toward a natural settlement of their troubles than did their leaders. The parliament of Prussia foreshadowed reforms that were still important and pressing for the Weimar republic, while the constitution of Kremsier solved the problems of administering territories of mixed populations better than the government of Vienna ever settled the question, and better than the Austrian or Hungarian or Croat rebels showed any signs of doing while they were in power. In fact, it was in these parliaments that the real creativity of the period lay, not in the short-lived improvisations of governments themselves provisional, nor yet in the spectacle of popular force which yet did not succeed in destroying the forces of reaction. The greatest failure of all in 1848 was that the men who had power never really trusted the people.

Was nothing gained by all the year of revolution, either from the violence or from the quiet talk? The answer is very little. Some revolutions shake up society so that when the pieces fall together again they are in a new pattern which permits growth in a new direction. In 1848 that hardly happened. The Austrian serfs were freed, but did this make up for the extra repression on all other Austrian subjects? Italy made a new start toward greater freedom, but Germany was disillusioned about freedom. Some old illusions were destroyed, but the new myths created by men like Marx and Bismarck were as one-sided as the ones they supplanted and failed equally to represent a synthesis of values. The test of whether a revolution is successful is not whether some power with a new name exercises the same essential restraints as before (which happened to Europe in 1870), but whether some important group has won some important new freedom—economic, political, social, or religious.

Out of 1848 and its struggles no important new freedom was wrested. Instead men lost confidence in freedom and imagined they had made a great advance in sophistication by turning from idealism to cynicism. After 1848 classes and nations played power politics, each unashamed to get what it could each for itself with very little thought for the common welfare of society. This was not realism, though it was called *Realpolitik*. In 1870 this policy brought a new chance to win many of the specific demands of the 1848 revolutionaries, yet no one can say that the basic questions of justice and cooperation among classes and nations were settled at that time. For these problems failure was worse than mere failure, for no new chance arose. In 1914, at the time of the next continental explosion, many of the powers that had been half rotten in 1848 disappeared for good, but with them disappeared a good part of the class and nation structure itself. For the appeal of totalitarianism comes partly from its indifference to these problems which had seemed so unyielding to solution. Today millions of classless, stateless people crowd the continent in hatred and despair—and in a way they are the end product of the futility and ruthlessness of the 1848 revolutions.

Bibliography

In the following bibliography, annotation is omitted for those titles which are self-explanatory, those which are described in the text, and those too well-known to require comment.

For a vantage point from which to compare twentieth-century ideas with nineteenth, I have found particularly valuable Karl Mannheim, *Man and Society in an Age of Reconstruction* (London, 1940), A. D. L. Lindsay, *Essentials of Democracy* (Philadelphia, 1929) and Jacques Barzun, *Romanticism and the Modern Ego* (Boston, 1943). Of course no one who studies revolutions should fail to consult Crane Brinton, *The Anatomy of Revolution* (New York, 1938).

Escape from Freedom, by Erich Fromm (New York, 1941) breaks ground in its analysis of the psychological sources of all modern history. Hannah Arendt, *The Origins of Totalitarianism* (New York, 1951) deals profoundly with the texture of social life in nineteenth- and twentieth-century Europe.

I · GENERAL

Works Dealing with Several of the 1848 Revolutions, or with Nineteenth-Century Thought

Actes du Congrès Historique du Centenaire de la Révolution de 1848. Paris, 1948. Introduction by R. Fawtier.

Carr, E. H. *The Romantic Exiles: a Nineteenth Century Portrait Gallery.* New York, 1933.

Corti, Count Egan. *The Reign of the House of Rothschild.* Tr. by Brian and Beatrix Lunn, London, 1928.

Fetjö, François, Ed. *Opening of an Era, 1848. An Historical Symposium.* London, 1949.

Fisher, H. A. L. *The Republican Tradition in Europe.* London, 1911.

Hyndman, H. M. *Commercial Crises of the Nineteenth Century.* London, 1892. Chapter 4 deals with crisis of 1847.

Kohn, Hans. "The End of 1848," *Current History*, May, 1949.

Namier, L. B. *1848: the Revolution of the Intellectuals.* New York, 1946. The author deals with all the revolutions, but he is most interested in, and most enlightening on the problem of Slavic nationalities.

Postgate, R. W. *Revolution from 1789 to 1906.* London, 1920. An invaluable collection of documents with notes and introductions, emphasizing always the proletarian revolt.

Rothfels, Hans. "1848: One Hundred Years After," jmh, xx, 1948.

Ruggiero, Guido de. *The History of European Liberalism.* Tr. by R. G. Collingwood. London, 1927. The philosophy of liberalism in different European countries in the Nineteenth Century.

Russell, Bertrand. *Freedom versus Organization. 1814-1914.* New York, 1934.

Weill, Georges, *L'éveil des nationalités et le mouvement libéral, 1815-1848.* Paris, 1930.

Whitridge, Arnold. *Men in Crisis.* New York, 1949.

Wilson, Edmund. *To the Finland Station.* New York, 1940. A history of nineteenth-century radical thought, starting with Michelet, and including a good deal about Marx and Engels.

Woodward, E. L. *Three Studies in European Convertatism: Metternich Guizot, the Catholic Church in the Nineteenth Century.* London, 1929.

The periodical *1848 et les révolutions du XIX siècle,* published by the Société d'Histoire de la Révolution de 1848, became in December 1950 *Révue des révolutions contemporaines.* Under both titles its files are invaluable for this period.

II · FRANCE

MEMOIRS OF PARTICIPANTS

Nearly everyone who took part in the revolution of 1848 either wrote a special book to defend his part, or described the revolution at length in his memoirs.

D'Alton-Shée, Comte Edmond. *Mes mémoires, 1826-1848.* Paris, 1869, 2 vol.

———. *Souvenirs de 1847 et de 1848.* Paris, 1879. D'Alton-Shée was a liberal peer who helped with the February banquet but for whom the revolution soon went too far.

Arago, François. "Autobiography" in *Biographies of Distinguished Scientific Men.* London, 1857. More about his scientific than his political career.

Barrot, Odilon. *Mémoires posthumes.* Paris, 1875, 4 vol. This conceited parlementarian includes a full though prejudiced account of the whole revolution.

Blanc, Louis. *1848: Historical Revelations.* London, 1858. In pretending to answer Lord Normanby's account (see below), Louis Blanc gives his own interpretation of what was done and what should have been done by the provisional government.

Caussidière, Marc. *Mémoires de M. Caussidière, ex-préfet de police et représentant du peuple.* Paris, 1849, 2 vol.

BIBLIOGRAPHY

Chénu, Adolphe. *Les conspirateurs. Les sociétés secrètes. La préfecture de police sous Caussidière.* Paris, 1850. Confessions of a police spy.

Delahodde, Lucien. *History of the Secret Societies and of the Republican Party of France from 1830 to 1848.* Philadelphia, 1856.

Du Camp, Maxime. *Souvenirs de l'année 1848.* Paris, 1876. Flaubert's friend, and a member of the national guard. Flaubert later put the experiences which they shared together into his novel, *Une éducation sentimentale.*

Dumas, Alexandre. *Révélations sur l'arrestation d'Emile Thomas.* Paris, 1848. Translated as an appendix in *The Last King* (London, 1915). Dumas was Thomas' most ardent defender.

Falloux du Coudray, F. A. P. Vicomte de. *Mémoires d'un royaliste.* Paris, 1888, 2 vol.

Girardin, Emile. *Journal d'un journaliste au secret.* Paris, 1848.

Herzen, Alexander. *Lettres de France et d'Italie, 1847-1852.* Translated by Mme. N. H. Geneva, 1871.

————. *My Past and Thoughts.* Translated by Constance Garnett. London, 1924-27, 6 vol. Herzen was one of the most intelligent and feeling men alive in 1848. His observations are always magnificant.

Hugo, Victor. *Choses Vues.* Paris, 1913. Hugo's diary was pungent. For his mature reaction to 1848, read *Les Misérables,* which has a chapter devoted to one of the 1848 barricades.

Lamartine, Alphonse de. *History of the French Revolution of 1848.* Translated by Francis Durivage and Wm. S. Chase. Boston, 1849. A gilded apology.

Lemoine, Edouard. *Abdication du roi Louis-Philippe recontée par lui-même.* Paris, 1851. Brief, sympathetic account of a conversation with the ex-King in England.

Normanby, C. H. P. Marquis of. *A Year of Revolution. From a Journal kept in Paris in 1848.* London, 1857. The British ambassador's view, to which Louis Blanc retorted. (See above.)

Persigny, Fialin, duc de. *Mémoires.* Paris, 1896. Louis Napoleon's campaign manager and friend.

Proudhon, P. J. *Les confessions d'un révolutionnaire, pour servir à l'histoire de la révolution de février.* Paris, 1851.

Sand, George. *Souvenirs de 1848.* Paris, 1882. Reflective rather than historical. Brief.

Senior, Nassau William. *Journals kept in France and Italy from 1848 to 1852.* London, 1871.

423

BIBLIOGRAPHY

Senior, Nassau William. *Conversations with Thiers, Guizot and other distinguished persons during the Second Empire.* London, 1878.

Thomas, Emile. *Histoire des ateliers nationaux.* Paris, 1848.

Tocqueville, Alexis de. *The Recollections of Alexis de Tocqueville.* Translated by A. de Mattos. London, 1896. Tocqueville took part in the revolution as a national guard and as a member of the Constitutional Assembly. Guizot said of him that he judged democracy as a vanquished aristocrat who realized his conquerors were right. Tocqueville wrote of the leaders of the revolution keenly but very harshly, yet he realized that the poor people in June were fighting for what they had been told was right.

Eyewitness Accounts

d'Alméras, Henri. *La vie parisienne sous la République de 1848.* Paris, n.d. Built around quotations from eyewitnesses, lively but incomplete.

Apponyi, Rudolf, graf. *Vingt-cinq ans à Paris, 1826-1852,* 4 vol. Paris, 1913-1926. Son of the Austrian ambassador.

Bonde, Florence. *Paris in '48: Letters from a Resident Describing the Events.* London, 1903. A foolish Irish girl. Useful only for recording the wild kind of anti-republican rumors that got started.

Bouteiller, Paul. *La Révolution Française de 1848 vue par les Hongrois.* Paris, 1949.

Cass, Lewis. *France: its King, Court and Government. By an American.* New York, 1840. Cass was American Minister to France from 1836-1840. This volume, written for Americans of 1840, emphasizes both Louis Philippe's court ceremonials and his American adventures.

Girardin, Delphine de. *Lettres parisiennes 1840-1848.* Vol. v of her *Oeuvres complètes,* Paris, 1860. The wife of the publisher of *La Presse,* a well-known poetess, contributed a newspaper column of Parisian comment.

Heine, Heinrich. *French Affairs. Letters from Paris.* Translated by Charles Godfrey Leland. London, 1893, 2 vol.

Ménard, Louis. "Prologue d'une révolution," reprinted in *Cahiers de la Quinzaine,* v. Paris, 1903-1904. Originally published in Paris in 1849, by one of the most bitter of the defeated side of the June 1848 insurrection.

Mitchell, D. G. *The Battle Summer: Being Transcripts from Personal Observation in Paris during the Year 1848. By I. K. Marvel.* New York, 1850.

Rush, Richard. *Occasional Productions . . . Including a Glance at the*

424

BIBLIOGRAPHY

Court and Government of Louis Philippe and the French Revolution of 1848, while the Author Resided as Minister from the United States at Paris. Philadelphia, 1860.

Vandam, Albert Dresden. *An Englishman in Paris.* New York, 1892. One of the most observant eyewitnesses.

THE REVOLUTIONARY PRESS

Dayot, A. P. M. *Journées révolutionnaires: 1830, 1848, d'après des peintures, sculptures, dessins, etc., du temps.* Paris, 1897. Poorly reproduced but interesting set of cartoons, lithographs, and portraits of the period.

Delmas, Gaëtan. *Curiosités révolutionnaires. Les journaux rouges: histoire critique de tous les journaux ultra-républicaines publiées à Paris depuis le 24 février jusqu'au 1ᵉʳ octobre 1848.* Paris, 1848. A catalogue for contemporary collectors.

Delvau, Alfred. *Les murailles révolutionnaires.* Paris, 1852. Elaborate, hand-tinted facsimiles of all the wall placards which adorned Paris during the first two months of the republic. Delvau seems never to have finished his job past that point.

Richomme, Charles. *Journées de l'insurrection de juin, 1848, par un garde national, précédées des murs de Paris, Journal de la rue, collection des principales affiches opposées de février a juin, 1848.* Paris, 1848.

Wallon, Henri. *La Presse de 1848, ou revue critique des journeaux publiés à Paris depuis la révolution de février jusqu'à la fin de décembre.* Paris, 1849. A reactionary editor lists all journals of the period named, classifying them as "socialist" (bad), or "political" (good). Essentially another catalogue.

HISTORIES WRITTEN BY CONTEMPORARIES

Marx, Karl. *The Class Struggles in France, 1848-1850.* New York, 1924. This is what Marx (or Engels) wrote for the *Neue Rheinische Zeitung* shortly after the events. The Marxian economic interpretation of history is here brilliantly applied for the first time, with strikingly original and sharp effect.

Stein, Lorenz von. *Geschichte der sozialen Bewegung in Frankreich von 1789 bis auf unsere Tage.* Leipzig, 1850, 3 vol. Stein analyzes revolutions in a way that almost does the work of both Marx and Crane Brinton. With the idea that freedom means the highest development of each person's personality, Stein shows how the social order prevents it.

Stern, Daniel. *Histoire de la révolution de 1848.* Paris, 2nd ed. 1862.

4 2 5

BIBLIOGRAPHY

2 vol. Daniel Stern was the pen name of the Comtesse d'Agoult, Liszt's mistress and the mother of Cosima Wagner. Her history of the revolution of 1848 is by far the best full account written by a contemporary. Later, during the Empire, she maintained the only republican salon in Paris.

CONTEMPORARY ESSAYS ON ECONOMICS AND POLITICS

Blanc, Louis. *The History of Ten Years, 1830-1840*. Translated by Walter Kelly. Philadelphia, 1848. Louis Blanc's indictment of the bourgeois civilization of Louis Philippe's France was important in rousing different ideals. The French edition, of course, was published in 1840.

————. *The Organization of Work*. Translated by M. P. Dickoré. Cincinnati, 1911. A translation of the first edition. Blanc wrote many versions of his famous pamphlet.

Blanqui, Jerome Adolphe. *Des Classes ouvrières en 1848*. Paris, 1849. This Blanqui, the revolutionist's brother, was sent by the Academy to study labor conditions at the end of 1848. Though he ridiculed the socialist solution, he showed up and condemned the misery of working class housing, child labor, unemployment, and the results of low wages.

Boncour, P. *Lamennais*. Paris, 1928. A collection of quotations from the unfrocked priest whose poetical, early Christian version of Christianity had tremendous effect in Europe just before 1848.

Corbon, Anthyme, *Le secret du peuple de Paris*. Paris, 1863. Corbon, one of the worker members of the Constitutional Assembly, describes his fellow workers in a vivid, almost Freudian way. His thesis is that moralists and educators never get very far in improving the people because they do not touch their passions. Under the prevailing social conditions, workers did not have scope to use their passions and abilities, and repression of these passions upset their whole personalities. Corbon had a vision beyond his age.

Guizot, F. P. G. *Democracy in France*. New York, 1849. From exile Guizot urged France to return to the family, religion, the class system, lest democracy lead the nation into anarchy.

Michelet, Jules. *Le Peuple*. Paris, 1865. Originally written in 1846, when Michelet still adored the people.

MODERN HISTORICAL STUDIES CONCERNING MEMBERS OF THE PROVISIONAL GOVERNMENT

Cahen, Georges. "Louis Blanc et la Commission du Luxembourg," *Annales de l'Ecole Libre des Sciences Politiques*, Volume XII, Paris, 1897.

BIBLIOGRAPHY

Calman, Alvin R. *Ledru-Rollin and the Second French Republic*. New York, 1922.

Cherest, Aimé. *La vie et les œuvres de A. T. Marie*. Paris, 1873. A favorable biography. Includes Marie's notes.

Droz, Heinrich A. *Lamartine und die Revolution von 1848*. Zurich, 1919. Anti-Lamartine. Compares what really happened in the first few days of February revolution with Lamartine's official account of them. A pedantic study.

Guillemin, Henri. *Lamartine, l'homme et l'œuvre*. Paris, 1940. Interesting and modern, not exhaustive.

Ibos, General P. E. M. *Le général Cavaignac, un dictateur républicain*. Paris, 1930. The military author sees nothing unfavorable in his military subject.

Keller, Paul. *Louis Blanc und die Revolution von 1848*. Zurich, 1926.

Whitehouse, R. H. *Life of Lamartine*. London, 1918, 2 vol. Reviewed by J. S. Schapiro in the *Political Science Quarterly*, Vol. 34, as "a study of the poetic temperament in politics." With British reserve, Whitehouse lays out the course of Lamartine's psychological development.

MODERN STUDIES ON BARBÈS AND BLANQUI

None of these materials are adequate, and it is difficult to find out answers to even simple questions in any available sources.

Dommanget, V. M. *Blanqui*. Librarie de l'humanité, Paris, 1924.

———. *Blanqui à Belle-Ile*. Paris, 1935. After 1848 Belle-Ile was Blanqui's prison, where he carried on political conversations and correspondence. His life at this time is better documented than during the revolution.

Jeanjean, J. F. *Armand Barbès: 1809-1870*. Paris, 1909. Volume I of this work goes through April 1848. I was unable to locate Volume II, if it was ever printed, in this country.

Stewart, Neil. *Blanqui*. London, 1939. Elementary communist propaganda.

Wassermann, Suzanne. *Les Clubs de Barbès et de Blanqui en 1848*. Paris, 1913. A useful, day-by-day account of these clubs.

MODERN STUDIES WHICH DEAL WITH LOUIS NAPOLEON DURING THE PERIOD OF THE SECOND REPUBLIC

Boon, Hendrik N. *Rêve et réalité dans l'œuvre économique et sociale de Napoleon III*. The Hague, 1936.

Cheetham, F. H. *Louis Napoleon and the Genesis of the Second Empire*. New York, 1909.

BIBLIOGRAPHY

Guedalla, Philip. *The Second Empire: Bonapartism, the Prince, the President, the Emperor.* New York, 1922. An unconvincing job of debunking. Guedalla attributes Napoleon's success to the ineptness of his opponents, or to historic irony, and makes it thereby inconsequential.

Guérard, Albert. *Napoleon III.* Cambridge, Mass., 1943. An interesting, up-to-date, sympathetic account. The author believes Napoleon was the one ruler of his age who built for the twentieth century.

Lebey, André. *Louis-Napoléon Bonaparte et la Révolution de 1848.* Paris, 1907-1908. 2 vol. Long-winded.

Robert-Pimienta, Robert. *La propagande bonapartiste en 1848.* Paris, 1911.

Simpson, F. A. *Louis Napoleon and the Recovery of France, 1848-1856.* New York, 1923.

————. *The Rise of Louis Napoleon.* New York, 2nd ed., 1925. Simpson's biography, though eulogistic, is both extraordinarily interesting and extraordinarily convincing.

MODERN STUDIES OF MISCELLANEOUS PEOPLE CONCERNED WITH THE FRENCH REVOLUTION OF 1848

Allison, J. M. S. *Thiers and the French Monarchy.* Boston, 1926.

Charpentier, John. *George Sand.* Paris, 1936.

Grant, Elliott M. *Victor Hugo during the Second Republic.* Northampton, N.Y., 1935.

Josephson, Matthew. *Victor Hugo.* Garden City, N.Y., 1942.

Monin, Georges. "George Sand et la république de février, 1848," *Révolution française,* Vol. 37, 1899.

Monod, V. Marie-Octave. *Daniel Stern.* Paris, 1937. A fine life of Marie d'Agoult, the historian of 1848, whose personal story was not only highly dramatic but full of social implications.

Puech, J. L. *La vie et l'œuvre de Flora Tristan.* Paris, 1925. Flora Tristan was a French feminist and socialist who died in 1844 on a trip around France to teach the workers their rights. Her life, involving a trip to Peru, a husband who shot at her and kidnapped their children, is dramatic enough for a movie. Its value for a study of 1848 lies in its connection with working conditions and early socialist thought.

Reclus, M. Maurice. *Emile de Girardin.* Paris, 1934. Highly entertaining.

Zévaès, A. B. *La chute de Louis-Philippe.* Paris, 1930. A good example of the popular, vivid histories which have been written recently in France for popular consumption. This one is full of detail, but lacks a bibliography.

BIBLIOGRAPHY

Modern Histories and Monographs on 1848 in France

Benoist, Charles. "L'Homme de 1848," *Revue des deux mondes*, 1913.

Cassou, Jean. *Quarante-huit*. Paris, 1939. A thoughtful critique of the soul of 1848, the end of romanticism, the squalor and hope of the workers, the fear and indifference of the bourgeoisie.

Crémieux, Albert. *La Révolution de février*. Paris, 1912. A standard monograph on the February days which manages to be charming. It uses eye-witness accounts only. Its thesis is that the revolution was carried through by the working classes, not the so-called leaders.

Duchon, Paul. "Les élections de 1848," *Revue de Paris*, 1936.

France Illustration. May 1, 1948. A special centenary number of this famous magazine, devoted to a review of the year 1848.

McKay, Donald Cope. *The National Workshops: a study in the French Revolution of 1848*. Cambridge, Mass., 1933.

Renard, Georges. *La République de 1848*. Vol. ix of *Histoire socialiste*, Paris, 1905.

Schmidt, Charles. *Les journées de juin, 1848*. Paris, 1926. Popular and none too accurate.

Modern Material Not Specifically About 1848
but Useful as Background

Clapham, J. H. *Economic Development of France and Germany, 1815-1914*. 2nd ed., Cambridge, 1923.

Cuvillier, M.-A. *Un journal d'ouvriers: l'Atelier, 1840-1850*. Paris, 1914.

Dickinson, G. Lowes. *Revolution and Reaction in Modern France*. London, 1892. A fine little book, covering the period 1789 through 1871.

Elton, Godfrey. *The Revolutionary Idea in France, 1789-1871*. 2nd ed., London, 1931. Anti-Marxian.

Gray, Alexander. *The Socialist Tradition*. London, 1946. Contains chapters on Blanc and Proudhon, and their forerunners, Saint-Simon and Fourier.

Louis, Paul. *Histoire de la classe ouvrière*. Paris, 1927. Full of statistics.

Maigron, M. *Le romantisme et les moeurs*. Paris, 1910. The writer believes that the drenching of life with romance in the 1820's and 1830's led to a general falsity in social relationships, evidenced by the prevalence of suicide and adultery, as well as a general incapacity on the part of individuals to face life.

BIBLIOGRAPHY

Michel, H. *L'Idée de l'état: essai sur l'histoire des théories sociales et politiques en France depuis la Révolution.* Paris, 1896. Including essays on Blanc, Lamartine, Proudhon.

Soltau, Roger. *French Political Thought in the Nineteenth Century.* New Haven, 1932.

Weill, G. *Histoire du parti républicain en France de 1814 à 1870.* Revised edition, Paris, 1928. An admirable survey.

III · GERMANY

Source Books

Klein, Tim. *1848, der Vorkampf deutscher Einheit.* Leipzig, 1914. Dr. Klein, sure that 1848 was a struggle for unity, not, as the Weimar historians would have it, for freedom, made a compilation of all sorts of documents, excerpts of published accounts, philosophical explanation—telling a complete story of 1848 in the words of those who lived through it.

Legge, J. G. *Rhyme and Revolution in Germany. A Study in German History, Life, Literature and Character: 1813-1850.* London, 1918. Legge took over Klein's work, not exactly verbatim, and with a very different set of comments, tending to show that Germany had always been hopelessly nationalistic, ruthless, and power-mad. Not trustworthy as history, but has sources hard to find elsewhere.

Memoirs and Letters, Having to Do with the Court Circle Around Frederick William IV

Bailleu, P. and G. Schuster. *Correspondence of Empress Augusta.* Berlin, 1912. Volume I contains her letters written during 1848 as Princess of Prussia.

Bunsen, Frances. *A Memoir of Baron Bunsen.* London, 1868, 2 vol. More personal than political. Bunsen was the Prussian representative in London, besides being Frederick William's only liberal friend.

Frederick William IV. *Briefwechsel zwischen König Friedrich Wilhelm IV und dem Reichsverweser Erzherzog Johann von Osterreich.* Frankfort, 1924.

———. *Briefwechsel mit L. Camphausen.* Ed. by Brandenburg. Berlin, 1906.

Gerlach, Leopold von. *Denkwürdigkeiten.* Berlin, 1891, 2 vol. Gerlach was one of the King's most conservative friends. His day by day accounts of conversations at court tell a good deal about court feeling.

BIBLIOGRAPHY

Radowitz, Josef von. *Nachgelassene Briefe und Aufzeichnungen zur Geschichte der Jahre 1848-1853*. Ed. by Walter Möring, Berlin and Stuttgart, 1922.

MISCELLANEOUS MEMOIRS AND LETTERS

Bamberger, Ludwig. *Politische Schriften von 1848-68*. Berlin, 1895.

Bergsträsser, Ludwig, ed. *Das Frankfurter Parlament in Briefen und Tagebüchern*. Frankfurt, 1929. Chiefly valuable for a complete set of Blum's letters to his family from the Frankfurt Assembly. Contains letters from some others too.

Born, Stephan. *Erinnerungen eines Achtundvierzigers*. Leipzig, 1898.

Corvin, Otto von. *A Life of Adventure*. London, 1871. Corvin's life was highly romantic, and his account of it most entertaining. He was in Paris in February, joined the German Legion there, fought in Baden and commanded at the siege of Rastatt, for which he was imprisoned. His book is valuable not only for his revolutionary exploits but for its description of Germany in the period leading up to 1848.

Hohenlohe-Ingelfingen, Kraft. *Aus meinem Leben*. Berlin, 1897, 4 vol. The observations of a straitlaced soldier.

Schurz, Carl. *Reminiscences*. New York, 1907. Schurz was not yet twenty when the revolution broke. His adventures show how romantic life could be for young Germany.

Siemens, Werner. *Personal Recollections*. New York, 1893. One of the inventors of the electric telegraph tells a little about 1848.

Unruh, Hans Viktor von. *Erinnerungen aus dem Leben von H. V. v. Unruh*. Ed. H. v. Poschinger, 1895. The President of the Prussian National Assembly.

Wagner, Richard, *My Life*. New York, 1911. 2 vol.

EYEWITNESS ACCOUNTS OF THE REVOLUTION IN PRUSSIA

Angerstein, Wilhelm. *Seit 1848: Beiträge zur preussischen Geschichte*. Vol. I, *Die Berliner Märzereignisse in Jahre 1848*. Leipzig, 1864.

Boerner, Paul. *Erinnerungen eines Revolutionärs: Skizzen aus dem Jahre 1848*. 1920, 2 vol.

Busch, Wilhelm. *Die Berliner Märztage von 1848*. München, Oldenbourg, 1899.

Circourt, Adolphe de. *Souvenirs d'une mission à Berlin en 1848*. Paris, 1908. A conservative but observant friend of Lamartine, sent to Berlin to keep peace between France and Germany.

Donelson, Andrew Jackson. "The American Minister in Berlin on the Revolution of March, 1848." AHR, Vol. 23, 1918.

BIBLIOGRAPHY

Gneist, Rudolf. *Berliner Zustände: Politische Skizzen aus der Zeit vom 18 März 1848 bis 18 März 1849*. Berlin, 1849. Tells of working classes.

Perthes, Otto. "Beiträge zur Geschichte der Märztage 1848." In *Preussische Jahrbücher*, Berlin, June 1889.

Springer, R. *Berlins Strassen, Kneipen und Klubs im Jahre 1848*. Berlin, 1850. Very interesting.

Vitzthum von Eckstadt, E. K. *Berlin und Wien in den Jahren 1845-1852*. Stuttgart, 1886. A young, well-connected Saxon diplomat, who describes Berlin before the revolution, Vienna during it.

THE BADEN REVOLUTIONISTS

Hecker, Friedrich. *Die Erhebung des Volkes in Baden für die deutsche Republik in Frühjahr 1848*. Basel, 1848.

Herwegh, Emma. *Zur Geschichte der deutschen demokratischen Legion aus Paris*. Grünberg, 1849.

Mieroslawski, General Ludwig. *Berichte . . . über den Feldzug in Baden*. Bern, 1849.

Struve, Amalie. *Erinnerungen aus den badischen Freiheitskämpfen*. Hamburg, 1850.

Struve, Gustav. *Geschichte der drei Völkershebungen in Baden*. Bern, 1849.

HISTORY AS WRITTEN BY CONTEMPORARIES

Becker, Bernhard. *Die Reaktion in Deutschland gegen die Revolution von 1848*. Vienna, 1869. An early but very clever study of the maneuvers of the reaction.

Engels, Friedrich. *Germany: Revolution and Counter-revolution*. New York, 1933. The material Engels wrote for the New York *Tribune* in 1851. Appendix contains a history of the Communist League. Engels has a wonderfully clear point of view and fine style.

Heller, Robert. *Brustbilder aus der Paulskirche*. Leipzig, 1849. Dull.

Laube, Heinrich. *Das erste deutsche Parlament*. Leipzig, 1849, 3 vol. An orderly history with many quotations from speeches, and some color.

POLITICAL PAMPHLETS AND SPEECHES SHOWING THE SPIRIT OF THE AGE

Arnim, Bettina von. *Dies Buch gehört dem König*. 2nd ed. Berlin, 1852. The author, who had fallen in love with the aged Goethe as a young girl and made herself famous by publishing his letters, by 1848 was the *enfant terrible* of Berlin society. She wrote this book before 1848, to explain to the King how the other half of his people lived, and had to spend a short while in prison because it was not properly censored.

Petzet, W. and O. E. Sutter. *Der Geist der Paulskirche. Aus den Reden der Nationalversammlung.* Frankfurt, 1923. Speeches of the Frankfurt Assembly, edited with a view to justifying the Weimar Republic and the eternal German love of freedom.

Radowitz, J. M. von. *Deutschland und Friedrich Wilhelm IV.* 2nd ed. Hamburg, 1848. This pamphlet appeared anonymously, and was influential in turning Germans to the idea of the King of Prussia as their natural leader.

Vermeil, Edmond. *Henri Heine, ses vues sur l'Allemagne et les révolutions européennes.* Paris, 1939. Second half is made up of quotations from Heine, who hated the romantic sickness of Germany and is made out as foreseeing Nazism.

Wagner, Richard. *L'Art et la révolution.* Brussels, 1898. Written in July 1849, from Switzerland, hot from Wagner's part in the revolution.

MODERN HISTORIES OF THE GERMAN REVOLUTION

Blum, Hans. *Die deutsche Revolution, 1848-49. Eine Jubiläumsgabe für das deutsche Volk.* Leipzig, 1897. The son of Robert Blum, no revolutionary himself, wrote a huge volume, full of pictures, portraits, caricatures, facsimiles of proclamations as well as narrative.

Brandenburg, E. *Die deutsche Revolution 1848.* Leipzig, 1919. First-class little narrative.

Dahlinger, Charles W. *The German Revolution of 1849.* New York, 1903. The third Baden uprising.

Ellis, William Ashton. *1849.* London, 1892. The Saxon revolution.

Fiedler, Fritz. *Die Berliner Märzrevolution 1848 und die Belagerung von Paris 1870-71.* Jena, 1926. A critique of Hohenlohe's reporting.

Hohlfeld, Johannes. *Die deutsche Revolution 1848-49.* Leipzig, 1948.

Lüders, Gustav. *Die demokratische Bewegung in Berlin im oktober 1848.* Berlin, 1909.

Matter, P. *La Prusse et la révolution de 1848.* Paris, 1903.

Mommsen, Wilhelm. *Grösse und Versagen des Deutschen Bürgertums. Ein Beitrag zur Geschichte der Jahre 1848-1849.* Stuttgart, 1949. One of the books unpublishable under Hitler. Mommsen gives enough quotations to show all points of view, but his own judgments are discriminating. A fine book.

Pascal, Roy. "The Frankfurt Parliament, 1848, and the Drang Nach Osten," JMH, June 1846.

Quarck, Max. *Die erste deutsche Arbeiterbewegung; Geschichte der Arbeiterverbrüderung 1848-49.* Leipzig, 1924.

BIBLIOGRAPHY

Rachfahl, Felix. *Deutschland, König Friedrich Wilhelm IV und die Berliner Märzrevolution.* Halle, 1901. A refutation of Sybel and Perthes.

Valentin, Veit. *1848.* New York, 1940. A translation of excerpts from his long German history of 1848, not remarkably enlightening to an American reader.

————. *Geschichte der deutschen Revolution 1848-49.* Berlin, 1930, 2 vol. The most complete, standard study.

MODERN BIOGRAPHICAL STUDIES OF MEN IMPORTANT IN 1848

Carr, E. H. *Michael Bakunin.* London, 1937. An admirably written study—all that a biography should be.

Caspary, Anna. *Ludolf Camphausens Leben.* Stuttgart, 1902. Overly personal, dull, unimportant.

De la Faverie, Schalck. "Robert Blum," *La Révolution de 1848.* Vol. XVI, 1919-1920. Straightforward account of Blum's life.

Fleury, Victor. *Le poète Georges Herwegh.* Paris, 1911. Unenlightening.

Freytag, Gustav, *Karl Mathy: Geschichte seines Lebens.* Leipzig, 1870. Mathy was the leader of the Baden moderates.

Friedensburg, Wilhelm. *Stephan Born und die Organisationsbestrebungen der Berliner Arbeiterschaft, 1840-Sept. 1848.* Leipzig, 1923.

Geiger, Ludwig. *Bettina von Arnim und Friedrich Wilhelm IV.* Frankfurt, 1902.

Kohn, Hans. "Arndt and German Nationalism," AHR, July, 1949.

Lenz, Max. "Bismarcks Plan einer Gegenrevolution im März 1848." *Sitzungsberichte der preussischen Akademie der Wissenschaften,* Berlin, 1930.

Lewalter, Ernst. *Friedrich Wilhelm: das Schicksal eines Geistes.* Berlin, 1938. An interesting study of the King of Prussia's education and character.

Meinecke, Friedrich. *Radowitz und die deutsche Revolution.* Berlin, 1913.

Newman, Ernest. *The Life of Richard Wagner.* New York. Volume II, from 1848-1860, came out in 1937.

Studt, Bernhard. *Bismarck als Mitarbeiter der "Kreuzzeitung" in den Jahren 1848 und 1849.* Blankenese, 1903. Largely a collection of Bismarck's opinions, as he expressed them in his paper. A running and vivid commentary.

Wentzcke, Paul. "Zur Geschichte Heinrich von Gagerns. Seine Burschenschafterzeit und seine deutsche Politik," *Quellen und Darstel-*

lungen zur Geschichte der Burschenschaft und der deutschen Einheitsbewegung. Vol. I, Heidelberg, 1910.

Wyndham, Horace. *The Magnificent Montez.* London, 1935. One example of the inaccurate and sensational literature which is all that Lola Montez has ever had devoted to her.

STUDIES OF MARX

Barzun, Jacques. *Darwin, Marx, Wagner: Critique of a Heritage.* Boston, 1941. A savage attack on the characters, originality and philosophical influence of these three.

Bloom, Solomon. *The World of Nations.* New York, 1940. Bloom concludes that Marx was not a nationalist, though he made some nationalistic statements.

Mayer, Gustav. *Friedrich Engels . . . a Biography.* New York, 1936.

MODERN WORKS OF MORE GENERAL HISTORY WHICH TOUCH ON 1848 IN GERMANY

Gazley, J. G. *American Opinion of German Unification.* New York, 1926.

Hayes, C. J. H. *The Historical Evolution of Modern Nationalism.* New York, 1931.

Meinecke, Friedrich. *Weltbürgertum und Nationalstaat. Studien zur Genesis des deutschen Nationalstaates.* München and Berlin, 1908.

Sybel, Heinrich von. *The Founding of the German Empire by William I.* New York, 1890.

Taylor, A. J. P. *The Course of German History. A Survey of the Development of Germany since 1815.* New York, 1946. This, though brilliant, shows touches of the anti-German fever that besets British scholars during every war. It is particularly interesting on the relations between Germans and Slavs.

Treitschke, H. von. *History of Germany in the Nineteenth Century, 1815-1848.* Tr. by Eden and Cedar Paul. New York, 1915-19. 7 vol. Offensive in its nationalism, anti-Semitism, anti-liberalism, but undeniably interesting.

Ward, Sir A. W. *Germany, 1815-1890.* Cambridge, England, 1918, 3 vol.

IV · AUSTRIA

MATERIAL BY CONTEMPORARIES

Andrian-Werburg, Victor. *De l'Autriche et de son avenir.* Paris, 1843. One of the books, printed abroad and smuggled widely into Austria, which did the most to show up the bad system of government.

BIBLIOGRAPHY

Auerbach, Berthold. *A Narrative of Events in Vienna from Latour to Windischgrätz.* Tr. by Taylor, London, 1849. The author, who was to become a distinguished writer, went to Vienna to observe events and wrote a day-by-day account.

Frankl, Ludwig August. *Erinnerungen.* Ed. Stefan Hock, Prague, 1910. Not valuable, except for interesting bits about the Reading Club.

Füster, Anton. *Memorien vom März 1848 bis Juli 1849.* Frankfurt, 1850. 2 vol. The chaplain of the Academic Legion.

Hartig, Count Franz de Paula von. *Genesis: or Details of the Late Austrian Revolution, by an Officer of State.* London, 1853. Interesting analysis of how the Austrian machine ran. From a conservative official.

Helfert, J. A. von. *Die Wiener Journalistik im Jahre 1848.* Vienna, 1877.

———. *Der Wiener Parnass im Jahre 1848.* Vienna, 1882. These two books quote extensively from the daily press of 1848 in Vienna. The second gives a poem for every day of the year.

Hübner, Count Joseph Alexander von. *Une année de ma vie.* Paris, 1891. A gay young Austrian diplomat, lively, intelligent, but not critical.

Hügel, Baron Carl von. "Story of the Escape of Prince Metternich." Volume I of *National Review,* London, 1883.

Kudlich, Hans. *Rückblicke und Erinnerungen.* Vienna, 1873.

Pichler, Adolf. *Aus den März-und-Oktobertagen zu Wien.* Innsbruck, 1850.

Pillersdorf, Baron Franz von. *Austria in 1848 and 1849.* London, 1850. The first liberal minister's indictment of his predecessors and successors is so vague it is hard to figure out what he means.

Schütte, Anton. *Die Wiener Oktober-Revolution. Aus dem Tagebuche des Dr. Schütte.* Prague, 1848.

Schuselka, Franz. *Das Revolutionsjahr März 1848-März 1849.* Vienna, 1850. Relatively uninformative.

Stiles, William H. *Austria in 1848-49.* New York, 1852. 2 vol. The American Chargé d'Affaires at Vienna wrote the longest and most careful contemporary history. He covers the whole empire, Hungary and Lombardy as well as Vienna. Honest, careful, impartial.

Wiesner, Adolph. *Denkwürdigkeiten der österreichischen Zensur.* Stuttgart, 1847. Wiesner was thrown into prison with thieves on account of dramatic works criticizing Austrian policy. This is an appeal for better conditions.

See also the work by Vitzthum, listed under Prussia.

BIBLIOGRAPHY

WORKS BY MODERN HISTORIANS CONCERNING THE AUSTRIAN
REVOLUTION AND ITS PERSONAGES

Bibl, Viktor. *Metternich, der Dämon Österreichs*. Leipzig, 1936.

————. *Die Niederösterreichischen Stände im Vormärz*. Vienna, 1911.

Blum, Jerome. *Noble Landowners and Agriculture in Austria, 1815-1848: A Study in the Origins of the Peasant Emancipation of 1848*. Baltimore, 1948.

————. "Transportation and Industry in Austria, 1815-1848," JMH, March, 1943.

Brügel, Ludwig. *Geschichte der Oesterreichischen Sozialdemokratie*. Vienna, 1922. Tedious compilation of sources without generalization.

Cecil, Algernon. *Metternich, 1773-1859: a Study of his Period and Personality*. New York, 1933. Admiring.

Charmatz, R. *Adolf Fischhof*. Stuttgart and Berlin, 1910.

de Coudray, Helene. *Metternich*. London, 1935.

Friedjung, H. *Oesterreich von 1848 bis 1860*. Stuttgart and Berlin, 1908-1912. A standard work. Pro-Austrian, anti-Hungarian.

Goldmark, Josephine. *Pilgrims of '48: One Man's Part in the Austrian Revolution of 1848 and a Family Migration to America*. New Haven, 1930. Charming and scholarly account of the author's grandfather's part in the revolution.

Heller, Eduard. *Mitteleuropa's Vorkämpfer: Fürst Felix zu Schwarzenberg*. Vienna, 1933. Defends Schwarzenberg's policy as one that might reasonably have saved Central Europe in 1918.

Jászi, Oscar. *The Dissolution of the Hapsburg Monarchy*. Chicago, 1929.

Kann, Robert A. *The Multinational Empire: Nationalism and Reform in the Hapsburg Monarchy, 1848-1918*. New York, 1950.

Kriebel, Hermann. *Feldmarschall Fürst Windisch-Graetz, 1787-1862*. Vienna, 1929: A pamphlet issued by the Windischgrätz family.

Maurice, C. E. *The Revolutionary Movement of 1848-1849 in Italy, Austria-Hungary and Germany*. London, 1887. Stuffy and often inaccurate about details. But one of the first books to give the Slav problem prominence.

Mayr, Josef Karl. *Metternichs geheimer Briefdienst; Postlagen und Postkurse*. Vienna, 1935.

Molisch, Paul. "Die Wiener Akademische Legion und ihr Anteil an den Verfassungskämpfen des Jahres 1848," *Archiv für österreichische Geschichte*. 1924.

Oberhummer, Hermann. *Die Wienerpolizei im Revolutionsjahr 1848*, Vienna, 1928.

BIBLIOGRAPHY

Presland, John. *Vae Victis. The Life of Ludwig von Benedek.* London, 1934. An excellent biography. Even though General Benedek's chief fame came in 1866, this life is so careful and so understanding that it throws a great deal of light on the 1848 period, as indeed on every point that it touches.

Redlich, Joseph. *Emperor Francis Joseph of Austria.* New York, 1929. Translation from a great Austrian historian.

————. *Das æsterreichische Staats- und Reichsproblem.* Leipzig, 1920-1926.

Schwarzenberg, Adolph. *Prince Felix zu Schwarzenberg, Prime Minister of Austria, 1848-1852.* New York, 1926.

Taylor, A. J. P. *The Hapsburg Monarchy.* London, 1941.

Zenker, E. V. *Die Wiener Revolution 1848 in ihren sozialen Voraussetzungen und Beziehungen.* Vienna, 1897. Fine study of workers, peasants, and the social aspects of the Vienna revolution. Objective and sympathetic.

V · HUNGARY

Social Conditions in Hungary as Seen by Contemporaries

Eötvös, Baron Jozsef. *The Village Notary.* Tr. by Otto Wenckstern, London, 1850. A novel intended to expose the evils of local government to Hungarians.

Metternich-Winneburg, Prince C. L. W. *Aphoristische Bemerkungen über die ungarischen Zustände zu Ende des Jahres 1844, mitgetheilt vom Fürsten Metternich.* (n.p., n.d.)

Paget, John. *Hungary and Transylvania, with remarks on their Condition, Social, Political and Economical.* London, 1839. Descriptions of every phase of life seen by a traveler, adorned with delightful sketches.

Quin, Michael J. *A Steam Voyage down the Danube.* Paris, 1836.

Smith, J. Toulmin. *Parallels between the Constitution and Constitutional History of England and Hungary.* Boston, 1850.

Tkalac, E. I. von. *Jugenderinnerungen aus Kroatien.* Leipzig, 1894.

The Hungarian War as Told at the Time

Beck, Baroness Wilhelmine von. *Personal Adventures during the Late War of Independence in Hungary.* London, 1850. Adventures of a spy on the Hungarian side who impersonated a baroness but was exposed as a lady's maid.

Brace, Charles Loring. *Hungary in 1851.* New York, 1852. The first

BIBLIOGRAPHY

American allowed in Hungary after the war, who went to study
the condition of the lower classes, was imprisoned for his curiosity.

Chasles, Philarète. *Scènes des camps et bivouacs hongrois, 1848-1849.*
Paris, 1879. An imaginary but graphic account of an officer under
Jellačič, and his female aide-de-camp.

*Correspondence relative to the Affairs of Hungary 1847-1849. Pre-
sented to both Houses of Parliament by order of Her Majesty.*
The British ambassador at Vienna was unfavorable to Hungary,
and besides could get little news from behind the lines. Contains
important proclamations and speeches otherwise unavailable in
English.

*Correspondence respecting the Refugees from Hungary within the
Turkish Dominions.* London, 1851.

Czetz, Johann. *Bem's Feldzug in Siebenbürgen.* Hamburg, 1850.

Görgei, Arthur. *My Life and Acts in Hungary in the Years 1848-1849.*
London, 1852. 2 vol.

Iranyi, Daniel, and Charles-Louis Chassin. *Histoire politique de la
révolution de Hongroie, 1847-1849.* Paris, 1859. Iranyi was a
Hungarian revolutionary. This 2-volume work the best near-
contemporary history.

Klapka, George. *Memoirs of the War of Independence in Hungary.*
London, 1850.

Kmety, George. *A Refutation of some of the Principal Misstatements
in Görgei's "Life and Actions in Hungary in the Years 1848-
1849."* London.

Kossuth, Ludwig. *Die Katastrophe in Ungarn.* Leipzig, 1849. Kossuth's
first, angry, reaction, just after his arrival in Turkey.

Leiningen-Westerburg, Charles. *The Letters and Journal (1848-1849)
of Count Charles Leiningen-Westerburg, General in the Hungarian Army.* Ed. by Henry Marczali, London, 1911.

Pridham, Charles. *Kossuth and Magyar Land; or, Personal Adventures
during the War in Hungary.* London, 1851. This *Times* correspondent took so long getting to Hungary that the war was over
before his arrival.

Pulszky, Franz. *Meine Zeit, mein Leben.* Pressburg, 1881. The Hungarian envoy to London. Knew all the important Hungarians and
was present at many historic conversations, all faithfully recorded.

Pulszky, Trezsi. *Memoirs of a Hungarian Lady.* London, 1850. A
charming story of life on the Pulszky estate in Hungary, and of
the part of the author's husband in the war.

BIBLIOGRAPHY

Scenes of the Civil War in Hungary in 1848 and 1849 with the Personal Adventures of an Austrian Officer. Philadelphia, 1850.

Schlesinger, Max. *The War in Hungary, 1848-1849.* Translated by John Edward Taylor. London, 1850. Colorful and fervidly pro-Hungarian.

Schütte, Dr. Anton. *Ungarn und der ungarische Unabhängigkeitskrieg.* Dresden, 1850. 2 vol. Lively and interesting. More scholarly than Schlesinger.

Szemere, Bartholemew. *Hungary from 1848-1860.* London, 1860. Letters to Cobden about Hungary's rebirth, by the ex-leader of the pure republicans in 1848.

Teleki, Ladislas. *De l'Intervention russe.* Paris, 1849.

Ujhazy, Ladislaus. *A Brief Explanatory Report as to the Termination of the Hungarian Struggle.* New York, 1850.

Wiesner, A. C. *Ungarns Fall und Görgey's Verrath.* Zurich, 1849.

MODERN WORKS BEARING ON THE HUNGARIAN REVOLUTION

Angyal, D. "Le comte Etienne Széchenyi," *Revue des études hongroises et finno-ougriennes.* Vol. VI, 1926.

Hartley, M. *The Man Who Saved Austria. The Life and Times of Baron Jellačič.* London, 1912. Favorable, written to please the Jellačič family. Worse than that, unperceptive.

Knatchball-Hugessen, C. M., Lord Brabourne. *The Political Evolution of the Hungarian Nation.* London, 1908. 2 vol. Documented history of the Hungarian constitution.

Jánossy, Dionys V. "Die russische Intervention in Ungarn im Jahre 1849," *Jahrbuch des Wiener ungarischen historischen Instituts.* Budapest, 1931.

Kerchnawe, Hugo. *Feldmarschall Fürst Windisch-Grätz und die Russenhilfe, 1848.* Innsbruck, 1930. The Prince's grandson is eager to prove that the Fieldmarshal was not instrumental in calling for Russian aid.

Schiemann, Theodor. *Geschichte Russlands unter Kaiser Nikolaus I.* Berlin, 1909-1919. 4 vol.

Sproxton, Charles. *Palmerston and the Hungarian Revolution.* Cambridge, England, 1919.

Zarek, Otto. *Kossuth.* Translated by Lynton Hudson. London, 1937. Strongly prejudiced in Kossuth's favor.

VI · ITALY

MEMOIRS AND ACCOUNTS WRITTEN BY CONTEMPORARIES

d'Azeglio, Constance. *Souvenirs historiques.* Turin, 1884.

d'Azeglio, Massimo. *Austrian Assassinations in Lombardy*. London, 1848.

————. *L'Italie de 1847 à 1865: correspondence politique*. Paris, 1867.

————. *Recollections*. Translated by Count Maffei. London, 1868. These recollections unfortunately go up only to 1846.

Cattaneo, Carlo. *L'Insurrection de Milan en 1848*. Paris, 1848.

Colomb, P. H. *Memoires of Admiral the right honorable Sir Astley Cooper Key*. London, 1898. Key was in charge of a British warship at Cività Vecchia during the siege of Rome.

Correspondence respecting the Affairs of Italy. British Parliamentary papers, including the communications between the Foreign Office and the consuls and British diplomats in Italy. Four volumes cover the period from 1846 to March 1849, and there is a separate volume for the *Affairs of Rome*.

Dandolo, Emilio. *The Italian Volunteers and the Lombard Rifle Brigade*. London, 1851.

Eliot, Frances. *Roman Gossip*. London, 1896. A British lady, the daughter of Lord Minto, tells many good anecdotes and gives a colorful picture of what Rome looked like.

Ellesmere, Francis Egerton Lord (translator). *Military Events in Italy, 1848-1849*. London, 1851. Translated from the German of a Swiss mercenary, William Meyer Ott. Ott was careless of political fact, but gave good views of military life. He was strongly pro-Austria and pro-Pope, although Ellesmere disclaims bias on his part.

Farini, Luigi Carlo. *The Roman State from 1815 to 1850*. Translated by Gladstone. London, 1851-1854, 4 vol. Farini was one of the bright young men who occupied various official posts under Pius' liberal administration.

Ferrero, Gabriel Maximilien. *Journal d'un officier de la Brigade de Savoie sur la campagne de Lombardie*. Turin, 1848.

Garibaldi, Guiseppe. *Memoirs*. Edited by Alexandre Dumas. Translated and with introduction by R. S. Garnett. New York, 1931. One of several variant editions of the *Memoirs*.

Holyoake, G. J. *Bygones Worth Remembering*. New York, 1905. A friend of Mazzini gives a few sidelights on Mazzini's life in exile.

Honan, Michael B. *The Personal Adventures of "Our Own Correspondent" in Italy*. New York, 1852. The London *Times* reporter who covered the campaigns in Italy colors his story with sex and adventure like many modern journalists. His report is more interesting for the story of how newspapers operated in those days than for the ground he covered, for he tried to leave out material that he had previously printed in the *Times*.

James, Henry. *William Wetmore Story and His Friends*. Edinburgh, 1903, 2 vol. Includes about 30 pages of a diary kept during the siege of Rome by Story, a Boston aristocrat.

Lesseps, Ferdinand de. *Ma mission à Rome*. Paris, 1849.

———. *Réponse au Ministère et au Conseil d'Etat*. Paris, 1849.

———. *Recollections of Forty Years*. London, 1887. Lesseps could never get beyond rehashing the documentary evidence concerning his mission to Rome and his mistreatment by his superiors.

Mailand und der Lombardische Aufstand, märz 1848. Frankfurt, 1856. Probably written by Helfert. A very pro-Austrian account.

Mazzini, Guiseppe. *Life and Writings*. London, 1891, 6 vol.

Minghetti, Marco. *Miei ricordi*. Turin, 1889. 3 vol. Minghetti was Minister of Public Works under Pius in early 1848. He was in constant correspondence with men like d'Azeglio and quotes most of their letters.

Morozzo della Rocca, Enrico. *The Autobiography of a Veteran, 1807-1893*. Translated by Janet Ross, New York, 1898. A friend of Charles Albert.

Orsini, Felice. *Memoirs and Adventures Written by Himself*. Translated by George Carbonel, Edinburg, 1857. Orsini was a revolutionist who ended his life by trying to bomb Napoleon III. Has interesting documents unearthed by the Roman Republic concerning the papal government.

Ossoli, Margaret Fuller. *Memoirs*. Boston, 1852.

Pasolini, Count Guiseppe. *Memoirs*. Compiled by his son, translated by Lady Dalhousie. London, 1885. A young layman who knew Pope Pius IX well before his elevation, and who was one of his trusted advisers during the months before the flight to Gaeta.

Pellico, Silvio. *My Ten Years' Imprisonment*. Translated by Thomas Roscoe. London, 1886.

Radetzky, Joseph Wenzel. *Briefe an seine Tochter Friederike, 1847-1857*. Vienna, 1892.

Richards, E. F. *Mazzini's Letters to an English Family, 1844-1854*. London, 1920. Mazzini's letters to the Ashurst family give a charming picture of his humor, variety of interest, affection, and political opinions.

See also the work by Hübner referred to under Austria.

BIBLIOGRAPHY

Modern Works Dealing with Events and Figures of 1848 in Italy

Arno, Wolf-Schneider von. *Der Feldherr Radetzky.* Vienna, 1933. A glorification of the old empire.

Agresti, Olivia Rosetti. *Giovanni Costa: His Life, Work and Times.* London, 1904. One chapter on Costa's part in the Roman revolution.

Barr, Stringfellow. *Mazzini, Portrait of an Exile.* New York, 1935. Not a full-length study, but psychologically interesting, full of Mazzini's letters.

Belluzzi, Raffaele. *La retirata di Garibaldi da Roma nel 1849.* Rome, 1899.

Berkeley, G. F.-H. and J. *Italy in the Making, 1815-1846.* Cambridge, England, 1932.

————. *Italy in the Making, June 1846 to January 1848.* Cambridge, 1936.

————. *Italy in the Making, January 1848 to November 1848.* Cambridge, England, 1940. These three volumes are in immense detail, based on everything there is to read, including archives. The books are interesting, the battle descriptions admirable. But the evils of the nineteenth century were deeper than the authors saw, perhaps because of their pro-Catholic bias, and they also seem to misunderstand the twentieth century, however much that counts in a work of history.

Bourgeois, Emile and E. Clermont. *Rome et Napoléon III.* Paris, 1907. Standard and admirable.

Ciasca, Raffaelle. *L'origine del "Programma per l'opinione nazionale italiana" del 1847-1848.* Milan, 1916. The author traces the evolution of the idea of those reforms which would require a united Italy, culminating in a kind of common program for all liberals worked out by d'Azeglio.

Costa de Beauregard, Marie Charles Albert. *Les dernières années du roi Charles-Albert.* Paris, 1890. An interesting, detailed, subtle psychological study by a devoted courtier.

Curàtulo, G. E. *Il dessidio tra Mazzini e Garibaldi.* Milan, 1928.

Demarco, Domenico. *Una rivoluzione sociale: la repubblica romana del 1849.* Naples, 1944. A fine and much needed study of the social aspects of the Roman republic.

Frischauer, Paul. *Garibaldi: the Man and the Nation.* London, 1935. Well written, clever, sensational.

Giovagnoli, R. *Ciceruacchio e Don Pirlone.* Rome, 1894. Misleadingly promises to be a study of Ciceruacchio and the comic paper, "Don Pirlone," issued in Rome under the republic.

Greenfield, Kent Roberts. *Economics and Liberalism in the Risorgimento: a Study of Nationalism in Lombardy*. Baltimore, 1934. The author feels, quite correctly, that Mazzini, and "exasperated idealism" have been overrated as factors in making Italy. He studies economic motives very intelligently, though his unspoken assumption is that nationalism would always be on the side of economic interest, which was not uniformly the case in 1848.

Griffith, Gwilym O. *Mazzini: Prophet of Modern Europe*. London, 1932. Admirably written biography.

Gualtieri, Luigi. *Memorie di Ugo Bassi*. Bologna, 1861.

Hoettinger, Franz Ferdinand. *Radetzky: ein Stuck Österreich*. Leipzig, 1934. A shameless glorification.

Johnston, R. M. *The Roman Theocracy and the Republic 1846-1849*. London, 1901. Anti-papal. Well documented.

Larg, David Glass. *Giuseppe Garibaldi: a Biography*. London, 1934. Entertaining, possibly inaccurate.

Maguire, John Francis. *Pontificate of Pius the Ninth*. London, 1870. The clerical position.

Martinengo-Cesaresco, Evelyn. *Italian Characters in the Age of Unification*. London, new ed., 1901. This countess knew most of the figures she writes about.

Masi, Ernesto. *Nell' ottocento*. Milan, 1905.

Matter, Paul. *Cavour et l'unité italienne*. Paris, 1926.

Monti, Antonio. *Un dramma fra gli esuli*. Milan, 1921. Mazzini's relations with Cattaneo in Milan in April 1848.

Nielsen, Fredrik Kristian. *The History of the Papacy in the XIXth Century*. New York, 1906, 2 vol. The work of a Danish Protestant. Sound.

Omodeo, Adolfo. *L'età del risorgimento italiano*. Messina, 1931.

Pailleron, M. L. "Une ennemie de l'Autriche." *Revue des deux mondes*, vol. 26, 1915. About Princess Belgiojoso.

Prato, Guiseppe. *Fatti e dottrine alla vigilia del 1848*. Turin, 1921. Study of the Piedmont Agricultural Society, with ramifications in every branch of public life.

Salvemini, Gaetano. *Mazzini*. Florence, 1925. Analysis of Mazzini's opinions on all subjects, with much quotation, and comparison of his actions with his words.

Taylor, A. J. P. *The Italian Problem in European Diplomacy, 1847-1849*. Manchester, 1934. Using archives at Paris, Vienna and

London, the author shows the nature of the interest of other powers in the fate of Italy.

Trevelyan, G. M. *Garibaldi's Defence of the Roman Republic.* London, 1907.

Vidal, Cesar. *Charles-Albert et le risorgimento italien.* Paris, 1927.

Whitehouse, H. Remsen. *A Revolutionary Princess: Christina Belgiojoso-Trivulzio, Her Life and Times. 1808-1871.* London, 1906.

Whyte, Arthur James B. *The Early Life and Letters of Cavour. 1810-1848.* Oxford, 1925.

――――. *The Political Life and Letters of Cavour, 1848-1861.* London, 1930.

Books on Venice in 1848

Binzer, Augustin von. *Venedig im Jahre 1844.* Pest, 1845. A guidebook, with an excellent map.

Debrunner, Jean. *Mémoires.* Zurich, 1850. The captain of the Swiss volunteer regiment at Venice. Also published in German.

Flagg, Edmund. *Venice, the City of the Sea from the Invasion by Napoleon in 1797 to the Capitulation of Radetzky in 1849.* New York, 1853, 2 vol. Flagg, the American consul at Venice, wrote, says Manin's editor, "with that mixture of calm and enthusiasm peculiar to the Anglo-Saxon race." Manin, who oddly enough did not know him at Venice, called his book the best and most exact account he had seen.

Helfert, Joseph Alexander von. *Aus Boehmen nach Italien, märz 1848.* Frankfurt. 1862. Detailed, lively account of the author's journey from Prague, to Vienna, to Venice.

La Forge, Anatole de. *Histoire de la république de Venise sous Manin.* Paris, 1853. 2 vol.

Manin, Daniele. *Documents et pièces authentiques laissés par Daniel Manin.* Edited by F. Planat de la Faye. Paris, 1860, 2 vol. Intelligently chosen and annotated selection of official documents and papers left by Manin.

Trevelyan, G. M. *Manin and the Venetian Revolution of 1848.* London, 1923.

VII · THE BRITISH ISLES

Contemporary Writers on Great Britain and Ireland in 1848

Cavour, Camillo. *Thoughts on Ireland.* London, 1868. First published in 1844. Cavour argued strongly for the union with Great Britain, mainly on economic grounds.

BIBLIOGRAPHY

Doheny, Michael. *The Felon's Track, or History of the Attempted Outbreak in Ireland.* Dublin, 1920. Doheny was one of the men engaged in the abortive uprising of July 1848.

Duffy, Sir Charles Gavan. *Four Years of Irish History.* London, 1883.

———. *Young Ireland.* London, 1880. These two ponderous volumes tell more than anyone would want to know about the activities, conversations, differences of the Young Ireland group between 1840 and 1848.

Engels, Frederick. *The Condition of the Working Class in England in 1844.* London, 1892. A work in which Engels developed his theory of the proletariat "in embryo" as he says.

Fontane, Theodore. *Journeys to England in Victoria's Early Days, 1844-1859.* London, 1939. A delightfully observant German.

Lamartine, Alphonse de. *England in 1850.* New York, 1851.

Meagher, Thomas Francis. *Meagher of the Sword.* Dublin, 1939. Speeches by the most glamorous of the Young Ireland party, before and during his various trials for sedition.

Mitchel, John. *Jail Journal.* New York, 1854.

———. *The Last Conquest of Ireland (Perhaps).* New York, 1878. The second of these books deals with the events of 1848, the first with Mitchel's trip in a prison ship to Tasmania.

Speeches from the Dock. Edited by Seán ua Ceallaigh. Dublin, 1945. The courtroom oratory of the victims of British justice in Ireland from 1798 on.

MODERN WORKS ON GREAT BRITAIN AND IRELAND IN 1848

This list of books on Britain makes no pretense at completeness. For Ireland, where materials are scarce, this bibliography shows the important sources for the 1848 uprising, such as it was. But the enormous literature about Chartism is outside the scope of this list—here are given only a few titles that have helped for the special purposes of this history.

Aldington, Richard. *The Duke.* New York, 1943. A life of Wellington.

Bell, H. C. F. *Life of Palmerston.* 1936, 2 vol.

Cecil, Algernon. *British Foreign Secretaries.* New York, 1927.

Slossen, P. W. *The Decline of the Chartist Movement.* New York, 1916.

West, Julius. *A History of the Chartist Movement.* London, 1920.

IRELAND

Connolly, James. *Labour in Ireland.* Dublin, 1917. Socialist history by a socialist "martyr," of 1916.

BIBLIOGRAPHY

Dillon, William. *Life of John Mitchel*. London, 1888, 2 vol.

Fogarty, L. *James Finton Lalor*. Dublin, 1918.

Laughton, J. K. *Memoirs of the Life and Correspondence of Henry Reeve*. 1898. 2 vol. Reeve was the editor of the London *Times*. Letters to him from Lord Clarendon, Lord Lieutenant of Ireland, are interesting, from the government point of view.

Mansergh, Nicholas. *Ireland in the Age of Reform and Revolution*. London, 1920. Based on views of continentals—Mazzini, Marx, Cavour—tries to show how Ireland was tied up with the continent.

Ryan, Desmond. *The Phoenix Flame*. London, 1937. This study of Fenianism has an introduction on the heritage of 1848.

White, Terence de Vere. *The Road of Excess*. Dublin, 1946. A life of Isaac Butt, whose chief fame came later, but whose apprenticeship in 1848 was instructive and is here well presented.

BIBLIOGRAPHY

Index

INDEX

Azeglio, d', Marchioness Constance, 313, 357

Azeglio, d', Marquis Massimo, 327, 347, 382; youth, 311; attitude toward women, 312; tours Italy, 1845, 318-322; hatred of Austria, 319; views, 323, 339; on Turin, 325; organizes procession, 330; on war, 357; serves under Victor Emmanuel, 359, 360; on freedom, 414-415

Azeglio, d', Marquis Robert, 328

Bach, Alexander, Austrian Minister, 253n., 256, 273

Baden, Grand Duchy of, 168-180

Baden, Grand Duke of. *See* Leopold.

Bakunin, Michael, Russian revolutionary, 182-184

Balbo, Cesare, Italian writer, 327, 330

balloons, used in war, 343, 399

Balzac, Honoré de, 30

Bandiera brothers, 318, 326

Bank of France, 66

Banquets, campaign of, 24; Lamartine's, 11; Paris, 25-28, 39

Barbès, Armand, French radical leader, 22, 62; Club of the Revolution, 62; attacks Blanqui, 63; on April 16, 74-75; in Assembly, 78; on May 15, 80, 81, 82; imprisoned, 83

barricades, *Paris*: February, 31, 33, 34; June, 89, 92. *Berlin*: 118-120. *Dresden*: 184. *Vienna*: 225. *Milan*: 340-341, 343, 344, 355. *Rome*, 373

Barrot, Odilon, French politician, in banquet campaign, 24-28, 32; on revolution, 33; in ministry, 34, 36; on provisional government, 44; in Assembly, 78; under Napoleon, 102

Bassi, Ugo, Garibaldi's chaplain, 378, 379

Batthyanyi, Count Louis, heads Hungarian Ministry, 272; refused audience, 273; on Croats, 277; fails to hold military frontier, 281; meets Jellačič, 282; meets Ferdinand, 282; forms second cabinet, 284; enlists in army, 286; executed, 304

Bavaria, Kingdom of, 180-181

Belgiojoso, Princess Christina, 313; at Milan, 347-348; at Rome, 375-376

Bem, Joseph, Polish officer, 242; in charge of Viennese defense, 242-243; escapes, 249, 249n.; in Transylvanian campaign, 291-292, 293; flees to Turkey, 305

Berlin, description before 1848, 110-112; in March, 1848, 116-119; in October, 1848, 136-137

Bismarck, Prince Otto von, 84, 115, 145, 166, 412, 418; in United Diet, 127; Augusta appeals to, 134; advises Frederick William, 137

Blanc, Louis, 14, 16, 39, 40, 280, 312, 391, 412, 413, 416; early life, 19; *Organization of Work*, 19-20; at first session of provisional government, 43-45; heads left wing of provisional government, 47, 48; frightened by workers' march, 60; Luxembourg Commission, 67-69; feared, 77; in Assembly, 78; voted out of office, 79; on May 15, 82; endorses Napoleon, 84; in England, 406; character, 418

Blanqui, Adolphe, French economist, 86-87, 96

Blanqui, Auguste, French radical leader, 14-15, 22, 74; opposed to provisional government, 47; organizes March 17th demonstration, 60; sets up Central Republican Society, 61; appearance, 61; doctrine, 61-62; hurt by Taschereau scandal, 63; on May 15, 81; imprisoned, 83

Blum, Robert, German radical leader, 182, 312, 412, 419; early life, 150; popularity, 151; in Frankfurt Assembly, 154; on Archduke John, 155; on war, 156; on Malmö, 158; goes to Vienna, 160, 244, 245; execution, 161, 249, 250, 255

Bodelschwingh, E. von, Minister of the Interior, 118, 121, 124

Boerner, Paul, Berlin student, 115, 178

Bohemia, Kingdom of, 4, 193, 262. *See also* Czechs.

Bonaparte family, 56

Born, Stephan, German worker, 134, 144; youth and opinions, 131; organizes Berlin workers, 132, 418; in Saxon revolution, 183, 185

Boston Tea Party, inspires Milanese, 338

Bourbon, House of, restoration, 12

Brandenburg, Count von, 137

Bréa, General, French officer, 92

bread riots, Berlin, 112

Brentano, Lorenz, German lawyer, 174, 175, 176

bridge, at Buda-Pest, 265, 291; at Venice, 381, 395, 397

Brinton, Crane, on Lamartine, 75

British diplomacy, reaction to Second Republic, 51; reaction to Schleswig-Holstein war, 158. *See also* Lord Palmerston.

INDEX

INDEX